Technology Best Practices

Robert H. Spencer
and
Randolph P. Johnston

JOHN WILEY & SONS, INC.

This book is printed on acid-free paper. ∞

Copyright © 2003 by Robert H. Spencer and Randolph P. Johnston All rights reserved.

Published by John Wiley & Sons, Inc., Hoboken, New Jersey.

Published simultaneously in Canada.

This publication is designed to provide accurate and authoritative information in regard to the subject matter covered. It is sold with the understanding that the publisher is not engaged in rendering legal, accounting, or other professional services. If legal advice or other expert assistance is required, the services of a competent professional person should be sought.

ISBN: 0-471-20376-9

For more information about Wiley products, visit our web site at www.Wiley.com.

Printed in the United States of America.

10 9 8 7 6 5 4 3 2 1

Contents

Preface

The problem with writing a book on technology is that new options may become available tomorrow that we have not even dreamed of yet. These new technologies hold out the hope of greater realization, greater profits, and a better world. These promises surface each year with each new innovation. Still, management asks, "Where are the promised profits? What is enough to spend on technology? What is the best way to work smart with technology?"

No matter how much technology has changed over the past 30 years, there are certain unalienable principals and practices that simply do not change over time. These include proper planning and implementation, training, and review of practices. Other procedures and techniques, such as implementing strong security and monitoring how technology is used, deserve consistent attention but are usually ignored until an incident shows the need for diligence. These are the practices this book will endeavor to explore, explain, and present.

Why *Technology Best Practices*? Because one size does not fit all. From our combined 60 years of experience in the technology profession, we have learned that there is a right way and a wrong way to implement technology. The right solution for one user may be the wrong solution for another. So, why *Technology Best Practices*? This same experience teaches there are practices and procedures proven with time that do work when all factors are taken into consideration. As implementers of these practices, we need to know the objectives of the organization at the beginning. Taking short cuts and not funding technology at appropriate levels also consistently result in failures in the extreme. Why? Because a failed network upgrade, software implementation, or communications infrastructure may be catastrophic to the business as a whole. PCs are no longer personal systems that have a limited impact when they fail. Today, PCs are used as network servers, communications servers, database servers, and wide area network gateways. When there is a failure, everyone feels it immediately. In researching this book, we talked with the best of the best in many fields. We have known many of these experts over the years and respect them, not only for their success, but also for how they became successful. This book incorporates insights from both users and abusers of technology.

CHAPTER ONE

Why *Technology Best Practices*?

HOW TO MANAGE THE TECHNOLOGY?

To manage technology, it is necessary to coordinate people, hardware, and software resources. "You can do *anything* with technology if you are willing to spend enough money and time." This statement is not a fantasy and contains a large amount of truth. However, it is important to carefully select, successfully implement, and continuously manage technology to accomplish business goals. So many organizations spend money on technology and do not reap the results because of poor implementation, lack of training, or incorrect selection. It is appalling when technology is implemented for technology's sake. This book can serve as a guide for an organization's decision-making process on technology.

Technical skills are not a prerequisite for managing technology. The desire to ask questions, manage projects, and look at possibilities is a large part of the battle. The *how* of managing technology will be a cooperative effort between a technology steering committee, internal information technology (IT) staff, and contractors who provide installation and support services. A mix of in-house and out-of-house support based on size, response time needs, complexity, and other factors is needed. The *how* of managing technology will be explained with planning, policies, and procedures.

WHO SHOULD MANAGE THE TECHNOLOGY?

The information technology steering committee (ITSC) should manage the organization's technology. Information technology was traditionally managed by a professional data processing staff that managed the centralized mainframe or minicomputer, and provided all of the organization's core IT functions. This is still a reasonable approach for larger organizations, but a balance of people that support core processing as well as productivity work is needed. Regardless of size, the organization must have a strategy to provide help and recovery in the event of failure, and backup on a daily basis. In a small organization, the one person who is considered *computer literate* will often handle all

IT tasks. Organizations of all sizes should have a plan to accomplish the IT items that make sense for the business strategy.

The IT Steering Committee should recommend the strategy of the organization, and the IT manager should execute the projects selected by the IT Steering Committee. The organization, function, and responsibilities of this group are covered later in the book. *Computer gurus* in small organizations can have a small group recommend projects, but will probably manage most of the implementations themselves. It is rare to recommend that an IT or management information systems (MIS) manager control the IT decisions for an organization, although most are quite competent and capable of doing so. The process of discussing IT needs is a way to discover new technologies that can help the business educate, gain agreement, and monitor implementations. If IT makes the decisions unaided, all of the issues, solutions, and needs of the users may not be considered.

The *who* that accomplishes these tasks will have a major influence on the success or failure of the business. Several studies have pointed out that technology automation will make the typical office worker 25 percent more productive and effective. When considering that four people can do the work of five with automation, it should be easy to justify technology expenditures for these gains.

WHAT SHOULD BE MANAGED?

All aspects of technology! This may sound like an exaggeration, but every single aspect of technology in the business, from the copiers to the phone systems to the computers to the software to the training, should be considered. If a business process has any element of technology involved, it should be considered and reviewed on a regular basis. New, better, and potentially less expensive or revolutionary methods should also be considered.

Politics in the organization may be one of the bigger stumbling blocks to comprehensively managing technology. Because of some historical decision, copiers may be under one person's control, while phone systems are the responsibility of someone else and an MIS department may manage IT. However, as shown in the chapters on communications, the organization may be better served by consolidated voice and data over the same lines. From a technology perspective, it is always better to coordinate all aspects of the technology used in a business. In large businesses, it can be very challenging to get your arms around all of the items to be considered. It becomes even more challenging without a technology background and people who are explaining things in *geek speak*. Have the discipline to ask for a simpler explanation, if needed. Use an old management technique of asking questions. With technical people, it is helpful to ask the same question at least three times in different forms to make sure that you understand the answer. Another management technique that works well with technical people is to ask one more question *after* you think you understand everything. This extra question routinely unveils the true issues or complications, and clearly helps your understanding.

Walking into someone else's political territory can, at times, be career limiting. But managing technology correctly is so critical that it is important to be a leader and take the risk.

WHEN SHOULD TECHNOLOGY BE MANAGED?

Continuously! Each project deserves daily or weekly management. The minimum management that makes sense is an annual review. Quarterly or monthly reviews makes even better sense. The technology review does not need to take a lot of time, but it should include a status update on all open projects, any significant issues, and any new technologies that should be considered.

Most new technology functions added to business can be accomplished in a few weeks to a few months. If the project can be clearly defined, it is a candidate for being outsourced. A project that is outsourced will have to be managed more carefully than one using in-house IT staff.

Other chapters in this book will explain procedures that should be developed and followed every day, week, month, quarter, and year. Some tasks will take a minimal amount of time, and others will require a day or more to complete. However, if the technology is not managed, the outages will cost your organization far more than the time invested to manage the resources properly.

WHY MANAGE TECHNOLOGY?

It is less expensive to manage technology implementations than to leave these resources alone. In an earlier book, the five-component model of computing, originally developed by Dr. David Kroenke, was discussed. This approach to computing explains how all computing systems have five basic components: hardware, software, data, procedures, and people. If any one of the five components fails, the systems will not function properly and not produce the desired results. The five-component model is one approach to managing all of the computing resources. When considering making a change, it is reasonable to ask how the change will affect each one of the five components. For example, there may be a need for a faster, larger capacity tape backup system. If the tape system is upgraded, how does it affect the hardware (probably need to be replaced)? How does the upgrade affect the software (possibly requires an upgrade)? How does the new backup system affect the data (possibly makes old backups inaccessible)? How does an upgrade affect the procedures (perhaps it eliminates some tape rotations, changes or start times)? How does the change in the tape system affect the people (new training, different procedures, down time)? Using the five-component model as a framework to ask questions can answer many of the *whys* of technology.

WHERE SHOULD TECHNOLOGY BE MANAGED?

Everywhere it is used. It goes without saying that technology is becoming more portable and geographically dispersed. These issues alone point out some of the items that need to be managed. For example, what happens if a mobile user's portable computer is stolen? How confidential is the data? How do we get this user productive again as quickly as possible? If this is the third time this year a computer has been stolen from this user, this is a chronic problem.

Communications technologies also change the *where* of computing by allowing Internet Access worldwide, remote access, wireless access, wide area network access, and other options that will be discussed in later chapters. But the key point (or question) for now is: what are the hardware, software, data, procedural, and people factors to be considered when managing the location of technology use? Many companies begin using personal digital assistants to later find that their most valuable company asset, the client database, is loaded on a non-secure handheld device. Other companies implement wireless without turning on the security options, and then realize that hackers can drive by in cars and get access to their local area network and private company information. The technology manager's job is to think about and prevent these situations before they occur.

INSIGHTS AND ADMONITIONS

Technology is such a broad field that there are many opinions on how to accomplish similar tasks. The recommendations for technology best practices reflect what are considered to be the best methods available right now, but there can be dozens of correct ways to do anything recommended. The procedures described and the policies recommended are the best insight currently available.

Since business conditions, legal requirements, and the technology being used will change over time, the supplemental web site for this book *www.technologybestpractices.com* is a source of updated supplemental material. The intent is to always make the best decisions for business, using the best technology available, complying with regulations that result in the best customer service you can provide, augmented by technology. If anything in this material conflicts with that view, be assured that it was not written clearly; new technology has made an old methodology obsolete; or business requirements have changed.

FRAMEWORK OF THE BOOK

The book is divided into two major halves. The first half of the book is focused on technology and contingency planning, policies, procedures, and managing IT resources and people. The second half of the text is focused on understanding the basic components of technology including software of all kinds, hardware, communications including local area networking, wide area networking, remote access, Internet, and telecommunications. Finally, the book closes with discussions of future technologies to watch. Visit the web site *www.technologybestpractices.com* often to see a current list of recommendations by product category, including pricing.

CONCLUSION

This book is intended to give the reader collective insights from observing and helping companies implement technology, using the best practices available. There are many right ways to implement technology, and there are many wrong ways. Hopefully, this book will provide answers to many of the intriguing issues that that come up while considering the technology to implement for an organization.

CHAPTER TWO

Technology Planning Best Practices

THE PLANNING PROCESS

Research at MIT, conducted by the Sloan Business School, shows that the "likelihood of success in utilizing information technology to increase productivity is a function of several technical and non-technical factors." (*The Profit Initiative,* MIT Sloan School of Management, Cambridge, MA.) To attain success, there are three prerequisites—a careful determination of strategic applications, an intelligent selection of technologies, and an ability to incorporate appropriate changes into the organizational structure. Failure to take into consideration even one of these factors will lead to failures in the overall technology implementation and adoption process.

Despite all of the technological advances during this century, white-collar workers still spend a large amount of their time retrieving information from various sources in order to perform their jobs. Some information resides on computers of different makes and types; some exists on paper and other traditional media, and some must be accessed through personal interactions. The increasing complexity of data processing systems seems to create bottlenecks to information storage and retrieval rather than improving the flow of information. Often the integrity of the data is called into question because of redundant information stored on decentralized systems. Even the validity of information can be questioned because of a lack of integrity checking.

Managers continually improve and augment technology in the hope that technology, in itself, will increase productivity and thereby increase profits. Arguably, technology does make a difference. Technology also falls short of meeting expectations. As more and more capital and human resources are committed to technology, management has amplified the need for a greater return on investment (ROI). The hope is that technology can help greatly reduce inefficiencies and waste. Over the past several years, there have been a number of studies released by PriceWaterhouseCoopers, Deloitte & Touche and other consulting firms that seem to confirm:

- Work activity is generally highly fragmented, causing waste and inefficiency.
- Despite substantial investment in information systems, few business processes are truly enabled by technology.

- A large percentage of the time spent on administrative work such as unnecessary reviewing, reworking, and redundant recording and reconciling of data between departments does not add value.

Everyone from the international consulting firms to the ivory towers of academia agrees that more planning must go into the technology acquisition and deployment process. Planning helps determine more than what technology to purchase; it identifies the objectives of the technology to be deployed, how it is to be deployed, and the benefits that are to be derived. Planning requires a lengthy and serious review of the organization from the perspective of how information flows, what is necessary, what is not, and what is redundant. The planning process does not start with identifying the latest and greatest technology, even if that is where many technology professionals like to begin. *Planning begins with determining what your people do, how they do it, and where technology can be used to leverage resources such as people.*

Most companies are not using technology effectively to manage the flow of information through their organization. Technology, in itself, cannot create efficiencies, or inefficiencies. In the tasks they perform, the users create these. The technology planning process documents the existing information flow in the organization, and determines how these processes could be more effective or offer greater returns on the investment. One management theory that emerged in the mid-nineties, the *theory of constraint* (TOC), was first introduced by Eliyahu Goldratt, in *The Goal,* a book about the challenges of maximizing manufacturing performance. Goldratt's theories apply to other industries as well. Constraint theory is based on the reality that every operation's maximum output is constrained by some resource. Tools can help find the constraint(s) and manage them most effectively. TOC has developed into its own academic school of thought on recognizing and solving business constraints. While an in-depth study of TOC is well beyond the scope of this book, TOC does make very interesting reading. There is a plethora of material on the Internet on this subject. TOC reinforces the need to constantly review how tasks are performed and to develop optimum workflows to benefit the organization. Every business benefits from recognizing where it is constrained and then doing something about it.

Identifying constraints can be simply translated as: How can it be determined where procedures are not working well? What processes are not efficient and need to be re-engineered so that fewer resources are needed to accomplish a given task? The following information formalizes the process of planning and documenting technology requirements.

USING PROCESS ENGINEERING TO IMPROVE INFORMATION FLOW

"Without process, companies decay into a spiral of chaos and internal conflict." (Michael Hammer, author of *Beyond Reengineering: How the Process-Centered Organization Is Changing Our Work and Our Lives*). During the 1970s and 1980s, process engineering dominated chemical, pharmaceutical, mining and some types of manufacturing industries. For the past several years, the business community has been applying the principals of process engineering to improve workflow management and better enable the use of technology. In his latest book, *The Agenda: What Every Business Must Do to Dominate the Decade,* Hammer defines process as " . . . a technical term with a precise definition: an organized group of related activities that together create a result of value . . . "

An example of a process might be accounts payable (yes, accounts payable could be composed more than one process. But this needs to be simple, so that readers do not go screaming from the room!) The accounts payable process might be composed of these high-level activities (each high-level activity might be broken down into specific steps with sample forms and the names of each person involved in the activity):

- *Daily.*   Receive invoices from vendors.
- *Daily.*   Route invoices to inventory control for verification of receipt.
- *Daily.*   Enter verified invoices from inventory control into computer.
- *Weekly.*   Determine which invoices to pay based on discounts.
- *Weekly.*   Make payments and write checks.
- *Monthly.*   Report all payments to accounting to close period.
- *Monthly.*   Reconcile payments made to bank account balance.
- *Annually.*   Summarize all payments and prepare annual reports.

Most departmental activities will be more complicated. The point here is to list all the activities that make up the accounts payable process. Then, list all the activities for each area of the accounting department, then move on to marketing, sales, inventory control, shipping and distribution, and so forth. The next step will be to visually show how documents, or data, move through the organization. Workflow diagramming will be discussed next.

Documenting Processes by Workflow

Workflow defines how information flows through your organization This information is also called transactions; a purchase, a check, a receivable, or a contact are all considered types of transactions in the real world. Experience shows that as physical pieces of paper flow through a business, electronic transactions flow inside your computer network. If the flow of information is cumbersome or inefficient, in the real world, constraints that cost money will be created. The first step in the planning process is to analyze current workflow and how information flows through your organization to determine where the constraints are. Once constraints are identified, more effective ways of accomplishing the activities will be designed.

Why do constraints occur in the first place? There are many reasons: organizational layering, a high reliance on paper for decisions and transactions, excessive points of control, and redundant operations that develop over time. Essentially, people view the organization in which they work not as a complete system, but as a series of distinct departments and functions. While it is important to dissect an organization and analyze specific workflows, it is critical to put the pieces back together and evaluate the integration of individual workflows. Evaluating how these support the business operating model as well as continually identifying potential constraints is key for improvement.

In the accounts payable example above, an invoice received for payment is forwarded to inventory control to be validated. Someone has to validate that the item was received and disbursed. The process analysis of accounts payable did not include what happened to the invoice in inventory control. That will be picked up later when the inventory control department processes are analyzed. Yet, at some point how that document got to inventory control and back to accounts payable must be considered. The process might flow better if either inventory notifies accounts payable every time they receive inventory, or if all invoices should are routed to inventory control before going to accounts payable to create a much more efficient flow of information. The complete analysis should show a total, holistic view of your organization. If more businesses took the time to analyze the activities of their employees and created processes that made everyone more efficient, the result would be greater productivity and less cost.

So, why does business not view the organization holistically and spend the time to develop more efficient workflows? When planning for technology, the inclination is to approach technical issues such as hardware, software and communications first. Technology professionals are well prepared for and comfortable with these types of activities. When management says that the network is too slow, or people are not entering transactions quickly enough, the tendency is to turn to the hardware and software to solve the problem. However, before technology professionals can develop an overall strategy for the organization and determine the technology that will best support the organization's business model, management must insure that time is taken to flow the processes and identify the activities performed by users.

A workflow consists of a collection of activities that support a specific process. Classic examples of a workflow can range from tracking the activities in the accounts payable department as shown above or a claim management in an insurance company. What about production scheduling in a manufacturing company or patient care within a hospital? Within each of these larger workflows, there exist micro-workflows. Each department or group within an organization has many workflows that move information through an organization. Some of these workflows may appear to be independent of each other, such as an accounts payable process and an inventory control process. However, as shown in the example above, they are not independent. It is rare to find a process in an organization that has a significant economic impact and is also isolated; all workflows flow together. Finding activities in workflow diagrams that are not linked to other processes should set off flashing lights and sirens! Most processes should tie together and should be highly structured and highly repetitive. The objective of strategic technology planning is to improve the efficiencies of performing processes through automation and create productivity gains.

Today, the definition of workflow is much broader, and not only encompasses the traditional *production* workflow areas, but also includes administrative and ad-hoc processing as well. Administrative workflow is structured and repetitive, but usually includes fewer participants and lower throughput. Consider an accounting department with accounts payable, receivable, and payroll functions. The tasks to complete each of the accounting support functions may be performed by multiple participants in the accounting department, or a few who perform specific tasks at given times. In all cases, the tasks performed are repetitive in nature and should be performed the same way each time they are executed. Ad-hoc tasks are considered unstructured and spontaneous, again with a low number of participants and low volume. Many organizations have procedures for structured tasks, such as insurance claim filing, manufacturing processes, or processing a mortgage application. However, virtually no documented procedures exist for administrative and ad-hoc workflows in many organizations.

The objective of this book is not to teach you how to design effective workflows, but to introduce workflow management as a best practice for diagramming, or flowing the processes you identified in the organization. Those who would like to delve more into the subject can consult the Workflow Management Coalition (*www.wfmc.org*). This group has developed standards as well as a framework for establishment of workflow standards. While this level of workflow analysis and flow diagramming are beyond most small businesses, there is valuable information available through the coalition. For purposes here, readers only need to understand the concept of workflow, to have the basic skills to diagram the activities in a process and to then tie multiple processes together. With this level of understanding, critical processes can be flowed, analyzed, and improved. This diagramming can be done using simple tools such as Microsoft Visio. It is also fine to prepare the diagram by hand using a simple flow chart template from your local bookstore or art shop. Samples of such diagrams are included later in this chapter.

What Kind of Benefits Can You Expect from Process Engineering?

Now that the terminologies and tools are understood, the reasons an organization begins a process engineering project can be considered. Technology professionals will often find themselves needing to convice management to fund a processing engineering project. Such projects nearly always result in increased productivity, reduction of operating costs, and improved performance, good reasons to consider process engineering as a strategic process. Process engineering does not have to be performed by a high-level consultant, but does require a disciplined approach. The people managing the project should know the business and the industry.

The reason to begin the process engineering project may be to define current problems, needs, and applications in order to improve your business or increase productivity. Once completed, it is a good idea to update your diagrams and documentation every five to ten years to correct workflow errors that creep into an organization because of change, mergers or acquisition. This happens, for instance, when an operation moves to a new location, building, or warehouse. Employees will attempt to apply the processes they know, but because the flow changes in the new location, the old workflow does not work efficiently. Costly errors will be introduced without anyone realizing it. New employees, or reassignment of employees who are not correctly trained for their new position, also introduce changes in the workflow and create activities that do not flow properly, resulting in inefficiencies and reduced productivity.

Best Practice Examples—*What Not to Do!*

After 25 years in the same location, a large financial institution built a new large building across town. The new facility had all the modern conveniences and the most current technology money could buy. New furniture, new phone system, new computers—it was a great working environment. A few weeks after the bank relocated its staff, the president called, explaining that they were having problems with their accounting software and asking for help fixing the problems.

A definition of the problems and an assessment of the current operating environment was the place to begin. The problem appeared to be that invoices were not getting posted and paid. The bank was losing discounts, as well as being close to incurring some serious fines from other institutions. To assess the current operating environment, staff interviews were conducted and the workflow processes were observed for a few days. Based on this review, the technology was working just fine. It was the workflow in the new building that had created bottlenecks and caused documents to be lost, or data not to be entered on a timely basis.

Accounting staff, who had worked next to each other for many years, were now at opposite ends of the building. Workflow that had developed over many years was suddenly interrupted because of the new location. Staff, who had communicated simply by turning toward the other person asking a question or passing a form by hand, found that asking questions and sharing common documents was now cumbersome.

In designing the new location, individual needs such as well lighted offices and ample work space were top on the list. But, management and the designers had failed to conduct a process review and to flow these processes in the new building. They did not fully consider the actual tasks being performed and had not created new workflows to meet the new building design. After meeting with the appropriate staff and flowing transactions across the operations, the payable problem was resolved. As an added benefit, other potential problems were uncovered and corrected before they became an issue. And, other activities were made more efficient. No change in technology was needed.

In another example of how costly not having a well-defined workflow process can be, a large company asked for assistance in identifying a new accounting solution. This company was successful and had done a good job of managing their manufacturing and inventory control area, but had never really focused on the processes in accounting and marketing. The management of this process engineering project began by developing the *As Is* document showing the current critical workflow processes and defining activities that key people performed. The *As Is* and *To Be* procedures will be more fully defined later in this chapter. They are the flow diagrams that help visualize what people do and how they interface with each other—they are workflow diagrams. The process of flowing invoices through the payment process showed that the invoice receipt clerk logged the invoice, compared it to the original purchase order, and then made a copy. The clerk filed the copy in the vendor's folder prior to sending the original to accounting to be paid. Then, an accounts payable clerk entered the invoice data into the accounts payable accounting software, and literally passed the hardcopy invoice to a second clerk in the next cubicle. The second clerk was responsible for pulling up the transaction on a computer screen and comparing what was entered to the hardcopy invoice for data entry errors.

Once the data verification was complete, the second accounts payable clerk made another copy of the original invoice. The clerk filed the copy in a vendor file kept in accounts payable, before sending the original back to the invoice receipt clerk. When the original hardcopy receipt returned, the invoice receipt clerk removed the copy they had made only hours earlier, threw the copy in the trash and filed the original! After observing and diagramming this process, we asked "Why?" The explanation was that at least eight years ago, an invoice had been lost from a vendor who was very good friends with the CEO. This had developed into a major incident causing the CEO to come down to accounting and say some very unpleasant things.

As a result of this incident, the controller put in place a procedure to ensure that each department tracked an invoice all the way through the process and that everyone had *covered* themselves, so that such a thing never happened again. (After all, no one wants too many visits from the CEO!)

The copies made by accounts payable were kept until the file cabinets were filled, then they were boxed and sent to an off-site storage facility where, to the best of our knowledge, they were stored, for a fee, forever! Add to this the lost productivity by having three people enter the same information in two different parts of the system; processing an invoice was a very expensive and resource-intensive activity.

After diagramming the workflow for this process, we worked with management and staff to make changes to the company's software and developed new written procedures for paying invoices. Now invoice data is only entered once at the point of origin and verified in accounts payable before a check is issued. Simple modification to workflow not only saved a lot of money, it shortened the time it takes to pay vendors and process invoices.

Both companies described above were so impressed that they approved and funded an expanded process engineering project for all departments and the development of new written procedures. The cost savings were significant.

Nine Steps to Best Practice Process Engineering

As the two examples show, the results of process engineering are improved workflows. The process engineering methodology requires that the activities that create processes be *engineered* rather than be allowed to simply evolve, as is usually the case. As an organization matures, procedures develop over time. A process engineering effort must address all parts of the organization: jobs, skills, structure, information technology, management systems, business processes, and even values and beliefs. An undertaking of this magnitude probably seems overwhelming. However, the process engineering methodology is scalable; that is, it can be applied within a single department or process, or it can be applied to the entire organization.

Keep in mind that because process engineering crosses departments and impacts individuals throughout the organization, a process engineering team must represent the various departments affected equally to get the buy-in needed to succeed. Members of the project team must feel empowered to challenge old assumptions; there must be an executive-level sponsor who can move across departments to resolve issues that arise (and they will), and a project manager who can lead the group and keep them moving forward.

In an article by Frank Tait titled "Enterprise Process Engineering: A Template Tailored for Higher Education," published by *Cause/Effect* (*www.educase.edu*), a practitioner's journal about managing and using Information resources on college and university campuses (Volume 22, Number 1, 1999), the author identifies nine steps necessary to ensure successful Enterprise Process Engineering. We have taken those nine steps identified by Tait and adapted them into nine best practice steps that fit general business as follows:

1. Create the process engineering team.
2. Identify strategic objectives.
3. Define how to measure success.
4. Diagram existing workflow—the As Is.
5. Identify affected and involved parties.
6. Design new workflow—the To Be.
7. Model business processes.
8. Apply best practices.
9. Review and refine on a recurring basis.

1. Create the Process Engineering Team.

Process engineering begins, as most projects begin, with a committee. Information technology staff should not attempt this project by themselves. The committee should also include as many representatives of each department as appropriate. It is best to start small, perhaps with the accounting department, or inventory control, and then expand to encompass other areas.

The committee should have representatives from the functional areas of the department, or departments, being reviewed. Input from as many people as possible is useful, but the committee needs to be small enough to be manageable. For a small business, three to five people could represent the entire company. For larger organizations, it may be necessary to have a supervisory committee that has oversight for functional area subcommittees. Experience has shown that three to five is the right number, and certainly no more than seven. With more than seven, you do not have a committee, you have a mob!

The diagram in Exhibit 2.1 shows a small process engineering planning team with a few sub-committees. These organization charts are easy to prepare using the Microsoft Organization Chart 2.0 object in Word. (From Word click on Insert/Object and then scroll down until you see chart object and press enter. Word 2002 users have a nice new tool for creating a number of organization and process diagrams.) Other drawing or diagram tools can also be used to diagram the committee and list the responsibilities clearly. The diagram should have details on the members and their areas of responsibility.

Exhibit 2.1

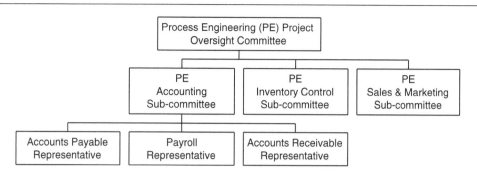

2. *Identify Strategic Objectives.*

Depending on the scope of the process engineering initiative, the strategic objectives could be broad and apply to the entire organization. Defining strategic objectives could be limited to a single department, such as improving the payroll process but could also encompass the strategic business objectives of the entire organization as well. These could be as broad as expanding plant facilities, adding additional products or services, integrating new departments or staff from a potential merger or acquisition. Or, objectives may be more efficiency oriented and focus on improving workflow to reduce costs as demonstrated in the examples earlier.

It is best to begin with the organization's business plan and review the overall objectives of the company. Then, dissect these to determine how broad objectives can be achieved by improving narrow processes performed in each department. Success in this phase will be determined by the group's ability to document objectives at all levels.

As functional areas define their objectives, information technology professionals will need to listen closely as team members discuss current problems or needs so that they can offer technology-based solutions or tools to help engineer new activities, thus creating new workflows.

3. *Define How to Measure Success.*

In his article, Frank Tait refers to a similar step he calls *Determine important metrics.* These are referred to as successes in the business world, and successes are usually measured in positive financial results. The process engineering team must determine how to measure if the process engineering project is successful. Tait says that measurements can be determined in part by creating a set of questions that relate to the objectives of the organization, global and departmental, and then answering these questions. The questionnaire might include, "How do we know when we're successful?" and "How will we know if we did something better than it was done before?" Examples of measurements include the time it takes to complete a process, such as creating an order, processing an order, making payments, running payroll, responding to customer inquiry, changing a product specification and so forth.

Measurements must address the question to each manager involved, "What's in it for me?" Since process engineering is an expensive and resource intensive activity, the team must have buy-in from each department, as well as the entire organization. And buy-in only comes if the participants believe that the process will result in positive results, such as improved workflow, increased profits, or reduced costs. Showing management a defined way to measure the success of this project will go a long way toward being able to expand and continue the project throughout the organization.

4.   *Diagram Existing Workflow—the As Is.*

Where tasks are being reengineered, it is necessary to flow the current processes first in order to visually show how tasks are currently accomplished and to identify steps to be re-engineered. The workflow diagramming process is not usually done by the committee, but is assigned to a person, or persons (who may also be committee members), knowledgeable with the area(s) being evaluated. The committee defines how the workflow analysis is to be done and the person(s) performing the diagramming is to proceed. This is important to insure that, as each area is diagrammed, the methodology is consistent throughout the organization. A best practice is to involve those with a wider range of knowledge and with no preconceived prejudices; this may be outside consultants or other knowledgeable persons who have been through a similar project and have some good experience to share.

Where individuals were asked to create diagrams (simple flow charts) to show how they performed their duties, critical steps were left out because the steps had been taken for granted. An exercise used in seminars is for the attendees to take a blank piece of paper and write a very detailed procedure on how to accomplish the process of tying a shoelace. They must include a diagram (flow chart) of all the steps (activities) in the process. This is an activity that almost everyone has each done daily, for many years. In fact, the process is so second nature that trying to describe the steps and diagram it becomes extremely tedious.

When someone too close to the actual process is assigned to document and diagram it, there is an extremely high amount of errors. Here a team approach may be better, with the person documenting the process interviewing the workers and making notes. They then document and diagram the process. With input from the workers, the end result will be more complete and much more accurate.

This step is extremely labor intensive, but probably the most critical. The team responsible for flowing existing processes must record processes, sub-processes, and tasks, and then review each one. This can be done manually with paper and pencil, with software that automates the process, or with a combination of manual efforts and software to complete the diagrams. The team needs to ask how people downstream are using the information and the work generated by each task and determine who does what and why. This process is also referred to as business-process-review (BPR) or *as-is analysis.*

In addition, the team should assign each process a name that clearly reflects what the process does. Some authors use an *end-to-end* naming convention, such as *approve payables and issue check,* or *accounts payables.* This convention can become unwieldy, but it has the advantage of conveying a continuous flow. The team also must clarify every term associated with the process by developing a data element dictionary so that naming conventions are standardized throughout. For example, what is the precise definition of *customer, order approval,* and so forth? Smaller companies with limited resources do not need to go to this level of exactness, but larger companies or holding companies with several operating companies should consider the benefits of standardizing their approach.

5. *Identify Affected and Involved Parties.*

Process engineering is about change, and where there is change, someone will be affected. The achievement of the team's strategic objectives depends upon success across the organization. The team must consider ahead of time anyone who might be an affected party in the change process and attempt, where appropriate, to include them in the design process. Tait's article identified owners, actors, and stakeholders, titles that fit just as well in business as they do in academia. I have adapted the roles Tait defined as follows:

Process owners perform and own the process. For example, the people in the accounting office are the primary process owners in accounting; salespersons are often the owners of sales processes such as writing orders, or checking on inventory balances. A process owner can be a person or an organizational entity. All processes identified must have at least one owner.

Process actors are the *customers* or *suppliers* of the process who are outside of the process owner's organization. For example, a vendor, or client might be an actor to one of the organization's processes. For example, a vendor would be a supplier. A vendor could also be a customer at the same time, but is performing a different role, so do not get confused. These are just labels we attach to help focus on the participants.

Process stakeholders are process actors who have a special, mission-critical interest in the process, either as process-output recipients, or as super process owners. For example, while the federal government may be an *actor* in the *payroll tax payment* process, it is not a stakeholder. However, in a manufacturing or sales process, the marketing department is a stakeholder because part of its mission depends on the proper execution of manufacturing or sales related processes.

In this phase, everyone affected by the project has a chance to review the As Is documentation and diagramming and make comments. This is also where the committee will receive input on changes that would improve workflow, make activities more efficient, and improve operations. Be careful. Many *actors* and *stakeholders* are quick to comment on processes they do not own, or to criticize other *owners,* but sometimes are reluctant to consider the processes they own as having problems. This is where things start getting a little sticky and you need to review *Basic Diplomacy 101.*

6. *Design New Workflow—the To Be.*

According to Michael Hammer, a process is "a related group of activities that together create a result of value to a customer." According to PricewaterhouseCoopers, "Process engineering deconstructs processes and rebuilds them in a way that creates the most value for an institution. It promotes change aimed at improving the quality and timeliness, and reducing the cost, of cross-functional business processes."

A process typically starts with a trigger action and ends in a result, involving numerous departments along the way. For example, a staff member might ask, "How do I go about getting office space for a new faculty member?" In contrast, process re-engineering poses the question, "What needs to happen when a new faculty member comes on board?" The answer includes assigning office space, a computer, and a desk, and initiating human resources activities like payroll. By taking a process, rather than a departmental approach, the institution achieves minimal waste and a highly efficient value-oriented workflow.

In this phase, the input from Phase 4, *Diagram existing workflow—the As Is,* and Phase 6, *Identify affected and involved parties,* will be assembled to begin changing the As Is to the To Be. The To Be diagrams and workflow documentation show the improvements to be derived, along with where changes must be made.

7. Model Business Processes.

Before making wide sweeping changes as a result of Phase 6, *Design new workflows,* the committee should review each change in the To Be and actually prototype the changes prior to placing them into production. An important best practice is to make changes gradually, so as not to *shock* or adversely affect the overall operations. Change sampling allows the process engineering committee to fine tune new workflows, so that the fullest benefits are derived from the re-engineering process.

A successful re-engineering plan takes into account the need for phased-in approaches, and the challenges of implementing processes, while maintaining ongoing operations.

8. Apply Best Practices.

This book is all about best practices, right? So, the authors should know which *best practices* are the best, right? This definition of a best practice is posted at *www.searchVB.com:* "A best practice is any technique or methodology that, through experience and research, has proven to reliably lead to a desired result. A commitment to using the best practices in any field is a commitment to using all the knowledge and technology at one's disposal to ensure success."

A commitment to best practice methodologies is a commitment to research, discuss, and test new ideas and practices before putting them into place. Organizations must be willing to change directions quickly if an idea or practice proves not to be viable. Organizations must be willing to identify failures as quickly as they identify successes and adapt quickly without laying blame or criticizing others.

Applying best practices means being able to constantly benchmark results. The American Productivity & Quality Center (APQC) believes that benchmarking is not simply about a comparative analysis, site briefings, or crunching numbers. Benchmarks are helpful in setting goals and selecting which organizations to learn from, because they typically show how much improvement is needed.

So, a best practice is a superior method or an innovative process that contributes to improved performance. The test of a best practice is not whether it is the ultimate example; rather, the test is whether it works in the situation. The company must research the ways other organizations are doing a particular process and then consider the findings from their own company's viewpoint. This method allows the team to use the best practices it has identified as a template for determining which processes can be re-engineered and what the new process should look like.

According to APQC, organizations that use benchmarking to discover best practices provide exceptional customer service, have reallocated resources, use enabling technologies, and have a system to measure improvements. An APQC study of best practices in the use of technology found that a key enabler is to examine the business process itself, not to simply automate a process in the hope of benefits resulting.

The APQC website, *www.apqc.org,* offers detailed information on the benchmarking process as well as methodology for conducting your own best practices benchmark for your company.

9.   Review and Refine on a Recurring Basis.

Like most successful projects, process engineering does not end when the first pass is complete. In fact, many businesses report that, even on the third or fourth review of processes in their organization over as many years, they are still finding ways to renew, recreate, and redefine processes to make the company more efficient and profitable.

Among the items to be evaluated on a recurring basis are document processing, work relationships, and data flow. Based on its findings, the committee should refine workflow and practices, improve quality, and facilitate the management of change within the organization. Companies that have proactively embraced process engineering have trained staff and created micro versions of the PE team, both inside departments and at remote locations, and empowered them to continue the PE process as an ongoing effort.

Creating Workflow Diagrams and Reports

Now that the importance of preparing workflow documentation and diagrams has been discussed, some tools as well as practices for how to prepare the diagrams and documentation will be helpful. The tools should be as simple and easy to use as possible. Larger organizations will sometimes need to use more sophisticated software programs to assist them in workflow design and linking activities. Most medium and small businesses can accomplish their goals with only a small investment.

Two inexpensive software application tools every information technology department should have are Microsoft Project® and Microsoft Visio®. Microsoft Project® is a reasonably inexpensive and simple project management tool. Microsoft Visio® is unquestionably one of the best diagramming tools on the market for its price. Each of these applications cost under $400 for a single user version; both can be used for many purposes. So, this is an investment in software that can be used over and over for many different projects.

Microsoft Project® can be used to flow key elements of the process engineering effort such as timelines and milestones. Human resources can be assigned and reports printed to show time required as well as due dates for assignments. Having a project management tool is critical to quickly identify overlapping tasks, and tasks that can run concurrently.

Microsoft Visio® is used as a diagramming tool to graphically flow tasks. The first step is to create a series of diagrams for critical departments, areas, or tasks that currently exist. This process is called the *As Is*. Mapping the As Is accomplishes three objectives. First, it seeks to identify points of weakness in the existing system. Second, it identifies areas where productivity, or data flow, may be improved. And finally, it provides specific input to vendors. Vendors can more easily determine what is needed where and how applicable their products are to the organization. Diagrams help prevent assumptions that often occur in written or oral presentations. The adage *one picture is worth a thousand words* could not be more true.

Some organizations may find creating the diagrams overwhelming, particularly if they have never used such a tool before. Also, many individuals may be involved in the process. IT people should help guide the process and coordinate the PE effort, but should not be expected to create the diagrams. The diagrams may be created by the functional area staff, but this staff may be so close to the process being diagrammed that they miss important activities. If an external consultant is not used, consider using staff from other departments to diagram the processes. This best practice has proven beneficial as a way of introducing staff to what happens in other areas of the organization.

It is often a good idea to begin with a broad general diagram of the organization. This will indicate what areas need to be detailed, as well as pointing out obvious areas of concern or needs. In Exhibit 2.2, the author identifies several areas where data had to be rekeyed because the company's software could not share information between departments. The diagram further stresses that in several instances, data exists in one part of the organization that was not transferred or that was lost because of the applications being used. This diagram makes a simple point and provides a visual of the problem areas.

After each of the general diagrams is complete, the process engineering committee will review them and combine individual diagrams into a complete picture of the organization. Each specific area, such as customer service, sales, marketing and accounting will then be assigned for more detailed diagramming of the activities in each of those areas. In reviewing each process and the workflow activities to be diagramed, the committee members should also begin collecting sample forms and reports, and interviewing each worker about the data elements used in performing their job or tasks. Gathering this information now will save time later, and the information will be used in preparing the data element dictionaries (which is a listing of all the data that is collected and what it is used for and who it is used by), as well as other documentation you will need to manage your technology.

The number of diagrams you will generate varies, depending on the size of your organization and the number of activities that make up a process. It will also depend on how many processes you want to document. The level of detail required will also vary depending on your organization's needs. It is a fine line between not having enough information and having too much. If in doubt, err on the side of too much, if possible!

Exhibit 2.2

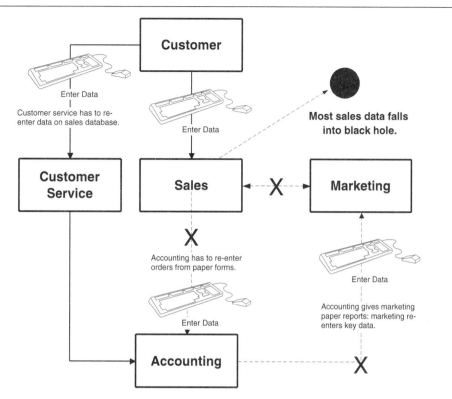

After the As Is diagrams have been prepared, reviewed, and finalized, the next step is to prepare the To Be. The To Be diagrams represent improvements on processes from the way they are done today. It is possible to add, remove, or change the activities and how information flows through the organization. The To Be diagrams correct flaws in workflow discovered in the As Is as well as enhancements to processes that are identified in the PE project. Like the As Is diagrams, some of the To Be diagrams will be very basic and others will be very detailed. The diagram in Exhibit 2.3 shows how the organization would like the sales flow process to work on a very general level versus how it is currently working today (Exhibit 2.2).

Visually comparing Exhibits 2.2 and 2.3 shows how the To Be recognized where inefficiencies existed and recreated the flow. Additional documentation that maps out the application programming changes, or new program requirements that will be needed to make the To Be happen, are not seen here.

While Visio provides a vast array of diagram graphics and representations to the user, it is important that the process engineering committee insure that the diagrams are consistent in both look and feel. Having some diagrams flow left to right and others flow down can be very confusing and can create errors in the workflow analysis. Having a broad mix of images used in the diagram can also cause incorrect interpretation of the diagrams and create confusion. A best practice is always to *Keep it simple!* Having one

Exhibit 2.3

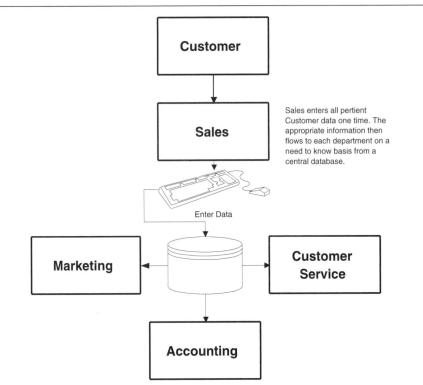

Sales enters all pertient Customer data one time. The appropriate information then flows to each department on a need to know basis from a central database.

of the technology staff, or a knowledgeable person in the organization, train the persons who will be creating the Visio diagrams is an excellent idea. The agreed upon methods for diagramming processes can also be conveyed at the same time.

Exhibit 2.4 shows a simple workflow for a single task in the sales department. This was an actual workflow (changed enough to protect the innocent). The task is Sales Forecasting, which everyone would agree is important to determining manufacturing needs, inventory to order, shipping requirements and billing.

This gives a better idea of a To Be workflow diagram. Exhibits 2.2 and 2.3 were very general, a 30,000-foot flyover of the process. Exhibit 2.4 is intended to be a ground-level view of what is actually being done at a reasonably detailed level. In fact, the more detail (pertinent facts only) at this point, the better. Notice that to the right of each graphic are the comments or observations made during the interviews when the activity flow was being charted. Note also the references to other processes, as well as data elements collected. This is the level of detail that will be collected.

As stated earlier, the end result of process engineering is change, and many individuals are adverse to change. This aversion results in the continuance of errors, loss of potential revenue, and could ultimately result in the potential failure of the company. Process engineering is most commonly done in conjunction with the procurement or

Exhibit 2.4

Sales Forecasting Process

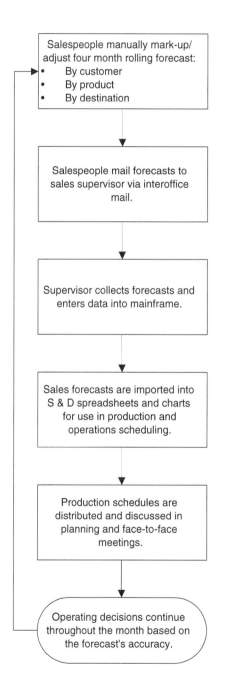

Observations

- Admin Assistant currently prints and mails.
- Forecast includes prior month's actual and three months projected sales.
- Note close link to Projecting Customer Sales vs. Production Process (MIP4)
- Includes account deletions.

- New step in process as of a few weeks ago. Forecasts previously went to accounting for mainframe entry.
- Deadline to Supervisor is 20th of the month.

- Supervisor is working with assistant so forecast entry will transition to her.
- Completed by 24th of month.

- Occurs approximately 24th to 25th of the month.
- Manager monitors product needs to support sales.
- Liaison between sales and refining.

- Occurs around the 1st of the month, with schedules reviewed weekly in various meetings.
- Includes all remote manufacturing locations and warehousing.

The flowchart boxes read:

- Salespeople manually mark-up/ adjust four month rolling forecast:
  - By customer
  - By product
  - By destination
- Salespeople mail forecasts to sales supervisor via interoffice mail.
- Supervisor collects forecasts and enters data into mainframe.
- Sales forecasts are imported into S & D spreadsheets and charts for use in production and operations scheduling.
- Production schedules are distributed and discussed in planning and face-to-face meetings.
- Operating decisions continue throughout the month based on the forecast's accuracy.

replacement of new automation systems (developing the requirements definition and request for proposal documents). Why is information technology so intimately involved in the process? Because process engineering will provide IT with a blueprint of where the needs are and what resources are needed. While a tremendous amount of effort is expended up front, this information is invaluable to information technology professionals who must plan out current and future systems based on the needs of the organization. Without this process, it is simply a blind guess.

Summary of Process Engineering

The following summarizes how these projects can be divided into smaller phases for better management.

- *Phase I:* Get input from all users (*owners*) as well as customers and vendors (*actors*) where appropriate. Include all significant *stakeholders*. Separate personal agendas from facts. When in doubt, validate. Be sensitive to organizational consequences. Create a committee of knowledgeable persons to lead the project. IT is a participant, but does not dictate. Draw a general diagram first. Document and diagram As Is processes through the organization. Next, create detail diagrams to the level needed. Look for obvious problems first, particularly problems that can be quickly, easily and cheaply corrected. These are *home runs* that can win people over to the project quickly. It is almost always possible to find problems that can be quickly corrected to win over some friends.
- *Phase II:* Prepare a list of common elements and questions. Prepare narrative of conceptual design. Prepare To Be diagrams to optimize workflow and correct errors. Look for sign-off. Start new diagramming at the point of customer contact. This is called customer centric, another best practice in today's business world to create systems that are entirely customer driven. Address ownership of data and resistance to activity measurement issues. Prepare the data element dictionary. The three steps in functional design are: 1. Identify the sequence of data use. 2. Describe all the reports, forms, and so forth needed by users. 3. Combine this information with new data maps and conceptual design narrative.
- *Phase III:* Develop technical specifications using staff, external consultant, IT and software suppliers. Consider process fit, resources, features, reliability, scalability, customization, size, code, linkages, software developer, and so forth.
- *Phase IV:* Evaluate any custom changes needed to code, and the screens and reports following prototype testing. Design training program to support culture, processes and technology. Have a detailed implementation plan written and reviewed by everyone affected to include milestone dates and objectives. Be realistic in expectation! Move forward.

The diagram in Exhibit 2.5 reflects the objective of each phase and the tasks to be accomplished.

Exhibit 2.5

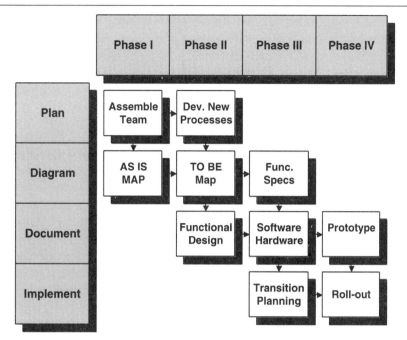

This diagram is very simple but conveys the message. What is not shown here is that the process is never ending. Reviewing processes and improving them on an on-going basis must continue.

Now that the workflow diagrams are complete, the user's needs are well documented, and the objectives are understood, the written strategic technology plan to deliver the most beneficial technologies for your organization is the next step.

DEVELOPING THE STRATEGIC TECHNOLOGY PLAN

Organizations develop technology best practices by methodically documenting, reviewing, changing, and documenting some more. Every purchase, every new software application, server, workstation and so forth is purchased not because something broke, or version 2.0 was released, but because it was to be implemented as part of an approved plan. Strategic planning begins with the development of a written plan of action. The plan has several components. This section defines each of the recommended components of a strategic technology plan. The actual plan may vary depending on the size of the business, resources, and objectives. Each of the sections below represents a section of the strategic technology plan. Begin with the vision statement.

Determining the Vision

The strategic technology plan begins with a vision statement. This is not a verbose and eloquent statement plastered on all walls and stalls, but a simple vision statement for the information technology (IT) department that helps them focus on the purpose of the plan objectives so that they do not wander off the first time some great new technology is released.

This is a vision statement for information technology developed for a client as part of developing their strategic technology plan.

It is the vision of the information technology department to create a seamless, integrated system of databases and applications supported by hardware and accessible by any internal or external resource with appropriate access rights through enterprise-wide services.

Notice that this vision statement is simple and straightforward. It is not the vision of IT to make more products, sell more products, or create new products. In the example above, the vision for IT is to create a technology infrastructure that supports the organization. If a vendor releases a new product, or announces a new direction, consult the vision statement and ask if this merits a change in direction. Sometimes the organization should adjust to take advantage of the new technology. More likely than not, the organization should continue on course, even if it means finding another vendor.

Do not be fooled by this short, simple, one sentence example. The wording of this vision statement took hours of work with the client. It was reviewed by every member of the IT department, and by senior management, to ensure that the statement reflected not only what IT felt its vision to be, but what management believed the IT vision should be as a reflection of the greater company vision.

Project Objectives

Most information technology departments have multiple technology projects in progress at the same time. Some of these projects are planned and some are a reaction to a crisis. Problems occur when these projects are not coordinated. The objective of the strategic technology plan is to develop an umbrella, under which all technology projects can be developed, coordinated, and managed. As projects are added, completed, or changed, this document will be updated accordingly.

Project Scope

It is critical to define the scope of the project early on. In the preparation of the strategic technology plan, managers of each department should be consulted about their objectives and areas where they foresee the greatest needs. Information technology touches on every department in an organization. The plan must be seen as critical to the successful deployment of technology to increase efficiency and maintain or reduce overall operational cost.

It is critical that IT staff aggressively seek out all persons who might have constructive input to the planning process. As strange as it may sound, the strategic technology plan is as much for the rest of the organization as it is for IT. *It is the organization's strategic technology plan.* IT must be open to allowing departments and users define what they need. IT must then plan how to provide what is requested.

Project Approach

To complete the strategic technology plan, collect work papers and plans for each of the ongoing capital projects and miscellaneous technology projects. Assemble and prioritize the documentation for each of these projects. IT must then evaluate the status of all current projects and compare the resulting analysis to existing resources. Next, discuss each outstanding technology project with each department head to determine if current projects meet the organization's needs, if adequate resources are available, and where additional efforts are required.

In this section of the plan, detail your approach to each project, resources applied, and expected milestones. Tell the department heads that the milestones are estimates and not chiseled in concrete. They know things change and will appreciate knowing when projects fall behind because of a virus attack or a server crash. Update the timetable as quickly as possible and continue moving forward.

Benefits of Planning

Everyone knows it is difficult to take the time to prepare a written plan. However, this book is about best practices, not about just getting by. When several major systems will have to be updated or replaced, coordination within the department and the organization is critical. The plan must recognize that new methodologies are emerging that could be advantageous for the organization considering any major software and hardware enhancement. Such technologies use the Internet to include web browser viewers to access information and web development tools, such as Java and ActiveX to support real time applications. Over time, new hardware and software will continue to emerge.

In order to benefit from these technologies, the organization must first examine how it currently uses technology and what is needed to benefit from new emerging technologies. This plan will provide strategic technology options and, where possible, the steps to accomplish recommended strategies. In the end, the organization will be able to benefit from a unified approach, as well as recognize savings from consolidating efforts.

Preparing the Technology Assessment

The plan must begin with an assessment of the current state of technology in the organization. The portion of the assessment included in the plan should be as brief as possible based on the size of your organization. Detailed network hardware and software information should not be included in the strategic technology plan document as this document will be read by individuals outside of IT who would not appreciate lists of hardware components, software versions and other details. The technology assessment portion of the plan should reference detail documents that can be supplied upon request.

The plan should briefly describe the infrastructure and major software applications supported, such as financial, inventory, manufacturing, and so forth. The number of workstations, servers, printers, and remote locations served might be summarized. Include major action items for the budget section. For instance, if a server needs to be retired early, or the backup software vendor goes out of business, and an unplanned purchase is needed this year, document that in your findings. Unusual or unplanned rapid expansion of users might be defined here in preparation for more information later in the plan.

Defining the Technology Mission Statement

Do not confuse the mission statement with the vision statement. The vision statement provides an image of where the information technology department is headed while the mission statement defines what the department does. The mission statement is short, no more than two sentences. The following example was developed for the same organization as the vision statement above. Again, notice that this is short and simple—but took a lot of effort to word just the right way!

> *It is the mission of the information technology department to manage, coordinate and deploy organization-wide information technology resources to support effective delivery of automated services.*

Goals and Objectives

What are the goals and objectives of the IT department? If the function of IT is to simply to keep systems up and running, then the operation is in maintenance mode. This mode is tactical, not strategic, and not truly maximizing the use of technology in the organization. Such activities as backing up files, installing software, and replacing broken computer parts are tactical, not strategic, activities. Activities that explore software application potential, or deployment of systems to augment staff and increase productivity, are strategic approaches to technology. Information technology professionals in best practice organizations consider themselves as strategic to the organization.

The following nine steps are from a real plan, developed for a client who defined departmental goals and objectives to serve their organization in the year to come:

1. Create and maintain a centrally managed technology infrastructure that serves the needs of all departments and that fully supports users throughout the organization.
2. Create and maintain a dynamic network hardware and operating system platform that is reliable, secure, flexible and efficient.
3. Standardize a database technology that will support current and future applications systems' needs.
4. Provide state-of-the-art application software that embraces and supports current electronic data processing techniques.
5. Provide for the integration of applications systems and data, so that all data is available to all users and applications.

6. Enable all processes of the organization to be as electronically oriented as possible, so that information flows electronically, thus reducing or eliminating the creation and propagation of printed material.

7. Develop operating processes and procedures that insure data accountability, data backup, data recovery and data security.

8. Provide technology training and education for users to make them more productive and leverage the organization's investment in technology.

9. Provide on-going support for all users, establish technology standards and provide all departments with standards, policies and procedures to protect the technical and information resources of the organization.

SOFTWARE STRATEGY

Within the overall strategic technology plan is a software plan. The software plan begins by defining the current core processing applications and the hardware architecture that supports those applications. This statement does not detail specifics, but should list the core applications, vendor or brand in use, how long the applications have been in use, and the platform being supported.

A trend statement that describes IT's objective to incorporate emerging technology into the organization's infrastructure should follow. A best practice trend today shows IT attempting to identify and evaluate fully integrated software solutions for core applications. The objective of IT is to create an integrated solution for the organization's information needs and to provide a system capable of being accessed by employees and others, from simple and readily available tools, such as a common web browser interface. This is referred to as an e-business solution. Most business software providers today are writing their systems to benefit from Internet technology.

To assess future technology infrastructure, current software features and functions must be documented. Current applications may be client server-based, Unix-based, or may be running on a proprietary operating system with a limited economic life and targeted for replacement. Be sure to document all personal computer-based applications that are both stand-alone, as well as file server and print server-based. In the case of personal computer applications, define if information technology support staff must update and load patches at each individual workstation. This is cumbersome and not cost-effective. New planning should include applications that can be updated from a central server or workstation with the least amount of human intervention possible.

In many current environments, problem calls and inquiries for assistance require that technology support staff go directly to the system where assistance is needed. For businesses utilizing older technologies, the cost of maintenance and support is likely to be very high. This results in significant resources being dedicated to *maintenance mode* and minimal resources being available for future expansion and implementing new technologies. By identifying and replacing the applications that are the most labor intensive, it is possible to reduce the long-term cost of support and significantly reduce the total cost of ownership (TCO) to your organization.

There are three best practice software technology strategies that are crucial for any organization to implement a true e-business platform. These strategies use emerging technologies and web tools to radically change the way applications are processed, information is retrieved and updated, and users' general access to information. The goal of these strategies is to reduce the overall cost of technology, while increasing user productivity through ease of access and availability of information. The following is a general discussion of each of these strategies. A more detailed description of these hardware and software methodologies will be presented in later sections of this book

Thin Client

Thin client computing is an important strategy; it centralizes control in much the same manner as mainframe computers centralized processing a few decades ago. The deployment of a thin client solution could significantly reduce hardware and support costs for some organizations.

The thin client is a minimally configured personal computer. Applications are actually run on a thin client server, located in a central computer room, versus each user's personal computer. This is a key difference between a traditional personal computer workstation, called a *fat client,* and a thin client solution. Only screen images are sent to the thin client and keystrokes are returned to the terminal server for execution.

Cost benefits of thin client computing are:

- The thin client solution requires less bandwidth, thereby reducing communications cost.
- The thin client solution provides for easy Internet or dial-in access to applications at nearly network speeds.
- The thin client solution makes it possible to introduce new applications quickly, often adding life to older personal computers, since all the power resides in the terminal server hardware.
- The thin client solution creates a higher level of security, since users cannot introduce unauthorized applications and viruses into the network.

Since no solution is perfect, there are also drawbacks:

- Not all users can perform well in a thin client environment and not all applications perform properly as well. Therefore, it may be necessary to have a mixture of both thin clients and fat clients for the foreseeable future.
- Terminal server software and hardware is fairly expensive. The terminal server software is licensed according to user licenses.
- When the terminal server goes down, all the users go down! Since work is not distributed, everyone must wait for the system to return. Information technology will configure redundancy and fail safes for possible disasters. A best practice solution would be to develop a plan that would split users over two terminal servers. Then, if

either server crashes, at least half of the users can work. Including fail-safe backup and redundancy in your planning is important.

Exhibit 2.6 diagrams the logical infrastructure of a thin client solution.

Exhibit 2.6

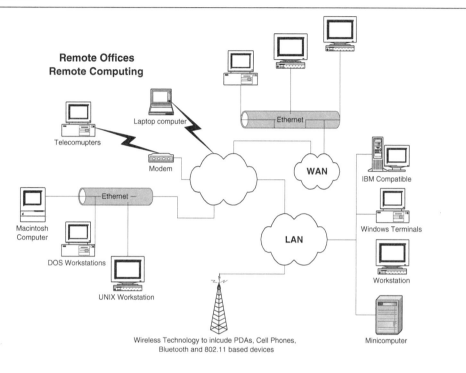

Remote Offices
Remote Computing

Laptop computer

Telecomupters

Modem

Ethernet

Macintosh
Computer

DOS Workstations

UNIX Workstation

Ethernet

WAN

LAN

IBM Compatible

Windows Terminals

Workstation

Wireless Technology to inlcude PDAs, Cell Phones,
Bluetooth and 802.11 based devices

Minicomputer

Browser Client

Web-enabled, browser-based applications are also an important technology strategy. This is an emerging technology and applications are still being developed to operate in this environment. For a period of time, it is expected that businesses will deploy both thin client and web-enabled applications as the transition evolves. Initially, thin client will help reduce the cost of supporting users and extend the economic life of older hardware. As web-enabled applications mature, and as resources for internal development become available, the IT support staff can migrate users to this technology.

Browser-based applications deliver solutions to users exclusively through a common web browser interface, such as Microsoft Internet Explorer® or Netscape Navigator®. In most cases, no special software is needed, as there is with the thin client strategy where a small applet, referred to as a client, must be stored at the workstation. Like thin client server computing, this model centralizes the applications and data providing for easy access. Browser-based computing is a viable long-term technology strategy for any organization and is key to fully implementing the larger e-business strategy.

Cost Benefits of the browser client are:

- The browser client solution requires less bandwidth than conventional networked fat clients, thereby reducing communication cost.
- The browser client solution provides for access to applications and data from either internal networks (Intranets) or via the World Wide Web (Internet.)
- The browser client solution makes it possible to introduce new, and update existing, applications quickly. This significantly reduces the personnel of supporting users.
- The browser client solution is more secure than traditional network environments and does not allow users to introduce unauthorized applications and viruses into the network.

Downsides to the browser-based solution are:

- Browser-based solutions are immature and just now coming to market. The migration will be gradual over the next few years.
- Information technology may need to bring Internet and Intranet development in-house, which could require additional resources and training.
- Since the development of browser-based solutions is in its infancy, organizations will need to develop several in-house applications to meet the unique needs of certain departments and to accelerate the implementation process. Unlike conventional applications, browser-based solutions are done in small applets that can be readily reused and are easy to develop and maintain.

Web-based Solutions

A more intensive and managed deployment of Internet, Intranet and Extranet solutions can minimize the cost of specialized software and allow unique user needs to be met. The Internet is a combination of tools and applications that includes vertical market applications (such as accounting and finance applications); content containers (pages of web content); communications; email and chat; video-based, HTML-based, and XML-based browsers; and search engines. It also includes products that support and generate viewing, sharing, communicating and operating on the World Wide Web and in Intranet and Extranet environments. A commonly accepted definition of an Intranet is an internal, corporate network that uses the same basic architecture, protocols, and applications as the Internet. Intranets use the applications that have developed around the web and offer seamless integration between corporate networks and the Internet itself. Intranets can store, retrieve, and distribute information in the form of electronic documents. They vary greatly in size and in scope. Thus, the applications used in their creation and utilization also vary.

An Extranet is a network that links business partners, suppliers, distributors, contractors, and increasingly, customers, to one another over the Internet by connecting their corporate intranets. Extranet use represents the third wave in the *net* evolution. Generalized Internet use marked the first phase and Intranet implementations constituted the second.

Companies increasingly view Extranets as the next logical step to web site and Intranet installations, typically using them to exchange information more efficiently and to stream-line commercial transactions. Extranets offer a variety of benefits, including improved time-to-market cycles, reduction in telecommunications costs, lower procurement costs, and closer relationships with business partners. One example of an Extranet is direct links between city and county law enforcement agencies, sharing criminal activity and officer deployment to leverage resources and provide a higher level of coverage.

The development of browser pages to access common, or specialized, databases requires trained staff, understanding of the tools to be used, and appropriate security that protects the privacy of sealed information. Because web-enabled technology is new, most information technology professionals recommend that organizations first prototype one department at a time and then expand throughout the organization as solutions are developed or purchased. Many organizations are approaching web-based solutions as they did custom programming solutions a couple of decades ago. As the development of custom code created benefits for the early users of automation, developing leading edge web-based applications can offer larger businesses advantages over their competitors.

Many organizations do not have the resources to deploy a technology enterprise all at once. In the beginning, as a best practice for developing web-enabled applications, the developer should focus on the development of *reusable* tools and applets that will make future development faster and less expensive. As information technology begins rolling out web-based solutions by department or functional area, tools, screen shots, database routines and so forth will be developed that can be used over and over again in other areas.

Cost benefits of the web-based solutions are:

- Many readers are likely to be horrified by the idea of returning to a time when organizations hired and managed a large programming staff to develop custom applications. With the advent of the Internet, this pattern is being repeated. Today, most claim little, if any, strategic advantages are derived from off-the-shelf technology. Any advantages are derived from how the software is used. Since web-based applications are a new frontier, the possibilities are endless. Each business can fashion an e-business technology strategy that is best for them.
- If development projects are well managed, a large percentage of the code can be developed as objects that can be used over and over, reducing the overall development cost, and making the applications less costly to maintain.
- Web-based solutions can be platform independent where nearly any browser can be the front end to a powerful database. Platform independent applications allow business the flexibility to run on Windows, DOS, Unix, Linux, workstations and servers, greatly reducing licensing and maintenance cost.

Downsides to the web-based solutions are:

- Some of the things that make web-based solutions a strategic weapon also create a downside in development cost, deployment, and long-term support.
- If the development of web-based solutions is not well managed, poorly documented and expensive applications to maintain and deploy will be created.

Emerging Software Technology

Defining emerging technology can be tricky. Software technology that is emerging when this book is written may not still be emerging when the book is published months later.

Emerging software may be defined as new applications, features, or benefits that might benefit your organization. For instance, Best Software released handheld accounting applications for the popular Palm Personal Digital Assistant (PDA). Other software vendors are following with mobile accounting applications. This represents a major departure from standard applications and so may be considered emerging software technology.

Another emerging software technology to watch is document management. Document management has many components—imaging, storage and retrieval, work flow management, and so forth. Document management is important because of the shift from external unstructured documents to internal structured and unstructured documents (structured and unstructured documents will be discussed in later chapters). Organizations need the tools to store and track documents in an electronic form. When considering document management solutions, information technology staff may be forced to standardize a single product for scanning, imaging, indexing and storing all document images throughout the organization. The information technology department must work closely with users to affect a planned rollout and provide training necessary. Because of the cost to scan, image, and index historical documents, information technology should view this process of implementation as a multi-year project.

HARDWARE STRATEGY

Software strategies were discussed first because software considerations should always come first. However, in reality, IT is often more comfortable with the hardware platform, is unwilling to adapt a multi-platform hardware strategy, and may force users in that direction. A best practice organization will always put software selection ahead of hardware concerns, making hardware a part of the cost of software implementation and thus including all costs in the return on investment calculation.

To begin this process, information technology professionals must fully document the current hardware inventory used throughout the organization or bring existing documentation up-to-date. This detail should not be included as part of the strategic technology plan because it is simply a list of technical reference information that might cloud the critical information in the plan. A simple paragraph can give a general overview of the current environment:

> *XYZ Company's existing mainframe environment consists of an NCR 3550 computer and associated peripherals. The NCR 3550, which was installed in 1991, was last upgraded with a new processor(s) and additional memory in 1997. The NCR 3550 basic architecture is dated and is reaching the end of its useful service life. In 1999, an NCR 4300 was purchased as a backup machine for the NCR 3550. The information technology department*

will be replacing the older NCR 3550 with a newer NCR 4455 in the second quarter of 2001. The replacement unit will be faster and less expensive than the existing units, which are several years old. XYZ has approximately 650 personal computer workstations that are Windows 95 and Windows 98 based. XYZ also has approximately 150 display only workstations, which will be replaced over the next 18 months as a part of this plan. Printers vary widely, but the most commonly used user/department printers are Hewlett Packard Laser Jet and Bubble Jet Printers. More detailed information of all workstation and printer resources is on file in the information technology department according to date of purchase and expected replacement date. This information can be provided to department heads upon request.

A description of current hardware may be more or less verbose. It is important to provide the readers as brief an overview of the current technology as possible without losing your audience. Many of the individuals reviewing the planning document, and approving the funding to proceed, will be nontechnical and may be intimidated or confused, by too much technical detail. An organization often brings in an independent consultant because management cannot communicate with their technical staff. Management may be intimidated by a language they do not understand, feel they do not have the expertise to judge what is important and what is optional. In reviewing the plans that IT present, consultants often find them to be complete and right on target. However, the plans are difficult to follow and understand. In an effort to *educate* management, IT often provides an abundance of detail, software, and cost information, without actual business justification for upgrading or changing direction. IT must remember that management nearly always has a *return on investment* (ROI) focus. Decisions to purchase new hardware and software must be backed up with justifications that translate into increased productivity, reduction in cost, or better leverage of resources.

The following defines a few specific hardware strategies that can be used to plan hardware acquisition and deployment as part of the strategic technology plan.

Network Server Strategies

Information technology is responsible for deploying hardware technology that supports the selected software strategies. This means user and server technology that supports both the thin client and browser-based software strategies described above. This will include thin-client workstations from Wyse® and other vendors who provide workstations with limited local resources as well as full-function personal computers where appropriate. Workstations should be supported by the most current Windows server operating system solutions and Citrix Metaframe® Servers, which will support multiple users from centrally located server farms. Workstations should be configured in standard images.

The trend today is toward a centralized, versus decentralized, server strategy. Where possible, IT should centralize all network servers serving the organization in a central computer room (the exception may be where two computer room facilities are used at remote locations and serve as backup for each other in the case of a disaster.) While this may not be entirely possible today, deployment of thin client and browser technology over the next few years will serve to naturally move information technology departments in that direction.

In a distributed environment, the typical IT department will have several servers, each with its own specific purpose. Microsoft, for instance, recommends that IT deploy one software service per physical box. This would mean having an exchange server, Internet information server, SQL database server, application server, print server and so forth. While it is easy for a vendor to recommend an approach, it could be very expensive and resource intensive to deploy software and hardware in this manner. When planning for the deployment of network servers, IT must consider not only the resources and cost related to multiple servers, but the impact on disaster recovery as well. Chapter 12 addresses best practices for contingency planning. Preparing to support the organization in the event of a disaster means careful planning of the deployment of your servers and communications infrastructure.

IT must therefore determine which services (mail, Internet access, database, etc.) can be grouped together, and may want to configure servers so that, should a server fail, another server can pick up those failed services until the failed services can be restored. The strategic technology plan should briefly address this issue. Keep details here to a minimum, as this is a planning document and should not overwhelm the reader.

Client Workstation Strategies

There has been a general adoption of desktop image management beginning in early 2000. The process has been highly successful at reducing user downtime and reducing the cost of system maintenance. According to studies released by Gartner Group, AMR research, Tolly Group, and others, it costs an organization more than $400, not including parts and lost productivity due to down time, every time a technician opens a workstation to repair it. The objective of IT is to reduce this cost and lost productivity. A more detailed explanation of the process and software used to image desktops is provided in Chapter 6.

There are several workstation strategies that IT can deploy—from fat clients that are fully equipped personal computers, to thin clients that are minimally equipped personal computers, and network computers that may have connection software embedded in the unit firmware. Many network computers have no floppy, compact disk player, or hard disk drive.

An important workstation strategy today is to extend the life of workstations. Deploying software solutions that are client-server based and using Windows Terminal Server or Citrix Metaframe does this. The software solution is discussed above, and in Chapter 4, in more detail. The strategic technology plan should define the ROI of the thin client solution and the intent of IT to deploy the technology to reduce maintenance and support costs, as well as extend the economic life of the user workstations.

Purchasing Strategies

In order for the organization to purchase equipment at the best possible price, the information technology department should work closely with purchasing to make large quantity bulk orders at key times when vendors are most likely to offer the best pricing to reduce inventory. By standardizing with a single vendor, limiting the number of models purchased, and purchasing on-site technical support, IT will significantly reduce the total cost of maintenance and support over the life of the equipment.

Deployment of Peripheral Components

Many organizations share printers between several individuals. But, best practice businesses are finding that it may be more beneficial to provide users who do a lot of printing with their own printers. There are several locations where user productivity can be increased by deploying additional printers. Information technology must also continue to upgrade and deploy printers, scanners, optical devices, handheld devices, and other technology as applications develop and benefits to the company can be identified.

Continuous System Upgrade and Replacement

Experience shows that because systems fail slowly, over time, not replacing units on a regular basis creates real costs in productivity. Further, as systems age, the cost of maintenance rapidly increases. When a large percent of technology is replaced at one time, the cost is difficult to fund and must be recovered over long periods of time.

The routine maintenance of existing hardware is severely lacking today. With the distribution of hardware to remote locations, many businesses neglect the importance of maintaining these systems. Sometimes maintenance can be as simple as cleaning monitor screens and keyboards on a regular basis. Several companies conducted studies on the cost of responding to problem calls versus preventative maintenance and found that preventative maintenance was much more beneficial. One maintenance strategy was to automatically clean and replace the toner cartridges in all laser printers on a regular basis rather than waiting for a call that a printer was out of toner. There might be some waste in cartridges not fully depleted, but this waste was offset by the benefits of worker productivity. At a specific time, a technician would make the rounds and clean and replace toner in all the printers. A large company with many printers might have more than one schedule for group printers and another for personal printers that are not heavily used. At cleaning time, the technician would test each printer to determine if it is properly aligned and working. They would also verify the users assigned to that printer and the degree to which it is used, to determine if the current printer is adequate or if an upgrade is needed to improve user productivity.

This routine maintenance and verification have a number of side benefits as well. During one strategic planning engagement, a printer purchased six months earlier that no one was using was found! Evidently, someone had identified a need and ordered the printer. IT had set the printer up. But, there were no instructions on who should be using that printer! Management was amazed, but acknowledged they had dropped the ball. In another engagement, a user in payroll was printing to a printer in accounts payable, some distance away from her desk. She did not know why she was using that printer, when there was a perfectly good one not 25 feet from her. But, she used to work in accounts payable and that was the printer she used there. When she changed offices, her system went with her; no one had contacted IT with the changes. The cost of traveling to her printer several times a day could have been avoided. Routine maintenance would have caught both of these situations and corrected them quickly.

Finally, make it easier for staff to replace mouse and keyboard attachments without calling IT. Several businesses today are placing a few mice and a couple of keyboards in the supply closet where they keep post-it notes, felt tip pens and paper clips. If a user is having problems with a keyboard or mouse, there is no waiting for IT to respond to the call. (Not to mention that IT professionals are a little expensive to spend their time changing out a mouse or keyboard!) The users simply request a replacement in the same manner they request other supplies (staples and pens) and replace the item. Company policy varies on how to dispose of the failed item. Some companies tell me they forward the failed component to IT, which then collects them, and does a quick repair check when there are no other demands (if that ever happens in IT!) Others log when a user pulls a keyboard or mouse for replacement, but then dispose of the old item. Since keyboard and mice run under $20 today, they are considered disposable. The log is useful because it tracks who is requesting a replacement, as well as how often. IT enters the information into a help desk problem-tracking program for future reporting. All in all, this is a very good approach to keeping users productive and letting IT stay focused on important technical issues.

The most successful strategy to combat maintenance problems is the development of an annual technology budget where a percentage of the organization's entire technology infrastructure is upgraded annually. As new technology is purchased, older technology is reassigned and the newer technology is deployed where the organization would benefit most. Today, many organizations budget to replace technology over a three-year cycle. By deploying thin client and browser or thin client technology, information technology can extend the useful life of workstations and servers from 2–3 years to 4–5 years.

COMMUNICATIONS INFRASTRUCTURE STRATEGY

Organization wide-area networks can reach a saturation point very quickly. This will have an adverse impact on productivity. Verifying data throughput and upgrading services on a regular basis can prevent a communications bottleneck from developing. IT should not wait for management or users to complain that communications can no longer efficiently handle the day-to-day tasks of backup of remote servers, Internet access, e-mail, and file transfers. Today, it is not enough to simply deploy fast wide-area network technology. IT must also focus on solutions that serve mobile users and the integration of data over a widely dispersed user base. Best practice businesses are returning to centralized data management, eliminating unnecessary duplication, and depending on centralized databases to increase data security and prevent information leaks.

A centralized communications structure that services internal, external and remote users requires high-speed, reliable, combinations of T-1, DSL, and broadband cable communications. See Chapter 9 for specifics on the implementation of remote technology.

In many organizations, the information technology departments have responsibility for managing the voice communications systems as well as data communications. The strategic technology plan might include migration into voice over Internet Protocol (IP) technology. Voice over IP (VoIP) is a key strategic technology for many enterprise businesses today. VoIP, as well as other voice-over-packet network technologies, such as those using frame relay and ATM, are designed to lower the total cost of ownership for telephone systems and to enable new applications for end users. The technology can also result in improved reliability and security. According to a study conducted by the Gartner Group and reported at *www.voipwatch.com* in October 2000, the VoIP market is maturing rapidly. Gartner estimated that, in the near future, more than half of public broadcast exchange (PBX) shipments would be VoIP based, which are servers running call management software and connected to a local area network (LAN).

The voice-over-IP market breaks into two segments: enterprise-type applications on a private network and wide-area services where a network operator packages voice traffic for transport across an IP network. VoIP technology has been around for several years, and is fairly stable with well-defined implementation processes. IP voice quality has improved and become less of an issue in recent years. Information technology must plan to integrate VoIP into its wide area network strategy to provide additional services to all departments, and to further reduce the cost of communications. One common application of VoIP is customer relationship management (CRM). By providing self-service applications that customers can use to interface with the business, an organization allows a customer to directly access product configurators to order items directly using Internet tools. The same systems can provide shipping or delivery information to customers without human intervention. VoIP systems can also be used to route voice messages to mailboxes for remote pickup or for routing of messages where the intended receiver is absent and someone else is answering inquiries. CPA4Sure, *www.cap4sure.com,* is an example of a company using this best practice to allow customers to set up an account, place orders and track delivery of these orders via the company's Internet/Extranet without having to contact help desk staff directly. New account information is routed to an account manager who then contacts the new customer directly (thereby not losing the *warm fuzzy* of person-to-person contact) and keeps customers aware of new product offerings, credit management, and other services.

Creating a comprehensive plan that involves sales and marketing staff, along with manufacturing and distribution, requires that IT receive input from several other departments. It must keep management from each department involved in the selection and deployment process.

DELIVERY SYSTEMS STRATEGY

The concept of defining and developing structured delivery systems is fairly new. Because of the number of platforms IT must serve, and the variations in applications and tools users require, delivery systems define how the right tools and applications are delivered to each user.

Standardizing which tools, such as Microsoft Internet Explorer or Netscape Navigator, are used for access, viewing, and modifying data is important. This technology is called web-enabled and truly represents the future of software development.

In the past, delivery system strategies have revolved around specific vendors, such as Microsoft. This has happened without most IT professionals considering all the possible ramifications. IT has often developed strategies they considered non-proprietary only to find out later that there were proprietary components that locked the company into a specific vendor, or product direction.

The minute a company starts to rely on a single technology, the provider of that technology controls not only the speed and reliability of the solution, but also its cost. Another problem surfaced in 2001, when Microsoft decided to change some of its licensing policies. Although Microsoft's products support standards, many of its products also have proprietary features that provide additional benefits. When Microsoft announced plans to change its licensing scheme, the customers that depended heavily on those proprietary features suddenly realized their choices had been minimized. They had lost much of the control over their own destiny. Because of this experience, some IT professionals are pushing toward less proprietary solutions.

Taking back control of your IT costs requires reducing your dependency on proprietary features in favor of standards. For example, base your directory services on lightweight directory access protocol (LDAP) and resist the temptation to take advantage of proprietary extensions offered in some solutions. This way, if the current LDAP directory is too slow or the provider is charging too much, it can more easily be replaced with one that is faster, cheaper, or more reliable.

Author's Note: Lightweight directory access protocol (LDAP) is a protocol for accessing online directory services. It runs directly over TCP, and can be used to access a standalone LDAP directory service or to access a directory service that is back-ended by X.500. There are several excellent explanations of LDAP on the Internet, search parameter LDAP.

Delivery of client and server browser-based applications is another area where companies can tie themselves to a specific vendor without realizing it. Again, Microsoft is an example. Microsoft elected not to include support for Java on its Windows XP CD. Microsoft requires customers to install the Microsoft virtual machine (Microsoft VM) for Java to run Java applications (*www.microsoft.com/java/*). Microsoft contends that their release of Java, while differing from the Sun Microcomputer release, takes optimal advantage of Windows, which is their objective.

There cannot be a delivery strategy that does not include the Internet in its many forms. As simple as it may seem, management may not share IT's understanding of the value of the Internet. Basically, your company Internet serves three basic purposes:

1. To act as the primary conduit for the flow of information from the company to your customers and vendors, regarding services provided by the company and the modalities for conducting business with your company.

2. To act as a central repository for all public use forms and historical documents generated by your company for general distribution to others.

3. To act as a public relations tool for your company, to provide a presence on the Internet, and provide customers and vendors with an alternate means of conducting business with your company.

Presenting a comprehensive plan to deploy information via the Internet is important. Management throughout your organization must not only understand the benefits to be derived, but also what resources they are to contribute. A company will not have the resources to implement an enterprise-wide Internet at once. Best practice suggests that information technology develop an implementation strategy based on information received from each department or group within the organization. The second phase is to develop a prototype project to demonstrate the effectiveness and benefits of the strategy. Review the prototype with management, and upon approval of resources to proceed, progress slowly on a department-by-department basis in order of relationship, or in order of greatest ROI by department.

Getting permission to move forward on development of the Internet may be the easiest part of the project. There are three possible options for the development and maintenance of an Internet site:

1. Contracting the site development out to a third-party service provider. This option does not always allow an organization to maintain a high level of quality and provide the most current information possible to constituents. Depending on an outside source for site development and maintenance has repeatedly been a sore subject for many IT managers.

2. Take all Internet servers in-house and assume full responsibility for the servers and all web development. This usually requires a significant increase in technical and support resources. This may not be the best alternative for a number of reasons. First, the expense of bringing the services in-house could minimize the level of quality the company could afford. Second, IT would have to bring in much higher bandwidth to support access to the Internet site. And third, IT may have to add additional security to ensure that internal servers remain secure.

3. Develop a hybrid of the options above. The best practice solution to long-term care and feeding of your Internet site is assigning responsibility where there is the greatest control with minimal resources.

   • Move responsibility for the company web site from your third-party provider in-house to IT. Assign that responsibility to someone on staff who fully understands the mission of your company. Assigning responsibility does not mean having to do the work; it means directing those who do the work and determining what needs to be done when.

   • Hire appropriate qualified Web engineering and design staff based on the size of your organization, who can make quick changes when needed and also maintain the internal company Intranet site. IT should take the responsibility for design and implementation. Base the site on the information gathered from throughout the organization.

- Contract with an outside party to host all web sites. This minimizes the potential threat of intrusion to the corporate network and reduces the start-up cost for hosting both the Internet and Intranet (see below.) IT can always retain the option of moving sites in-house at a later time.

Highly innovative companies consider their Intranet to be strategic to their company mission. When it comes to re-engineering information delivery systems, Intranets can provide tremendous returns for the cost. A company Intranet site should have three basic objectives:

1. To act as the primary conduit for the flow of internal information. This may be as generic as company policy and procedure manuals to more detailed information such as purchasing, human resources and inventory information.
2. To act as a central repository for all forms utilized by the company. Implementation of this concept allows for centralized forms management and the transition from the use of static and preprinted forms to the use of dynamic virtual forms.
3. To act as a test bed for the use of emerging *business-to-business* (b2b) and e-commerce business solutions before their use on the corporate Internet site. This procedure allows all departments to measure the impact of these new technologies on their internal business practices and to incorporate required changes prior to their deployment to the company's Internet site.

The overall objective of the strategic technology plan is to provide ever-increasing access to accurate information in a timely manner to employees of the organization and to those with a need to know. To accomplish this, IT must build and support a delivery system that incorporates each of the technologies described above. IT must:

- Build a high-speed internal communications backbone and infrastructure to include enhanced high-speed wiring, high-tech switches and routers, and fast gateways supported by third-party providers working with the company.
- Create and maintain an information portal that includes an Internet, Intranet and Extranets, where appropriate, to bring all the information of the company under one umbrella.
- Provide hardware and software applications appropriate to support the applications as they are rolled out to end-users.
- Develop a continuous update model for upgrading and maintaining quality hardware, software applications, and networks that increase user productivity by leveraging advancing technology.

EMERGING TECHNOLOGY STRATEGY

While focusing on the primary projects defined in the plan, it is important that information technology not lose sight of technology awareness and enlightenment as moving targets. Information technology must continue to be aware of and to evaluate new technologies as they emerge. These technologies, including handheld mobile devices such as Palm OS and Windows CE-based devices, hold a promise for those who need access to information, basic e-mail, and electronic books. Other technologies, such as Wireless Applications Protocol (WAP), define how wireless protocols such as Blue Tooth, 802.11 will be used to communicate between appliances. These range from wireless controllers for wireless devices to remote communications devices. Wireless technology is the future of technology, and information technology can make it a strategic part of the organization.

STAFFING AND EDUCATION STRATEGY

Not properly educating users to maximize the benefit of the technology has been one of the great failures of the past twenty years. That technology has not fulfilled the promises made by IT is a constant complaint of management. Perhaps the promises were too great, or IT did not do its job to document the expectations and to follow through. Business knows that realizing a better return on technology investments today means providing higher levels of education to end-users. A review of hundreds of acquisitions over the past decade reveals a recurring theme; many vendors had demonstrated product features and benefits that were never implemented when the software went live. In several cases, management even selected the product specifically because of a certain feature that was never used. When budgets were prepared and plans were made, training and education always went to the end of the list and was never completed. In some cases, businesses were on the verge of throwing out their current application and starting over. These companies needed to clean up their systems, upgrade their hardware, upgrade their software applications, and create a training program to put the technology to work for them. The results were exactly as expected. For the first time in years, managers claimed that the computers were working for them.

The greatest barrier information technology faces in deploying and supporting advanced technologies is the continued availability of knowledgeable and experienced technology staff. Information technology has made great advances over the past few years, but the struggle to attract and keep technicians continues. If IT is to carry out a plan to create and support the type of advanced technology seen today, information technology departments must have qualified technicians and developers. Over time, IT staff will be moved into new roles, but the information technology department must have staff during the transition between technologies to lay the framework for future development.

Companies must also change their focus on training employees to use the technology it has deployed. In the past, because of lack of staff, the focus has only been on training. That is, showing a user how to turn the system on, navigate to a few tools, and perhaps print documents. To truly benefit from technology, organizations must be proactive and institute a technology education program for all users. To educate users goes beyond surface utilization of the computer to providing more depth on the applications used and how to access information directly.

A best practice to achieve improved productivity and performance used by medium to large companies today includes the hiring of an *education coordinator*. The concept of the position of education coordinator (EC) is relatively new. The EC may be positioned in either information technology or employee services. One of the primary objectives of the EC is to evaluate staff knowledge and recommend training. The EC should be very familiar with the functions performed and the needs of each department. The EC does not have to be technical, but should have good skills with the computer and a good understanding of back-office applications such as word processing, spreadsheets and electronic mail.

The EC, after canvassing department heads and users, will map out a training plan to educate users for the best ROI. Some training may be low-level and ensure that users know how to access information, work with printers, send messages and so forth. However, most of the training will be more goal-oriented and relate directly to maximizing the benefits of application software. Education is a combination of classroom seminar lectures, hands-on exercises, and study. Rather than simply asking a vendor to come in and present a seminar on their product, the EC will develop a specific curriculum of the items to be covered. They will present the instructor with a list of specific questions, processes, or other inquiry about the product the company is using. The instructor will then prepare a presentation geared to the needs of the company. These presentations tend to be not so basic in nature and of much greater value.

To maximize the value of training, a best practice is to have each course attendee complete a course assessment at the end. Some companies may call these what they actually are—a test. But, some companies may not be able to call them tests. However, educators find that students are much more attentive if they know they are to be tested on the material presented. They will then try to stay awake (very important to learning), take notes, and ask questions when they don't understand something the instructor said. Course assessments have several objectives. They give an indication if the attendees understood what was presented. These assessments also show if the instructor did a good job. The course assessments should be prepared by the EC, not the instructor, based on the material requested. If 90 percent or more of the attendees miss a question, perhaps this is the presenter's fault. Some companies tie training into annual compensation. This provides employees with an incentive to attend seminars and improve their skills with the technology provided.

The EC works closely with department heads, as well as IT, to identify needs and potential areas where technology could be used to leverage staff and increase productivity. In order for the EC to be effective, management must carefully define the role and develop a method of tracking the value of the education to the company. It is important that this position is valued and is not simply seen as another overhead position. Most trainers can provide generic training for applications such as Microsoft Windows, Microsoft Office (Word, Excel, PowerPoint, etc.), the Internet and so forth. The EC will arrange training based on the needs of the users. The EC will define the course of seminar topics and work closely with the software vendors to ensure that the training given is targeted specifically to the needs of the organization.

The EC must understand the goals and objectives of the position and be able to convey these to management, so that success can be tracked. Not investing enough in this position, or staffing the position with the wrong person, can have a severe negative impact on the company. The compensation for this position must be tied to experience and expectations.

PLAN ASSUMPTIONS

Any plan projects into the future and requires the author to make some basic assumptions. In the field of computer technology, where directions can change very quickly because of financial issues, mergers, acquisitions, or market acceptance of a product, IT professionals must plan. But, those plans must be based on what is known, or believed, to be valid at a specific point in time. These beliefs are assumptions. IT must make assumptions that are as accurate as possible, and document the decision-making process thoroughly, should the assumptions require defense in the future. IT must plan, based on the mission of the organization, to implement technology that meets the needs of the organization.

Based on trends in the marketplace, IT may assume that web-enabled applications will be the future. IT might base this assumption on information from sources such as Microsoft's well-publicized Microsoft.NET initiative. The fundamental idea here is the shift from individual web sites or devices connected to the Internet, to constellations of computers, devices and services that work together to deliver broader, richer solutions. According to Microsoft, Microsoft.NET offers great opportunities for developers and partners. And, consumers benefit from an integrated, secure, and easy-to-use Internet experience. IT may also base the decision on reports published by other vendors. When making assumptions, be aware of the source of evidence. Who stands to benefit most from the Microsoft Microsoft.NET initiative? Microsoft would debate that it serves the mutual interest of all Microsoft customers. However, as discussed earlier, selecting a single vendor solution can also restrict an organization's future ability to navigate its own destiny. Yes, Microsoft.NET and other such products benefit the user, and take advantage of the operating system. But, what happens when the direction changes?

A best practice is to develop assumptions from third-party independent sources as well as personal knowledge. Even then, make certain that reports business decisions are based on are as unbiased as possible. If a specific vendor that is highly represented funds the report, that report should be suspect. The old adage that *figures don't lie but figurers do* is truer than you think. Do not fall into the trap of deciding what to do and then justifying it. Stay open to new developments and know what makes good business sense for the company. Act on that, not on what is comfortable.

Good assumptions are built around proven technologies and developing trends. It is easy to say that Internet-centric, web-enabled solutions are the future. But, what technologies are needed to support these solutions and is there fundamental support for them? Evolving solutions that will drive web-enabled applications include *application solutions providers* (ASP). Fast out of the gate, ASPs lost much of their steam in 2001. Yet, ASP solutions also apply to in-house hosted solutions and can be a strong fit in an overall plan. An organization, over time, might create an ASP environment where information technology delivers centralized applications and services based on building blocks such as *extensible markup language* (XML), and *structured query language* (SQL) in common database formats that are *open database compliant* (ODBC). This allows information to be inputted a minimum of times (hopefully once) and then shared across applications. Even highly vertical solutions like *geographical information systems* (GIS) can be integrated into a total Internet-wide enterprise solution. This assumption builds on multiple tools and accepted standards to create an objective that has economic benefits to the company.

SQL, XML, ODBC and SQL are all standards and tools that develop trends. But, IT must also focus on new assumptions of how these tools will be combined to create application solutions. Document management, Web-based applications (built on Java, Active X, and even Perl tools), client-server applications, and front-office tools like Microsoft Office and Star Office all integrate to create the e-business strategy. Exhibit 2.7 shows how IT creates an e-business-centric strategy. Use this research and these graphics to explain and justify assumptions.

There are several benefits to a fully integrated e-business strategy.

- Web-enabled applications require less processing power at the Client (user) workstation, and thus lower the overall cost of hardware upgrades and software licenses, while extending overall the economic life of the hardware.
- Databases are centrally stored and managed with less redundancy of information, meaning less opportunity for data to be entered erroneously. Centralized databases also provide a high degree of security and reliability ensuring fewer mistakes and less cost to maintain and support.

Exhibit 2.7

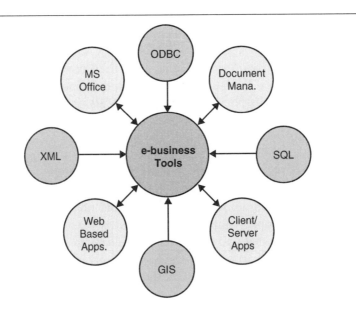

- Information is available universally, meaning that users may access the information from any client workstation that is authorized to attach itself to the Intranet and access data. Because the strategy is Internet based, the network can be extended to anyone with Internet access who has appropriate authority to access company data.

Complete the assumptions with referenced white papers, analysis, research documents, and reports. Keep the assumptions simple and straightforward. The assumptions will be justified in the budget and the project cost part of the plan.

CONCLUSION

The objective of this chapter was to introduce the best practice techniques generally associated with technology planning. The chapter has shown the steps to document that plan and develop a written strategic technology plan. The next chapter will cover best practices for managing existing technology as demands change and the infrastructure ages.

CHAPTER THREE

Policy and Procedures Best Practices

BENEFITS OF WRITTEN TECHNOLOGY POLICY AND PROCEDURES

In a perfect world, would it not be wonderful to prevent the majority of technology problems? Actually, even in our imperfect world, most problems can be prevented. There must be well-developed and well-written policy and procedure manuals that all technology users are trained to follow.

It takes time to document technology and define how it should be used. Then it takes time to distribute the information to all the users, who must read it, and then do what the manuals say. Policy and procedure statements are collectively referred to as *standard operating procedures,* or *standards.* Some might say that developing standards is a lot tougher to do than it sounds. Actually, it is not that difficult if best practices are followed. The returns are well worth the investment of time and resources.

Written standard policy and procedure manuals provide a methodology for documenting what employees should do (policy) and how they should do it (procedures). Many organizations have policy manuals in place for traditional activities, such as hiring new employees, terminating employees, requesting leave, company dress code and so forth. They may also have the traditional procedures for manufacturing products, filling an order, even closing financial transactions. Most of these are in place for either regulatory, insurance, or historical reasons, not as tools to improve productivity.

Where should the focus be? Today, a wider range of employees has access to corporate information, as well as open access to the Internet. Employees receive electronic mail at work and use instant messaging to talk to friends and family during business hours, costing businesses millions each year in lost productivity. Consider the following results of studies:

- Internet traffic is the second largest consumer of the overall corporate network. (*Ziff Davis Market Intelligence*)
- 30 to 40 percent of Internet use in the workplace is not related to business. (*IDC Research*)

- 70 percent of all Internet porn traffic occurs during the nine-to-five workday. (*SexTracker*)

Still, according to a survey conducted by Management Recruiters International, Inc. (*www.BrilliantPeople.com*) in 2001, only 64 percent of companies polled have formal Internet use policies. Restricting access seems to be the least attractive option for most companies.

As technology drives business today, it has become critical for management to place a greater importance on documenting how the technology should and should not be used. Written policies and procedures that exist for their own sake can standardize the organization into a quagmire and reduce creativity and innovation. But, a few very important statements that limit liability and streamline operations can help achieve maximum benefit from technology investment.

Hopefully, companies have formal policies and training programs related to race, religion or sexual preference in the work place. But what about abuse of technology for electronic communications? What about inappropriate or illegal use of the company's technology resources, such as personal computers, servers and web servers? Establishing an acceptable use policy is absolutely mandatory in today's litigious environment. Appropriate monitoring and reporting technology that identifies abuses that leave your company open to poor judgment by an employee must be implemented. This will be discussed in more detail later in this chapter. Beyond liability, what about inefficiencies and improved productivity? These can be much more critical to the organization on a day-to-day basis.

The more traditional areas of policy and procedure creation will be discussed later. A different type of policy than most IT managers think about will be covered first. This is the establishment of business rules, policies that affect your applications, as well as your hardware, and primarily pertain to how these technologies are applied in your organization.

BUSINESS RULES AS POLICY

There seems to be a growing crisis in the lack of standards in businesses in general, particularly in establishing and documenting policies as they relate to business rules. Business rules are policies and procedures that exist in computer systems and provide a foundation for the complex policies and constraints that govern the daily operation of a business. Business rules may be as simple as:

- When to print a report?
- Who should have access to information?
- How should printed reports be destroyed?

There are also more complex processes such as calculating commissions or the steps in calculating inventory levels. Over the past couple of decades, the rapid changes due to competitive pressures have required massive changes in information technology and the application of business policies. This rapid change, coupled with declining resources, has resulted in many organizations having complex systems filled with out-dated policies.

Consider a specific organization for a moment. Are the IT policies, the business rules, consistent and accurate throughout the organization? If policy is not consistent throughout the organization, the technology, and the processes it supports, will not function properly. The results can be devastating revenue losses and crippling lawsuits.

Unfortunately, most information technology professionals cannot simply look at an application and scan all business rules to ensure that they reflect changing business policies. Information systems are not able to give the user an abstracted view of the business policies and assumptions that drive an application's program logic. Because business policies are not necessarily separate from an application's code, but may not be a part of the application itself, validating the policies can be difficult.

To stress the value and the importance of establishing policies as business rules, consider spreadsheets as an example of technology where policies must be established. Any user can see the formulas and macros used in a common spreadsheet to make predictions and obtain results. Yet, what constitutes confirmation that the formulas and macros used in the creation of the spreadsheet are accurate and the results correct? Where are the policies that state the company standards for development of spreadsheets? In a best practice environment, such a policy might establish the use of a common library file folder where templates (standard workbook files) are stored. These are the reviewed and approved templates to which all users must adhere. Policy instructs that, if anyone needs to create a new template, they follow an established procedure of first stating the purpose of the new spreadsheet, providing a sample for review, and meeting with a review committee. This is done before using any information from the spreadsheet in any report or for any result, used by the company. This does not have to be a long and arduous task. If streamlined procedures are developed, it could take an hour or a day, depending on the complexity of the spreadsheet.

Why should there be this much trouble to validate a spreadsheet? Raymond R. Panko, University of Hawaii, says in his paper *What we know about Spreadsheet Errors,* "a number of consultants, based on practical experience, have said that 20 to 40 percent of all spreadsheets contain errors." This is from his own research (*www.panko.cba .hawaii.edu,*). A summary of Dr. Panko's study is also posted at the American Institute of Certified Public Accountants, *www.aicpa.org,* Dr. Panko shows error rates as high as 91 percent in the spreadsheets reviewed. It is also important to consider that, on the low side, at one point in the study, more than 20 percent of all spreadsheets reviewed had qualitative errors.

In a best practice environment, there should be policies that govern the creation of spreadsheets. This begins by defining who has the authority to create spreadsheets. Next, what process exists for validating that the spreadsheet is functioning properly? Finally, how can the spreadsheet be posted so that it can be shared with others? For the past few years, professionals have stated that such action stifles creativity. This has been found not to be true. Creative and innovative staff can use spreadsheets and still minimize potential errors. In the end, having data calculate correctly is the most important objective.

Organizations that document policy for spreadsheet creation have a simple but effective process. A library of approved templates are created and managed by a senior person in the organization. In some organizations, there may be several libraries and they are managed according to structure, such as department, group, and so forth. A list of each approved template is available, hopefully as part of the organization's Intranet. This is the first place someone goes when they need a spreadsheet to accomplish a task.

If a template does not exist, the next step is to create one. The person would draft a simple request, on a form or an e-mail message, defining the need and requesting authority to create the template. After approval is given, the template is created (that the template contains good documentation internally for all formulas, macros, etc. is a given.) When complete, the creator of the new spreadsheet asks someone else to review the finished product. This process, a peer-to-peer review, is no more complex than the spreadsheet being reviewed. Understand that the goal here is not to create more work, but to eliminate duplicate efforts and insure accuracy. So, more complex spreadsheets will take longer to review. Once the review is complete and the creator and reviewer sign off on the end product, it is sent to the library manager. The library manager adds the template to the appropriate directory, updates the template listing and responds to the creator to move forward. Products like Excel can be very self-documenting, so take advantage of this by including as much information as possible. Exhibit 3.1 is an example of using *File/Properties* to document a workbook. This, however, is not the policy, or business rule, but a result of the rule you put in place.

Exhibit 3.1

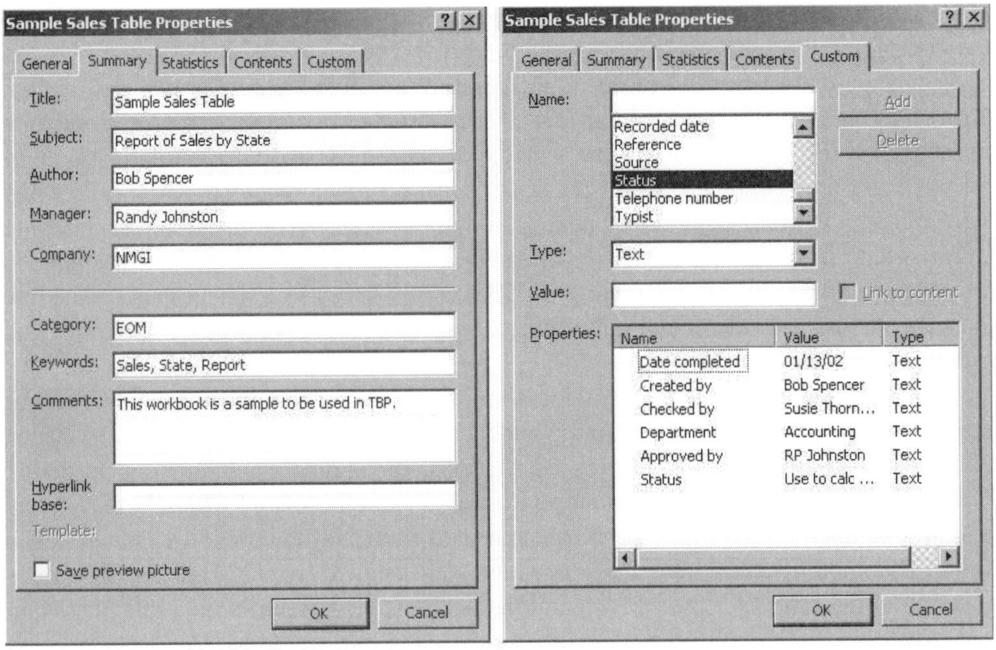

The policy might read as follows:

Policy 11.1

Use of File/Properties for validating and recording all templates
Effective date of last change January 13, 2002 17:26:36.

XYZ Company, in order to preserve the integrity of the results produced by all workbooks or assumptions made from workbooks, requires that all staff follow the following procedures:

All new workbooks calculating or representing information to be used by this company, or upon which any decision or representation will be based, must be approved by a senior manager. The senior manager will first verify that a similar workbook does not already exist. The senior manager will only accept new workbooks that have been approved by a supervisor or senior in charge. The workbook must have been approved in a peer-to-peer review. The workbook must be cataloged and stored in the appropriate data library where it will be stored in a read-only format to avoid possible modification by anyone but the authorized librarian. The creator will document their name, purpose of workbook, supervisor or owner of the workbook, and other pertinent information as shown in the example.

End of Policy

This is an example meant to demonstrate several important components. First, the title followed by an assigned indicator, and in this example, the department, policy identifier number and a revision number. This is followed by the date and time this policy was posted. The body of the policy follows the header information. A best practice is to keep the text short and to the point. If business rule policies are too verbose, they can be misleading and confusing. If the description seems confusing or too complex, consider separating it into two or more rules. Finally, within the rule is a procedure. Business rule policies are documented differently from operational policies, such as the acceptable use policies, privacy statement policy and so forth, where the procedures to enforce the policy are most likely separate, and the policy may actually be enforced by more than one procedure statement.

The example of the spreadsheet is used to convey the concept of a business rule as it applies to maintaining the integrity of data. Similar rules could be applied to Word processing templates for correspondence and so forth. Developing policies that reflect business rules to be applied to program applications are much more difficult and complex to set up.

When applications have been purchased from third parties, such as a financial accounting application, it is necessary to review how each transaction is processed and develop policies for handling those transactions in the company. Third-party applications, as opposed to in-house developed applications, are typically written for a broad cross-section of industries; therefore, they are generic in nature. Making them specific to a company means creating policy and procedures to deal with each type of transaction that enters the system, and reports produced from the system.

For the third-party applications, each transaction must be reviewed in the workflow (as defined in Chapter 2). And then, how the application processes these transactions must be addressed. Policy business rules might be created for such activities as paying commissions to sales reps and others. These policies must then be translated into procedures that can be accomplished in the application. At the same time, policy must reflect what is to be done if something changes. For example, if the way your company pays sales commission changes, how will the business rule change in all affected applications?

For in-house developed applications, a programmer must change the program logic when changing a business rule. The programmer probably would change the application in question, but could forget to address the many interdependencies with other applications. In other cases, the business unit might make the policy changes and not know about the underlying applications that need to be updated. The business rules must allow for all these possibilities.

There are three major reasons for the lack of consistency between documented policies (business rules), and what is actually done. First, the IT department may be focused on the technology and not be familiar enough with the business processes (procedures) and rules (policies.) Also, not enough automated tools exist to support business-rules management. Finally, there is not a strong link between data-modeling tools and the tools for implementing business rules.

Organizations tend to bring experts in at the front end of the development or acquisition process to define requirements; and at the final stage, before the application is deployed, to ensure it meets expectations. But, with issues such as deregulation and a major increase in the number of mergers and acquisitions, business rules are changing rapidly. Most IT organizations cannot keep up. The most significant problems develop over time, as the business rules that were applied when the application was brought online change; and IT does change the applications to be compliant. Consultants are often brought in to make recommendations to change accounting applications, because of the number of problems and errors that have crept into the system. Management assumes that the technology is to blame. Careful analysis shows that the new procedures are actually being followed, but are not supported by applicable policies. Or analysis may show that new people are using the applications and are not aware of how to use the system, that is, what policies to follow. In many cases, simply updating the business rules eliminates the cost of implementing entirely new systems.

Even developers with a thorough understanding of business policies often have difficulty translating that knowledge into procedural code. Data modeling is one of the first steps in a development project. The data model defines the structural business rules by defining the terms and facts connecting those rules. Unfortunately, there is usually no link between the application data model and the actual run-time system. Portions of the structural rules, as represented in the data model, are implemented in multiple systems and are inconsistently maintained across systems. There is no easy way to track more complex business rules.

Problems resulting from processes based on inconsistent policy (business rules) often occur below the surface, where management cannot see them. IT managers cannot be expected to tackle the problem alone because it is not, in itself, an IT problem. Instead, IT must work closely with management who can identify the policies that need to be changed.

The first step to developing the business rules and sound policies is to create a formal project team with members from the IT and business departments (this could be the same project team used to map the workflow processes). The company must then hold workshops to make sure the business experts and IT work together to define the company's business rules. Once these rules are clearly understood, the business scenarios supporting them are finalized and tested. The rules are then validated by a wider group of key business experts who run the operations that use these business rules globally.

Creating business rules can be a resource intensive task. And, there are not a lot of automated tools available to help in the process. Oracle Designer 2000 is one tool that can be used for capturing the data model. A Microsoft Access database can be created to capture the business rules and identify the owners of those rules. Excel spreadsheets can be used to capture and model the analysis data. More sophisticated technology can also be put to use during this phase of the project.

Ultimately, IT managers are responsible for managing the data necessary to carry their company into the next millennium. Whether it is a small company with a limited IT budget or a multibillion-dollar enterprise, one thing is clear—implementing an IT project requires the ability to make quantifiable decisions. Justifying massive project expenditures based on intuition or industry direction is simply not enough. A return-on-investment analysis provides the evidence business managers require. This approach can effectively bridge the communication gap between IT and business professionals. Making business professionals aware of policy's impact on how information systems perform is crucial to avoiding errors and improving productivity.

This concludes the discussion of best practice policies and procedures relating to business rules. Now, more traditional policies that govern the use of information systems, distribution of information, and systems security will be discussed.

REQUIRED POLICIES

Business rule policies that govern how users use software applications at an operations level improve productivity, reduce errors and increase employee efficiency. However, most information technology professionals are familiar with the policies that define proper use of company-owned technology.

Many of these policies have developed over the past two decades, starting with the introduction of personal computers into the workplace. Prior to personal computers, most businesses had either mainframe or mid-range systems where the interface between machine and human was centrally controlled by the software applications being processed. It was a kinder, gentler, albeit less exciting world. Direct interface with users was accomplished via *dumb* terminals. Users were limited to logging into specific applications assigned to them and could only perform a limited range of tasks. Younger readers may find this hard to imagine—but that is the way it was! Centralized computing was well managed, as was corporate data. The advent of the personal computer not only changed all that, but also allowed users to be more dynamic, to assume roles that they had not performed before, and to have greater access to company data.

To manage the use of computers in the early days, the personal computer use policy was developed. The personal computer use policy was intended to define how the new computers were to be used, to avoid illegal use of the computer as well as illegal distribution of company-licensed software and so forth. When these personal computers were linked together via local and company-wide networks, another policy, to manage which users had access to what data, was developed. This policy was the network use policy. Then, the Internet was brought into the workplace and an Internet use policy had to be created. Finally, everyone began receiving and sending electronic mail related to both company business and personal business, and the e-mail policy was born. There were too many policies to govern a single purpose, the acceptable use of the company-owned technology. Today, all of these policies have been merged into one comprehensive document known as the acceptable use policy.

The Acceptable Use Policy

The acceptable use policy defines the acceptable use of technology in the organization; this includes the hardware, software, and communications equipment the company provides. Everyone in the company must be expected to follow the written policy, without exception. The policy must be in writing to be effective. Many companies today also post the acceptable use policy, along with other policies, on the company Intranet for easy access.

Copyrighted Material

With the availability of information on the Internet today, the temptation to copy this information and use it for personal gain is almost overwhelming. Music and videos are distributed freely via a number of online entertainment sites. Many of these sites act as peer-to-peer exchanges where people can share music they have copied from CDs or movies they copied from DVD. If employees use your firm's computers to copy and distribute copyrighted material, music, text, or images, the company is liable and responsible! The first step is to explain to your employees that such activities will not be tolerated. The next step, to reinforce the point, is to have a statement in the acceptable use policy, such as:.

(*Note:* All sample wording provided herein is only an example. Please review the wording carefully and modify it to fit your specific needs and at the advice of legal counsel, as appropriate.)

> *Users will not violate copyright laws and their fair use provisions through inappropriate reproduction and/or distribution of music, movies, computer software, copyrighted text, images, and so on.*

Hacking Attempts

Computer hackers are very smart people who will not always use their own home computers to hack into unauthorized sites. No, hackers will come in early, work through lunch, and stay late. They may use their company's computer resources and Internet access to gain entry into sites they are not authorized to visit. Management can be held responsible for their employees' actions, even if they were not aware of what was being done. Therefore, management should take reasonable action to monitor employees, and to formally notify employees that such actions are not acceptable.

> *Users shall not use company computers or network facilities to gain unauthorized access to any computer systems. Using programs intended to gain access to unauthorized systems for any reason or purpose is strictly prohibited.*

Handheld Devices

Employees with access to company data may be able to print that data; transfer data to portable media and remove it from the office; or send information over the Internet. If these actions are not done within the scope of the performance of their duties, such activities are unauthorized, and may even be illegal.

Information leak is a colorful term for taking or distributing a company's confidential information. Actually, this idea is not new at all, but the vehicles for making it happen are new. In the early 1980s, managers became concerned that employees would copy confidential or private information onto floppy disks and take them when they left the company. Today, the number one cause of information leak is handheld devices and inappropriate use of the Internet.

Handheld devices include such devices as the popular palm, or pocket pc personal digital assistants (PDA). Handheld devices today are where the first microcomputers were twenty years ago. Many staff members bring small, convenient, and powerful tools into the workplace without the authorization or approval of management. A simple software application is loaded on the user's workstation and a docking station for the handheld is attached. With only a ten-minute install procedure, a user can synchronize the handheld device with the corporate personal information management system. In moments, the entire client database, contact information, manuals, and nearly any piece of information on the network can be transferred to these deceivingly small, but powerful devices, and then go with the employee out the door.

Keep in mind that policies are meant to offer protection from inadvertent events, as well as out and out fraud or theft. Companies should not necessarily close the door to handheld devices because of concern that confidential information may leave the office, as this technology may be beneficial to the organization. Handheld computers can make people more productive, save time, and increase productivity. Yet, these same tools are routinely removed from offices and carried about. They are lost in airports and left on tables at meetings. Without proper guidance, in the form of written policies and procedures, companies are exposed to an information leak. It is a best practice to include the following in acceptable use policy.

Users shall not connect unauthorized equipment to company equipment—including, but not limited to, handheld devices, docking stations, hubs, routers, printers, or other equipment connected to the company's network directly or via remote attachment.

Users shall only export or import information from handheld or portable computing devices where such devices have been authorized by the supervisor. In such a case, the user is personally responsible for protecting and safeguarding company-owned information. The device shall be password protected at all times, the user shall maintain possession of the device and shall make every effort to safeguard company information from unauthorized access.

Because we live in a world where employees come and go, it is also a good idea to include the following.

All electronic data is the property of the company and the user is required to protect this information to the degree possible for the security and privacy of those involved. Should the user leave the employ of the company, travel outside their authorized work area, or become incapacitated for a period of time, all company information is to be removed from portable data devices immediately.

Understand that the purpose of these statements is not to prevent either intentional or accidental occurrences of information leak but to ensure that employees are aware of their responsibilities and to document acceptable behavior.

Network Security

Many network administrators and managers feel comfortable with their system security, but consider this. While the application software may be password protected, so only authorized users can access information, the data itself may be accessible. With all operating systems today, file access rights must be declared according to user and user group rights. Failure to do this may make the files accessible by unauthorized persons. When mainframes ruled the day, only a select few even knew how to access data files, much less open them up and extract the information. Today, children have enough understanding of computers to open and view files. Many of your users have all the skills necessary to search for, open, and view data that is not properly secured.

Users shall not make unauthorized attempts to circumvent data protection schemes or uncover security loopholes. This includes creating and/or running programs that are designed to identify security loopholes and/or decrypt intentionally secure data. Users will not view or attempt to view data which has not been made available to them in the normal course of their duties.

Licensed Software

Business owners must take the loading and running of unauthorized software very seriously. Unauthorized programs and files may be transported into the company computer systems from home computers, via the Internet, or loaded directly by users without the approval of IT. One of the most obvious concerns is that files brought in from outside the company may carry computer viruses that jeopardize the safety of the computer and stored data. Another important reason to establish a policy against the unauthorized loading of data files or software is violation of possible licensing or copyrights that might exist. Companies must have a direct written statement, in the form of a policy, that they only allow the use of licensed, legal software.

Users will not violate terms of applicable software licensing agreements or copyright laws.

Users will not knowingly or carelessly run or install on any computer system or network, or give to another user a program intended to damage or to place excessive load on a computer system or network. This includes but is not limited to programs known as computer viruses, Trojan Horses, and worms.

Users will use company resources solely to conduct company business. Use of company resources for commercial activity, such as creating products or services for sale, is strictly prohibited.

Electronic Mail

What users can and cannot do with e-mail and instant messaging is a critical part of your acceptable use policy. Generally e-mail and instant messaging are referred to as electronic communications. There are at least three specific areas your acceptable use policy should address. These include:

1. Discriminatory activity.
2. Harassment in the workplace.
3. Displaying or distributing offensive material.

It is very clear that obscenity and pornography absolutely cannot be tolerated in the workplace. Aside from any personal reasons that may exist, it is against the law. With the emergence of e-evidence, the plaintiff's ability to subpoena e-mail messages and the history of sites a person visits, the ability to prove a case is significantly easier. Again, a business that does not have appropriate written policies in place and a method to monitor employees has little chance of defending itself in court.

Users will not use e-mail to harass or threaten others, or to send materials that could be deemed inappropriate, derogatory, prejudicial, or offensive. This includes sending repeated, unwanted e-mail to another user.

Users will not use e-mail on company-owned, company-sponsored or company-provided hardware or services to transmit any information, text, or images that could be deemed offensive, inappropriate, derogatory, prejudicial, or offensive.

Users will not initiate, propagate, or perpetuate electronic chain letters.

Users will not send mass mailings not directly associated with or in the routine performance of the course of duties or assignments. This includes multiple mailings to newsgroups, mailing lists, or individuals, for example, "spamming," "flooding," or "bombing."

Users will not forge the identity of a user or machine in an electronic communication.

Users will not transmit or reproduce materials that are slanderous or defamatory in nature, or that otherwise violate existing laws, regulations, policies, or that are considered to be generally inappropriate in a workplace.

Users will not display images or text that could be considered obscene, lewd, or sexually explicit or harassing.

There have been a number of reported incidences of individuals reading, reproducing, or transmitting information they should not have had access to in the first place. With the shift from using paper to electronic media, many individuals have become much too complacent about the privacy and security of confidential information. Rather than trying to define what people should and should not read, it may be best to simply state that if people do not believe they have access to information, they should not attempt to access that information.

Users will not attempt to monitor or tamper with another user's electronic communications, or read, copy, change, or delete another user's files or software without the explicit agreement of that user.

Each of the acceptable use policy items above addresses specific areas of concern. The following sample is intended as a guide in the development of a policy. The sample has been compiled from a number of best practice examples. Again, it is not intend-

Acceptable Use Policy

Sample Company encourages the sharing of information, comprehensive access to local and national facilities to create and disseminate information, and the free expression of ideas. General-access facilities and infrastructure are provided to further these purposes. There is an obligation on the part of those using these facilities and services to respect the intellectual and access rights of others—locally, nationally, and internationally.

Computing resources and facilities of Sample Company are the property of the company and shall be used for legitimate activity related to the performance of the duties and responsibilities of the users only, for administrative, public service, or approved contract purposes. Supervisors may, at their discretion, allow personal use of these resources by the employee that does not interfere with the institution or with the employee's ability to carry out company business. Individuals who disregard elements of this policy will be subject to appropriate disciplinary and/or legal action by Sample Company. Use of company computing facilities for personal or commercial use is not authorized. Use of company computing facilities for educational purposes must be consistent with other training and educational programs. The use of company computing facilities for higher education degree-seeking or certification programs may only be done with the specific written approval of the appropriate supervisor.

Individuals and noncompany organizations using the company's facilities to gain access to noncompany facilities must be cognizant of and observe the acceptable use policies of the company at all times.

Failure to observe these policies will result in the immediate disconnection or loss of use privileges, as well as possible disciplinary action or termination at the discretion of the offending party's supervisor or department head, based on the nature and severity of the offense.

Unauthorized viewing or use of another person's computer files, programs, or data is prohibited. All users should also be aware that all programs and all files are deemed to be the property of the company, unless the individual has a written agreement signed by an appropriate representative or officer of the company. Federal or state law may require disclosure of individual computer files that are deemed public records under the state public records statute. State and federal law may prohibit the disclosure of certain records as well.

Entry into a system, including the network system, by individuals not specifically authorized (by group or personally), or attempts to circumvent the protective mechanisms of any system, are prohibited. Deliberate attempts to degrade system performance or capability, or attempts to damage the systems, software, or intellectual property of others are prohibited.

The electronic mail and instant messaging systems of the company shall not be used for the *broadcasting* of unsolicited messages or for sending chain letters. The communication system shall not be used for the sending of material that would be considered obscene, offensive, or threatening by the recipient or another viewer of the material.

The company reserves the right to monitor and record the usage of all facilities and equipment, and all software that is the property of the company by ownership, lease, rent, sponsorship, or subsidy, if it has reason to believe that activities are taking place that are contrary to this policy or state or federal law or regulation, and as necessary to evaluate and maintain system efficiency. The company has the right to use information gained in this way in disciplinary or criminal proceedings.

The Federal Copyright Act nearly always protects commercial software. Use of company facilities or equipment for the purpose of copying computer software that does not contain specific permission to copy (some licenses do allow the making of one copy for backup) is prohibited. The unauthorized publishing of copyrighted material on a company server is prohibited, and users are responsible for the consequences of such unauthorized use.

An individual's access to computer resources may be suspended immediately upon the discovery of a violation of this policy.

Failure to comply with any of the above policies may result in termination of your network services, disciplinary action, and/or criminal prosecution. The company reserves the right to terminate any company network connection without notice if it is determined that any of the above policies are being violated.

ed for companies to extract this example and publish it as their own policy but to use it as a benchmark. As stated previously, legal counsel should be consulted.

Security and privacy are quickly becoming more important than ever before in the operation of your business. Every day, computer hackers are finding new ways to gain unauthorized entry into corporate information systems. With increased dedicated business Internet access, corporate America is putting information at a greater risk to exposure. Whether using the Internet to convey information between corporate sites, conducting business on the Internet, or using e-mail, all these activities increase the potential that business IT systems will be penetrated and confidential information will be stolen, or technology assets will be used illegally.

What is the source of these potential threats? The U.S. Department of Justice convicted a sixteen-year-old juvenile for hacking into the Department of Defense network. Going by the name *cOmrade*, the young hacker made his way into a military computer network used by the U.S. Defense Threat Reduction Agency (DTRA). News releases stated that cOmrade also managed to gain unauthorized access to a server located in Dulles, Virginia, and installed *backdoor* access to the server. The backdoor program collected more than 3,300 messages. In addition, the hacker found a way to discover at least nineteen user names and passwords of department employees' computer accounts. He also retrieved and downloaded proprietary software from NASA worth around $1.7 million. NASA uses the software to support the international space station's physical environment. In order to address the security breaches, computer systems at NASA were forcibly put out of business for twenty-one days in July of 1999. If this happens to the Department of Justice and NASA, what could be happening to corporate systems?

The Security Policy

Securing the technology assets of the company from intrusion has become the number one objective of today's technology professional. Protecting information systems and associated business assets from intrusion requires an understanding of how attacks occur and the source of threats. News stories of the external threats, such as those above, make good press. But, the truth is that organizations are more vulnerable to internal security threats. Intrusion may occur because a curious employee is bored and starts punching buttons. Or, a knowledgeable, but unhappy employee may decide to leave and do some serious damage before departing. Outside intruders, using sophisticated tools, can exploit operating system vulnerabilities. Intruders discover weaknesses in operating systems and application software programs by reverse engineering of the code. They literally take the code apart and determine which instructions do what. If system programmers leave backdoors (program code that allows entry that bypasses the system's usual security) open, they allow unauthorized access. Applying patches to off-the-shelf software and systems, or trusting firewalls (the electronic wall separating a company's computer network from the outside world) is not the answer. Reliance on these devices alone can provide a false sense of security, potentially giving hackers access into your system. Most people, even technologists, do not realize that, unless they are diligently maintained, firewalls become obsolete over time. The simplest of changes to the network can negate firewall settings.

The key to protecting a business is to recognize that the tools and techniques for hacking are constantly changing. Protection depends on understanding what hackers look for and how they use it to serve their ends. Understanding these techniques gives companies a better feel for how to protect their assets; and how to make sure their business stays securely operational. Securing a system today is the very first step in real protection. Keeping a system's protection current is essential to operating any information processor into the future. Keeping up with hacker technology means constant study. Professional hacker-trackers constantly monitor public or *open-source* channels, including hacker chat rooms, software, and hardware manufacturer's updates, web sites dedicated to security, security company product advances, and so on.

One employee told her supervisor that her Word and Excel documents were secure because she placed passwords on all documents containing confidential information. A quick visit to *www.lostpassword.com* completely burst her security bubble. There are a number of such sites on the Internet that offer software cheaply, or for free, that can remove the password or break into the default security protocol of well-known programs.

How secure are your systems? In the Joint Computer Security Institute/Federal Bureau of Investigation (CSI/FBI) 2001 Annual Report (which is something not expected to be mandatory reading), 35 percent of respondents reported a total loss of $377,828,700. Seventy percent of respondents with an Internet connection reported attacks from the outside, a 20 percent increase over the previous year. If you are having trouble explaining the security risk that exists today, visit *www.gocsi.com* for a copy of the most current FBI study.

Be prepared to lose some sleep! Understand that all the hackers are *not* outside your company. (After all, these folks have day jobs!) Most illegal system intrusions begin with employees breaking into company files, systems, and networks. Therefore, it is quite evident that a best practice includes security policies and avenues to enforce them.

All best practice companies implement strong security protocols and have their systems audited on a regular basis for lapses in security or possible attacks. There are several reputable companies that offer security audits and reviews. However, these services are not inexpensive. Penetration Testing, one type of security service, attempts to penetrate into your network from outside your firewall or point-of-entry. Security audit testing and reporting can run thousands of dollars, depending on the level of testing needed. The downside to having a security audit conducted is that the findings are only valid at the exact moment of the audit. Someone could turn off the firewall the moment the examiners leave and the system would not be secure. Some businesses, such as financial institutions, elect to have continuous testing that is a combination of automated software and human interaction to continuously test their systems' vulnerability to attack.

In addition to diligent testing of installed passwords, restricted data access, and fortified computer rooms, it is very important to have a written security policy. Since the development of security policies and procedures requires some detailed knowledge that many IT professionals may not have, there are several third-party vendors who sell predefined security policies. On the web, you can visit:

www.information-security-policies-and-standards.com
www.kirion.net/securitypolicy/
www.sans.org

More detailed security information is presented in later chapters and may be incorporated in the policy and procedure documentation.

The Privacy Policy

The convergence of electronic communications, commerce and the Internet has created a heightened state of concern over personal and private information. In 1999, 2000, and 2001, the Congress of the United States took decisive steps to protect an individual's private information, as well as how information collected but not owned may be used. The most significant and best-publicized act was the 1999 Gramm-Leach-Bliley Financial Modernization Act. Although this act focuses primarily on the banking community, it has far-reaching implications for other industries as well. For instance, as a result of the Gramm-Leach-Bliley Act, the Federal Trade Commission issued regulations directly affecting tax practitioners and other practitioners providing services to individuals. The Securities and Exchange Commission (SEC) has also come out with its own guidelines on privacy disclosures for investment advisors registered with the SEC.

There are several facets to the personal privacy issue. First, there is the well-publicized collection of information at a web site. This collection could be information keyed into an online form and then sold for private gain. The information keyed in to purchase a product falls into this category, as does the invasion of privacy by placing *cookies* on a user's system without their knowledge, or collecting specific information about a user through the use of intrusive software, called spy software, again without the user's knowledge. New Congressional laws are clear in regard to limiting the use of information for a purpose not agreed to by the individual supplying the data.

Today, common sites collect information on a premise generally known as opt-out. This simply means that at the bottom of a form, after the user has entered all content, there is a small disclosure statement asking the user to check a small box if they do not wish their information to be shared. If this box is not checked, and there are other methods of acknowledgment that barely satisfy existing privacy laws, the assumption is that permission is given. It is expected that Congress will enact laws that require sites to ask individuals to opt-in. That is, private information may not be used for any purpose, implied or explicit, without the express permission of the individual. Even if Congress does not pass such legislation soon, users themselves are beginning to turn away from entering confidential information without some guarantees of privacy. If users will not complete purchase forms, they cannot become customers and e-commerce will die a slow and agonizing death.

The second reason that privacy will continue to be an issue is the maturing of a technique commonly referred to as data mining. *Data mining* exploits an existing database, correlating data elements to create new information. Data mining is not new; the introduction of these techniques began with analysis of large mainframe databases. Today, there are several off-the-shelf software applications to assist in this process. With the emergence of open database compliant (ODBC) software, the underlying data is much easier to get to.

In some cases, how confidential information is used is an internal decision. In other cases, guidance is emerging in each profession as to what is appropriate and what is not.

The best advice for now may be: *If in doubt—don't do it!* For more detail of the extent of privacy regulation, visit *www.ots.treas.gov/rules.html* and review how stringent regulation is becoming for financial institutions.

Best practice dictates that every organization should have a published privacy statement. It is important to publish the privacy statement on your web site, as well as providing it to your customers in a written form. Your Internet privacy statement should be the same as your written privacy statement. A few best practices tips for the privacy statement are:

- Provide easy access for the privacy statement.
- Request a review by legal counsel for *defensibility*.
- Ensure that the staff knows the policy and that it is followed!
- Be clear on what to tell the customers.

The customers should know the following:

- The company understands the importance of protecting the privacy of customers.
- The company takes seriously the importance of safeguarding customer information.
- The company is committed to the customer's privacy.
- The staff is committed to personal privacy.
- The organization makes every effort to collect, retain, and use customer information only as it pertains to the ability to serve that customer.
- Employee access to personally identifiable information is limited to those with a need to know.
- The employees understand the importance of customer/client privacy and follow the company guidelines.

Organizations must never disclose personal or account information to unaffiliated third parties, except to transfer information to reputable agencies, or to help complete a customer-initiated transaction.

The following sample privacy statement is to provide guidance in understanding the type of information needed in a privacy statement. Companies should consult with legal counsel before posting a privacy policy on the Internet or distributing it to clients.

Sample Privacy Statement

Sample Company understands the importance of protecting the privacy of our customers and others who share personal or confidential data with us. We consider any personal information you may supply to us to be personal and confidential, and are committed to using this information solely for the purpose of providing superior service and convenient access to the right products and services.

We take our commitment to safeguarding customer's information seriously, which is why we have adopted the following principles.

- Sample Company makes every effort to collect, retain, and use customer information only where we believe it is useful (and as allowed by law) in administering Sample Company business and to provide products, services, and other opportunities to our customers.
- Sample Company limits employee access to personally identifiable information to those with a business reason for knowing such information.
- Sample Company stresses the importance of confidentiality and customer privacy in the education of its employees.
- Sample Company takes appropriate disciplinary measures to enforce employee privacy responsibilities.
- Sample Company does not disclose our customers' personal or account information to unaffiliated third parties, except for the transferring of information to reputable credit reporting agencies; or when the information is provided to help complete a customer-initiated transaction; or the customer requested the release of the information; or the disclosure is required or allowed by law.
- Sample Company maintains appropriate security standards and procedures regarding unauthorized access to customer information.
- If Sample Company provides personally identifiable information to a third party, the third party must adhere to similar privacy principles that provide for keeping such information confidential.

STANDARD OPERATING POLICY AND PROCEDURES

Why have written policy and procedures? Because, well-documented processes reduce errors, and improve productivity and increase profits.

Why doesn't everyone have written policy and procedure standards? Users say they do not have the time to develop them. IT says they do not have the time to develop them. *You never have time to do it right, but you always have time to do it over!* Taking the time to develop and implement quality procedures is not a cost. It has been proven many times over that best practice organizations that take advantage of well-documented procedures see positive economic gains from their efforts.

The objective of the information technology (IT) policy and procedures manual is to standardize certain practices, to improve the quality of service, to improve user and information technology department relations, and to improve communications. This manual is the complete authority governing practices in providing technology services to the various entities within the organization. Everyone must conform to its contents. Procedure development is often the result of extensive research and management approval before publication. IT must gain everyone's cooperation, so that procedures benefit both the users and the organization. The initial document is only a starting point. Users must be encouraged to participate in further development of practices by making recommendations for additions, deletions, or revisions to the contents of the manual. The procedure manual continues to grow and evolve as business and technology dictates.

The IT standard operating procedures (SOP) manual has lost its way over the past three decades. Early on, the SOP was a comprehensive and readily accessible source of reference for the processing of all information. As information processing became decentralized, or diluted, throughout the organization, development of written procedures got lost in the time constraints of other priorities. Over the years, the proper processes, if not the value altogether, for developing and maintaining technology related procedures has been all but lost. Many technology professionals report they have procedures, but then cannot actually produce a comprehensive manual. Procedures they refer to are often sparsely written memorandums that most of the users are not aware of and have not read. Or, worse, the procedures are floating in the ether of their minds—where no one but the user is aware that the procedures even exist.

To begin formally documenting a manual means gathering all the pieces from around the organization in order to standardize the form. From this point, the process of developing your SOP will be discussed as if it is going to print and distribution. However, it is best to not print a number of copies of the manual for distribution, but rather to post it on the Intranet for easy access.

To insure that the manual is effectively maintained for future growth and change, a format and page number scheme must be followed. Here is a common sample of a format to follow.

Identification: The manual chapter or primary topic.
Section: Section of manual chapter.
Subject: Subject of page.
Page number: Page number of subject description.
Subpage: Should inserts be required at later time.

For example:

Identification: Computer processing environment
Page: 2.3.1–001.00
Section: Backup procedures
Date: mm/dd/yy
Subject: Backup site, schedule, and retention

In a smaller organization, the manual numbering scheme does not need to be as sophisticated. However, always plan for growth and changes. All updates to procedures must be well coordinated. The distribution of updates should be based on a master list of recipients maintained by the IT department. Again, the first preference is not to print hardcopy, but to provide access to all users via the company's Intranet.

Procedures within Procedures

The maintenance of written procedures is most often the responsibility of a number of different individuals in various departments. Someone has to be in charge of the total collection. It works well for human resources, or a similar area, to manage the development of the procedures and coordinate the department where technology is effected. Best practice companies incorporate technology related procedures as an integrated component with other procedures such as *sales call procedure, purchase order requisition, leave request procedure,* and so forth. IT is involved with the development and approval of nearly all written procedures. This makes sense since technology permeates so much of what is done in a business today; it is often difficult to determine where the separation is.

Documented procedures will be procedures that are global in the organization. Human resource related activities are a good example; there will be procedures that are specific to a single department, such as *nightly server file backup procedure.* This procedure is most likely only relative to the IT department. A best practice method is to develop a procedure manual that separates procedures by each functional area. Having multiple procedure manuals (manual refers to both hardcopy and softcopy of all procedures) is not recommended. Rather, IT will develop procedures that only effect activities within certain departments. IT will have a section of the complete document just as human resources and the marketing department will each have a section.

There are also technology related procedures that are incorporated into procedures in other departments. For instance, if a company allows users to store files on a local personal computer and backup of those files are the responsibility of individual users, where does the procedure go? If the procedure is in the IT department section, will a new administrative assistant look there to determine company policy on backing up word processing and worksheet files? These procedures need to be in an administrative functions section that is referenced in several places from the policy manual. In this case, for example, IT would coordinate with department heads, establish a policy (users are or are not permitted to store files locally), and then develop a procedural description that tells users how to backup and secure their local data.

Some smaller organizations where stringent separation of functional areas is not necessary commingle procedures into a single all-encompassing manual. This is fine, but IT must be involved in the development of the procedures and see that the processes related to technology are consistent throughout.

The IT Policy and Procedure Manual

The information below defines the basis of a best practice procedure manual for IT. The procedures may be part of a larger collection, or may stand alone as a guide to IT personnel only. When the procedures affect users outside the IT department, either senior management or the information technology steering committee (ITSC) should review the procedures at least annually.

To make it easier to develop IT procedures from this book, samples are provided and descriptions of why and how to develop each are provided. The objective here is not to provide a manual that can be printed and put on the shelf. The manual might be pretty sitting there on the shelf, but it would also be pretty useless.

The following section defines the most common areas to be documented, and critical procedures that IT must document. This list is by no means inclusive and may vary, depending on the size and scope of your IT operations. This section begins with the 30,000-foot flyover of the IT procedure manual and then comes down to ground level with more detail in each area.

Information Technology Environment

There are a number of reasons to maintain written documentation of your technology infrastructure and establish the processes for maintaining and updating your technology.

Functional Description of IT

It is important to describe the technology environment of an organization. This is for the benefit of new IT staff as well as everyone who works in the company. The documentation should include

- *Locations.*   Where are the data center(s) located?
- *Organizational Structure.*   Define the report structure of the organization so people understand how IT is staffed and who does what.
- *Position Descriptions.*   Describe the IT staffing by function so that everyone is fully aware of their responsibilities. The IT manager often says, "We all wear many hats and do whatever is needed." In this case, there is a lot not getting done because everyone thinks it is someone else's job! This will be discussed more below with examples of current position descriptions.
- *Mission Statement.*   This is another important statement of who IT is. What is the corporate mission? Is it to be a maintenance group, to fix people's computers when they break? Or, is it to be a strategic element of the business responsible for innovation and bringing improvements that show up on the bottom-line? The mission statement sets the stage for what the IT department does.

Configuration Description

- System hardware.
- System software.
- Disk utilization.

Run Procedures

- Daily information technology log and run sheets.
- Computer room policy.

- Incident reporting.
- Operational policy for personal computers.

Backup Procedures

- Backup site, schedule, and retention.
- Backup of user workstations.
- Backup of off-site data sources.

Library Management

- General information.
- Library description.
- Housekeeping.

Security

- System log on and log off.
- Internet and Intranet security.
- Password storage and retention.
- Password protecting data files.

Printed Report Distribution Control

- Printing and distribution of sensitive information.
- Record retention and report tracking.

Physical Data Center Procedures

- Physical security.
  - Security policy.
  - Security alarm system.
  - Data security.
- Fire protection procedures.
  - Fire protection policy.
  - Fire safety training.
  - Materials storage.
- Electrical system procedures.
  - Power up and power down procedures.
  - UPS system testing.
- Disaster recovery procedures.

- ○ Disaster prevention.
- ○ Network backup system.
- ○ Process recovery.
- ○ Equipment replacement.
- ○ Standard forms.

Disaster Recovery Contingency Procedures

- Summary and scope of plan.
- Disaster definition.
- Recovery action plan.
- Recovery phases.
- Disaster recovery team.
- Individual responsibility.
- Notification.
- Organization and vendor contact list.

Description of Core Applications

Those software applications that are critical to a business are defined as core applications. Examples are financial accounting reporting software, manufacturing and distribution software, and even secondary applications such as asset management software. In a professional services firm, billing software could be a core application. These applications are typically run from a central server(s) and are fully managed by IT.

Defining the core applications in company procedures provides a central location for information and also defines how these applications are to be used in the organization.

Description of Back-Office Applications

Back-office applications are the support programs used in organizations. Microsoft Office, Coral Office, or IBM Smart Suite are examples of back-office applications. This section also includes applications such as Adobe Acrobat, Internet Browser, FTP software, and so forth. There could be a long list of back-office applications, but remember, this list defines the organization's authorized software. If the software is not listed here —it is not authorized! Standardizing software and documenting it in procedures provides much better control and the ability to manage software more effectively.

Functional Description of IT

The functional description procedures should define:

- *Locations.* Describe where resources are located. If staff is maintained in multiple locations, describe where they are assigned and the functional responsibilities of each group. Include address and contact information, if it is not restricted.

INFORMATION TECHNOLOGY ORGANIZATION STRUCTURE

Describe the reporting structure of the IT organization so it is clear how IT staff is organized, who IT is, what IT does, and to whom IT reports. A visual, such as the example in Exhibit 3.2, helps users easily understand how IT is structured. The highest level management positions may be omitted if appropriate. The visual may include additional positions such as the web master or developer, programming staff, or the database administrator. Notice that the information technology steering committee reports to the IT director. The ITSC should work closely with IT in an advisory capacity and provide direction to IT. The ITSC will be presented in more detail later in this chapter.

Position Descriptions

Again, while position descriptions are not strictly procedures, they do define what has to be done and by whom. Position descriptions, which used to be called job descriptions

Exhibit 3.2

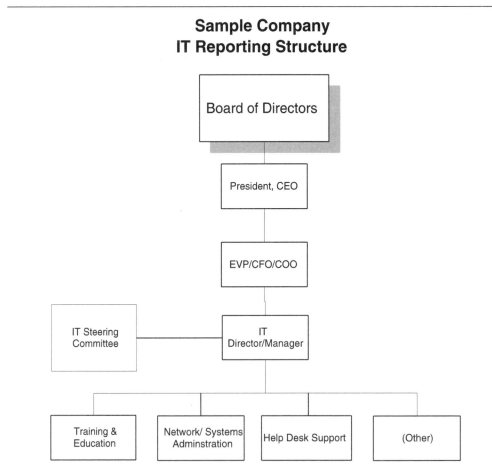

Sample Company
IT Reporting Structure

back when people were actually expected to do something, are fundamental to structuring the organization. Someone performs all processes within IT, and the position description document defines who performs what functions. If a function is not assigned to a specific person, with an appropriate backup assigned in case of absence, there is a greater risk that an important task will be missed. Everyone must be fully aware of his or her responsibilities ensuring that critical tasks are performed regularly, and at the appropriate time. As mentioned earlier, IT managers often say, "We all wear many hats and do whatever is needed." In these cases, there is a lot not getting done because everyone thinks someone else is doing it! The following position descriptions identify processes, or tasks, that must be performed in a modern IT department. With the exception of the IT director, multiple persons may occupy the other positions.

Some position descriptions are not included because they are very specific to the platform and type of business. For instance, many larger organizations have system operators that maintain and support the services on mainframe computers. Based on unique needs and the tasks to be performed, use the following to adapt or develop unique position descriptions. A word of caution—do not tailor position descriptions to individuals. They are developed around the tasks and processes required, then the position is staffed with a qualified technician or professional to perform those processes.

Director of Information Technology

The information technology director performs duties under the direct supervision of a senior manager or officer of the company. Over the years, the IT department has appeared, under many different names, of course, all over the company organization chart. The preference here is for IT to report to the chief operating officer or the chief financial officer. Many consultants would disagree that the IT should come under the CFO, or an equivalent position such as the controller. This prejudice against placing IT under the accounting department is because of the history of an abuse of power by accounting. There is no problem with IT reporting through these channels as long as the company officer understands that IT must serve everyone in the organization and that accounting does not have any special hold on information or technology resources. An organization where it is beneficial for IT to report directly to the CEO is rare. This is not a good idea because the chief executive officer rarely has the time to devote proper attention to the technology department and coordinate its demands.

If the organization is large enough, there may be a chief information officer, or CIO. This is a very high-level position, and the person occupying it should be more interested in *the big picture* than the day-to-day events of the IT department. The CIO is a strategic position that is mostly involved with planning. For instance, the CIO is included in high-level meetings concerning new products, planned mergers or acquisitions, or major changes in the company that would either affect be or affected by technology. The IT director, or manager, is more involved on a day-to-day basis at an operating level. Again, depending on the size of the company and the IT staff, the IT director should spend most of their time managing and not actually *doing*. Yet, in the real world, the head of the IT department may be very involved at a working level.

The IT director is responsible for the day-to-day operations of the information technology department. The director is responsible for implementing and maintaining the technology infrastructure of the organization and overseeing the resources to support its users. The director is required to demonstrate a high level of understanding of technology, and the ability to recognize the resources needed and guide those resources to their assignments. The responsibilities of the director are:

- Directs and coordinates all approved programs, projects and major activities of the information technology (IT) department.
- Supervises and directs all IT staff.
- Maintains and develops efficient computer usage.
- Reviews performance of IT personnel and equipment on a regular and consistent basis.
- Ensures all applications and programs are maintained to the highest degree of security.
- Directs professional development and departmental staff training programs.
- Evaluates applicability of new technical developments.
- Develops IT methods and standards.
- Evaluates equipment requirements and analyzes available equipment capabilities.
- Responsible for all communications equipment and network infrastructure.
- Responsible for all voice communications and all communication lines.
- Documents current systems operations.
- Applies current technology to solution of problems.
- Defines systems security and control procedures.
- Develops systems testing and conversion plans.

Network Administrator(s)

During the past decade the primary functions of the IT department have evolved from a single computer focus to focusing on a network of many interrelated devices. A box focus refers to a time when all applications were centralized and processing took place on a single mainframe processor. This was 30 years ago. Twenty years ago, the number of these centralized systems increased dramatically as midrange systems dominated medium, and even many small businesses. Still, the theme of technology was centralized processing. About this time, personal computers entered the business arena and rapidly proliferated. As these personal computers became more powerful, they took on many of the tasks that had been performed by midrange and mainframe computers. These high-end personal computers adopted the term server. Operating systems evolved that linked these servers together so that applications were distributed to many servers linked on the same network. This network with all attached servers, workstations (now called clients), printers and other devices became the dominant computing power.

This network of codependent devices had to be administered by technology professionals who had trained and been certified on one or more personal computer network operating systems (NOS). The network administrator, also referred to as a network manager, is typically the highest-level technologist in the organization. As the senior technology professional, the network administrator(s) manages the servers to include loading and upgrading NOS and application software. They typically add and remove users and manage the system backup. When there is a crisis, the network administrator corrects the problems.

The network administrator is responsible for all physical aspects of the network and communications. This position will create new users, change security as directed, and remove users. The network administrator oversees contractors for all locations, and insures that work performed is according to the organization's guidelines, in a timely manner. The network administrator reports directly to and makes recommendations to the IT director. The responsibilities of the network administrator are:

- Oversees and coordinates all network hardware, servers, and desktop systems to include any third-party interfaces, ISP interfaces and communications interfaces.
- Reviews performance of technical support and contract personnel on a regular and consistent basis.
- Ensures all systems are maintained to the highest degree of operations.
- Maintains and tests backup disaster recovery systems.
- Maintains expertise in current technical methods and standards.
- Responsible for the design and implementation of new systems.
- Maintains documentation for all current systems and standards.

Help Desk Technician(s)

The help desk technician has routine direct contact with users. The help desk is the first point of contact for any problems a user may have. The help desk technician has a medium level of expertise on a wide number of applications and operating systems and receives technical direction from a senior technician, such as the network administrator. The responsibilities of the help desk technician are:

- Oversees and coordinates all user workstations.
- Responds to and resolves end user requests for help.
- Maintains manual and automated help desk reports.
- Tracks all end user hardware and software configurations.
- Maintains most current authorized software for all users.
- Adds and deletes users and changes passwords as necessary.
- Maintains current knowledge about the operating characteristics and maintenance requirements of peripheral devices that are assigned.
- Maintains knowledge of current standards applicable to the operation of peripherals and the handling of input and output media.
- Maintains an orderly and current library of systems documentation and technical information.
- Keeps supply storage areas orderly and accessible.

Web Administrator(s)

The web administrator is responsible for coordinating the posting of information to organization-owned or -managed web sites. The web administrator prepares storyboards for web artists and content developers to integrate into sites and approves all material created. The web administrator acts as technical liaison to third-party contractors. The web administrator has general knowledge of web-based tools, but is not required to develop web design graphics. The responsibilities of the web administrator are:

- Works closely with all department heads to review changes and implement web-based content.
- Point of contact for all Internet Service Providers to resolve issues and initiate action.
- Develops and updates the Intranet site(s).
- Maintains the organization's internal Intranet site.
- Possesses a general knowledge of HTML. XML, Java and ActiveX, as well as other web-based tools.
- Manages the organization's images and PDF databases.

Database Administrator(s)

The database administrator is responsible for maintaining interactive structure query language (SQL) databases. This includes low-level report generation and posting data updates. The responsibilities of the database administrator are:

- Has a working knowledge of vendor SQL database structures and query language.
- Meets with information technology steering committee (ITSC) and user staff on a regular basis to determine needs.
- Develops screen and hardcopy reports for user staff from SQL files.
- Manages all of the organization's databases, internal and external.
- Works closely with IT technical staff to help resolve technical issues.

Mission Statement

Why is an IT mission statement needed? Everyone needs focus, and perhaps IT professionals need focus more than anyone else in the organization. Because they work in a field that changes at an incredible rate, and deal with the problems related to the speed of this evolution, focus is very important. The mission statement creates this focus. If taken seriously, the mission statement is a constant reminder of the purpose of IT. Keep the mission statement short and to the point. A single sentence or two is all that is needed. With a longer statement, the mission becomes diluted. Here is one possible example.

It is the mission of the information technology department to provide all services required to meet the current and future information systems needs of this organization in the most efficient, effective and economic manner possible.

Information Technology Steering Committee (ITSC)

The information technology steering committee (ITSC) is a partnership between IT and the technology user community. The information technology steering committee should be a collective group representing the users of all technology services within the organization. Rather than have information technology establish the priorities of tasks to be performed and resources required, the information technology steering committee assists in the establishment of priorities and funding of resources. The ITSC takes on the burden and responsibility of defining where IT should focus and prioritizes tasks to be done. The ITSC does not have supervisory authority over IT; the ITSC is not in a position to tell IT what to do. The ITSC is an advisory body. As always, it is senior management that directs the activities of IT. There are always demands on IT resources, such as routine hardware and software maintenance and responding to help desk support requests, which are managed by the IT director. The ITSC is rarely involved with the day-to-day routine tasks. The exception is that the ITSC reviews summary reports of help desk activity so they can see where the support calls are coming from and the time IT is spending supporting users. In reviewing this information, the ITSC will often request, and fund, more training or additional upgrades for the benefit of their users. But, this is a side benefit of the ITSC. The real objectives of the ITSC are to prioritize project assignments to IT and to support IT in acquiring additional resources when needed.

A good example might be that IT has received a request from accounting to install an upgrade to the accounting system migrating from a proprietary database system to a SQL database. At the same time, the vice-president of manufacturing sends a message to IT that they are extending their product line and need to add an additional 30 items to the inventory system. This will involve creation of multiple warehouses, bin locations and a new numbering scheme. On top of all this, the marketing department calls with the good news that they have identified a new customer relationship management solution and are ready to have it installed—and yesterday would be great!

For this particular IT department with limited resources, the problem is obvious. Too many tasks, not enough resources—now who decides the order of priority? In most organizations, IT is left to make the decision which usually means IT tries to make everyone happy, without the proper resources, and ends up making everyone angry. Or, IT meets the demands of the squeaky wheel. Well, the squeaky wheel gets the oil. Those who are the loudest in their demands get the attention first. No matter which direction IT goes, it will be the loser, because it is not in the position to make these decisions.

Enter the ITSC. The ITSC is an independent body composed of users and representing the best interest of the users and the company. They must agree among themselves who has the greater priority, or they must convince management to provide additional resources. This method works much better than the approach many companies take. In many companies, IT goes to senior management, throws up their hands, and says, "You decide!" Best practice companies make good use of the ITSC, which is an on-going group. Members rotate on some predetermined schedule so as not to get stale. Membership is, for the most part, voluntary and most members *should not be* technical either by vocation or avocation. The ITSC must be composed of average users who understand the primary business of the company and are interested in what is in the best interest of the company.

Now that we have covered what an ITSC does, what it is its composition? How is an ITSC assembled? The information technology steering committee should include user representatives, non-IT management, if possible, and either the IT director or network administrator. In a larger organization, the help desk supervisor may come in to the meeting for a brief update report and question and answer session. It is strongly recommended that the size of the committee be limited. The best numbers are five or seven. In a very large organization, there may be a tier effect where there are subcommittees for technology in each functional area reporting up to the ITSC. Why five or seven? Because experience has shown that more than seven people are not a committee; they are a mob, and much less gets accomplished. If the company can handle a larger group, go for it. But, remember this warning.

The ITSC is to meet on a regular basis. I hate meetings! You can drag me to a meeting kicking and screaming, and I will be the first one out the door when it is over. Make the meetings worthwhile! Require each committee member to submit agenda items to the chairperson several days prior to the meeting. The ITSC chairperson should compile the agenda items, plus the standard IT department reporting items, and publish an agenda at least 24 hours before a meeting. A rule of thumb is, if there is no agenda, there must not be a reason to meet! Do not hand an agenda out at the meeting; no one will have time to review it and gather his or her comments and input. If I walk into a meeting and am handed an agenda for the first time, I know there is a hidden agenda, that decisions have already been made, or that someone is not a good leader. If any of these cases are true, there is no need for this meeting.

The last tip for ITSC meetings is: *keep them short and to the point—stick to the agenda*. No meeting should take longer than 50 minutes. If a meeting takes longer than 50 minutes, then either there are too many items on the agenda, and more than one meeting is needed to make the appropriate decisions. Or, there is too much discussion and the meeting needs to draw to a close. Studies show that people lose their focus in meetings that last more than 50 minutes. They are thinking about everything but the meeting. Time to send them back to work.

INFRASTRUCTURE STANDARDS

A fairly brief description of the organization's infrastructure should be placed in the standards and procedures manual. This is not the place for a detailed listing of every component, every workstation computer and printer, every modem, switch and router. Begin with a brief statement of the standard hardware and then move on to the standard software. When either changes, update the manual.

Hardware and Software Procurement

Study after study indicates that the cost of maintaining hardware is on the rise. Part of the cost is labor and materials necessary to support multiple models of hardware and versions of software. Best practice organizations document procedures for the procurement of standard components. On an annual basis, they review their standard workstation and server parameters and publish any changes that are appropriate. In an organization where hardware and software is purchased at departmental levels, this is critical. There have been several costly situations where departments did their own procurement, without notifying IT. And then, IT was assigned to support the purchase 90 days to a year later. Two to three years later, as this older equipment was failing, the end result was tremendous overhead in maintenance, which IT often absorbs in its budget. Supporting a number of different hardware vendors and various drivers for internal components not only results in a nightmare for IT, but also in a huge cost to the company in lost productivity and erroneous processing.

Best practice organizations today are striving to standardize vendor products, even when an older model is replaced. They attempt to review purchases down to the component level and purchase similar hardware components that use the same drivers. When supporting several hundred personal computers with limited technical resources, taking 45 minutes to find a video driver is not affordable.

There are a number of variations on how technology related items like hardware and software are purchased. Getting control of purchases really begins with the ITSC. Simply telling everyone that IT is now in charge and will do all buying may not work. Explaining the cost to the ITSC and getting the users buy-in and help, and enforcing written technology procurement policies is the only way to go. Where there is not ITSC, the IT director must get senior management, department heads and the organization's purchasing department to support the standardization.

Hardware and Software Maintenance

Beyond simply maintaining the organization's technology while hardware and software is in service, technicians need written procedures for:

- The length of time to spend trouble shooting a problem.
- When to take action to replace suspect components.
- Disposing of worn or non-functional inventory.
- Procurement process for new or replacement parts.
- Recording and storage of software licenses.

Information Technology Log and Run Sheets

This section may not be applicable to smaller companies that do not have dedicated operations staff. Applications such as batch posting processes, inventory updates, batch accounts payable processing, or batch report generation are normally found in larger organizations, such as financial institutions, large retail organizations, hospitals and so forth. These are processes performed by a systems operator. IT will maintain a daily IT run log of all processes executed by IT Operations during each 24-hour period. Run sheets that describe each daily job processed by IT will support the daily information technology log.

All production runs processed by IT staff should be documented and stored for easy reference. The run sheets are typically arranged in alphabetical order by process, or by run date. On the run sheet, provide a brief narrative of the process and include a flow diagram of the entire process stream. All files, reports, and so forth are indicated on the diagram. In addition to the run sheets, include a current listing of any script code, control language code (larger and mainframe system) and entry parameters to be input from the systems operator.

The IT director, or senior staff technician, should review the run log daily to insure that all processes were run correctly and there were no exceptions during processing that were not correctly handled.

Where some run processes may be automatic, and performed by the computers on a predetermined schedule without human intervention, the senior IT person on staff should review the computerized log files daily to insure that the processes are performing properly. Examples of such processes include nightly backup routines and updating of virus definition files.

Processing Center (or Data Center) Policy

Select a default name to assign that magic room where the primary systems, servers, and communications equipment are stored—processing center, computer room or data center (the room stays the same; only the size of the boxes and the name changes) policies must be established that are supported by procedures that protect the operating environment of that room.

Security

Unauthorized personnel should not be allowed in the computer room unless accompanied by an information technology employee. The door to the computer room should not be left open. A best practice is to place a cipher, or some other type of lock, on all entrance doors. The combination to the computer room door is not to be released to anyone. A published list of those persons with authorization to enter the computer room is to be posted near all entrances. A sign-in book is an excellent idea, so there is a written record of any visits from parties not on the authorized access list.

The following is a brief example of an access policy statement. Make sure a procedure for modifying and posting changes to the access list is included, as well as assigning responsibility for changing the cipher lock codes.

Make sure the IT staff as well as co-workers know that the computer room is a restricted area and not for entertaining and casual visits. The IT director will set the tone for security in an organization and is responsible for enforcing the policies and procedures put in place—ignoring any one policy is the same as ignoring all of them!

Personnel shall under no circumstances allow access to anyone that cannot be properly identified or that is not expected. This policy must be strictly adhered to during off-hours and on weekends. There shall be no exceptions, including friends and relatives. If this is a problem, contact the appropriate security officer for the organization for clearance.

The Sample Company Data Center (computer room, or whatever language works), located at 123 Main Street, second floor, is a restricted area. Access is limited to those persons with a need for entry; a list of those persons will be posted outside the main hall entry door. The cipher lock combination will be changed quarterly, or whenever the access list changes, and all persons will be notified of the new access code. IT staff is not authorized to allow anyone access or ingress to the data center without the express permission of the director, information technology department or the president (or other senior ranking corporate officer, depending on the specific organizational structure).

Individuals who have been entrusted with keys, passwords, or combinations must take appropriate measures to ensure their safekeeping and protection. Under no circumstance should any key, password or combination be given to another individual without the express permission of the appropriate security officer. This may create some inconvenience when dealing with cleaning crews, and so forth, but it is essential for proper security.

It is just as important to protect data center computer resources from the inside as outside. The IT director is responsible for enforcing a security policy and related procedures that ensure the intellectual resources of the organization are protected. Inside security begins with the user identification code and password necessary to gain access. Enforcing a strict code and password policy will not guarantee a secure system, but will be an excellent beginning. A best practice standard recommends that user ID's be at least a twelve character alphanumeric identifier. It is strongly recommended that the user ID log in not be less than seven alphanumeric characters. For an individual user, the user ID may be a meaningful representation of the characters in the user's name or an agreed upon numbering convention. Some sample user ID's include:

- First name and the first letter of the user's last name.
- First and middle initial and user's last name.
- Some organizations assign an employee a unique number that is not confidential, but not widely known by everyone in the organization. These may be used with the approval of human resources, who ensures that the number is not confidential or restricted.

The user password may be the most abused standard in all organizations. Users must learn that security breaches are real and that proper security measures must be observed at all times. Every user must be assigned a password that is effective, but not overly restrictive. A best practice password is a five-to-ten character alphanumeric password. Many organizations initially set up new users so that the password is set the same as the user ID at the first log in. At the time of the first log in, the user assigns a password. In most cases, the network administrator can override and change any user's password if it is necessary to enter the system and remove a user, or if a user forgets the password and needs IT to assign a new one.

Users must change their passwords periodically to avoid the system being compromised. While standards vary, a reasonable policy is for passwords to expire every 60 days. The system will notify the user, prior to password expiration, to change to a new password. If all warnings, including the final one, are ignored, the user cannot log on to the system but must notify the help desk and request a new password. This request should be logged as a support request. After two password abuses, a new password is not assigned until requested by the person's supervisor. If abuses continue, the issue should be taken to the ITSC for action.

Cleanliness

There have been many incidents that could have been avoided if the computer room had simply been kept free of debris, dangerous chemicals, and excess parts and components. It is a best practice to keep the computer room, service and support area (where maintenance and setup is done), and staff work areas neat, clean, and orderly. All surfaces and display screens should be cleaned daily. Printers will be cleaned on a regular scheduled basis. It is not enough to simply tell staff to *clean up*. The written procedures specify what is to be done daily, weekly, monthly and so forth, as well as by whom. For example:

The network administrator will be responsible for cleaning all monitors and surface areas on a daily basis as well as ensuring that all trash and debris are removed from the computer room on a scheduled basis. Once a month, the help desk supervisor will take inventory of all usable parts and store these properly while discarding broken, or unusable parts and components. For items of value over $500, which have been booked to fixed assets, IT will coordinate the disposal of property with the accounting department.

Help Desk Policy and Procedures

Well-defined and documented policy and procedure statements must support the help desk. This includes having a standardized support request form (SRF) and a log book to document outstanding SRFs. The log book could be either a manual log, or an automated system with databases storing SRF and log book information for reporting.

The responsibility for implementing policy and managing procedures falls to the help desk supervisor in a large organization with a number of support technicians, or the network administrator, or IT director or manager in a smaller organization.

If the resolution involves a change to any equipment, project, program, or procedure, a change request form should be completed so that inventory and fixed assets may be adjusted.

It is always a best practice to provide work flow diagrams of all procedures that document processes. Visual diagrams like the one in Exhibit 3.3 save time and effort in reading a process description and interpreting the instructions.

Exhibit 3.3

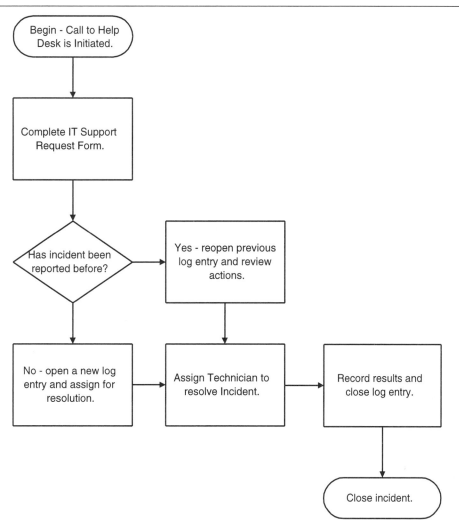

The support request form will be used by the information technology department to report a problem that occurs with any technology related equipment, project, program, or procedure.

The following is a sample form. Again, modify the form to best fit your needs, but keep it simple! Keep the form fairly easy to use and understand, so that reporting is simplified and usable.

Support Request Log

The support request log book is a journal of all the SRFs that are open and closed (see Exhibit 3.4). As part of the call tracking process, the help desk technician will enter each

Information Technology Help Desk Report

Sample Company Anytown, USA

Support request number _____ Reopened call appends: _____

Call taken: date ___/___/___ at _____:_____:_____ By: _____

Support related to: Software ( ) Hardware ( ) Network ( ) Other ( )

Name of requestor: _____ System ID: _____

Description:

_____

_____

_____

(Include as much detail as possible using the back of form if needed.)

Assigned to: _____ (Specify if not within 30 minutes of taking call.)

Action taken:

_____

_____

_____

(Include as much detail as possible using the back of form if needed.)

If a change request if necessary, enter change request #: _____

User signoff on action taken: _____

Date and time SRF closed: _____/_____/_____ _____:_____:_____

Log entry closed and from filed by: _____

Exhibit 3.4   Sample Support Request Log

Control Number	Date Opened and Date Closed	Opened by/Closed by	Assigned to

incident on the support request form and then make a single entry in the log. When the incident is closed, the on-duty help desk technician makes the notation in the log.

The log entry has been shortened for reasons of space. The logbook will be much improved by separate entry fields for dates opened, closed, and by whom. The help desk will replicate this report format and place it in a binder to be maintained for review and action by the IT director. This information should be summarized and reported to the information technology steering committee at each meeting, including incidences that have been resolved since the last meeting and those remaining. Some discussion of repeat offenders or specific problem types can be identified and resolutions discussed. The reporting of incidents and analysis of what is causing failures to occur is the single most important reason for instituting a formal help desk.

BACKUP AND RECOVERY PROCEDURES

The next critical area is backup of critical media and recovery procedures.

- It is essential that all files be backed up in a regular and timely manner.
- All critical backup diskettes must be stored in a secure and acceptable location, preferably in a locking fireproof cabinet away from the PC.
- Backup media must be properly identified and dated.
- All backup files must be in synchronization with one another. If a job updates several files, all those files must be backed up at the same time.

Backup Site, Schedule and Retention

The written procedures must document precisely how data backups are completed, the retention of all information, where the backup files are to be stored, and when they can be destroyed. The procedures must also define validation of backup files through restoration and testing. Actual business contingency and disaster recovery processes are covered in Chapter 4, but these processes need to be documented in the policy and procedures manual for everyone. All backups of programs and files must be stored in an appropriate fire and heatproof safe or vault. Several generations of previous backups must be retained in the event that such backups are needed.

The difference between a fireproof safe or vault versus a heatproof one is significant. Many people have been saddened when they find out the difference after a catastrophic failure. Many safes and vaults, particularly older units, are only fire-rated. Since these were used for storing paper documents and negotiable instruments (money or stock certificates), they were perfectly functional.

However, safes and vaults used to store magnetic media are a different story. These units must be highly heat-resistant. The destruction threshold for magnetic media, which is primarily composed of glass and various types of plastic, is much lower than the combustion level of paper. Disks and other storage media can be rendered useless long before the heat is high enough to ignite or burn paper.

The procedures must also document exactly what the backup schedule is—who is to do it, and who is responsible for removing the backup media offsite or to an appropriate storage area. Be sure to define the rotation schedule if backup media is to be returned to the computer room, after a period of time, to be reused.

Some organizations only back up program and operating systems files when an update occurs, whereas data files are backed up daily. Make sure there is a restore procedure that can rapidly bring the systems back to an operating environment as quickly as possible.

The backup media retention policy is a serious decision, and must be in writing. The number of copies to be maintained depends on the size of the organization. Do not be in the position of losing critical files over the cost of a quality backup unit and adequate media. Test partial and full system restores on a regular basis.

- *System backups.*   monthly
- *Master files (daily).*   6-day cycle
- *Master files (quarterly).*   3-month cycle
- *Furniture and equipment files (pcs).*   8-disk cycle
- *Offsite full system and data files (weekly).*   4-disk cycle
- *Other miscellaneous (servers, daily and weekly).*   4/8-version cycle

Control and Destruction of Printed Reports

Due to legislative action during 2000 and 2001, security and privacy of confidential information is high on the list of IT priorities today. Even more stringent regulations can be expected over the next few years. IT is responsible for protecting information from printed reports that contain sensitive information, such as customer address, account balances, and so forth. It is the responsibility of all employees to respect and protect the privacy of their customers and the intellectual properties of the company. Reports may also contain sensitive information pertaining to the operation of the company and related entities. It is the responsibility of all employees to limit access of such information to only those with a need to know and to protect the information from access by unauthorized individuals. This needs to be conveyed to all employees at all levels. If confidentiality of information is breached, disciplinary action should be taken.

In larger organizations where reports are printed centrally, all reports are to be delivered to only those authorized to receive them within the organization. IT will create a distribution list for use by the courier in the delivery of daily reports. Users must not leave reports containing sensitive information on their desks when they are away from their work area. Highly sensitive information is to be locked away or secured when not being used. Access to areas where sensitive data is in constant use will be limited to authorized individuals. Reports containing sensitive information should go to shred bins to be shredded and disposed of periodically to protect the privacy of the organization and its customers.

Disposal of Confidential Material

All companies today have a tremendous responsibility for maintaining the security and confidentiality of all sensitive data. This includes customer information, as well as programs and file listings, dumps, run sheets, documentation, and so forth. It is imperative that all employees understand the importance of the confidentiality of account information. They should understand that their company has a fiduciary responsibility and could violate that trust by releasing information to unauthorized individuals. To prevent confidential and sensitive information from getting into the wrong hands, all information should be shredded, as described above.

All other trash from the data center should be placed in a trash receptacle and picked up by a trash collection service on a consistent basis. All reports or hardcopy sheets should be shredded and properly disposed of in shred boxes.

CONCLUSION

This chapter has attempted to highlight the most critical areas for documenting technical policy and procedures. Fortunately, there is a wealth of material written on the subject. It is critical to remember that written policies and procedures are not an option, and are not the product of idle hands. Policies and procedures are not something to do between more important projects, or because there is nothing better to do at the moment. Written standards are the basis for a best practice organization.

CHAPTER FOUR

Business Contingency Planning

CONTINGENCY PLANS—DISASTER RECOVERY AND BUSINESS RESUMPTION

Business contingency planning could have been covered in either the planning chapter or the policy and procedure chapter, but the subject is important enough to deserve a chapter of its own. Business contingency planning goes by a number of names, business resumption contingency plans (BRCP), business continuity planning, and disaster recovery planning. These will be referred to collectively as *contingency plans.*

There is more than one approach to contingency planning. The traditional approach is to prepare a plan in case information systems fail as the result of a major storm or fire damage. These are disasters; no doubt about it, but the risk of one of these events occurring is relatively small compared to other events that happen every day. These daily events can cost a business far more than a single catastrophic failure. Contingency planning today must go further than sending backups to off-site storage, or even having a remote alternate processing site. True contingency planning is about keeping the business afloat during a number of unforeseen emergencies.

Because technology has permeated the workplace much more than a decade ago, contingency plans must focus more on the workplace and the processes performed. The plan should detail how the recovery process will take place from the human perspective. Getting the technology back online may be the least of the problems.

In preparation for year 2000, many organizations developed contingency plans for critical information systems. However, these plans were geared to a specific event, program failure, and are not comprehensive enough. Organizations must review their plans and update them. Organizations must go beyond their information systems and develop comprehensive contingency plans for all critical resources.

After the tragic events of September 11, 2001, many organizations initiated a review of their internal contingency plans. Organizations affected by the terrorist attack that had tested contingency plans were up and running, at least at a minimal level, very quickly. Organizations must ensure they can rapidly provide a minimally acceptable level of critical services during a disaster.

As recent events have shown, organizations can experience a sudden disruption of their operations. The disruption can be minimal, with a power outage for an hour or two, or a building and its contents could be destroyed by a sudden explosion or fire. Threats to your business can be natural, human, or technical. To be effective, contingency plans should consider potential disasters at all levels. The plans should assume that the business could not continue operating at its physical location, due to a natural disaster or some other unforeseen event, for an extended period.

Contingency planning includes five phases:

1. Establish organizational planning guidelines.
2. Business impact analysis (the risk assessment).
3. Develop detailed contingency plans.
4. Validate.
5. Communicate the plan.

Each phrase will now be discussed.

Phase 1. Establish Organizational Planning Guidelines

The Board of Directors and senior management can either develop appropriate contingency plans or designate the task to a formal emergency response team (ERT). The ERT will be described in more detail later in this chapter. In either case, the board and senior management always retain the responsibility for the plan's development and approval, along with sufficient resources to ensure the plan's success.

Depending on the organization's size and complexity, the ERT can consist of one or two individuals, or could be composed of management and staff, appropriate third-party vendors and/or consultants. ERT members should represent all areas of the business. Group members should understand that their objective is to initially develop and then ensure updated, viable contingency plans.

A critical system or service is any internal or external system or service that would have a negative material impact on operations or financial condition. It is important to note that specific critical systems may be components of a number of core business processes and may serve as an interface between and among the operations of core business processes. In identifying criticality, management should consider the customer's needs. For example, if the business relies extensively on electronic systems to conduct business, all of the components that constitute this process are likely to be critical.

Phase 2. Business Impact Analysis (the Risk Assessment)

Organizations must ask themselves, "What system or service would significantly impact the continued operation of the business?" "If this system or service were non-operational, how long could the business continue to function without it?" These questions assist management in assessing the business risk. In performing a business impact analysis, organizations should consider:

- The critical system(s) or service(s).
- Type of failure events.
- Minimum acceptable service levels.
- Probability of occurrence.
- Failure scenarios.

Organizations should prioritize these risks and develop appropriate contingency plans. When a small business evaluates its risk, it is important to consider that, in the event of a catastrophic event, a small, one-location business like a bank may take on more risk because it has fewer financial and human resources available.

Critical System or Service

A critical system or service can be physical (building, roadway, parking lot, or ingress to your business), human (employees, members, consultants) or technical (hardware, software, interfaces, external systems, power sources, telecommunications). The ERT should work with department staff to determine critical activities. For example, staff should review the network diagram, a picture of all the internal and external systems and their interface, and include each process or interface associated with the critical service.

Other possible critical systems can be applications and the associated files stored on an employee's hard drive to document board minutes or reconcile ledger accounts or bank statements. Organizations can survive interruptions if they evaluate their exposure and prepare for a full range of disasters. Part of the process is to identify events that can impede operations. The traditional approach is to attempt to identify all possible events and prepare a plan that responds to each of these.

Type of Failure Events

Localized events like water leaks, fire, robbery, bomb threat, building damage, employee strike, threats against employees, simultaneous, temporary or permanent loss of several key employees, vendor failure, computer viruses, sabotage, hardware damage, biological threat, are more controllable. They have a direct effect and it is possible to plan for them.

External events are more difficult to manage. These disruptive events include power outages, communication disruptions, storms that result in hurricane, tornado, earthquake, floods, snowstorm and ice damage) and do commonly occur. Road closures due to damage or scheduled construction, explosions, striking employees at an adjacent business, chemical spills, protests, and riots may also affect business indirectly and are less manageable. These types of events have an impact radius of one mile, 50 miles and 100 miles.

Statewide or national events, strikes, and security threats, such as the terrorist attack that occurred on September 11, loss of service by the communications provider, or third-party service provider could affect business. In today's global economy, many companies depend on products or services outside their geographic area and even outside national boundaries.

Minimum Acceptable Service Levels

The ERT should establish minimum acceptable service levels based on the duration of failure events. Practical categories include: immediate (one day or less), short-term (one to three days), intermediate (three to ten days), and long-term (greater than ten days). In evaluating minimum levels, organizations should consider:

- Minimum number of employees required.
- Ability to bring in outside human resources.
- Amount of service or system down time before it will affect the ability to continue servicing the customer.
- Regulatory requirements.
- Financial impact on the business (business checking accounts, line of credit advances, cash needs, etc.).
- Vendor and outside source list including addresses, phone numbers, cell phone numbers, pager numbers, and contact people (service bureau, online banking provider, security company, power company, etc.).
- List of current systems and equipment including model number, version, and manufacturer with address, phone number, and contact person.
- Legal and liability issues.
- Security.

Probability of Occurrence

Evaluate the likelihood of a specific event occurring. If the business operates in a southern state, the likelihood of a snow or ice storm is remote. A business located along the southern coastline might be more vulnerable to hurricanes, and a midwestern business could be affected by tornados. The same theory applies to other natural disasters. Human or technical failures affect everyone regardless of the threat or location.

Failure Scenarios

The traditional approach to disaster recovery focuses on specific failures and addresses a strategy for each. While this approach is less effective, because of the potential for a business to be affected by statewide, national or international events, many managers are more comfortable with this type of planning. Once management determines critical systems or services, identifies failure events, establishes duration categories, and determines minimum acceptable service levels, they should rank event probability and criticality in developing failure scenarios. This is where to establish minimal levels of acceptable risk, and how much to spend in advance to avoid, or recover from, potential failures.

This is one method for identifying potential risk of failures and measuring your response. A large number of financial institutions use the best practice risk analysis method to determine where the greatest threats of failure are located. This approach is recommended by regulatory agencies auditing the institutions.

A *dependency* is the critical system or service. An *event* is the type of disaster. *Duration* is the defined time frame the critical system would be out of service. *Probability* is the likelihood of occurrence. And, *criticality* is how much of an impact the failure would have on operations over the duration period. The *probability* and *criticality* must be measured. Any number of scales might be used. However, the most effective is a scale of one to five, with five being the most likely event to occur or most critical system, and one being the least likely to occur or least critical system.

Exhibit 4.1 illustrates three scenarios—power supply outage (failure 1-A to 1-D), power outage (failure 2-A to 2-D), and employees not able to report for work (failure 3-A to 3-D). For example, failure scenario 3 considers the same failure event, employees unable to report for work, over four different timeframes, 3-A, immediate, to 3-D, long-term. The probability that no employees are available to report for work for more than ten days, failure scenario 3-D (identified as long-term) is very low (1), while the impact of having no employees for more than ten days would be very high (5).

For some businesses that are *seasonal,* or experience an extremely high volume of business at specific times of the year (tax season in a public accounting firm for instance), there could be a ranking for *period*. The period could represent a season, or specific time frame, where a low- or medium-ranked failure might be more critical. This will be unique to each business, but warrants additional discussion among management.

Exhibit 4.1

Failure	Dependency	Event	Duration	Probability	Criticality
1-A	Serv. Supplier	Local Power Out	Immediate	2	2
1-B	Serv. Supplier	Local Power Out	Short-term	2	3
1-C	Serv. Supplier	Local Power Out	Intermediate	1	4
1-D	Serv. Supplier	Local Power Out	Long-term	1	5
2-A	Serv. Supplier	Remote Power Out	Immediate	5	3
2-B	Serv. Supplier	Remote Power Out	Short-term	4	5
2-C	Serv. Supplier	Remote Power Out	Intermediate	3	5
2-D	Serv. Supplier	Remote Power Out	Long-term	2	5
3-A	Employee	Cannot get to work	Immediate	3	3
3-B	Employee	Cannot get to work	Short-term	2	4
3-C	Employee	Cannot get to work	Intermediate	1	5
3-D	Employee	Cannot get to work	Long-term	1	5

Organizations should also realize that they may face simultaneous multiple failure scenarios, depending on the disaster. The development of failure scenarios will allow businesses to prioritize and develop appropriately detailed contingency plans. A failure scenario with a probability and criticality rating of five should have a higher degree of attention and more resources devoted to developing and implementing contingency plans than would a failure scenario with a probability and criticality rating of one. The failure scenarios must be periodically reviewed to ensure that probability and criticality ratings are still appropriate, given the changing environment and member expectations. Prior to increased terrorist activity, worldwide managers did not consider such scenarios in areas that previously had minimal threats. Today, a business in a large metropolitan area might place more resources to recovery in the event of a local or national attack, such as those we have seen in the past twelve months.

Every business should understand and accept that the process of formally assessing your level of risk is both time consuming and labor intensive. It should not be done too quickly or haphazardly. The result of the risk assessment defines where you will place your efforts and financial resources.

Phase 3. Develop Detailed Contingency Plan

Developing appropriately detailed and prioritized recovery plans for identified failure scenarios is the most important phase of contingency planning. To adequately respond to an emergency or disaster, a business must have well thought-out, documented and tested contingency strategies in place.

Begin by evaluating the options available and select the most cost-effective, practical, and appropriate strategy for the size and complexity of the business. The contingency strategies for a professional services firm, a financial institution and a manufacturer will all be different. The primary goal should be to maximize the functionality and speed of recovery and minimize cost. When considering critical information systems, any organization that uses an online service provider, or any outside third-party service provider, should evaluate the adequacy of the provider's contingency plans and ensure that the recovery plans are compatible with the service provider's plans. If the business depends on third-party relationships for such activities as distribution or shipping, your plan must include alternative providers for this service. The plan may include changing the operation strategies to split services provided by a single vendor or to two vendors to allow for an alternate channel, in the event of disaster.

Do not do this without careful analysis. One client suffered a loss of online services due to a loss of the communications lines. Even though the client had contracted for services from two different vendors, and had been using both vendors for an extended period of time, they did not realize, until the failure occurred, that both vendors contracted with the same vendor for Internet gateway connectivity. When that *second tier* vendor failed, both of their channels to the Internet failed, and they were unable to conduct business at an acceptable level for an extended period of time. They finally recovered, but at an economic loss that was not anticipated.

This is not an unusual story. Contingency planning for the year 2000 date bug revealed that companies had a high degree of exposure because their support vendors were using, or being supplied by, a common vendor two and three levels down the chain.

The business contingency plan focuses on the impact of a disruption. It must include the steps to be taken to recover critical activities in the event staff is unavailable, electronic and/or paper information is gone, and the building or other tangible assets are destroyed or unreachable. Each section of the plan should stand alone. The plan should incorporate:

- Approximate cost of implementation in terms of personnel and financial resources.
- Staffing requirements, such as replacement personnel, extraordinary staff expenses and safety and health factors.
- Sufficient detail so that employees can implement the contingency plan effectively.

The ERT assembles individual department, or group level, plans into a comprehensive organization-wide contingency plan. With a comprehensive plan, management can easily update the individual plans as services or systems change.

Phase 4.   Validate

To ensure the contingency plan actually works (which is very important when all is said and done), the plan should be tested at least annually, or whenever a significant change takes place. This is critical because business organizations change quickly today. When a merger, an acquisition, or change in management occurs, the plan must be reviewed for effectiveness. Appropriate changes must be made and tested immediately.

The test should determine if the organization could recover to an acceptable level of business within the time frame stated in the contingency plan. Examples of validation methods include, but are not limited to, simulations, role-play, walk-through, and alternate site reviews.

It is a best practice policy for organizations to utilize a qualified, independent party, such as an internal auditor, external auditor, consultant, or employees not directly involved, to develop and validate the contingency plan. The independent party's responsibilities include:

- Assessing the planning process.
- Reviewing the resulting plans.
- Testing the contingency plan's scope and evaluating the test results.
- Determining if management has appropriate follow-up and corrective actions.
- Evaluating the adequacy of management reporting and oversight.
- Verifying that the disaster recovery site has the current hardware, software, and environmental systems available to recover according to the plan recovery process.

Management should retain the necessary documentation that includes the scope and type of tests performed, and a sufficient audit trail to determine the success of each test with appropriate follow-up.

Phase 5.   Communicate the Plan

The contingency plan must outline a program to notify employees, members, third-party vendors, bonding companies, news media, law enforcement, regulators, insurance companies, and other outside parties about the disruption and the impact on operations. Notification can involve television, radio, newspapers, mail, or a combination of these methods.

In a failure or disaster situation, it is important to convey the information clearly and quickly to appropriate individuals outside the organization. It is important to notify customers that might be expecting shipments or other services so they can plan accordingly. Notify financial institutions, particularly if emergency cash reserves or lines of credit will be needed during the recovery process.

Many organizations plan what actions to take in the event of a disaster well, but fail to realize the resources required to initiate the recovery process and keep the business afloat during very difficult times. It is always a good idea to have a line of credit, or cash reserves, set aside for such a business interruption. Notify your insurance company. Many companies fail to call their insurance provider quickly enough, and as a result, may not recover as many of their expenditures as expected. In many cases when a company notifies their insurance provider quickly, the insurance company is able to bring additional resources to the fore and provide valuable assistance. Always communicate to your insurance provider that there is a written contingency plan, perhaps even providing a copy of the plan to them. Doing so will help you during the recovery process, and may even positively affect the premiums paid for disaster related coverage. Most insurance companies can be helpful during a crisis.

Some businesses may be required to report a failure or disaster to the appropriate regulatory body within a specific time frame. Failure to do this can create unnecessary problems. Institutions that have failed to do this quickly enough have been cited. In some cases, the failure was human oversight. Do not forget that catastrophic failures can be extremely stressful on the business. Failure to notify appropriate parties could occur simply because someone, in the midst of chaos, forgot. In other cases, failure to notify an important customer, business partner, or regulatory agency happened simply because everyone thought it was someone else's job! The contingency plan must clearly define where each communication responsibility lies.

Employees

Since the organization cannot know in advance which employees will be available during a disaster, it should communicate the plans and the procedures for responding to failure events to all employees. All employees should receive a copy of the plan and be fully aware of what is expected of them. In addition, the organization should store copies of the plan at a secure backup location or other site in the event the copies at the primary site are not available.

Many organizations fail to consider staffing as critical to failure recovery. Management must address these issues before a failure occurs. For instance, a major outage or storm could affect employees' ability to get to work. If there are employees responsible for their family's childcare or health care in the event of a disaster, the plan must clearly define what is expected. If these employees recognize that they could be personally affected by a storm or other disaster, they should advise management that they might not be able to respond as the plan dictates, so that the plan can be adjusted.

To be fully prepared for a disaster, a business must ensure that employees are cross-trained in a number of different positions. Identify specific positions that might be suspended during a crisis and either advise these persons not to report to work, or assign them to alternate tasks as a part of the recovery process. For instance, if major computer systems are off-line for an extended period of time, marketing may not be a high priority. However, marketing staff might be needed to take and fill orders manually. Being aware of employee limitations is also critical. If a marketing or an accounting staff person is reassigned to help relocate inventory and is unable to perform these tasks— during the disaster is not the time to discover that!

Operations Manual

Management should have each staff member develop detailed operating instructions. This will assist staff not familiar with the duties to continue critical functions. Operating instructions can also help the organization hire temporary staff not familiar with operations of specific businesses.

Training and Testing

Employees should receive annual contingency plan training. To be certain the operations manual provides satisfactory instructions, management may simulate a disruption by suddenly changing employee duties. Training and testing are very specific to each business. Many businesses do not extend training to an actual simulation because of the cost involved. However, conference room training and seminar based instruction is still necessary so that employees are aware of the recovery process theory and what will be expected of them.

When developing their plans, organizations can seek guidance from a wide range of sources. These sources include trade associations, industry periodicals, bonding companies, insurance companies, resources on the Internet, consultants, and seminars.

Nearly every business agrees on the importance of business contingency planning. Many also say that it is something they plan to get to. While they know it is important, they just can not afford to do it right now! Hurricanes in south Florida, mudslides in the west, and fires in the north are disasters that no one could have predicted, that resulted in financial losses. One seminar participant described a natural disaster that affected a business in California a few years ago. The company had continually postponed developing a written plan. When the earthquake occurred, the company did not survive the trauma. After more than five years, the owner was just beginning to recover financially. The cost of contingency planning is small compared to the result of not planning.

BEST PRACTICE APPROACH TO BUSINESS CONTINGENCY PLANNING

Management today must be keenly aware of how technology has caused the work environment to become very sensitive to disasters that affect that technology. Imagine, for a moment, that a business's computers, network, and servers all just go down. "What can be done next?" "What would be the impact on the business?" The impact is different for each business, but consider the impact on a professional services firm. This could be a public accounting or law practice, or an architectural or engineering firm. These types of businesses are easy to use as an example of the cost of a failure, because they bill their clients based on hours worked. Time is the inventory, and if that inventory is not used every minute, the time can never be reclaimed for sale at a later time. It is lost!

Assume there is a staff of 100, all with an average billing rate of $100 per hour, just to make the math easy. It is tax season, or the middle of a major case, or designing a high-rise building. How long can the business stand losing $10,000 every hour? Perhaps this scenario is a bit over dramatic, but then again, maybe not. Most business environments today are so dependent on technology that the loss of systems for any extended period of time can be catastrophic. There have been reports of companies who never recovered from a major loss due to catastrophic failure. This failure may have been caused by simple mechanical failure, a force of nature like a hurricane or tornado, or a simple brownout or planned blackout.

A few years ago, one major food manufacturer and distributor was nearly shut down because of an upgrade to a new software application. The information technology department had moved forward with a significant upgrade. But, all affected departments were not aware of it. Recovery options for an upgrade failure were not properly planned. The upgrade failed. The company could continue to make its product, but trucks were waiting to deliver, and store shelves were empty. The company was so tied to its technology that it could not take orders, track shipments, or do billing.

This was by any definition a disaster—an internal disaster, caused by a failure to plan properly perhaps—but no less a disaster. Buildings did not burn, employees were ready and able to work, services were all in place. But the business could not continue in any normal capacity. Managers who think of a disaster only in terms of catastrophic failure should rethink their definition.

It is time to begin addressing failures at multiple levels and preparing plans to avoid or recover from each. The phases outlined previously focused on defining disasters by specific type, assigning a probability to each, and assessing how critical the failure would be to a business. This is the traditional approach. Experience has taught us that it is more effective to include a definition of failure, regardless of the cause, in the planning and then develop a course of action. If a computer center is destroyed, along with the building that houses the primary place of operations, the needs are the same whether a tornado or a fire destroyed the building.

RANKING FAILURES BY LEVEL

A best practice approach to contingency planning is to divide and define potential failures into levels and then prepare recovery strategies at each level. This discussion will maintain that there are at least four levels of disasters with risks of loss at each level. Although all disasters cannot be prevented, the possibility for some can be minimized, resulting in significant economic savings.

In the past, management's focus has always been on preventing or minimizing the possibility of large-scale failures. Today, our experience indicates that the cumulative loss from small technology failures, called level 1 failures, is actually greater than for a single level 4 failure, a catastrophic failure. It is as important to a business to plan contingencies for these smaller failures as to plan for broader failures with more far-reaching impact.

The four levels of failure will be defined and how to minimize risk or exposure to each will be discussed. The contingency plan model should define, in more detail, the failures that fall into each level, depending on the specific business.

Level 1 Failures

- A level 1 failure can be remedied in less than four hours.
- A level 1 failure is defined as having a very limited impact.
- A level 1 failure typically impacts a single person or very small group.

An example of a level 1 failure might be a printer that is out of toner, a network interface card or network connection that fails, or a software application that fails because security was not assigned. A single workstation might be down because of a failed network interface card, or because the user cannot attach to data files stored on a central network.

Level 1 failures can be remedied fairly quickly. This happens every day in offices without serious thought. That is the problem! The costs of level 1 failures mount up over a year. This cost could be significant. It is not possible to know when level 1 failures will occur, but it is possible to develop contingency plans for rapid response, or for preventing them from occurring in advance. "How can a network card failing be avoided?" "How can a printer be kept from running out of toner?" Chapter 5 will discuss best practice methods for managing technology more effectively, including the creation of a help desk to record support calls and to track where failures occur. By analyzing the information report for technical support calls, management can develop strategies to minimize the impact of these failures.

The business contingency plan should support help desk policies at level one and provide the resources IT needs to prevent support calls from recurring.

Level 2 Failures

- A level 2 failure can be remedied in less than twenty-four hours.
- A level 2 failure has an economic impact, but is not considered significant.
- A level 2 failure affects a larger group of users or network segment.

An example of a level 2 failure might be a communications device such as a CSU/DSU, or a network server that brings down all users in a department. A truck that runs into the phone pole in front of the office, taking down local communications to the main office, could create a level 2 failure.

There is no way to prevent a level 2 failure from occurring. But it is important to minimize the impact. What will the staff do when a level 2 failure occurs? Will inventory items be lost? Will errors occur that could result in a lawsuit or loss of a customer? The effects of level 2 failures are minimized by testing the written business contingency plan. This plan is meant to instruct staff what they should do, who to call, and what actions to take. A level 2 failure, if not attended to quickly, can escalate into a level 3 or 4 failures.

Level 3 Failures

- A level 3 failure can be remedied in less than seventy-two hours.
- A level 3 failure has a significant economic impact.
- A level 3 failure affects a significant number of mission critical users.

When a level 3 failure is declared, the business must determine whether it is necessary to implement the organization's business contingency plan. Level 3 failures can escalate to level 4 very quickly. The defined period of time for a level 3 failure is less than seventy-two hours, or three business days. Beyond three working days, the potential for loss increases dramatically. When a business suffers a failure for this length of time, they typically fall back to a manual system. These systems weaken and fail rapidly beyond three days. The staff may become hurried or lax in recording information, or maintaining that information for later entry when the computer system returns. Many businesses cannot afford to be down even for three days. Imagine a public accounting firm that loses its computers on March 9, just before corporate returns are due to be filed! In this case, a level 3 would immediately be catastrophic and activation of a higher level of response would be declared.

Level 4 Failures

- A level 4 failure is a catastrophic failure.
- A level 4 failure has a significant economic impact.
- A level 4 failure automatically activates the ERT and business contingency plan.

The objective of the business contingency plan is to allow the company to continue to operate during a disaster, even if at a diminished level. The goal is to be self-sufficient to the lowest level possible. Catastrophic failures may be brought on by a number of disasters as described above. The attitude of *when* and not *if* is very helpful in preparing for level 4 failures.

Level 4 failures assume the activation of the business contingency plan and the need to acquire equipment, software, and relocation to an alternate site. Once the recovery process begins, recovery teams will be dispatched according to assignment, and the organization will be establishing temporary sites of operations. This includes activating an alternate processing site for the processing center, establishment of a network, procurement of workstations and communication lines. Some of the staff will be assigned to acquire folding tables, chairs and materials such as paper, writing utensils, calculators and so forth. This chapter will focus on contingency planning for technology and technology support. But, sections of the plan must be included for each functional area of the business with definitions of what is to be done in each area.

CREATING EMERGENCY RESPONSE TEAMS

Planning for emergency response in the aftermath of a disaster is a complex task. Preparation for, response to, and recovery from a disaster affecting the functions of the organization requires the cooperative efforts of many support organizations. These organizations need to work with the functional areas supporting the *business* of the company.

The business contingency plan is a formal document that records the objective of the overall plan. Who is responsible? How will the recovery take place? Involvement in and commitment to this process begins in the boardroom, not the back room. There must be a commitment from the highest level of the organization. Like all good projects, the planning process begins in committee. Depending on the size of the organization, there are three well-defined groups:

- Contingency management steering committee (CMSC)
- Emergency response teams (ERT)
- Functional area recovery management (FARM) teams

In a larger business with multiple locations, or multiple operating companies, the CMSC is the highest-level committee and is composed of an executive level committee representative of the entire organization. The CMSC ultimately supports and approves the plan. The development and execution of the plan is most often delegated to the ERT. The ERT is chaired by the president, senior vice-president for operations, or other senior manager, and is composed of representatives of each functional area and the head of information technology, referred to here as the IT manager.

In many businesses, the Comptroller or CFO is also a part of the ERT because they have the checkbook and the authority to authorize immediate funding. The ERT either develops the plan or assigns responsibility and approves the final written document before forwarding it on for the CEO or board of directors to approve. In medium or small organizations, the ERT also is responsible for executing the plan. In larger organizations with several functional departments or multiple operating entities (companies), the FARM teams are assigned to specific areas and are responsible for executing the plan and coordinating recovery at the direction of the ERT.

For example, in a financial institution, there could be a teller FARM and loan FARM at each branch, an accounting FARM for the accounting department, and so forth. In a manufacturing environment, there could be a shop FARM, a warehouse FARM, a supply FARM, and so forth. In a large CPA firm, there might be a FARM for each office or department. A FARM is not needed in a small office. The duties of the ERT and the FARM will be discussed in more detail.

The CMSC authorizes and supports the plan by approving it and then by providing resources to test and implement it. The ERT develops and manages the plan and the FARM executes the plan. A number of teams are created to execute the plan; these will be discussed in more detail later. Keep in mind that the number of teams and their responsibilities will vary with the size of the organization. But no matter what size the organization is, there are certain basic functions that must be included.

The goal here is to maintain an acceptable level of operations while minimizing risk. Therefore, the plan must identify the critical functions of your organization and the resources required to support them. The plan must provide guidelines for ensuring that needed personnel and resources are available for both disaster preparation and response, and that the proper steps will be carried out to permit the timely restoration of services.

In the event of a disaster affecting any of the functional areas, the ERT serves as liaison between the functional area(s) affected, as well as outside organizations providing major services. These services include support provided by security, personnel, and public information on behalf of the company.

The ERT must ensure that the plan undergoes a formal review, at least annually. This review should confirm the incorporation of all changes since the prior examination. This complete review of the plan could result in major revisions to the plan document. These revisions should be distributed to all authorized personnel, who should exchange their old plans for the newly revised plans.

The ERT does more than simply activating the plan and overseeing its execution. This is very much a hands-on process. Besides the functional area recovery management teams (FARM), there are other teams that are either staffed by members of the ERT, or in larger organizations, are subcommittees that report to the ERT.

These teams have general responsibilities that are critical to the recovery process. The following are the most common functions. There may be others depending on your business.

- The damage assessment/salvage team reports directly to the ERT, evaluates the initial status of the damaged area, and estimates the time to reoccupy the facility and the salvage value of the remaining equipment. This team draws members from functional areas, as well as finance and information systems, and appropriate support suppliers/vendors. Following the assessment of damage, the team is responsible for salvaging equipment, data, and supplies; identifying which resources remain; and determining their future utilization in rebuilding the data center and recovery from the disaster. The members of the damage assessment team become the salvage team.

  The damage assessment/salvage team are usually the first people on-site when a disaster occurs. They canvas the site, determining the extent of the disaster and providing input to the ERT about the equipment and systems that can be salvaged and what must be replaced. Replacement may include temporary systems to restore information services, as well as procurement of workstations, printers and other items necessary to conduct business. Since they may need to enter damaged buildings or contaminated areas, the team may require special training. In a business that deals with potentially dangerous chemicals, this may include special training for hazardous materials.

- The transportation team members are responsible for transporting resources, personnel, equipment, and materials to alternate sites set up to conduct business during the disaster. This team draws members from various segments of the organization. Employees whose normal duties are interrupted during the disaster are ideal to staff the transportation team. A representative of the information technology department must also be on this team to assist with the movement of servers, workstations and other components needed to reestablish the network. Someone on the team is responsible for acquiring temporary transportation, ranging from vans for carrying people, to trucks or vans for moving sensitive equipment and office supplies. In some cases, a third-party moving company will be hired to move heavier items. Arrangements for this service must be made in advance and documented in the written plan.

Transporting of staff and equipment is often overlooked in the planning process. There are very detailed contingency plans that identify an alternate site, where desk, chairs, and computers are to be purchased, and even who is to staff the alternate site; but nothing that identifies how equipment is to be moved and who is responsible for setup and assisting with this phase of recovery. The plan sounds great, but obviously fails when tested. One of the most important aspects of developing the business contingency plan is including the detail. It is the *little things* that can send the company into a tailspin at a very critical time.

Many employees who are displaced by an emergency would like to help in the recovery process, rather than being sent home, often without pay. But, the employees must sign a release and be physically able to perform the duties assigned. This is another good reason for documenting all tasks in the contingency plan well ahead of time.

- The public information team is the company representative to the public. They interface with the media, the general public and staff who are not directly participating in the recovery process. An administrator, the human resource/personnel officer or a team from both areas may handle public information. The organization must carefully prepare a plan defining what information is to be provided and who is authorized to represent the company.

This is an example of how quickly things can go wrong, even if a disaster does not really exist. During one particular year 2000 (Y2K) conversion, a financial institution converted their systems to new software and hardware at the end of 1999. The information systems conversion went smoothly. The only problem was that the institution decided this would also be a good time to update their phone system! As it turned out, all the phone lines did not come up as expected. After being closed for three days to complete the conversion, the bank opened for business. The Y2K conversion had been well advertised, but many depositors still showed up to check account balances in person, at local ATM machines, and over the phone. The phones could not meet demand, and by mid-morning, the bank was inundated with depositors who were concerned about their hard earned cash. With long lines outside the bank and phones going unanswered, it did not take long for the local television news people to show up with cameras in hand. Who did they approach? The first teller they could find! The teller, who was doing a great job, had not been trained to handle such aggressive questions from an overzealous reporter with a camera in his face. It took a while to calm things down. Fortunately this story did not make the 6 o'clock news, but it came very close.

Many organizations fail to assign responsibility to an appropriate person to deal with public announcements, communications with employees, and releases to the media. The person appointed to the public information team should be someone who knows how to deal with the public and is trained to make responses appropriate to the best interest of the company. This is often a high level executive, director of marketing, or director of human resources. It is usually not a good idea for this person to be head of the ERT, because that person will most likely have their hands full already. Make sure the staff knows who is responsible for answering questions and that staff is cautioned not to make any comments.

While the focus on technology related failures continues here, consider another type of catastrophic event that has happened more than once over the past few years. The president or several board members are on a plane that is missing or confirmed down. The loss of key management positions could adversely impact business, as could misinformation that might be inadvertently released by an uninformed employee. Do the employees know what to do when the call comes?

- The communications team is responsible for establishing voice and data communications between the affected site and the remainder of the organization or ensuring that communications is rerouted to an alternative location. The recommendation, again depending on the size of the company, is that one or more persons be assigned specifically to deal with the telephone company, Internet service providers, and other communications services providers. CEOs have told me that there is no way this is a full time job. They have obviously never dealt with the phone company! The IT manager should not be expected to deal with network and voice communications issues during a disaster. Their first priority will be the restoration of data services and getting mission critical systems up and running. There may be more than a single person involved. For instance, rerouting of voice communications may fall to one department, while data services go to another. But, all employees dealing with communications issues must be able to communicate and coordinate services.

- Other teams. Specialty teams will vary depending upon your business. For instance, a Hazmat team may be required for hazardous materials handling. Best practice recommends that specific individuals be assigned to contact insurance companies to advise them that the company is in recovery mode and will keep them informed. Special security may need to be addressed so someone might contract local law enforcement to provide temporary security, to protect valuable property, or to keep people away from dangerous areas. Someone from human resources is assigned to keep personnel apprised of the recovery process and direct them where needed.

Again, depending on the size of the organization. some of the teams identified above may be a team of one. It is more important to identify the task to be done, and ensure that a person is assigned that task, as well as a backup. Do not operate under the assumption that all employees will be available during a disaster. Prepare for a worse case scenario by having one or more alternates that are responsible for stepping in.

There must also be a reporting mechanism in place where all recovery teams, including FARMS, report back to the ERT. The ERT is typically operating from a war room. If the main building is inaccessible, the war room may be located in a trailer in the parking lot, or an alternate location. Once recovery begins, the best practice is to continue to recover around the clock, if possible, until the level of operation defined in your plan is established, and then continue until all sites are restored and you return to normal operations.

PREPARING LISTS

As mentioned before, there are a number of lists that must be prepared as part of the contingency plan. These lists must be maintained and up-to-date. These lists include general, as well as functional information. A general list includes:

- ERT and FARM task list.
- Employee contact list.
- Vendor contact list.
- Customer contact list (if appropriate).

Functional lists include information such as the fixed asset listing (this is helpful when replacing damaged items.) IT should provide current hardware and software inventory lists (these are often kept as part of the policy and procedures manual. This is fine, as long as the list is maintained and easily available in hardcopy format in the event of a catastrophic failure.) For a manufacturer, the list might include machines and parts inventory. For a financial institution, it might include vault, ATM and other information for recovery.

The lists should be consistent in format, so that they are complete and easy to read. In the event of a catastrophic failure, there is often chaos and confusion. It is easy to make mistakes and to take inappropriate actions that could create unnecessary cost or even create potential liability for the company. Accurate and consistent lists will help eliminate some of these possibilities.

Confidentiality of List

These lists contain confidential or, at the least, sensitive information in nearly all cases. It is the responsibility of the company to protect this information. When a list is updated, all expired copies must be destroyed according to company policy. Human resources or personnel will advise employees and others from whom the information is being collected of the intended use for the information and how it is to be retained. Some organizations may be limited in the information that can be collected and will have to adjust their plan accordingly.

Sample List

ERT and FARM Task List

Task ID: 1

Task Assignment: Activate emergency control center (the war room!)

Description: Activating emergency control center involves opening the designated area for recovery, allowing the ERT to have a central place to traffic all requests and to coordinate the recovery process. The assigned employee will open the room, establish communications lines, set up work areas to include associated supplies, and be on-site to brief ERT and FARM members as they arrive.

Assigned to: *Employee name*

Alternate: *Employee name*

Team Responsibility: ERT

Comment:

Information about teams, team positions, and the tasks assigned to them is necessary to ensure that all tasks are complete. The information is printed in alphabetical order by the task sequential order and team name. ERT coordinators use this information to review the tasks assigned to each team position and verify that all team business continuity tasks are preidentified and assigned to a team position.

Employee Contact List by Name

Detailed information for each employee is listed in alphabetical order by employee last name. The ERT will use this information when their plans are executed to notify and mobilize employees, and to locate the employee's home address, in the event the employee is injured or employee assistance is required. A record of all contacts to, or on behalf of, an employee should be recorded.

Employee Name: Hill, Mary A.

Position: Assistant Controller

Department or Duty Station: Accounting

Office Phone or Extension: 555-123-4567

Home or non-work Phone: 555-222-2525

Cell Phone: 555-333-3636

Other Contact (specify relationship): Mother, Susie 555-880-4569

Other Contact (specify relationship): Husband, Bill 555-880-1234

In some organizations, additional information may be helpful in a catastrophic failure, such as:

Blood Type: A+
Organ Donor: Yes
Glasses or Contacts: Yes
Day Care or School Contact:

Software Inventory List

In a disaster, critical information may be lost that would cost the organization a significant amount to replace. Software licenses are a good example. If all copies of software licenses are kept in IT, which is common, they might be lost in case of fire. The company could be forced to repurchase legal licenses as the business recovers. This is a shame, since the company already has legal rights to use the software but cannot provide proof. It is a best practice to maintain a list of all software owned and used by the organization. Store this with other critical lists at an alternate site for rapid recovery. Be sure to categorize the software in terms of use so that software that is needed immediately will be recovered first.

Name of Licensed Owner: *The company name*
Licensed for use at: 100 Main Street, Any Town, USA 12345
Name of Software: Norton AntiVirus Corporate Edition
Version: 7.5
Purchase: 01/01/02
License Number: 123456 (be sure to double check this carefully)
Activation Number: (good idea to store Microsoft's activation number)
Functional Software Description: Used on all systems to protect against rogue software attacks.
Used by: Employee name or workstation identification

(Variations of this list include a table list where common information is only entered once, followed by a table listing of software by license number, user and so forth to save space.)

Equipment Inventory List

As with software, some damaged hardware may be able to be replaced or recovered with the proper documentation. At the least, unused maintenance fees paid in advance may be reclaimed. However, the most important purpose of the equipment list is to speed the recovery process and to know what hardware each user uses, as well as to list shared network hardware such as servers, switches, routers, and so forth. Do not forget to include uninterruptible power supplies, personal digital assistances, cell phones, and other, often overlooked, components. The equipment information is printed in alphabetical order by equipment type. ERT coordinators use this information to ensure that current and correct information about the equipment is maintained and that procedures are established for replacing the equipment, and determining alternate site requirements.

Equipment Type: File Server
Equipment Group: Network
Description: Pentium IV 1.8 GHz 1GB
   RAM 5-40GB Fast-SCSI Fixed disk
Model #: 12345
Purchased: 01/02/01
Maintenance Through: 02/02/04 BTU
Vendor ID: KVA
Vendor Name: Maintenance
Serial #: Connection Type
Status: Quantity Required
Device Address:
Weight (lbs):
Maintenance Level:
Current Value:
Salvage Value:
Insurance Coverage:
Lead Time:

Supplies List

Information about supplies, the current quantity on hand and the daily usage for each supply should be documented. The information is printed in inventory code order. This list must be as comprehensive as possible to facilitate both short-term and long-term recovery with minimal lost time.

Inventory ID: 22112
Description: Payroll checks
Current Location: Accounting safe (primary stock)
Lead Time: 30 days to restock
Vendor number: 12345
Primary Vendor: Gulf Coast Printing
Contact: Mrs. Smith

Phone: 555-878-4574
Offsite Vault: Y
Quantity: 150
Rotated: Quarterly
Category: Checks—Secure Forms

TESTING THE CONTINGENCY PLAN

Testing the plan is an essential element of preparedness. Partial tests of individual components and recovery plans of specific FARM teams should be carried out on a regular basis. The ERT provides support to assist a functional area's recovery. These teams work with the FARM of the affected area to restore services and provide assistance at the operation level.

Contingency plans can be tested in a number of ways. Obviously, a plan is tested best in conditions that most closely mimic a true disaster. However, such aggressive testing can disrupt business unnecessarily and lead to unnecessary cost. On a number of cases, I have conducted a reaction test by downing a server, or network hub, and observing how employees react. If the plan has been communicated to supervisors and staff, they should know exactly what to do. If the plan has not been communicated properly, chaos results. Knowing how staff responds to even a short-term outage tells a lot about how successful the recovery process will be.

Many best practice organizations test a portion of the plan on an annual basis. Determine if the plan is still viable with a "desktop review" (a verbal exam) of the untested portions on the plan. If there are major changes in the business, a merger or acquisition, or a change in a service provider for instance; the plan should be thoroughly reviewed and appropriate changes made. Critical lists, such as vendor contacts, employee contact information and so forth should be reviewed and updated quarterly. Some organizations do this through human resources and update hardcopy lists whenever staff that has been assigned a recovery task changes. Whatever method used, make sure that the plan is always as current as is reasonably possible.

CONTINGENCY PLAN—RESPONSE AND RECOVERY

There are six required responses to a disaster, or to a failure that could evolve into a disaster. Each of these points must be addressed in the business contingency plan.

1. Identify a point of failure and determine a disaster condition.
2. Notify the persons responsible for recovery.
3. Declare an emergency and initiate the contingency plan.
4. Activate the designated alternate processing site, if appropriate.

5. Disseminate information.
6. Provide support services to aid recovery.

The next step is to lay out the format of the plan developed on the six points listed above. The following assumes that all critical systems, network components, and software needed to run the business's mission-critical processes have already been documented. These may be included in the body of the contingency plan. But most often, they are a part of your policy and procedures manual with copies stored at a remote location. *Note: Off-site copies should include hardcopy as well as softcopy.* In the event of an emergency, time is precious as is the speed of the response. You do not want to lose time finding a computer and printer so you can disseminate information. All vendor and supplier contacts and the items ordered from them should be listed so that additional stock may be ordered in an emergency.

The disaster recovery strategy explained below applies specifically to a disaster that disables the main data center. This functional area provides computer and major network support to core applications. Especially at risk are the critical applications, those designated as level 4 systems. The business contingency plan provides for recovering the capacity to support these critical applications within seventy-two hours. The subsections below summarize the provisions of the plan and explain the context in which the organization's contingency plan operates. The contingency plan complements the strategies for restoring the data processing capabilities normally provided by the information technology department. The disaster recovery phases are described as follows.

Emergency Declaration Phase

The emergency declaration phase begins with the initial response to a disaster. During this phase, the existing emergency plans and procedures direct efforts to protect life and property, the primary goal of initial response. Security over the area is established as local support services, such as the police and fire departments, are enlisted through existing mechanisms. The chairperson of the ERT is alerted and begins to monitor the situation.

If the emergency appears to affect the main data center (or other critical facility or service), either through damage to the technology infrastructure or support facilities, or if access to the facility is prohibited, the ERT chairperson will closely monitor the event and notify ERT personnel as required to assist in damage assessment. Once access to the facility is permitted, an assessment of the damage is made to determine the estimated length of the outage. If access to the facility is precluded, then the estimate includes the time until the effect of the disaster on the facility can be evaluated.

If the estimated outage is less than seventy-two hours, recovery will be initiated under normal operational recovery procedures. If the outage is estimated to be longer than seventy-two hours, the chairperson activates the ERT. The business continuity plan is officially activated. The recovery process then moves into the back-up phase. Under some conditions, it is advisable to notify the ERT that a disaster has occurred, even if the event is expected to last less than seventy-two hours. The ERT remains active until recovery is complete to ensure that the organization will be ready in the event the situation changes.

Alternate Site Activation Phase

Normally, the alternate site activation phase begins with outages lasting longer than seventy-two hours, or when management deems that the emergency warrants activating the backup processing site. In the initial stage of this phase, the goal is to resume processing critical applications. Processing may resume either at the main data center or at a designated hot site, depending on the assessment of damage to equipment and the physical structure of the building.

In the alternate site activation phase, the initial hot site must support critical applications for whatever time frame is necessary to recreate a permanent site. During this period, processing of these systems resumes, possibly in a degraded mode, up to the capacity of the hot site. If the damaged area requires a longer period of reconstruction, then the second stage of this phase commences. During the second stage, a shell facility (a pre-engineered temporary processing facility) is assembled and placed in a designated area.

A hot site provides equipment capable of processing applications and supporting communications as defined in the contract agreement. When a hot site is activated, the assumption is that the company will be required to provide no or minimal physical equipment. The company will be expected to provide programs and data, and in some cases, an operator. Many hot site providers will provide one or more operators at an additional cost, leaving the staff to concentrate on getting the site back online. A shell facility normally comes equipped with power and communications *stubs* to connect to. Shell facilities assume the company is providing all necessary hardware, software, and staff. Shell facilities tend to be for time frames much longer than a week or two.

Recovery Phase

The time required for recovery of the functional area and the eventual restoration of normal processing depends on the damage caused by the disaster. The time frame for recovery can vary from several days to several months. In either case, the recovery process begins immediately after the disaster and takes place in parallel with backup operations at the designated hot site. The primary goal is to restore normal operations as soon as possible. The definition of *normal* is relative to each company. In the short-term, the organization must be able to perform at a diminished level and still meet mission critical objectives.

The recovery phase incorporates all steps necessary to bring mission-critical functions back up to an acceptable service level. Restoring operating systems procedures, applications and data (databases), and networks must usually be done before any processing can begin. Documentation for this phase includes documenting the time required from the moment that the disaster is declared and ERT activates the plan, to bringing an alternate processing site operational and validating databases. In a reduced capacity, what is really needed must be determined. A best practice is to categorize all software and processes according to function. Critical functions are most important followed by essential and necessary functions. As time becomes available, the more desirable, but not required, functions are brought up. The following provides one approach for placing functions into categories.

Category 1—Critical functions are must have functions such as manufacturing, order entry, environmental control, and so forth. Without these systems, the company shuts down.

Category 2—Essential functions (there is sometimes a fine line between *critical* and *essential*) are employee time keeping, shipping, product ordering, and so forth. The company could do business without essential functions for a short time, but the impact would be significant. The company might also elect to use manual processes for a period of time until system resources are available.

Category 3—Necessary functions are accounting, financial reporting, accounts payable, and payroll. These activities could stop for a short period of time, as long as information was kept manually for automated entry and processing later.

Category 4—Desirable functions are everything else such as spreadsheets, word processing, graphics tools and e-mail.

I do know of companies that are so dependent on spreadsheets that for them, restoring this software would be essential, if not critical. You be the judge, but make sure that there is input from each department. What shipping and receiving considers critical may vary from what accounting needs to do their job.

There are also short-term options that the company can deploy during a crisis. One company set up temporary payroll using a low cost accounting software package, like Peachtree or QuickBooks, to generate payroll checks for employees during the crisis. Once the operation was fully recovered and it was business as usual, the data was reentered, along with all necessary adjustments, into the regular company accounting system.

With the power of personal computers today, there are a number of personal computer-based applications that support sales, inventory, shipping and invoicing. While these are not a viable long-term solution, the ERT might work with IT to use such software as part of the short-term recovery process. When this option is elected, the applications and data conversion should be well-tested before the software is used in survival mode!

The final sections of the plan should describe the FARM teams, the people who manage the recovery process, and their responsibilities. This will differ drastically by company. Do not forget a section on disaster recovery procedures that includes building evacuation and what to do in case of medical emergency, fire, hurricane, tornado, and so forth. Specific action items and designation of responsibility are discussed in this section.

The losses resulting for computer downtime will only increase in the future unless business learns to plan for and manage such failures. The power outages of early 2001 along the west coast may be only the beginning of national power outages that could result in systems failures. The above documentation may seem like a lot of useless paperwork and testing. But unless business learns a lesson from the past and prepares for contingencies, the risk of failures will only increase.

BUSINESS CONTINGENCY PLAN MODEL

The purpose of the model plan that follows is to provide a point of reference for your own plan development. The content of each organization's plan will be a direct result of the organization's risk assessment and decisions made on the potential for failure, expected length of failures, and the organization's financial ability to weather the interruption in service.

The knowledge gained from the risk assessment is assembled in the organization's contingency plan. The format of the model plan is to be followed to assure continuity between organization plans, which will be incorporated into the statewide contingency plan. There are many variations to contingency plan design. The following outline is a simple best practice approach.

1.0   Plan Objectives

The primary objectives of the plan are:

- To provide the organization with a tested vehicle which, when executed, will permit an efficient, timely resumption of the interrupted business operations.
- To ensure the continuity of the organization's business.
- To minimize the inconvenience and potential disruption to customers and clients.
- To minimize the impact to the company's public image.

1.0   Scope of Plan

The business contingency plan includes the strategies, actions and procedures to resume the business operations and functions associated with the organization. A key portion of this plan is the successful restoration of information systems and communications.

2.0   Plan Assumptions

The plan should state the assumptions made in its development. Plan assumptions are often not documented in the plan process, but are really a vital component. Assumptions are not only appropriate; they are necessary. Since most people cannot actually see into the future, assumptions are used to develop the structure the plan is built around. In the beginning of the chapter, we stated that it was impossible to design a plan based on every conceivable failure or disaster. It would be too long and not be complete because there would always be something that no one considered, such as the attack of September 11, 2001.

Assumptions must be made, and documented in the plan, regarding available personnel, available recovery equipment, and estimated damage. The assumptions must have some basis in logic and experience. Management will review and provide input into the assumptions made and advise of changes.

Examples of plan assumptions might include:

- In the event of a level 4 failure causing the shutdown of the primary place of business, the appointed ERT member would be authorized to negotiate temporary workspace sufficient to support 40 employees.
- In the event of a level 4 failure, the president of the organization is authorized to activate a $500,000 line of credit pre-approved by Big City Bank under agreement 123XYZ on February 12, 2002.
- In the event of a level 3 failure that renders the main database server inoperable, the IT manager is authorized to replace this server through the fastest means possible and authorized to expend up to $25,000 to this end without requesting additional authority.

This last example is included because of an experience we had two years ago where a server did fail while I was on site with a client conducting a technology assessment. The server took a power surge that basically fried the insides (we will not go into the how and why!) As the IT manager was frantically attempting to locate a partner to approve an order, I asked him why he did not simply go pick up a computer at the local electronics store to get the server back online quickly and then resolve the issue more completely after users were back at work. "I don't have the authority to do that," was the reply. In the meantime, the company was losing several thousands of dollars for each hour the server was down. This was not a best practice approach. Plan ahead.

3.0   Time Frames

Time frame is the period of time between the occurrence of the disruption event and the time when a given business function must restore some level of service. Time frames define, based on the level of failure, how long restoration should take. Some plans refer to this as acceptable down time. I do not like that phrase because the answer is zero. Time frames should give a realistic milestone for restoration.

The key here is *realistic*. Do not create timelines that will only look good to management. Do not succumb to pressure to make the number look better. If restoration of a server will take six hours, then putting four on a piece of paper will only create problems elsewhere in the plan. If management determines that six hours to recover a server is not acceptable, then the alternative is to deploy technology that can be recovered quicker and accept the cost of doing so.

4.0   Contingency Strategies

Resumption of time-sensitive business operations is dependent on availability of the resources required to support the associated functions and processes. Those resources include:

- Work area for personnel equipped with workstations, printers, networks, and data communications.
- Furniture and fixtures.
- Voice communications (telephone, inbound lines, long distance, cell phones).
- Connectivity to mainframe, midrange, client/server and mini-computer application systems (data communications).

A great example of contingency strategies gone bad occurred a few years ago. I was testing a disaster recovery plan for a small city. The IT department executed the plan to the letter and did a great job. The alternate processing site was set up, data was restored to a temporary server, voice and data communications were in place. A happy and joyful group turned to me and said, "Well, what do you think?" "Well done," I replied, "now can you print me a general ledger report for the past month?" As the IT manager turned to execute the report, his face suddenly became red as the realization set in that no one had remembered to bring a printer, because the printer was not included in the plan!

It is the small things that will get us every time. Of course, no harm was done here. This is why we test the plan in the first place. Having well thought out, documented, and tested contingency strategies will save the day in the end.

5.0 Disaster Definition

A *disaster* is defined as the unplanned loss of processing capability, for any reason, for some predetermined amount of time, as defined by the organization.

6.0 Plan Implementation Phases

The plan is organized into four phases: response, resumption, recovery and restoration. In the response phase, an event has occurred that interrupts business processing. The extent of impact to personnel, equipment and facility is to be determined. If a disaster is declared, it is done during the response phase. The alternate site is activated, if necessary. The resumption phase details the tasks, personnel and equipment necessary to resume mission-critical business functions. The response phase details the task, personnel and equipment necessary to resume minimal operations to full business functions. The restoration phase provides guidance during the cutover from the alternate processing site and the home site.

7.0 Emergency Response Teams

Recovery personnel are arranged into teams during each phase of the plan. Some teams will participate throughout the plan; some teams will only be activated to perform a specific task for a specific phase. The teams will be composed of a team leader, a backup team leader and staff. Examples of teams include:

- Damage assessment/salvage team
- Transportation team
- Public information team
- Communications team
- Specialty teams

8.0 Team Responsibility

Each team is assigned a detailed list of activities called tasks. The team is responsible for performing their designated tasks to accomplish a pre-defined objective within each phase. Each phase has specific tasks that need to be accomplished for the orderly recovery of the business function.

9.0 Plan Administration

Administration of the plan is the responsibility of a designated individual, such as an ERT coordinator. As the custodian and administrator of the business contingency plan, the ERT coordinator must have a thorough knowledge of all plan contents. Responsibility for maintaining specific sections of the plan resides with each team leader in accordance with the team's objectives and functional responsibilities of response, resumption, recovery and restoration.

Should a plan review necessitate any changes or updates, the ERT coordinator is responsible for generating the changes and issuing the updates. Individuals in responsible management positions will be periodically called upon to provide information necessary for maintaining a viable plan and exercise recovery capability.

10.0 Procedures

The primary objective of the ERT coordinator is to maintain response, resumption, recovery and restoration information current by promptly processing changes to the plan. Plan administration addresses those activities necessary for maintaining a viable business contingency plan.

Changes to the plan must be promptly processed. Specific plan administration activities ensure that the plan is maintained in a current state, and include:

- Conducting regular reviews, at least annually, of the business contingency plan by the ERT and the contingency management steering committee (CMSC).
- Reviewing and updating, quarterly, the business contingency plan by the ERT.
- Developing administrative procedures to control changes within the business contingency plan and to control distribution of the plan.
- Planning, developing, scheduling, and executing exercises to test the business contingency plan, including analysis of test findings.

11.0 Plan Distribution

The business contingency plan is a restricted document, since it contains proprietary information. For the purposes of this plan, proprietary information is defined as information that could have a negative impact on the organization or its customers if improperly released, and could be valuable to external parties. Proprietary information is all nonpublished information rightfully obtained, developed or produced by or for the organization and/or its employee(s) for the benefit of the company. Proprietary information is owned by the organization, not by the employee. Each individual possessing a copy of the business contingency plan is responsible for the protection of the proprietary information.

This document is classified as confidential. This plan is also restricted since it contains the organization's strategy for recovery of applications systems and time-sensitive data, and the names, addresses and telephone numbers of employees. Therefore, the plan is distributed on a need-to-know basis only.

CONCLUSION

This chapter has provided approaches for contingency planning for small and medium companies to very large organizations. Tailoring a plan to fit the size of the organization is critical to success. It is also important to design plans that cover a wide variety of potential failures and to put processes in place appropriate to the level of risk faced. Think of contingency planning as health insurance for the company. You will allocate resources and make the monetary commitment so that the business will continue to thrive in adversity while growing back to predisaster levels. Make the employees an important part of the recovery process, and test the plan regularly to validate that changes have not circumvented the steps you have put in place.

CHAPTER FIVE

Managing Technology Best Practices

Several years ago, I spoke at a national conference to a large room of technology professionals that included network administrators, database administrators, and others. I posed the question "What was the perfect user environment?" Somewhat tongue-in-cheek, one person responded, "One that the user never touched!" As humorous as that may sound, it is closer to the truth than most people responsible for managing the technology infrastructure of an organization would like to admit. In a perfect world, we could all start with a clean slate with new computers, pristine software installs, and the best network architecture that money could buy. Nothing would ever break, and all software would be compatible with all other software packages. Database administration would be easy and straightforward. Information would only exist in one place. Since this perfect world does not exist, technologists spend most of their professional career trying to get as close as possible.

This chapter will provide best practice recommendations for managing technology. The emphasis of the chapter is how to avoid common problems, such as incompatible hardware and software and user errors, that so much time is not spent attempting to repair the damage after it is done. We will focus on specific areas where most problems begin and end for information technology support staff. This includes selecting and deploying hardware and software and securing the infrastructure. The next chapter will focus on people issues, such as staff, training users, and managing the help desk.

SELECTING AND DEPLOYING SOFTWARE

With all the changes that have occurred over the past thirty plus years in technology, one basic principal remains the same—the software comes first. Yet, in too many cases, either management or information technology (IT) staff will attempt to begin with hardware selection as the primary consideration. I absolutely guarantee that if a software application meets a company's needs, there is hardware available that will process that application!

There are many reasons why hardware tends to be the first consideration. One reason might be the financial investment that the organization has in their existing hardware. Even more common is that the IT staff is very *comfortable* with the hardware and operating systems they have and are reluctant to change. If an organization is making software choices for either of these reasons without considering all possible options, they are doing their company a grave injustice! If senior managers have not kept up with changes in technology, they may not know that software databases are much easier to integrate today than a decade ago. Or, if they still believe a new server costs tens of thousands of dollars, they will be pleasantly surprised that systems today are less expensive as well as more powerful than ever.

Hardware selection and integration options will be explained more in the next section of this chapter. For now, let us begin with the software and assume that we can make all platforms work together. Beginning with this assumption allows the users to really focus on the solution and not begin eliminating options too early in the process.

Earlier chapters laid out planning processes for selecting software, such as determining the existing operating environment (the As Is); then refining that into the best possible operating environment (the To Be). In this chapter, we will assume you have done the needs analysis and requirements definition and have selected the software of choice to deploy to your users. Or, perhaps you already have software installed that works great. But, the cost of deploying updates to the software, supporting users, and maintaining the applications is too high, error prone, or ineffective. If this applies to you, then we need to develop best practice methodologies for you to deploy and support software.

Software deployment is the process of installing application programs on a system (workstation or server) and making that application and the data it supports available to users. The software manufacturer has usually been pushed to provide software deployment. If a company has ever installed a productivity suite such as Microsoft Office or an accounting application, it has been through an install process. Obviously, the DOS days are gone where you could simply copy the files into folders, on the hard drive, and execute a single filename to be up and running. In fact, it is hard to believe that could ever be done! This type of software was called monolithic, meaning the executable was self-contained. The software required few, if any, external resources, and no executable program cared whether any other program even existed.

The evolution of distributed networks left the central mainframe behind. Widely disbursed systems (wide area networks) radically change how software is deployed to endusers. The *sneakerware* (running from system to system with a handful of floppy disks or a CD) approach to installing software no longer works. The deployment dilemma has also been compounded by the evolution of software development. Back in the dark ages, a programmer would not think of releasing a program containing a *bug,* or a line of code that did not function properly. Today, it seems to be standard practice to release software that has not been fully tested or is not complete, and then update it multiple times during its life cycle. At one time, a company did not release more than one or two updates a year; now there may be as many as six to twelve. This puts a tremendous cost burden on the IT to update systems with the most current release and then to respond to user questions after the update is deployed.

MANAGING SHARED FILES AND DYNAMIC LINKED LIBRARIES

To understand the issues IT faces today in deploying and maintaining software, we must first understand how software works. The relationship between the manufacturer of the operating system and the application used must also be understood. Since Microsoft dominates so much of the business technology deployed, this section will focus on how Microsoft compliant applications are written and deployed, and where those issues are.

Microsoft Windows drastically changed the way software is deployed. Windows ushered in the era of component software. Through common interfaces, software today does *dynamic linking*. Dynamic linked software makes use of common libraries, as well as private libraries, through which common programs are shared between applications. Some of these library routines may have been developed by Microsoft, and are part of the operating system. Some may be shared applications acquired from third parties by your application provider. Any program in any library can talk to any other program in any other library. Today, it could be argued that software development efforts are primarily focused on building new applications from smaller, more adaptable *applets*, creating new applications in the process.

Microsoft, in its Windows Operating System (OS), releases application programming interface (API) instructions to software developers. Developers then use these APIs to leverage common program code. The result of this effort is dynamic linked libraries or DLLs. Microsoft Windows ships with a number of these; others are acquired from third-party vendors. These DLLs make Windows-centric tasks, such as resizing, moving, opening, and closing windows much easier and more standard across applications.

Microsoft promotes new technology and functionality through upgrades to their libraries. These libraries do not ship as part of the operating system release, but are distributed to software manufacturers as part of development kits. These libraries are called *redistributables*, and software manufacturers are encouraged to use and to ship these redistributables as a part of their software application. Examples of redistributables include: Open Database Connectivity (ODBC), Microsoft Data Access Components (MDAC), Visual Basic Runtime, and Microsoft Common Controls. The list of Microsoft redistributable files numbers in the hundreds, if not thousands. Third-party software vendors also develop and sell redistributable software for software manufacturers to incorporate into their applications, such as Adobe Acrobat Reader and Macromedia Flash.

Redistributable software, generally called libraries or dynamic linked libraries (DLL), are examples of component software written by programmers other than a primary application vendor and then sold to an application vendor to incorporate into their application. Sounds great! This method creates standardization, a common pool of programs, allows code to be easily reused, and shortens the development cost and time. In theory, all these good things happen. Making the link between the Windows application and its underlying libraries is a very complex task. The diagram in Exhibit 5.1 illustrates how programs link together. Note that an application makes a call to a DLL library for a component program (perhaps to open an ODBC database, or to display a calendar window on the screen to select a date). The DLLs sit on top of the shipped operating system and must interact directly with the operating system. But the DLLs did not ship

Exhibit 5.1

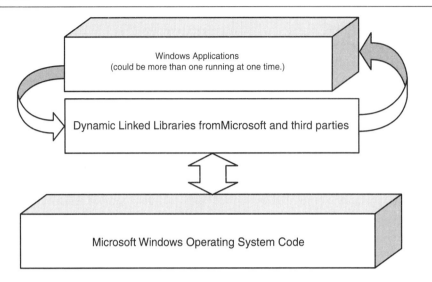

with the operating system and were not part of the original install (hence they are redistributable.)

DLLs can be the root of many of the problems encountered when deploying software. It is important to understand them thoroughly. In focusing on the diagram above, remember that the user may be running more than one application at a time. So, there may be multiple calls to load shared libraries as well as operating system calls loading programs into memory. As hard as Windows tries, it cannot always remember which DLL belongs to whom. If the software manufacturer does not do their job well enough, they do not always load and release DLLs properly either.

Problems in most deployments occur almost immediately. Problems most often occur because of the type of linking the software manufacturer invokes. One method of linking is to embed a call to a DLL inside the executable, called *static linking*. Static linking often works the best. The software manufacturer installs its own libraries, or copies library files from the shared folder into its folder where it can control the environment. This is great, except it also results in increased disk usage and library files appearing in multiple folders, which can be very confusing over time.

Another method is *dynamic linking.* Software manufacturers that use this approach wait until a library routine is needed then assume it is a common routine that will be in the shared libraries! This is a great idea in that installs are leaner (not as much code to load); dynamic linking minimizes redundant libraries and multiple occurrences of code; and the operating system can manage the libraries. Now, rejoice and think, "That's the solution I want!"

But, consider that there are two types of dynamic linking, implicit and explicit. With implicit linking, there is a list of predefined libraries and executables required; the program knows this list ahead of time and checks that all libraries are available. This works well; when the executable loads into system memory, the operating system will attempt to find all the libraries needed at that time. The alternative, explicit linking, occurs when the application needs the library routine and not before. To understand the difference between implicit and explicit library loading, consider the Microsoft Excel user. I do not need to take the time for Excel to find every linked library routine when I load the program because I may not intend to print a file, or change a cell format, or execute a Sum/Product function. I only want to find those things when, and if, I need them.

Static linking guarantees the correct API call for the exact version the program wants every time. Because it is embedded in the executable dynamic linking, and reduces the physical size of the executable, dynamic linking may benefit by loading components that have been updated since the initial install.

To deploy (install) or just troubleshoot software that runs on Windows Operating System computers, I recommend you visit Microsoft's software developer site for the Software Developer Kit (SDK) at *www.microsoft.com/msdownload/platformsdk/sdkupdate/*. There are a number of redistributables here, as well as more information on how Microsoft maintains shared libraries and implements static and dynamic linking. If you are struggling with DLL issues of your own, even as you are reading this book, you might consider downloading *Dependency Walker*. Dependency Walker is a well-recognized profiling tool that is freeware developed by Steve Miller, a Microsoft developer, who keeps this utility up-to-date with the latest Microsoft operating system releases. A free version of this software ships with Microsoft Developer Studio. You can download it from *www.dependencywalker.com*. Just in case you think this chapter is written for IT people in large technology centers with hundreds of users and hundreds of computers running high-end enterprise applications, consider what a neat tool Dependency Walker is for trouble shooting even a small single user application like QuickBooks. The screen shot in Exhibit 5.2 is of several of the DLLs called QuickBooks Pro 2001. You can use this to find where a DLL is used and by what application. If you have a little programming background, you can find what the DLL does.

Dependency Walker is a free utility that scans any 32-bit or 64-bit Windows module (exe, dll, ocx, sys, etc.) including ones designed for Windows CE and builds a hierarchical tree diagram of all dependent modules. For each module found, it lists all the functions exported by that module, and which of those functions are actually being called by other modules. Another view displays the minimum set of required files, along with detailed information about each file, including a full path to the file, base address, version numbers, machine type, debug information, and more. This utility is also very useful for troubleshooting system errors related to loading and executing program modules. Dependency Walker detects many common application problems such as missing modules, invalid modules, import/export mismatches, circular dependency errors, mismatched machine types of modules, and module initialization failures. Dependency Walker runs on Windows 95, 98, Me, NT, 2000, and XP. The program handles all types of module dependencies, including implicit, explicit (dynamic/runtime), forwarded, delay-loaded, and injected.

Now that there is a pretty good understanding of a key underlying approach to Windows compatible software, this chapter is almost ready to continue with defining best practices for deploying software. But, before leaving the DLL and shared library discussion, I want to clarify an issue I hear discussed in technology circles. "Why does

Exhibit 5.2

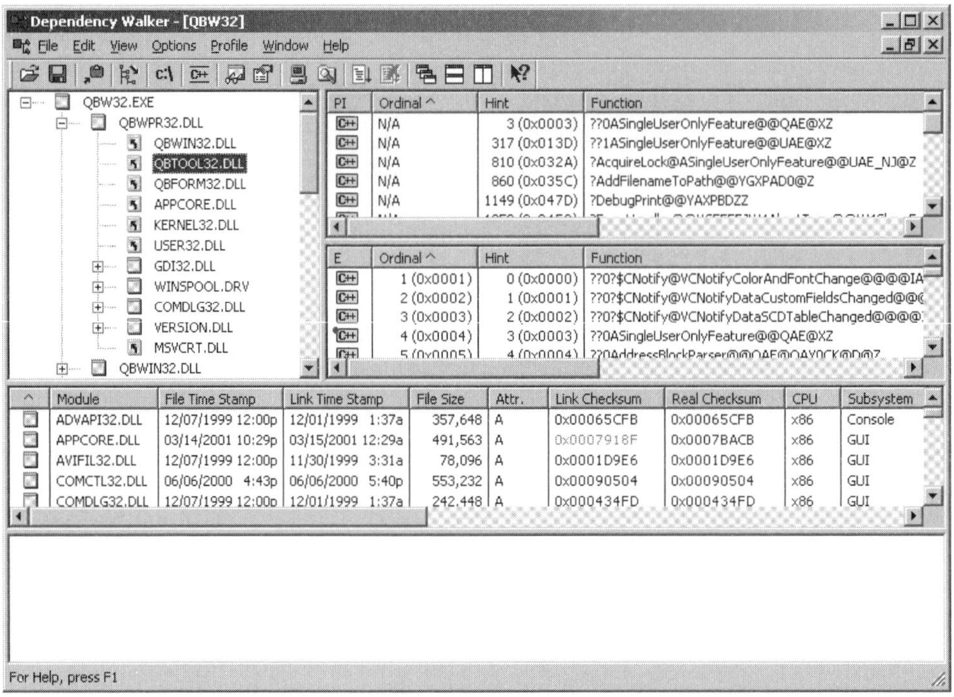

Microsoft allow non-Microsoft applications, and programmers, to store DLL and other files in the primary Windows Operating System folder?" (This statement is usually followed by words that are not appropriate to repeat in a book of this high caliber.) The simple act of loading files in the Windows primary folder (could be/Windows/System, or/WINNT/System, or whatever folder was installed in the operating system at load time) has long been at the root of both install and deployment, as well as uninstall issues. Why does Microsoft let this happen?

Since Windows was introduced, Microsoft has always stored its libraries within the system folder under the primary Windows folder. Microsoft's intent has been to maintain this folder as a repository for the operating system's files. However, nothing prevents software manufacturers from using this folder. In fact, manufacturers place their applications' shared files into this folder specifically because the operating system defaults first to the Windows and Windows system folders when an application needs a library, making search time much less for the application.

The creation of the deployment engine and setting up the install routine will be discussed. It is possible to move DLL and other library files to a folder other than the Windows primary folder. It is not an easy decision because of search time, duplicating files across multiple folders, and modifying the software manufacturers intended to install. However, there may also be a number of benefits—including being the only option when applications conflict over DLL version.

MANAGING DEPLOYMENT THROUGH STANDARDIZATION

Those of us who have supported Windows Operating System environments for the past decade are very familiar with *DLL hell*. DLL hell is the primary reason that *locked-down* systems exist. In fact, large corporations commonly have rather rigid policies in place to regulate and insure that shared library versions remain consistent. These processes range from limiting what the end users can install to physically restoring the Windows system folder integrity when the computer boots. Many IT managers prefer to lockdown users systems, which means to protect the system to the limit so that users cannot install software, printers, or even change the look of their desktop icons.

As the diagram in Exhibit 5.3 indicates, the best practice is to implement hardware and software standards, but not to the point where the cost of support savings restricts users' productivity and innovation.

DEPLOYMENT AS A COST OF SOFTWARE INVESTMENT

Nearly all technology professionals who are responsible for deploying software have said some *unkind* things about software developers during the deployment process. Yet, many of the issues that arise during deployment are as much our own fault as that of the software manufacturers. Software manufacturers know that ease of installation, deployment, and cost of support are key to the success of their product in the long run. However, in today's complex environment, programmers simply cannot anticipate every possible configuration, conflict, or incompatibility.

Exhibit 5.3

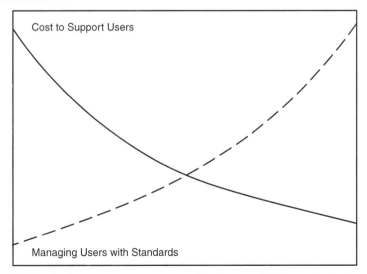

Cost to Support Users

Managing Users with Standards

No Standards   Hardware and Software Standards

When selecting a software product, users often believe that the tough work is over when the software is selected. If implementation expectations are not realistic, IT often suffers. In the beginning of the selection process, management and users must be made aware that compatibility and long term support are as much a part of the selection process as how the application works.

Once the selection committee has determined the application of choice, the next step involves calculating the cost of deployment. The cost of the software must include the purchase cost and the complete cost of deployment (installation, configuration, training, and support.) This total cost is the investment the company will make in the product over time. The money saved by using the new software is the benefit cost.

How is the cost of deployment determined? Immediately after the application of choice is selected, IT begins testing product compatibility and piloting the deployment process.

TESTING A DEPLOYMENT STRATEGY

Part of the software selection process should be to determine the cost and methodology for deploying the software, as well as getting an idea of the long-term cost to support the product. While this is a best practice, I am amazed that many businesses do not even consider deployment of the software in the purchase process! To accurately determine the total cost of ownership for the software considered, the distribution methodology must be tested on a representative sample group of users. This is ideally done before purchasing the software. The point of the pilot test is to deploy the application using as representative a selection of target systems as possible. Then the deployment process is initiated exactly as the product is deployed throughout the organization. A much smaller representative pilot deployment allows you to measure how easily the product will deploy. It is much easier to track, and recover from, problems with a pilot group than in the middle of a full-blown deployment.

The first requirement of the pilot test is to find a good variety of target computers, groups, and users. Some variety in this initial test will allow you to evaluate a large number of potential configuration or deployment issues. If remote and mobile users are a concern, they should be included in the pilot group as well. Large applications can be tricky to deploy from a central point and can cause a drain on network resources. Testing for this possibility is important as well. If a pilot test detects a substantial drain on network resources or bandwidth, alternative methods can be adopted quickly and the test resumed. For instance, for very large deployments, a deployment server may be tested as it offloads network traffic through multiple network connection points. In software management terminology, these deployment servers are known as software distribution points or SDPs. SDPs are not difficult to create and allow companies to deploy and support software during normal duty hours over very large networks. Pilot testing must include deploying through firewalls, routers, over virtual private networks (VPNs), and dial-up connections, so that all possible conditions can be tested ahead of time. Any modifications that need to occur as a result of the pilot test should be documented and included with compatibility testing and conflict resolution documentation.

Many IT professionals may feel that their job ends with the application deployment. Not so. IT should work closely with the users during pilot testing to validate that the application is working as expected, that users have full access to databases, and that all users who require access to the application have it. Again, note discrepancies and configuration issues during the application testing period and document the adjustments.

Just to repeat, pilot testing of an application serves two purposes. First, pilot testing allows the user to validate that the application works as expected. I have had users reject a selected application during the pilot test because they realized that the product does not actually work the way they expected. This is a critical point in the decision process. Current studies show that an average accounting software application has a seven year economic life. In reality, many businesses keep their accounting software much longer. Making the wrong software choice can stay with a company for a very long time!

Second, pilot testing allows IT to analyze the deployment and support cost of the product and plan the full deployment process. I have never had a product rejected during the pilot testing phase. This is where IT gets the most support from the vendor in terms of modifying the install procedures, answering deployment questions and providing support. The vendor wants to make the sale, so they work hard to ensure that IT can deploy the package with the least amount of problems.

If you carefully review the software manufacturer's install process, document it and test it in a pilot test, can you change the install process? How would you go about changing the way you deploy and support an application?

PREPARING A DEPLOYMENT METHODOLOGY

Most computer professionals and users assume that software has to be deployed (installed) the way the software manufacturer says. This is not necessarily true! In order to avoid such traumatic issues as DDL and shared file conflicts, analyze the manufacturer's suggested deployment process and modify it to better fit your environment. Of course, careful planning takes time at the front end of the process, but taking this time to really understand the deployment and customize it to fit your needs will pay off later, when you begin large scale rollout and support of the application.

Most manufacturers do not worry about how customers will deploy their software until the last item in the development cycle. That is not entirely a true statement. Software manufacturers realize that deployment is important, but for most developers, deployment is the last item on the list before they roll the product out to customers. Since most projects are behind schedule and over budget, guess what happens when it comes time to *throw together* an install routine? Another issue is the vast number of computer configurations out in the real world. No software developer could anticipate every possible combination of hardware, or what other manufacturers' software that might be running with their product. Developers do work hard to make their products bulletproof. They do not want the product to fail, but sometimes their idea of an ideal install is just not what is ideal for you.

While there are many exceptions, the process to install a computer application generally involves the following steps:

- Transferring files from their media to your system.
- Creating folders and distributing the copied files to their final location.
- Establishing shared library connections and registering with the OS.
- Final steps include desktop setup, icons, and autoloader script.

Each of these processes will be reviewed below so you can see where you can make modifications to the manufacturer's process. Most manufacturers use canned or third party software for the install process. These include Windows Installer Service, Install-Shield, and Wise Solutions. Reviewing these and other options are well beyond this book, but anyone who has ever installed a software application has seen these product screens. Technical information about Windows Installer can be found at *msdn. Microsoft.com*. InstallShield's website is located at *InstallShield.com*. Wise Solution's website is located at *WiseSolutions.com*. It would be worthwhile for people who regularly install software to spend time becoming acquainted with each of these applications at their websites.

Transferring Files to a System

Most installations begin with transfer files. When software applications could fit on a few floppy disks, this was an easy task. Today, however, all the application files are stored on one or more CD-ROM or DVD platters. The initial transfer program moves these files to the hard drive before the installation process continues. It is important to track exactly what files are moved where during the install process. To do this, you can use a number of file compare and desktop image tools to capture before and after snapshots of the system. Imaging software, discussed later in this book, creates an image of the desktop as it exists at that moment in time. Reports can be printed showing directories and file contents. There are routines that are used to compare file directories before and after installation. This is important documentation when installing new applications, as many software developers install files into the Windows core directory or other shared library folders. It is important to know what files are stored where.

Again, I will not compare or recommend specific software here, because needs vary and each company needs to select the right tools. The AppDeploy website, *www.appdeploy.com*, has great information about all the most popular imaging software packages as well as comparison information.

Creating Folders and Distributing the Copied Files to Their Final Location

The application media usually contains highly compressed files. After these files are copied to the hard drive, they are decompressed and stored in temporary folders. This is a great time, if possible, to pause the install process. Make sure that the Windows temporary folder is cleared before pausing the install process; many applications store their files here during the transfer process. Others may store the files in a temporary folder under the application assigned folder. (Many vendors such as Real, Adobe, and Symantec create Temp folders.) Most software manufacturers compress the application files and deploy them to the systems by using an extractor to place the files into a single folder on the user's computer. The next step is to join files or move files to the folder where the application wants the files to reside. Stopping the install after the files are copied to disk and then listing temporary folder contents helps you understand what files are being deployed.

Establishing Shared Library Connections and Registering with the OS

As discussed previously, shared files include Dynamic Load Library (DLL), system files, and other files used by more than one application to perform some function. Software manufacturers vary in how they deal with shared libraries. Some will maintain their own library and not depend on the operating system having the file available. Others will look for a specific library file, and if it is present, not load a new version. Still others will simply write their files to shared libraries and not be concerned that they might be overwriting a version used by another application (these are very bad developers!)

Reviewing the installation script files included in the setup folder can help you understand how a particular application install works. If you don't have the hours needed to analyze these files, ask the vendor to provide a summary document of the install process.

Since Windows 95, Microsoft has used the registry to manage how programs execute and how they relate to the operating system. Prior to Windows 95, many of the *behavior* commands might be found in the Autoexec.bat, System.ini, Win.ini and other files. Applications would write over each other and no one checked for conflicts. The registry was meant to overcome those issues. For the most part, the registry works. There are, of course, issues from time to time. The registry maintains a profile for each local account, so any software that requires initialization of specific user profiles has to be installed multiple times as each user logs on. This requirement is true even if the files go to the same physical location, because each user's registry entry must be initialed. Current trends in application design attempt to make this process easier by relying on the software application to populate the user registry data on first launch. This registry process can inhibit a clean *silent* install. A silent install happens when an application can be deployed to all users, and the application installs itself without any operator intervention. If you have installed an application that displayed a message to reboot the system, or enter a license number, or login—you have installed a noisy application. Noisy applications are messy to install and difficult to deal with if there are a large number of desktops to deploy.

Final Steps Include Desktop Setup, Icons, and Autoloader Script

The final deployment steps may include creating an application icon and placing it in the desktop folder, the system quick launch tray, or the start menu. This final step is where you are often asked to reboot before the install is completed. This reboot is needed to complete updating of the registry. To remove this noise from an install, scripting may be used to force an unattended reboot of the system, or the install might be suspended until the next time a user logged on, at which time the load process would resume and the install complete. Depending on the environment, you should be careful of this second alternative, as it can be confusing to users when they log in and the system behaves differently than expected.

Scripting has been used since the beginning of computers. Script files contain commands that the computer executes one at a time until finished. A script is like a program; it is a set of instructions. However, scripts are very basic and have limited functionality. Script files can be used to create an unattended, or silent, installation. Scripts can be as simple as a text file with a few commands, or as complex as a VBScript or JavaScript file. There are a number of alternative scripting languages as varied as the computer professionals that use them. Each scripting language has its own strengths and weaknesses. When it comes to selecting a script language, pick one that will efficiently do the job and still be maintainable, extensible, and reusable. A key factor in deciding on a scripting language is the availability of support and freeware scripts. For popular scripting languages such as VBScript, many common distribution solutions already exist. The following websites will provide you sources for other scripting tools as well as links to other sites—*www.desktopengineer.com*, *www.winscriptingsolutions.com* and *www. appdeploy.com*. Having a few scripting tools in the support tool kit is a wise idea. Besides being useful for installations and deployments, scripts can help manage a number of automated activities that support people need from time to time.

Once you fully understand how the software manufacturer intended the application to be deployed, you are ready to either accept it as is, or begin modifying the installer to fit your purposes. During the pilot test, there is the opportunity to test the install first as intended and then tweak it to work with your environment. A call to the software manufacturer can save a lot of time. This will be a grueling task the first time you do it. However, the upside is that after you have analyzed and changed a couple of installs, it becomes much easier. The flexibility and control gained over the install process makes the effort worthwhile.

MANAGING THE SOFTWARE

The standard install steps and suggestions for manually reviewing each step as to where files were placed, changes to the registry, and so forth were discussed in the previous section. For smaller organizations with a tight IT budget, brute force may be needed to manage the deployment and user support. However, there are software tools available on the market to help manage software. A good software management tool distributes and installs software. It includes a wide range of support modules—reporting, license tracking, network usage, and policy tracking. The obvious advantage to using software management tools is that much of the effort is automated from software distribution to removal. Software management software comes in several forms, at a basic level. The role of software management software encompasses the following:

- Inventory functions keep a record of what applications are currently installed by user.
- Licensing can either record all active licenses by application, or may actually track licenses in use to available licenses so license usage can be metered and managed.
- Warehousing physically provides storage space for the desktop images being deployed.
- Managing functions provide automated support for the distributed software.
- Reporting functions provide utilization and status reports.

The primary goal of management software is to provide a centrally managed location for the bulk of software distribution tasks. Centrally managed implies ease of administration and clearly defined status of installed software and pending software releases. Even if the process is automated, there must be processes in place to manage both software and hardware at all times.

Inventory

In a best practice environment, it is critical to maintain a current listing of all software and hardware inventory. This list should contain detailed information about the user, client workstation, network, and server software installed within an organization. Inventory information is used for troubleshooting, license compliance, and strategic planning. It would be great to be able to collect and update this information automatically, but the cost of such software may be beyond many companies. An ideal inventory would include license terms and conditions, date of acquisition, user names and location, system installation details, maintenance agreements, usage monitoring, history, and other relevant data. This type of information is often kept as part of the help desk, which will be discussed later.

For small companies, this inventory could be a spreadsheet or hard copy journal. In this case, the inventory is manually updated and contains minimal information about the software. The objective is to meet minimum requirements to avoid breach of license challenges, and provide upgrade proof and volume purchase leverage. A more advanced software inventory includes regular inventory of software from purchasing through distribution. At this level, the inventory process would be used with asset-tracking and system-discovery tools.

Licensing

License tracking and licensing monitoring are critical components of managed software. Many of the software deployment tools have some mechanism for either tracking the number of licensees installed, or for monitoring license usage. The advantage to having licensing centrally managed is that IT staff has an immediate record of license status. In larger organizations, managing licenses can be complicated. For instance, many companies use software metering to manage the use and control the number of licenses. If you have 50 licenses to use a specific software application, then the fifty-first user to request, or open, that application will receive a message that no licenses are available. Software management programs deal with metering in various ways. Some software management applications will record the fact that a user is waiting for an application license to become available and will notify the user when it does. Others may track the occurrences of *unavailable* notices, and provide reports that advise IT when it might be time to purchase additional licenses to meet demand. Licensing is a serious issue for IT to manage and is becoming more critical as the number of lawsuits rise nationally. Large and small software manufacturers are more commonly resorting to legal avenues to restrict the illegal use of software, and to generate additional cash flow. Some software manufacturers recently rolled out a *turn in your boss* campaign to encourage disgruntled employees to blow the whistle on employers who condone the use of illegal or unlicensed software.

Warehousing

Warehousing is the physical storage of distributable images. A popular best practice technique today is the creation of desktop images of a tested and validated install. This image includes all the software a user needs at their desktop. In an image-managed environment, IT will install, or update, an image with the most current software release or update. Then IT distributes the updated image to the desktops. This has the effect of providing the most current software at the desktop, but it also refreshes the entire disk image. This method is also commonly referred to as cloning. Cloning is quickly becoming the most popular method of software distribution and end user support. Warehousing maintains all the images deployed on a server and distributes the software across the network. There are, of course, variations of this theme. Warehousing can be done manually using an older server to store the images and keeping track of deployed licensed software in a spreadsheet or database for reporting. Warehousing is recommended for any organization over 30 users, or an organization with multiple locations, which make support difficult.

Policy Management

Policy management allows IT to assign individual users to specific groups. Simply by belonging to a managed group, the user has access to the appropriate authorized software for that group. Users can be members of multiple groups, if necessary. Managed groups is not a new concept to Novell Netware or Microsoft NT users. However, policy management is slow to catch on because it is usually found only in higher-end software, used primarily by very large organizations, or organizations where staff often changes position.

Manage Components

There has been much talk over the past few years about self-healing applications. Self-healing programs will detect when a needed file is missing, or damaged, and will automatically request a replacement. The manage components feature provides automatic self-healing of distributed packages. Self-healing can be done at the server side by monitoring client systems and keeping a record of the install status, or by responding to a client request for a replacement file. Some versions of component management tools also provide for catastrophic system failure recovery. In the case of software failure, the recovery component will transfer the appropriate image to the user workstation and notify IT that redeployment has taken place. Finally, managed software is included in regular reports. These reports should include details such as software type, revision, user name, and user identification by software title, and a record of valid software installs versus failed installs.

Reporting

With built-in reporting, systems administrators have immediate access to the software status reports, license usage, and other important statistics. Additional reporting functions include auditing and management reports, as well as network status and loads over time.

LONG-TERM SOFTWARE SUPPORT

IT professionals who are responsible for supporting end users know that as important as the deployment process is, deployment is only the beginning. The real work begins after software is deployed and users begin using the application. After a software application is deployed to users, IT is responsible for monitoring the software to make sure it continues to function correctly. IT must be prepared to respond rapidly when a software failure occurs. IT is better able to support users if users are knowledgeable about the software and hardware assigned to them; educating users will be discussed in the next chapter. However, there are several best practice methodologies for supporting end users.

Time after time, I experience IT departments that I consider to be in strictly maintenance mode. Maintenance mode means that the IT technical staff is in a reactive posture. When a user calls, they respond and attempt to fix the call; they then wait for the next user with a problem. The problem with maintenance mode is that IT will never get ahead and rarely has the time to create a future vision or to introduce new technology into the environment. Maintenance mode technicians swap out network cards, change a broken mouse or keyboard, and replace toner cartridges in printers! While all of these tasks need to be done, they should be assigned to the appropriate person. For instance, a best practice principal is to store spare keyboards and mice in the supply closet along with stationary and felt tip pins. The user can replace the malfunctioning keyboard or mouse themselves. The user either disposes of the broken item, or places it at a designated location for IT to diagnose later.

The same is true for replacing and maintaining printers. This is a task that can be assigned to administrative support staff and does not require higher paid professional technicians. In a best practice IT department, fixing problems is a small part of the department's responsibilities. IT also acts as the central repository for the historical records pertaining to software and hardware inventory, compatibility issues, and problems requiring an IT response. Historical records contain valuable information about areas such as compatibility testing and any conflict resolution processes that have arisen. Historical support information is invaluable for quickly resolving issues as they arise. But more importantly, the historical information can be used to prevent problems from reccurring in the future.

Perfect software would never fail. Unfortunately, we do not often run into perfect software. Therefore, an important aspect of software support is repairing software that becomes damaged. The key is how to implement a validation and subsequent repair process that occurs before the damaged resource is encountered by the application. A damaged resource could be a printer that is removed, or a rights access that has changed. Most of the time, when referring to a damaged resource, we mean program files that have been accidentally moved, deleted, or have become damaged (perhaps in the write process).

Some automated support software will conduct a limited scan of program files, portions of a desktop image, or server image, and compare the scan results to the master image stored on the image server. If differences are found, the software will attempt to correct the discrepancy automatically. This is a great way to anticipate and repair problems before they can affect user productivity. However, this type of technology requires a very robust operating environment. The operating environment needs to include high-end user workstations, servers, and network bandwidth to support the validation and file/image transfer process. With Microsoft Windows NT and 2000, the operating system protects system files through a function called Windows File Protection. Whenever the operating system detects an attempt to replace any of these special system files, a corresponding restore sequence is initiated to restore the system to its acceptable state. While this process works great for system files, it does not support third-party application files. However, the Windows Installer service can detect missing, corrupt, or the wrong version of key files or other installable resources. When corruption is detected, the Windows Installer service can restore the appropriate component, which may be multiple files, from the originating source image.

IT departments in small to medium companies are limited in support resources; the department may often be one or two people. Yet, small companies have the same needs as large companies. The good news is that the software and hardware needs of small companies may not be as great as larger companies with hundreds of user workstations that IT must support. Also, in smaller companies, some of the support needs are pushed, intentionally or by default, to the end user. I have noticed that there is more of a maintenance mode attitude in small businesses where the IT staff wears many hats. Whatever their size, businesses that do not include their technology staff in long-range planning and keep them apprised of changes in the organization's business plan are doing themselves a grave injustice. Professional technology staff must see themselves as having value that goes beyond maintenance. They should be free to recommend solutions that bring greater benefits to the organization. In this way of thinking, the purpose of IT is not to maintain technology but to provide technology that augments the organization's ability to meets its mission objectives, whatever those may be.

Licensing and license tracking is a necessary evil that management must address. There are a number of reasons why a business must conform to the licensing agreement of the software manufacturers whose products they use. But the main reason is—it is the law! I hear comments such as, "they have plenty of money," or "it does not really matter if I buy legal licenses because they are never going to come after me." This attitude is wrong on a number of levels. It is the responsibility of IT to track and report license usage and to insure that management is apprised of licensing issues as they change.

Licensing requirements are determined initially when the software product is purchased. IT must continue to monitor licensing and procure additional licensing as new users are added. This has to be watched very closely. With most traditional software, like Microsoft Office for instance, while it is possible to buy additional licenses, the company will not send a refund if the number of users drops. So, you must carefully judge when and where new licenses are really needed.

A key aspect to support in the software deployment process is to ensure that the company maintains license conformance. As soon as all licenses are consumed, an alert should be triggered to investigate the software's status. In some cases, license metering may be an effective tool. A software metering tool knows how many licenses are available and will monitor activation by each user. When the limit of licenses has been reached, another instance of the software cannot be run. Usually, the user will be asked if he or she wants to wait for a license to become available, or to try again later. The type of software license has a lot to do with how much flexibility is available. Some software is licensed per user. Thus, the software can be installed any number of times; however, only the assigned user can use the software. Other software is licensed per computer. This licensing scheme means that the software can be installed on only one computer, no matter which user is actually using it. Another form of software license is a site license. This license method is the most flexible arrangement and allows any number of installations as long as each user is within the same company. For applications such as accounting, or manufacturing, it is ideal to obtain a site license so the use is legal; but it is not necessary to track actual usage. Low-end applications like Microsoft Office, Abode Acrobat, and most accounting applications are user or computer license driven as discussed above. These require more resources to track.

An important tip before we leave the discussion of licensing. In support and business contingency planning, it is a good idea to maintain either the original licenses or copies of the licenses off-site in a secure damage proof safe. There have been disasters where documents supporting legal licenses were destroyed; and the company had no recourse but to repurchase everything. This is a real shame since they had paid for the license once and should have the right to use the software, but all licenses were destroyed. Do not expect the software manufacturer to maintain the licensing information, even if you diligently completed the forms and mailed them in. For accounting and other major applications, ask if they maintain licensing information should your licenses be destroyed for any reason.

MANAGING THE UPDATE AND UNINSTALL PROCESS

When a software application is installed, that application may have to be removed. Most of us assume that the uninstall day will be way down the road. With any luck, we will be retired on our fishing boat and it will be someone else's problem. Shame on you! The truth is we all need to deal with uninstalling applications and should have a methodology for handling this process, just as we do for deploying the software in the first place. As a side note, some software manufacturers and developers refer to this process as *decommissioning;* however, the term uninstall is more widely accepted.

Technology staff who have done an application uninstall, for multiple systems or a single desktop, know that an uninstall, if done incorrectly, can cause more problems than an initial install. The staff may be at the mercy of the software manufacturer to provide an uninstall routine that reverses their application install. This means that files and file folders are removed, and the application is unregistered by removing keys from the registry. Sounds pretty easy until shared folders are considered.

Several times I have uninstalled an application, and the uninstall utility would begin deleting files, only to stop when it came to shared files and ask if I wanted to remove a file. If this has happened to you, your response may have been the same as mine, "How in the heck would I know?" To be safe, we often respond to not delete the file, because if the program does not know, I sure do not know. The result is that older versions of DLL and shared files are left behind, or orphaned. This takes up space, clutters the registry, and will eventually cause problems.

A best practice when removing, or uninstalling, an application is to pull up your initial install documentation with snapshots before and after the install of all directories and the registry file. Review what files were added where and what changes were made to the registry. This can be used to put the system state back the way it was before that application was initially installed. Of course, there are still no guarantees. The second issue IT must deal with when uninstalling an application is that over time, after the application was installed, the computer state has been modified to accept other new applications or program updates. So, returning a workstation to the state it was in before the application you intend to remove was installed, is not really an option. You will need to review install maps for all changes made to the environment to determine if a file is needed by any other applications.

If the software deployed uses desktop cloning, or images discussed above, the job may be much easier. Using images, it is possible to simply create new images, test and deploy them. Creating an image from scratch is sometimes more efficient and easier in the long run than attempting to remove or modify existing user workstations.

Where strong standards are not enforced, users sometimes take it upon themselves to remove applications from their systems. I once had an IT manager tell me they felt that "the more computer savvy a user was, the greater the potential for problems." For instance, a long time computer user who went back to the DOS days had no problem going to a command prompt, locating the application folder (or the folder they thought was the application folder) and deleting it. Delete the application icon from the desktop —and voila, application gone! We know that in the Windows world, it is not this easy. But, registry keys are still there; shared files are still sitting happily in the Windows/

System folder or the WINNT/System folder. These shared files are likely to stay there until they cause a conflict with another application, or you reformat the disk!

For local installs, the first step is to remove the application via the control panel Add/Remove programs feature. If the application did not register itself with Add/Remove, and is not present on the list of applications installed; the next place to look for an uninstall program is in that applications program folder. Before deciding to remove the application folder, check the program manual or help files on the original install CD for uninstall instructions. If this step is needed to delete the application, search the registry using the Regedit program to attempt to remove as many references to the program as possible. This is the least desirable method for program removal. For uninstalling programs across multiple systems, go back to the original installation routine and reverse the process, cleaning the application from each system.

Updating Software

Updating is mentioned after uninstalling because many software manufacturers actually uninstall the prior version and then install the new or more current version. Others perform the update process by only transferring specific files, then rejoining programs and updating the registry. Regardless of the method the software provider uses, your own methodology should be similar to that used for the original deployment. Before deploying an update, pilot test it first. Map drive and registry changes along the way, in order to be comfortable with the changes the update process makes to the computer state. Once the pilot test is done, you may either use the update service provided by the software manufacturer, or decide to write your own script to deploy the update.

SELECTING AND DEPLOYING HARDWARE

The systems deployed today are far more complex than any we have worked with in the past. Conflicts between the operating system and hardware drivers are frequent. A later chapter will define specific hardware, as well as software recommendations. We will attempt to keep these updated on the technology best practices website at *www.technologybestpractices.com*.

IT professionals use different criteria to select hardware than management. Users have yet another concept of what they need. Hardware must be acquired to fit the software selection implemented; and the hardware must support the mission of the user. I have observed the frustrations of IT managers firsthand over the years as they strive to keep the hardware infrastructure viable in the face of constant cost issues. The problem is that IT technicians fail to understand management's questions. If IT takes a request to management for new user workstations, laptops, or a new server, they are routinely greeted with the comment, "How much does it cost?" What IT actually hears is "This costs too much!" Thus, IT attempts to constantly reduce the cost of IT until it actually impairs their ability to serve the organization and the client effectively. You should not waste money when purchasing hardware; searching for best pricing is the right thing to do. However, keep in mind that purchasing the least expensive hardware will cost more in lost productivity and maintenance cost over the economic life of the hardware.

It is a best practice to purchase and deploy name brand hardware where possible. Just because a second or third tier manufacturer product may cost a little less does not mean that you will be able to support the product for less over the next three to four years. Some technicians say they can build systems from components much cheaper than they can purchase the completed system. There are a few cases where this may be true. But, there is much more to the process. Those companies that elect to build their own systems must adhere strictly to well-defined and documented standards as to what components they will use. This means standardizing on motherboard, BIOS, controllers, video cards, hard drives, floppy drives, CD drives, and so forth.

STANDARDIZATION REDUCES THE COST OF SUPPORT

Economic Life is how long the user intends to productively use the hardware you are deploying. The economic life for a network switch or router may be between five and seven years if it is purchased at the top of the economic life cycle. The economic life of laptops seems to be around two to three years, depending on how well staff exercises care in transporting and using the laptop systems. The economic life of a server today is three to four years, mostly because of the rapid evolution of the Windows network operating system over the past decade. Linux or Unix-based servers generally have a longer economic life than Windows-based servers. The economic life of workstations today is four to five years, if the systems are properly configured when purchased. If a system three years into its economic life cycle is purchased, there may be less productive use out of the system. Higher-end Pentium IV-based systems with high speed ECC memory provide a longer life cycle. IT departments that deploy thin client or web enabled applications can expect a longer economic life. The life cycle of a product is the number of years the product can be expected to provide useful service. It is important to understand that useful service does not imply that the machine runs until it dies! By the time a workstation reaches the point where it has to be rebooted several times a day because the system is freezing up, it is impacting the productivity of the user. Management must always keep in mind that the user is the most expensive resource in the business, not the technology. The technology enables the users to be more productive. Faulty technology hinders the user's ability to be productive! Just because the image on a five-year-old monitor can still be seen does not mean that it is not impacting the health and productivity of the user.

Standardizing, as much as possible, reduces the cost of support. Most technicians will say that the time it takes to diagnose a problem is directly proportionate to their experience and knowledge of the components. If an organization simply purchases the least expensive system each time a new system is procured, without consideration of long-term support costs, they will end up with a large variety of hardware, many sets of drivers, and different quality components to support. The end result is greater support costs and less productive users.

Best practice organizations review their standard configurations two to three times a year to determine where adjustments should be made. These adjustments are kept to minimum unless economic benefits can be defined. If purchasing is not centralized, the standards are published as part of the company standards manuals to ensure departmental compliance. In organizations where strict standards are not enforced, IT is strongly advised to bill back support costs to each department on a per incident basis.

USERS CAN LOWER SUPPORT COSTS

Many organizations today do not empower users to take corrective action, do not provide training, or simply overlook the opportunity and benefits self-support can bring. Best practice methods allow users to take certain corrective actions to remedy common problems, replace broken components without calling IT, and research problems on their own. If they are trained how to respond when there is a problem, users can significantly lower the cost of supporting technology. Here is a list of common problems and what users should be trained to do before, or in lieu of, calling the help desk!

System Freeze

System lockup is one of the most recurring problems with Windows based computers. System hang-ups can be caused by either hardware or software failures; most often, the software is the problem. Many times a simple combination of software, or of keystrokes, can cause a system to hang. The accidental depression of the Ctrl or Alt keys while typing other letters or commands is one cause of system freezes. This actually creates an instruction to the software that it does not understand and causes it to stop.

When a system hangs, teach users to do the following. Pull out a piece of paper (if the company does not use a form for incident reporting) and make a note of all the applications running and exactly what the user was doing when the hang-up occurred. If they were typing a letter or updating a spreadsheet—specify exactly what the user was doing at the time, such as formatting a paragraph or range of cells. It is rare for someone to have a problem and then never have the same problem again. Keeping a log of problems can greatly improve the chances of finding a solution. Next, attempt to remove the offending program, or simply reboot your system, depending on what version of Windows you are running, as follows:

- Windows 2000 users should press Ctrl+Alt+Delete keys simultaneously. Now click on the task manager button and the applications tab. See if any of the active applications are listed as *Not Responding*. If so, click on this program to highlight that task and select the *End Task* button. There could be more than one program that is not responding. Continue to end each of these. Now close this window and return to the system. If it is not running properly, press Ctrl+Alt+Delete and select shut down to *reboot* the computer.

- Windows 95 and 98 users do not have the option to remove individual programs as easily. So, it may be best to reboot the system by pressing Ctrl+Alt+Delete twice. This may result in the system rebooting in safe mode (low resolution, low functionality.) As soon as the system is ready to use, click on start shutdown and reboot the system again.

No Power, or the Device Is Not Working

A user may call for support thinking that his or her system is broken when the problem is actually a disconnected power cable. If the system seems to have lost power, or the user loses the monitor display, train users to follow these steps before they call the help desk:

- Look on the front of the monitor for a green or yellow power indicator. If the monitor power indicator is yellow, solid, or blinking, it means the monitor has power, but has lost the image from the CPU. The CPU is referred to here as the main box that holds the drive components and motherboard. The central processing unit is usually considered to be the processor chip, but over the years the box itself has come to be known as the CPU.) If the monitor light is green, then it is receiving a signal from the CPU and the problem most likely lies with the CPU, or an application that is running. If there is no green light, there is no power to the monitor. Begin by checking the wall plug or UPS power strip and unplug and plug the monitor. If there is still no light, then pull the power connection from the back of the monitor and plug it in again, checking that both ends of the power cable are solidly connected. Next, make sure that if there is a power strip; it has a solid red light displayed. No light or a blinking red light indicates a problem with the power strip. This is also a great time to check the front of the CPU and the speakers for green lights to make sure they have power. No green lights—no power! Do not assume that the system has lost power; pressing the restart button on the CPU could result in losing data or corrupting data files. Pressing the power or restart buttons is a last resort effort!
- Once the user determines their monitor connections are solid and that they are receiving power, the next step is to check for power light on the CPU. Most CPUs have some type of green LED display light on the front panel. At the least, the user should have a fixed disk power indicator that they can see blink when there is disk activity. Sometimes pressing the enter key may cause this light to blink, indicating activity. If this happens, the problem is most likely a program-generated error. If there is no power light on the CPU, have the user check the power cable from the CPU back to the wall or UPS power strip to verify that the plugs are seated and that power is there. Many times cleaning crews, or the users themselves, may loosen the power connection when cleaning or moving around the computer.

Connecting or Reconnecting a Computer

There are many technicians who panic at the thought of users hooking up new devices to their computer, or moving computers from one location to another without *profes-*

sional help. In most cases, computer components have a number of unique cable connectors that attach to the computer CPU. If the user looks closely, it will be found that these connectors are one of a kind and that there is only one way to plug a cable connector into the CPU. Serial device and printer ports are beveled so that it is not easy to plug them in incorrectly. Phone cables use RJ-9 connectors that connect to a modem connector in the computer. These look like network connections, except network connections, called RJ-45, are larger than RJ-9 phone connectors. If the user is having a problem with their system or network, the first place to begin trouble shooting is to power down the system and remove all cables from the back of the CPU. Remind the user to count to ten slowly, to make sure all the power dissipates from the system's power supply. Then, plug all the cables in again, making sure they have tight, well-seated connections. This simple process often repairs a number of issues such as system hangs, flickering screens, network (or modem) not responding, and the like. One well-known best practice is, "Until proven otherwise, it is a cable problem!"

Network Connection Failure

Following, "The network seems awfully slow today!", network connection failure may be the third most common problem call. IT professionals know that a network connection becomes unavailable or slows down for a number of reasons. It may often be something beyond the user's control, and a technician must correct the problem at the server or network switches. However, users can be trained to do some basic diagnostics before they pick up the phone and call the help desk with a network issue.

First and foremost, teach users to shut down or restart the system before calling IT to determine if the system is simply frozen or has lost track of the network component. Then, educate users to call IT if the problem occurs persistently, more than once a month, so that IT can repair the system. Rebooting the system will help clear any errant network programs running in the background that may have gotten confused (hard to believe computers get confused, but they do.) This important step should perhaps have been included as an item by itself. Shutting down the workstation and then powering it back up can correct a significant number of problems. Windows is an extremely complex operating system. As discussed in the software section, different application programs will sometimes conflict under unique circumstances. It is a good idea for the user to note what he or she was doing when the failure occurred, and then restart the system. If the problem persists, then they should contact IT and provide a history of the problem.

If, after the user restarts the system and logs in, the network is unavailable, the user should double check the network cable connection to their system. If they, or their supervisor knows where the local hub or switch is, they should check it to see that lights are green and the hub *appears* to be functional. IT must understand that if the system is stored under a desk, or is not accessible, the user may be reluctant to crawl under the desk and check the connection. There is not an easy answer for this. Asking someone close by who does not mind crawling under the desk to give a hand is an option. One user might say, "Why should I do this? This is a job for IT." This may be a matter of company policy. In many cases, the user is best served by doing minor troubleshooting alone and getting back to work. IT may be in the middle of a major task where freeing a technician to check a network connection is considered a low priority. The user could be down for an hour or longer. Again, working as a team makes sense, and users will be more likely to do some of the minor troubleshooting described here if they are well-trained ahead of time and understand the benefits.

Train the users so that, when they unplug the network connection and plug it in again, they next look at the where the connection plugs into the CPU and should see several lights. Green lights and red lights and, sometimes, yellow lights. The colors of the lights may mean different things for different network interface cards. However, green is usually good and red is usually bad. The best the user may be able to do is determine if there are any lights, and if there are places for lights that are not on. This information can be sometimes valuable to the help desk when the support call is made, because they can check the network switches to see if the problem might be at their end.

Loss of Internet Connectivity

As the Internet becomes more critical to how users communicate today, IT is charged with keeping the information gateway open and flowing. Where the Internet gateway is via the network, the issue may be a network issue and the user should follow the steps outlined above.

If the user is using a modem to connect to the Internet, follow the network connectivity issues above as well, substituting modem lights for network interface card lights. Modem users verify they have a dial tone before calling IT. A dial tone can be lost for a number of reasons. If the user has a problem connecting to the Internet from a dial-up modem, ask the user to plug a regular phone into the modem line and call someone. Keep a spare single line analog phone in the IT department for just this purpose. Ask the user to pick the phone up to test the line. Even if the line is live and working, tell the user to call someone and talk for a few minutes, listening to the quality of the line. If the voices are not loud and clear, or if there is static, the user could be experiencing a bad connection and need to have the phone company check the line. In some organizations, the phone lines are under a department other than IT. Today, best practice organizations are putting all technology including phones, fax machines, cell phones, and so forth under IT as a common umbrella.

Finally, determine if the Internet connection is down or if the Internet gateway is unavailable. Here is the difference. A carrier, like AT&T, Sprint, MCI, local Bell service, or a cable service provider, provides a connection to an Internet service provider (ISP.) The ISP is the gateway to the Internet. It is possible to lose either of these and be unable to receive mail or use a browser. So, whom do you call? The easiest way to determine where the problem lies is to *Ping* the ISP. With only a little training, users can learn to operate the Ping program that comes with the Windows desktop operating system. To execute the program, click on Start/Run and type in Ping followed by a space and then the IP address, or domain name of any server address on the Internet. An IP address is a four-octet number where each octet is between 1 and 255. This may be a bit too much for the average user; tell them to type in the company's web server name or other web domain address, for example *www.technologybestpractices.com*. The Ping program will respond with how long it takes for the computer to reach the IP address being tested. If the Internet connection is not working, or the IP address is unavailable, Ping will return a message that says, "Destination is unreachable or not responding." Next, Ping the IP address of your ISP gateway (IT will have to provide this). If the first test responds that the two computers are talking, but the second test fails—the problem is with the ISP, not with the service provider. This is a simple test, but effective. Large IT shops may be hesitant to have users using tools like Ping. However, in small organizations with minimal or no technical resources, it is a viable procedure to follow.

Many small companies today use cable modems to access the Internet. Like modems and network switches, cable modems can be checked for connectivity lights on the front of the cable modem. Remember "green lights are good, red lights are bad."

Printer Not printing

In more that 80 percent of all printer help desk calls, the problem can be solved in one of two ways. First, the user should make sure the printer is powered on, and secondly, that it has toner. This is basic, but worth a check before the call is made for technical assistance. Many times printers, particularly network printers, can be turned off over weekends or holidays. Or perhaps, the nighttime cleanup people unplugged the printer to plug in a vacuum and did not plug it back in. Whatever the reason, this happens a lot and should be the very first thing checked. Next, if the user is having problems with the quality of the print, ask them to check the toner. Many printers, such as Hewlett-Packard Laser jet printers, will indicate on the front LCD display *Low Toner*. In most business today, this is where a small need becomes a crisis. A best practice would be to store a spare toner cartridge near each network printer and instruct users how to replace the cartridge. Another option is to store spare cartridges with copy paper and other supplies. The point is that a technician is not the only one who can replace toner. If the user is in a crisis and does not have a new cartridge handy, here is a little tip. Take out the old cartridge and shake it gently. Put the cartridge back in and they should be able to get another 25 to 50 pages out while waiting for the replacement to arrive.

Installing Local Applications

Many users take it upon themselves to install new updates to their software with or without permission from IT. It may be better for IT to prepare and educate the user ahead of time. For more complex software such as accounting software updates, fixed assets, or manufacturing applications, users should always follow the recommended procedures. Truth is, everyone should always follow the instructions. However, the instructions may not always work as expected. Problems arise when an install process is halted for any reason. More problems arise when users install an application without first checking to see if the operating system thinks it is already installed. A simple rule of thumb is often to uninstall an application before installing an update. This is particularly true for Windows politically correct software where the developer has followed Windows guidelines and registers itself with the operating system. Train users to know what applications are registered on their system by opening up the control panel and clicking on Add/Remove programs. While Windows 2000 Professional will give you the option to change or remove, older versions of Windows will only allow users to remove applications.

What To Do When Something No Longer Works

Computers are still dependable and predictable. If they change their behavior, it is because something caused the behavior to change. If a user's system suddenly fails where it worked correctly before, the user needs to be trained to ask, "What is different?" or "What have I done differently?" If problems occur, stop and consider what is different—a different printer, a new program update, a different sequence of keystrokes, commands or events that might cause the computer to act differently. If hardware has been added to the user's system, uninstall it and test again. Continue removing hardware peripherals until you find the offending device. USB devices, such as scanners, cameras, printers, and the like, are a problem in this regard; the computer may not be able to provide enough power to the device. Walk the user through uninstalling as many USB devices as possible and see if the problem goes away. Some devices, for example, do not get enough power from a hub, but work fine when connected directly to the computer. Others may not work on a USB port, because they want to take control and do not release access to other devices.

Out of Space Issues

A number of problems can occur because of disk space availability. Some of these problems present themselves in application errors and can make users believe the problem is a software issue. Anytime there is a disk save error, or the system is running much slower than it should, check for available disk space. Click on My Computer and then on each drive to determine free space. To help fix speed issues or system hang-ups, it is good to reorganize fixed disk drives a couple of times a year. In Windows terminology, this process is called defragging. At a minimum, users should be trained to defrag and reorganize their local disks drives if they store information locally. It is a best practice method to create script files that automatically execute these disk diagnostic and organization tools on a periodic basis such as one a month, or once a quarter.

What Users Need to Know before Calling IT

Computer users are often inclined to pick up the phone and call for help as soon as something goes wrong, then become angry when they are not given a quick solution. Before users call IT for help, they should:

- Review the problem completely, documenting the problem in writing. Writing down a description of the problem helps internalize it. Describe in detail the problem, what the user was doing when the problem occurred, and if the problem happened before.
- Make sure that users convey the urgency of the problem to the IT help desk. If the user is working on a project for the boss, or something on a deadline that will have

an adverse economic impact if it does not get out, it is important to let IT know this ahead of time. Most IT departments do not have idle hands sitting around waiting for something to break. There is usually more than one problem to deal with at a time, so users should be told when to expect support. Then, like the appliance repairperson, make sure you meet the expectation and arrive when, or before, expected.

- Don't assume IT knows what the user does. This is a big issue with applications, such as accounting systems. If accounts receivable, or inventory, or payroll is not posting correctly, the IT help desk people may not know the answer either. IT can help the user track down the vendor, pull a copy of maintenance agreements, sit in on conference calls, and do whatever it takes to help the user resolve the problem.

I have seen an unbelievable number of computer problems resolved by turning off the system, going to lunch, taking a coffee break, or going home (assuming it is not ten in the morning, of course.) In other words, take a break, walk away, and come back relaxed and ready to take an objective look at the problem. Suddenly the problem is not as large and ugly as it seemed at first glance!

One Size Does Not Fit All

Over standardization to the point of inhibiting productivity is one common error that many businesses make. While we routinely endorse the use of standardization, we do not support a common system configuration for everyone in the organization; some users may have specific needs that others do not. The following case examples bring this point more into focus.

After a careful review of the needs of a large group of mobile users for a strategic technology plan I was developing, I recommended two laptop model computers. The first recommendation was a fully configured laptop, and the second was a much smaller, lighter laptop (brand and model are not important to the example.) The large laptops were slated for power users and users who did not want to use an external monitor and keyboard. The smaller model was several pounds lighter, with a smaller profile, and only a 10-inch screen. This smaller model was intended for travelers who needed a machine on the road that was as light and portable as possible, to be used for electronic mail, web browsing, and word processing. I had the client test both models before recommending how to proceed. When it came time to order the systems, the technology staff complained that supporting two systems was "too much trouble"; they did not see why everyone should not have the larger units since they represented the *best* technology! According to IT, maintaining and supporting a single solution would be much easier. They also felt that the larger unit was a superior system.

In a second scenario, the controller of the same organization did not understand why I recommended dial-in connectivity services for staff that traveled frequently, via a national ISP, such as MindSpring, MSN, or AOL, which had local point of presence (POP) connections throughout most of the United States. The controller is a technology savvy person who does not travel out of town often, but does take his laptop home to work evenings and weekends. The controller said, "All I do is dial-in on an 800 number, connect to the mail-server, download my mail, disconnect, respond to my mail and repeat the process again. I see no reason why everyone cannot work this way!"

At face value, each of these arguments appears to have merit. After all, ease of support has traditionally been an important consideration. However, each of the examples also reinforces the *one size fits all* corporate technology mindset that often permeates large IT departments. Extensive research and experience working with technology users leads us to strongly disagree with this approach. Research says that if people are to be highly productive, IT must create an environment where technology solutions are tailored to the needs of the user. The need to make a large group more productive always outweighs the cost of a few support people.

In the first scenario above, the people who needed the smaller systems were physically unable to carry the heavier laptop machines on the road for extended periods of time. Secondly, the larger laptops were two to three thousand dollars more per system than the smaller units. Do not get sidetracked on the cost. The cost of the systems are not as important as the users' willingness to carry the machines with them, and actually use the technology on the road.

Further, our analysis showed that the mobile users needed to do research while on the road. If they were meeting with someone, they could research current news, company information and so forth online the night before and go into the meeting the next day with the most current information. The controller only used the office Internet link to do research and did not take into consideration the extended needs of others.

IT departments must consider the needs of the staff that will be using the technology. Where possible, it is fine to standardize, but not to the point that productivity suffers. The same is true for standardizing software. Where functionality is the same, users must defend their decision to be unique. A good example is the user who wants to stay with their favorite word processor or spreadsheet when the office is clearly migrating to another standard. The technology support staff should consider why the person wants to stay with what they have. This is often a simple fear of the unknown. Begin with training classes and provide a clear method for the user to transition. Provide tools for them to convert files in mass and show them differences in the commands, so the transition is as smooth and stress free as possible. More time must be spent on training and education as the technology used becomes more complex. We will give more attention to technology training and education in the next chapter.

Having the right laptop is important, but let us review the typical office setup as well. We have been involved in thousands of purchase decisions. We have helped organizations select and install systems, and have observed others in this process. It is interesting to observe the questions that are asked when planning new systems. It is even more interesting to observe that *no questions are asked!* Many times IT staff and retail vendors prepare proposals without ever observing users in action or surveying user needs.

Canvassing users and observing them at work is important to determine what tools will make them more productive. One of the first question I ask users is, "Are you right-handed or left-handed?" From an ergonomic viewpoint, this is a significant factor in the efficient use of computers. The hand you favor is important to how you work and how documents flow across your work area. Users will function best if the equipment is positioned correctly for them. With pencil and paper, it was easy; you simply adjusted your workspace to fit how you write. Typing and working with documents in an electronic workspace is just as important. Someone told me that they spend seven to eight hours a day on the computer, in Windows applications, taking help desk inquiries over the phone. Their job requires them to Alt+tab constantly between multiple application screens. It is stressful and time consuming. When I observed their workspace, I noticed they were using a four-year-old 15-inch monitor. The resolution was poor, as was the brightness of the screen. An obvious solution was to purchase a larger screen. The supervisor said they could not get the purchase request through because the monitor still worked! Think about this for a moment, before laughing at how ridiculous this sounds. Have you heard the same comment in your own office? Which is more expensive—the monitor or the person's lost productivity?

The next issue is lighting. Many older offices have lighting that is very poor for computing. Screen glare is a constant problem. Poor or inadequate lighting leads to eye ache, headaches, strain, stress, and time off work. This is a simple fact. Review the work space. Include appropriate modifications to allow for appropriate positioning of the computer hardware and adequate lighting in the deployment plan. If you are not convinced (or you are having problems convincing the person with the checkbook), set up a pilot project with a couple of real problem users. Measure their productivity before updating the workspace. Document what the users do in the environment. Measure their performance, number of characters typed per minute, documents processed (such as payroll or payable checks), and so forth. Then update the equipment, office layout, and lighting. After a short period for natural adjustment, measure productivity again. This is the written proof to take to management for justification.

I have written before about the printer myths. A printer myth is where management feels they are saving money by using a six-year-old laser printer and sharing it between four people. As part of the deployment plan development, observe (with a stop watch, if possible) how users print. How far is their work area from their primary printer? What is their travel time? Travel time is how long it takes to retrieve printed hardcopy and return to their desk. This should be done randomly and at multiple times, including end of the month, to get accurate measurements. Take the average times and multiply by the average hourly rate to come up with a pretty good idea of the lost productivity time. Make appropriate adjustments, but document the assumptions. It is important that the approach is logical and makes good business sense.

Then, plan the office layout with newer faster printers located closer to the users; and in some cases, individual printers for heavy users. Fifteen-page-per-minute personal laser printers are about $400 today. Over three years, what is the payback? This is hard return on investment (ROI) data that management can take to the bank and that you can use to back up your argument. There is no reason why ROI cannot be applied, or should not be applied, to every purchase decision. Where management's only argument is the cost of technology, it can be argued that *technology only costs when it is not used properly.*

The role of technology support is quickly moving from a maintenance function to proactively finding new ways business can leverage technology for improved profits. The technologist who focuses on maintenance and upkeep is not only limiting their value to the company; they may actually be causing the company economic harm. A best practice method is to require IT staff to regularly visit users, observe them in action, and ask them where they are having problems. Do not wait for the phone to ring with a problem. Be proactive! Just as there is not one car for everyone (if that is true, we would all drive Volkswagens), there is no one computer for everyone. As stated before, one size does not fit all. Hopefully, these best practices to managing and supporting users will help your organization.

MANAGING THE COST OF TECHNOLOGY

Managing technology cost means planning for new systems, new applications, major upgrades, network expansion, and so forth. Secondly, ongoing maintenance cost must also be managed. The planning aspect includes strategic planning and determining the cost of hardware and software to support each new objective. Ongoing costs that need to be managed include monthly support costs, such as personnel or third-party service providers, basic upgrades to memory and storage capacity, replacement of disposable components (e.g., the keyboard and mouse), communications, and supplies.

To manage the overall cost of technology, best practice organizations develop annual budgets to project the cost of supporting existing technology and new purchases. Planning and budgeting for existing technology begins with your technology infrastructure and must include:

- Desktops
- Laptops
- Printers
- Servers
- Networking equipment
- Communications
- Related hardware and software used in your organization

The cost of maintaining the technology infrastructure then, must include all costs related to hardware, software, and the personnel who support the infrastructure. There is also a cost for overhead, administration, and related costs that should be included. Preparing a technology budget is not solely the responsibility of the information technology (IT) department. IT must have input from other departments of the organization. For example, communications costs are often split between one or more vendors with phones on one bill, cell phones and pagers on one or more bills, and data communications provided by yet another third party. In other organizations, data communications is provided by the phone service vendor and billed on a single bill. In such cases, IT probably never sees the phone bill and may be completely unaware of increased charges and fees. By the time senior management becomes concerned over the cost of data communications, the costs are either above what they should be, or the organization has not benefited from evolving communications, as they should have.

Training is another item that is often unbudgeted. Most professionals agree that proper training enhances a business's ability to leverage its technology investment. Users who know the system and the organization's application software will be more productive, make fewer errors, and be able to better serve customers because they have a solid understanding of the application's capability. Training must be an annual budget line item, and it should be tracked somewhere. In the past, training was tracked in the personnel or human resources department. But technology-specific training should be tracked in the technology budget and measured as to the overall value of the training to the company.

CREATING THE TECHNOLOGY BUDGET

The first step to managing existing technology is to have a plan; the next step is to create a budget to fund that plan. The technology plan should include anticipated expansion or consolidation (i.e., additional users to be added or removed over the next one to three years). The plan should also include upgrading applications and targeting areas where training is needed. As the plan is reviewed and approved, each item will most likely have a cost. The budget determines the monetary cost of meeting new objectives, as well as the cost of supporting ongoing objectives (i.e., upgrading your core application each year to meet regulatory requirements).

Exhibit 5.4 is a sample budget sheet. Your budget should be more detailed than this sample, but detail can be tricky. The purpose of creating a budget is not to identify every item planned for purchase that year. The budget provides an idea of the resources that may be required in the future to support the technology infrastructure; the actual budget items will change over time. If there is a specific large dollar expense item pending, it is fine to put it in the budget—just do not make a habit of trying to identify each item in the budget plan.

A best practice technology budgeting method is to create what is commonly referred to as a three-year rolling budget. The first time you create the budget, lay out three years of expenses. In cases where actual estimates are not known, a percentage increase for years two and three can be projected. Maintenance or replacement of disposable items is a good example; maintenance cost and replacement of keyboards and mice will increase over time. Some items, such as software upgrades and maintenance cost, can be estimated for each year. Other items may be specific to a budget year. For instance, the servers are fine for the next year, but one of them needs to be replaced in the following budget year. Where budget numbers are unknown because of lack of experience, take a best guess and plug in a number. Track this number closely over time and revise it to more realistic estimates as your experience grows. At the end of each year:

- Compare actual costs to the original budget and review what happened. Remember, being under budget could be as bad (financially) as being over budget, if it meant you failed to execute your plan.

Exhibit 5.4   Sample Technology Budget

Plan Line Item	2002	2003	2004
Labor and Fees			
Administrative cost			
Payroll			
Meetings			
Overhead cost (other)			
Staff			
Network administrator			
Technician/help desk staff			
Services/fees (outsourced)			
Consulting services			
Maintenance (third-party)			
Support contracts			
Education			
Training non-technical staff			
Training technical staff			
Publications (technical)			
Conferences (technical)			
Subtotal			

- Review years two and three of the budget and determine what has changed over the past 12 months that might affect the next 24 months. Make adjustments.
- Add a third year to your budget.

Dealing with a three-year rolling budget allows planning, at least short-term, into the future. This allows scheduling and monitoring long-term projects and objectives that normally take more than 12 months to implement.

There are specific budgeting areas that should be included in the budget plan. Others may be added as appropriate for the organization, but do not remove items from this sample plan unless you are very certain they do not apply.

Labor and Fees Line Items

The first budget segment is labor and fees (see Exhibit 5.4), because this is typically the category where most of the technology expense is. Notice that there are identified line items for administrative cost. These are often ignored. Administrative cost should be broken into subaccounts for each funding entity or profit center to track cost back to that area.

The education section also includes additional technology support cost, such as training for operating and technical support staffs. There is a line item for technical publications IT staff should purchase, including books, newsletters, magazines, and specialized software. Most organizations also send a representative to at least one user or technical conference; that cost should be recorded here as well.

Hardware Budget Line Items

The next section is for budgeting hardware line items. The key items here include basic infrastructure costs. The word *network* could be used here as well; this includes all the components needed for all your computers to move information. The budget must also include *disposable* items. Disposable items include items that wear out faster because of repeated use, such as keyboards and mice. These items can be stored with supplies, such as writing materials and post-it notes, and drawn from inventory by staff as needed. Other items that might be included on the list are power supply equipment, computer racks, and so forth.

A frequent error made in technology budgets is not planning for expansion or growth. If you plan to hire ten new people next year, or to merge with another organization, do not forget to include new workstations and servers in the technology budget.

Communication Cost Line Items

The communications section of the budget should include the cost of all data lines. (Some organizations put their entire communications budget in IT; that is fine as well.) The next cost item is for the service provider who provides gateway access to the Internet, if you are accessing the Internet directly as most businesses do today.

Finally, any fees the organization pays for those persons who have remote access on a dial-up basis should be included. Note that communications hardware such as DSU/CSU, routers, and the like have not been included here. These are typically put under hardware. However, you can put communications equipment here, if that is the way you want to track it.

Software Cost Line Items

It is very important to budget for the anticipated cost of purchasing and upgrading software. Again, if you are planning to expand the number of users, the cost of operating

Exhibit 5.5   Sample Technology Budget

Plan Line Item	2002	2003	2004
Hardware			
Infrastructure			
Cable upgrade and testing			
Power protection			
Switch and router upgrades			
Disposable items			
Printers, scanners, cameras			
Keyboards, mice, other			
Servers (new)			
Servers (upgrades)			
Clients (new)			
Clients (upgrades)			
Subtotal	_____		

Exhibit 5.6   Sample Technology Budget

Plan Line Item	2002	2003	2004
Communications			
Connectivity (line cost)			
Internet gateway cost (ISP)			
Location 1			
Location 2			
Remote access cost (dial-ins)			
Subtotal	_____		

Exhibit 5.7   Sample Technology Budget

Plan Line Item	2002	2003	2004
Software			
Operating/network software			
Virus protection (upgrades/downloads)			
License (upgrades)			
License (new users)			
Subtotal	_____		
	_____		

system and application license fees must be included in the budget. Failure to plan for technology cost in advance of a merger or acquisition has led many organizations to a surprise shortfall in anticipated benefits, as well as short-term costs that had not been anticipated.

To make sure the budget is as accurate as possible, it is important to have IT involved early in the process. However, IT may not know all the strategic plans of each department. It is critical to have input from others and to have them coordinate the budget with IT to ensure that the budget includes future cost items.

Again, carefully review each of the budget line items and adjust as appropriate to the business. The most important consideration here is to have a budget and to follow it. As the plan changes, adjust the budget accordingly. At the end of each budget cycle, review actual costs and understand where discrepancies are and why they occurred. Remember a budget is a planning tool. It should not be set in concrete but should be kept as current and realistic as possible.

HARDENING THE SYSTEMS TO IMPROVE MANAGEMENT AND PROVIDE SECURITY

Most deployment plans address the cost of computers, schedules to minimize work disruption, installation of application software, and user training. But IT is not finished until they have included security issues. In this decade, the attention to security will grow dramatically as IT professionals rush to keep ahead of potential known, and unknown, threats. These threats come from without and from within. Internal security breaches rarely make it to the front page of news journals. According to some estimates, internal security breaches still represent as much as 51 percent of all unauthorized system accesses and the majority of thefts that occur. The discussion of computer security goes well beyond what can be covered in this book. We strongly suggest investing in several books and review websites that can provide more information. One of our favorites is Gibson Research Corporation *www.grc.com*, which is Steve Gibson's website. Steve is the author of Spin Rite and a number of other well-known utility softwares. We will use Steve's site to demonstrate a number of tools that can be used to secure and test systems on a regular basis.

This process of securing the technology infrastructure is called *hardening*. Hardening systems makes them more secure and better protects the interest of the organization.

Secure before Deployment

One of the best ways to secure technology is for IT to eliminate as many networked systems' vulnerabilities as possible. IT can also prevent security problems by securely configuring computers and networks before they are deployed. Vendors typically set computer defaults to minimally secure configurations; IT usually needs to change defaults to meet the specific organization's security requirements.

IT is far more likely to make decisions about configuring computers appropriately and consistently when they use a detailed, well-designed deployment plan that includes security as an item. In making such a plan, there will have to be tough decisions; there will be some hard trade-offs between usability and security.

Consistency is a key factor in security, because it fosters predictable behavior. Developing standards that insure consistency is important. Standards will make it easier for IT to maintain secure configurations and help to identify security problems more quickly. Security breeches often manifest themselves as deviations from predictable, expected behavior. To develop a security plan, the user workstation inventory lists should also include the security requirements appropriate for each user.

Network services should be annotated with the network services, such as electronic mail, access to the Web, domain name services, file transfers, and access to corporate databases, you plan to deploy. For each service, document whether the computer will be configured as a client, a server, or both (in the case of file and printer sharing).

Workstations are normally configured as clients for several network services. IT should document the planned behavior of those clients: the levels of access required, the type of access (read, write, etc.), and other aspects of the configurations required for client software.

There are three main security issues related to securing a workstation:

- *Confidentiality.* Information stored on the workstation may be disclosed inappropriately. This can happen when:
  - Unauthorized users gain access to the workstation.
  - Authorized users gain access to information that they are not supposed to see.
  - Authorized users inappropriately transmit information via the network.

- *Integrity.* The integrity of information stored on the workstation may be changed, either accidentally or maliciously.
- *Availability.* Authorized users may be unable to use the workstation, the network, or the information and services stored on each to perform their jobs. This can happen when:
  - ○ The information has been damaged, deleted, or otherwise rendered inaccessible (such as being encrypted or having its access privileges changed.)
  - ○ The computational resources of the workstation have been damaged or overloaded to the point of preventing authorized users' work.
  - ○ Access to services has been denied.

To secure a desktop workstation, a four-part approach is the best practice method and requires implementing security practices in the following areas:

1. Planning and executing the deployment of workstations.
2. Configuring workstations to prevent security incidents.
3. Maintaining the integrity of the deployed workstation.
4. Improving user awareness of security issues.

These four practices are designed to improve workstation security in several ways:

- They promote consistency. When the configuration and deployment of workstations is consistent, it is easier to manage security and to predict or identify use outside the norm.
- They help to maximize security on each workstation. This provides vital protection in case perimeter defenses fail. Host security is also a first line of defense against internal threats, which are more likely to occur than external threats via the network.
- They help to recognize security incidents sooner, help prepare to recover from security breaches, and prevent similar breaches from recurring. As a result, damages from security incidents can be reduced.

There is a more in-depth discussion of each of these practices at the Carnegie Mellon Software Engineering Institute's website *www.cert.org*.

Network servers are generally dedicated to single services. This usually simplifies the configuration and reduces the likelihood of configuration errors. It also can eliminate unexpected and unsafe interactions among the services that present opportunities for intruders. IT should keep a list of all services run on a server. In the case of Windows NT/2000, these services can be easily found under administration. IT should review these services periodically to determine if any unauthorized software is running. In some cases, it may be appropriate to offer more than one service on a single host computer. For example, the server software from many vendors combines the file transfer protocol (FTP) and the hypertext transfer protocol (HTTP) services in a single package. It may be appropriate for some organizations to provide access to public information via both protocols from the same server host. This is not recommended because this is a much less secure configuration.

Identify the network service software, both client and server, to be installed on the computer. Many operating system vendors bundle network service software for both clients and servers. You may choose to use those packages. For major services, however, third-party vendors may provide products that offer much better security. When making a choice, pay special attention to the ability of candidate packages to meet security requirements, and document the selection. Identify other application or utility software that will be installed on the computer. Include not only user-oriented application software, but also system-related software and security-related software.

Identify the Users or Categories of Users of the Computer

For workstations, you will sometimes be able to identify an individual who will be the primary user. But, more often, you will have to define categories of users. The categories are based on user roles that reflect their authorized activity. The roles are often based on similar work assignments and similar needs for access to particular information resources—system administrators, software developers, data entry personnel, and so forth. If appropriate, include categories of remote users and temporary or guest users.

For network servers, document the categories of users that will be allowed access to the provided services. For public servers connected to the Internet, the category of users is probably everyone. For internal servers, IT may need to categorize users by their organizational department, location, or responsibilities. Administrative users who will need access to administer the network server, as well as backup operators, should be included in a category of their own. Access to network servers should be restricted to only those administrators responsible for operating and maintaining the server.

In general, IT should prevent the use of a network server as a workstation. This will ensure that the server's users are restricted to those authorized to access the provided service and responsible for server administration. Correspondingly, IT should prevent having network services reside on and be provided by a user workstation. The security issues inherent with peer-to-peer networks is one reason larger IT organizations avoid them.

Determine Privileges by Category of User

To document privileges, create a matrix that shows users or user categories cross-listed with the privileges they possess. The privileges are customarily placed in groups that define the system resources or services a user can read, write, change, execute, create, delete, install, remove, turn on, or turn off. Most operating systems allow this, but do not provide printable documentation as a visual log.

Setup User and Data Authentication

Most microcomputer-based operating systems allow user authentication via the authentication capability provided at the desktop level.

There are usually two kinds of authentication for network servers: 1)   the kind provided with the operating system, commonly used for authenticating administrative users; and 2)   the kind provided by the network service software, commonly used for authenticating users of the service. A particular software implementation of a network service may use the provided authentication capability. Users of that service may need to have a local identity (usually a local account) on the server.

Authentication mechanisms are usually both technical and procedural. The most common approach is the use of passwords. But, other mechanisms, such as keys, tokens, and biometric devices, can be used. Biometrics is quickly becoming the most reliable and secure method. Biometric devices cost under $200 per workstation today and include fingerprint, voice, and retina identification.

Because authentication mechanisms, like passwords, require information to be accessible to the authentication software, IT must carefully document how that information will be protected. Authentication data is critical security information that requires a high level of protection.

For program and data files, the access controls provided by the operating system are the most common means used to enforce security via access privileges. IT might consider using encryption technologies to protect the confidentiality of sensitive information. Protection mechanisms should always be augmented by well-documented written user policies.

Intrusion Detection Strategies

Many of the common intrusion detection methods depend on the existence of various logs that systems produce and on the availability of auditing tools to analyze those logs. The IT security plan, part of the IT standard operating procedures, describes information that will be collected and managed to secure each computer. This will help IT select and install the appropriate software tools, and configure these tools to collect and manage network-wide security.

Maintain Adequate Backups to Restore System Integrity

To maintain the availability of services essential to a business, there should be some level of redundancy. For example, you may want to specify when to use hot, warm, and cold backups. Hot backups provide the capability to immediately switch configurations because the backup system runs in parallel with the primary system. Warm backups require some degree of reconfiguration before being used since they are not run in full parallel with operational systems. Cold backups must be started from a shutdown state and brought up-to-date before they are used.

It is common to develop the information content used by some network servers, such as those providing public services like the World Wide Web services on a different host. The authoritative version of this content is maintained (and backed up) on a second computer, and then transferred to the public server. This method makes it unnecessary to perform file backups of the Web page content itself. If the information is ever compromised, it can be restored by transferring a copy from the authoritative version.

However, backups of Web server logs are still required. Backups of configuration and installation information are also required unless there is a configuration management system that can be used to recover or rebuild a system from a trusted baseline.

Determining Who Connects to the Network

There are concerns relating to network connections that can affect the configuration and use of any one computer. Many organizations use a broadcast technology such as Ethernet for their local area networks. In these cases, information traversing a network segment can be seen by any computer on that segment. This suggests that you should only place *trusted* computers on the same network segment, or else encrypt information before transmitting it. Modems permit direct connectivity between one of the computers (and thus, potentially, the internal network) and the external networks reachable by the public telephone network. Many organizations forbid users to attach a modem to a workstation. It is a best practice method to not allow users to attach a modem to their workstation any time it is connected to the internal network.

It is also important to document the use of modems on a network server. As a general rule, do not attach modems to any servers other than servers whose purpose is to provide dial-in access. Some vendors may require direct modem access to provide a certain level of service. In this case, IT should establish procedures to enable the vendor to access the server via modem, and disconnecting the modem when it is not in use. Strong user authentication methods such as one-time passwords or token-based systems should be required for this type of access.

If the organization is small, it may be feasible to administer both workstations and network servers individually from their consoles. We recommend this method because it is the most secure. In most cases, however, workstations and servers are some distance from the offices of the system administrators. As a result, a significant amount of day-to-day administration is done from the administrator's workstation via the network. Providing the means for secure remote administration typically requires configuring the operating system and installing various software tools. This could include configuring the tools to encrypt administration commands and data that traverse the network between the target computer and the administrator's workstation. Administration procedures need to be defined and documented to configure the computer appropriately.

Secure Systems Not in Use

IT must determine the steps to ensure that the information contained on hardware being updated, replaced, removed from service, or disposed of is eliminated to the degree possible. For example, erase and reformat disks, rewrite tapes, and clear firmware passwords. The extent of the actions to take depends upon the sensitivity of the information. Hardware containing highly sensitive information may need to be physically destroyed to ensure that it cannot be used and that the information cannot be accessed. One best practice method is to remove and destroy fixed disk drives that might contain sensitive data. It is easier and less risky to simply remove and destroy such devices rather than take a chance on sensitive information leaking outside the organization.

Secure Systems before Deployment

Best practice indicates that IT must update computer deployment plans when relevant changes occur. New technologies, new security threats, updates to the network architecture, and the addition of new classes of users or new organizational units are sources of change.

The organization's security policy for networked systems should require that a detailed computer deployment plan be developed, implemented, and maintained whenever computers are being deployed. The plan must also provide access to those who require this information to perform their jobs. All new and updated servers should be installed, configured, and tested in a stand-alone mode or within test networks (i.e., not connected to operational networks) until they are completely configured and secure. Finally, all servers should present a warning banner to all users indicating that they are legally accountable for their actions and, by using the server, they consent to have their actions logged.

HARDEN SYSTEMS BY TESTING FOR VULNERABILITIES

How secure is your network? The Federal Reserve and insurers of banks and credit unions are so concerned about Internet connectivity and security of the information that many examiners are looking for proof of serious security testing. Across all types of industries, management is becoming more aware of the threats of unauthorized intrusion and has begun testing for it. The general term for this is penetration testing.

With penetration testing, a company hires someone to deliberately attempt to intrude into their system and discover and exploit vulnerabilities on their network. Typically, full-time security professionals (often consultants) perform this task. They use every known method to find vulnerabilities and penetrate the security of the network. They provide a deliverable to the company showing how they got in, the server's vulnerabilities, and what can be done to correct them. Depending on how far they get into the site, they can also prove the risk that the company faces by showing the internal data they collected.

The first decision management must make before conducting penetration testing is whether to have the security professional give the network administrators the scare of their life by not telling them what is about to happen. Or, should management engage the security professional to act as a liaison and work directly with the network administrators? There are real reasons for both options. It is up to you to determine which approach works.

The first option is meant to overcome the technical staff's attitude that they are so secure that no one can get in. Consider this the *wake up call* approach. The second option is intended to use security professionals to teach network administrators how to monitor and manage the network before and after the intrusion attempts.

There is a big argument about whether it is acceptable to give outside consultants inside information before executing penetration testing. After all, it is important to know just how far and how much information a determined intruder can get. However, not all intruders are working without inside information. Social engineering and inside information from employees can help any intruder get past even the best security. Disgruntled employees can be a big help to intruders or even take a direct part in an attack. So, when dealing with penetration testing, a combination of both approaches may be appropriate.

If you want to strengthen your organization's Internet security, you might do some research on the tools available for penetrating system security. There are a number of tools to test network security from the inside and the outside. Some of these are retail products and a number of excellent ones are shareware and freeware.

Penetration testing begins with a security audit to give a quick, efficient assessment of the security of information that can be obtained outside of an organization's controlled infrastructure. It focuses on the possibility of an unauthorized user outside of the organization exploiting known network and system vulnerabilities. There are several approaches to the security audit process, but generally they take place in the following phases:

- *Information gathering and active exploration.* This phase attempts to gather any information that is publicly available from external third-party sources. Examples of public information queries can include: DNS entries, domain registration information, published e-mail addresses, operating system identification, application identification, or online telephone directories. This is followed by a proactive examination of any system found during the first step.

- *Target identification and external vulnerability assessment.* This phase identifies potential services and vulnerabilities that may be exploited in the next phase, including the determination of a presumed network topology. This phase may include a modem detection attempt to determine if the site can be penetrated by dial-up connectivity (for those who leave PCs running in host mode overnight, or a modem turned on for the third-party software provider to dial-in and upload updates!)

- *Vulnerability verification.* Once the vulnerabilities are identified in the previous phases, the security professional will attempt to verify their test validity by intruding and exploring the systems. These tests are not intended to be disruptive to the operations, but be aware that disruptions can occur. For larger merchant sites, denial of service (DOS) attacks should be performed to determine if the systems are fully protected. DOS attacks are becoming extremely popular, as a way to shut down sites and steal CPU cycles for unauthorized processing.

- *Establishment and extraction.* Taking the testing to its final evolution means that the testers will attempt to access client files and move or copy files. They will attempt to establish a valid user id on the servers, and finally, they will provide the evidence of their penetration.

Where does IT go to engage these services, or buy the tools to offer their own security services? A few of the better known security services providers are PM Systems Corporation, a privately held company based in Chapin, South Carolina (*www.pmsyscorp.com*), Digital Defense Incorporated, in San Antonio, Texas (*www.*

digitaldefense.net), the Salinas Group, in New York, New York (*www.salinasgroup. com*), and finally Portculis Security Systems (*www.matrix0.org*). The vendors also offer a number of tools to purchase and use to measure the site's security or sell security services to clients.

Vendors, such as TelaFortis Systems, Inc. (*www.telafortis.com*) and Network Management Group, Inc (*www.nmgi.com*), provide other services such as a user's and site security handbook and assessments of your risk from internal mischief-makers.

Whether the information system is based on a Microsoft network, Unix, Linux, or another operating system, the default *out of the box* configuration is inherently insecure. Unless the system was installed yesterday and unless all of the applications and programs were released yesterday, it is certain that security weaknesses have been discovered and that patches are available. Installing patches, eliminating unnecessary weaknesses, and optimizing the system configuration will improve the network security. To harden systems from unauthorized access, all the current patches and service packs must be installed for all the software that is running. A daunting task at best, but a necessary one for a best practice organization.

PROTECTING THE SMALL TO MIDSIZE BUSINESS

Small and midsize businesses (SME) are targets for intrusion attacks via the Internet as much as large corporations and institutions. While we have attempted to address best practice methods for all businesses, some small organizations may feel left out because they lack the resources of larger organizations. Worse, they do not feel they are in danger. According to a recent report released by the Gartner Group, a large percentage of small businesses will suffer an intrusion between now and 2003. The report says that over half of those that manage their own network security and use the Internet for more than e-mail will be hit. It also says more than 60 percent of companies that are targeted will be unaware of the attacks, which are likely to include website hacking and the spreading of viruses. SMEs are especially vulnerable to malicious attacks because they usually cannot afford, or do not attract, personnel who have security experience. As a result, part-time employees or personnel without proper training or supervision often manage the company's network and Internet gateway accesses. SMEs also typically use regional ISPs that provide unknown levels of security, which puts them at a greater risk of an attack. Gartner suggests four best practice steps for SMEs to strengthen their network security:

1. *Security checkup.* SMEs connected to the Internet should consider contracting with a security firm to conduct an audit and risk assessment of their networks. The effort should include an internal network security audit and an external penetration test. That should take place whenever an SME makes major changes to its website or firewall, and at a minimum, once a year.

2. *Firewall configuration.* Ensuring that a proper firewall is installed is crucial. SMEs should focus on firewall appliances (*www.sonicwall.com*) that provide a base

level of security without requiring detailed security knowledge. SMEs should request quotes for managed firewall and intrusion detection services from ISPs.

3. *Boundary services.* Scanning incoming e-mail for viruses (more on this below) is a crucial security measure. SMEs can use either desktop or server-side antiviral protection. SMEs should take immediate action to disallow relay and halt the entry of spam into their environments.

4. *Consolidated remote access with strong authentication.* SMEs that provide dial-in access to e-mail and other enterprise systems should eliminate desktop modems and use consolidated modem pools and remote access servers. SMEs should require the use of hardware tokens to authenticate remote users.

According to Gartner, those four security measures will protect more than two-thirds of SMEs that are connected to the Internet. SMEs that manage highly sensitive environments, such as law firms, regional banks, independent insurance agencies, and state and local government agencies, should plan for additional precautions or outsource security operations to an experienced provider, according to one Gartner Group report.

Boundary services software is important to hardening system access and screening for harmful software agents. Boundary services software literally sits between the system or network and the Internet gateway. It guards against a number of types of intrusions. We reviewed four applications that fit into the category of boundary service software: Elron Software's Command View Message Inspector, Symantec's Mail-Gear, Content Technologies' Mail Sweeper, and Tumbleweed Communications' WorldSecure/Mail. These applications allow you to set up customized rules and use content-filtering engines, based on statistical processing or natural-language algorithms, to catch messages with confidential company information, inappropriate language, or large attachments that eat up network bandwidth. The most important feature of these products is their ability to scan e-mails and attachments for sensitive information on upcoming or current projects, legal information, and the like. They can be configured to scan e-mail messages for key words and phrases, and the products will find a message that contains those items. They will then discard the message and notify the user, send the message back to the user, or, in the case of Mail Sweeper and World-Secure/Mail, send it to a quarantine location for further evaluation by an administrator. All of these solutions permit setting up user exceptions so that trusted parties outside the organization can be kept in the e-mail loop on pertinent projects. Scanning for sensitive information, while an important feature, is also the most difficult to configure. Learning the rule-writing nuances of these products takes practice and patience.

These products are also important to help prevent, or minimize the threat, of libel suits. If you use an e-mail-filtering package in conjunction with a web-filtering solution to set up and enforce policies that monitor a user's use of the Web or prevent users from accessing inappropriate websites, you will be in a better position to defend against lawsuits or employee claims. Content Technologies, Elron Software, Tumbleweed Communications, and vendors such as Surf Watch offer separate web-filtering packages. An acceptable use policy that blocks or alerts managers and human resources departments to racist, sexist, or other blatantly libelous correspondence can protect a company from inadvertently creating a hostile work environment.

Finally, boundary services include e-mail filtering and can help the network and employees operate more efficiently. All four products listed above can block attachments based on file type, so executables and MP3 files can be kept off the network. MailSweeper and WorldSecure/Mail can even block messages based on attachment file size, a feature available in many e-mail systems as well. If you don't want to deprive employees of these files, MailSweeper and WorldSecure/Mail let you defer delivery of certain file types or sizes until the end of the day. This feature is important for networks with less bandwidth, as it cuts down on network traffic during business hours. The software's ability to recognize and eliminate spam mail and e-mail from known problem domains (web addresses) also helps keep the network clean and bug-free.

Unfortunately, a determined user can get around any of these products. None of them can scan http-based e-mails sent from free Internet accounts such as Yahoo! Mail or Hotmail. Elron and WorldTalk can take care of this problem via their web-filtering products. An e-mail-filtering system lets you control things that are within your control, such as the type and size of files users are sending via corporate e-mail accounts and their contents. It is still up to you to decide how rejected messages are handled. But, these packages may protect someone from the consequences of doing something he or she did not mean to do—like hitting the send button a moment too soon.

Securing a network from Internet and e-mail attacks does not have to cost a fortune. As an example of a best practice case, Network Management Group, Inc. (NMGI), Hutchinson, Kansas, implemented Linux mail gateways outside their existing firewall to filter e-mail for SPAM and viruses before they reach the internal network. This discussion may be a little too technical for some readers. But, those in either the Unix, or Linux, world will feel right at home. The purpose of presenting this solution is to show how much can be done to protect systems and eliminate SPAM with inexpensive shareware and freeware tools provided over the Internet. You do not have to spend a fortune to protect yourself!

NMGI used two Linux mail servers running Qmail (http://www.qmail.org.) The two servers act as primary and secondary servers for load balancing and redundancy for backup. At the heart of each server, NMGI runs Qmail-Scanner (http://qmail-scanner. sourceforge.net) on each message injected into the mail queue, whether the message is coming into, or going out of, the network. Qmail-Scanner can be integrated to work with nearly every major antivirus software vendor, as well as the Spam Assassin (*http: //spamassassin.org*) daemon for Unix and Linux. NMGI then chose to run Sophos for virus definitions, primarily because Sophos supports an excellent front-end tool called Sophie (*www.vanja.com/tools/sophie/*). Sophie loads the definitions into memory and provides access to them through Sophos' Libsavi libraries. This eliminates the need to execute a binary file for every new message accepted into the queue, reducing overall CPU time to process the message. The daemon then only needs to be restarted when new virus definitions are put in place. All *dat* files are updated automatically via the web. Trend (*www.antivirus.com*) is another antivirus vendor that provides libraries (Libsapi in this case) to their definitions. Trophie (*www.vanja.com/tools/trophie/*) has been written to utilize these libraries as a daemon.

Qmail-Scanner can be run even without an AV solution. It has an integrated perl-scanner that can do pattern matching on message headers such as *Subject: ILOVEYOU* which is a notorious visual basic script (VBS) virus. It can also be configured to disallow certain file extensions, restrict attachment size (stop large audio/video sharing via email), and do a number of other things.

In the most recent versions of Qmail-Scanner, support has been added for the Spam Assassin daemon *SPAMed*. This allows every message to be virus checked and spam checked in one pass. SpamAssassin uses a wide range of heuristic tests on mail headers and body text to identify spam based on a set of scoring rules. When SPAMed is run in this manner, it is known as global configuration. Managing user preferences is not possible because the mail delivery is not being done locally. This forces NMGI to use a higher spam threshold to eliminate the number of false-positives detected. In a single month, this solution tagged 11,186 messages as spam with less than 0.3 percent false-positives. This increases the number of false-negatives to over 4 percent but keeps the end users happy. Running SpamAssassin on a mail server hosting local accounts enables per-user configuration, allowing you to lower the threshold, and bring the number of false-negatives down while allowing users to white-list the false-positives.

Once the incoming mail has been scanned and determined to be clean, it is then delivered to the NMGI internal network via a port-forward on the firewall. This is one of the most secure methods of mail delivery that can be achieved. The firewall can be configured to accept the mail on a non-standard port, and only accept connections to that port from the mail gateway(s) doing the scanning. This prevents malicious users from delivering e-mail directly to an internal mail server bypassing the gateways.

As noted earlier, this entire solution is completely based on open-source solutions. A company could decide to integrate a corporate anti-virus solution, such as Symantec. Open AntiVirus (*www.openantivirus.org/*) hopes to be the solution to make this 100 percent free in the near future!

CONCLUSION

This chapter focused on aspects of managing technology where best practices can make a difference. It began with the deployment of software, because this is where it all begins. Most software problems can be identified and rectified in the deployment stage. Deployment occurs whether planned or not. If deployment is not planned, software can cost a lot of money for support and lost productivity. If deployment is planned, then deployment costs must be a part of the software investment analysis.

Hardware deployment and support are two other critical areas where IT must standardize and document their approach to provide users the right hardware.

Finally, we discussed issues about securing technology infrastructures and stressed the importance of deploying best practices methods for secure computing in this decade.

CHAPTER SIX

Managing Information Technology Staff and User Education

Technology professionals understand that their responsibilities only begin with planning and managing technology software and hardware. The greater responsibility, and perhaps the greater benefit to the organization, comes from how well IT staff is managed and the quality of training and education provided to users. Properly planned and executed, technology training and education increases end-user productivity and increases the utilization of technology. The education program must be formal, with documented processes and budget line items to ensure that both IT staff and users stay current. Best practice organizations know that the dollars spent on education are returned in the form of increased productivity.

EDUCATION AND TRAINING OF USERS AND INFORMATION TECHNOLOGY STAFF

Best Practice methods classify *education* and *training* as separate activities. Training is considered to be basic instruction—as in how *to do* something. In the early days of distributed systems, when personal computers first became widely deployed, users needed more training. Personal computing was not common and users needed very basic instructions, such as how to turn systems on and off as well as how to print. Training is also needed for signing onto networks and backing up files.

Education goes deeper into using technology. For instance, you may have a training session on Microsoft Excel to explain the basic features and functions. Taking the time to show users how to change options, styles, and use templates is important. As users become more familiar with a product like Excel, the number of sessions and the depth of training will change. Still, at least one training session is needed annually for new employees or users who have changed positions and now need to use Excel (as an example.) Best practice organizations take the next step and educate users on specific workbooks used in the business. For instance, the accounting department may have a number of workbooks for end-of-month reporting, creating graphs, or data analysis. A formal session to educate users on how these specific workbooks are used improves the user's ability to facilitate them.

Reading the example above, an IT professional may have thought, "Wait a minute, I'm no accountant! I can't teach accountants how to use Excel to do accounting!" They would be absolutely right. Training and education are organization-wide activities and not necessarily the total responsibility of IT alone. Many companies should consider having an education coordinator.

Role of the Education Coordinator

The greatest barrier facing IT in continuing to deploy and support advanced technologies is the continued availability of knowledgeable and experienced technology staff. IT has made great advancements over the past few years, but the struggle to attract and keep technicians continues. If best practice organizations plan to create and support emerging technologies, then IT must have qualified technical staff such as web administrators and content developers, database administrators, and so forth. The organization must also execute an education plan to allow users to maximize the organization's investment in technology.

This means the organization must create a focus on training employees to use the technology that is being deployed. Because there has been no one to manage and coordinate training and education in the past, the focus has been only on low-level training, such as showing a user how to turn the system on, navigate to a few tools, and perhaps print documents. To truly benefit from technology, organizations must be proactive and institute a technology education program for all users. Educating users goes beyond simply surface utilization of the computer to providing more depth on the applications being used and how to access information directly.

To this end, best practice organizations appoint an education coordinator. Today, the position of education coordinator is relatively new. The education coordinator may be in either IT or Human Resources. One of the primary objectives of the education coordinator is to evaluate staff knowledge and recommend training. The education coordinator should be very familiar with the functions performed and the needs of each department. The education coordinator does not have to be a technology professional, but should have good computer skills and a general understanding of the primary applications the business uses.

For instance, the education coordinator might conduct in-house training for front office applications like Microsoft Office and similar applications. The education coordinator also brings in outside trainers for specialized applications, such as accounting, manufacturing, or distribution. The education coordinator ensures that the trainers tailor their presentations to the specific needs of the organization, and do not simply present general product overviews. The education coordinator also prepares assessments for attendees to complete at the end of each training session to track the value and quality of the instruction given. These training assessments are extremely important. Going into the session, users know that they will be required to complete an assessment, which is very much like a *test* (the word test can be intimidating to attendees, so we avoid it).

This assessment lets management know if the trainer presented the information requested, and to what degree each of the attendees absorbed the information presented. If properly prepared, the assessment will also let the education coordinator know where specific users need additional help.

The education coordinator must work closely with department heads, as well as IT, to identify needs and potential areas where technology can be used to leverage staff and increase productivity. To be effective, the organization must carefully define the role of the education coordinator and develop a method of tracking the value of the education to the users. It is important that this position is seen to have value and not as simply another overhead position. Most trainers can provide generic training for applications such as Microsoft Windows, Microsoft Office (Word, Excel, PowerPoint, etc.), the Internet and so forth. The education coordinator will arrange training based on the needs of the users.

The education coordinator must understand the goals and objectives of the organization and be able to convey these to management, so that the success of the position can be tracked. Not investing enough in this position, or staffing the position with the wrong person, can have a severe negative impact on the company. In the beginning, the training of staff will be demanding. However, once the initial training cycle is complete, the demands on staff as well as the education coordinator will drop. For this reason, many companies assign the duties of the education coordinator to a person with other responsibilities if the company is not large enough to require an extensive year-round program. This does not mean that the position is not important and should not receive a high level of exposure. It just means that for the first year the education program is in effect, there will be a greater demand as everyone *catches up*. After that, there should be regular periodic training for new employees and those who have changed positions and need to be educated on applications that are new to them.

Training and Education Methods That Work

There is no one way to conduct effective education. In fact, one of the challenges for the education coordinator is to use a range of methods that best convey the knowledge and skills the company needs users to have. Since people learn in different ways, the education coordinator's goal should be to provide the type of education that the learner needs. The education coordinator, therefore, must be knowledgeable about the various methods for training and education. There are two mainstream theories of thought on how technology users learn. One theory believes the three primary learning mechanisms are visual, auditory, and kinesthetic (by doing.) Another more complex theory, called Multiple Intelligence Theory, believes there are eight learning mechanisms that include: math and logic, spatial, linguistic, music, kinesthetic, intrapersonal, interpersonal, and environmental. It is beyond the scope of this book to go into detail on these theories. To pursue more on the concept of multiple intelligence theory, research the work of Howard Gardner who developed this concept.

While multiple intelligence theory sounds very intriguing, understanding and managing a learning style that is divided into three categories, rather than eight, is much simpler. Therefore, we suggest that education coordinators focus on the three style learning model. Assessment tests can determine the dominant learning style, but we have found that observant interviewing can reveal much about a person's learning style. Remember that people do not learn through only one of the three styles. They usually need to have all styles present to learn most effectively.

When you are having a conversation with a visual learner, they will say things like, "I see what you mean" or "I can't picture that." Many of their phrases will have a visual word as a clue to the learner's style. An auditory learner will tend to have sound words present in their sentences. Phrases like "I hear you" or " sounds right to me" are good indicators of an auditory learner. Finally, a kinesthetic learner will tend to have more action words in their phrases. "Let's get to it" or "I can do this" are usually not words of action in this context, but rather the words of someone who has to do, touch, and feel the learning. When assessing people's learning needs, remember that they learn the most when they are taught in their primary style.

If the education coordinator is attempting to educate users how to get data out of a financial system, import it into a spreadsheet, and graph the results, they would design the training for three types of learners. Visual learners will need to be shown. So the instructor must show them what the data looks like in the financial system, illustrate how the import facility works, and demonstrate the many different ways of creating graphics. The auditory learner needs to hear more description and specific steps, while the kinesthetic learner will probably need to actually do the exercise of exporting data before they are comfortable with the process.

It is believed that users will learn most easily and quickly through their primary learning style. But sometimes multiple styles are needed to make training effective. We have been associated with a company, K2 Enterprises, *www.k2e.com,* that has provided technology-based continuing education to certified public accountants for a number of years. Our style is to discuss and demonstrate. In the case of Excel, we can discuss a specific function or feature and demonstrate with a screen projector and computer exactly how the function or feature works. This covers two of the primary learning mechanisms. However, we routinely have attendees who come to our seminars and complain that the session is not *hands on.* They are kinesthetic learners and want to actually do the exercises themselves.

Therefore, the best seminars would use computers to meet the requirements of all three primary learning mechanisms, right? Not necessarily. As we tell our seminar attendees, lecture style and hands-on style are dramatically different. Hands-on is not necessarily the best approach for all training sessions. In an eight-hour seminar, I can convey a lot more information by lecturing (discussing) and demonstrating than I can if everyone had a computer and were experimenting on their own. Hands-on sessions tend to cover a much lower level of content for beginner users who have not been exposed to what is being taught. In a kinesthetic learning environment, everyone in the seminar usually progresses at the learning rate of the slowest participant. This can be very frustrating and actually can be detrimental to those in the seminar who are quicker to grasp a new concept, tool, or process. In the case of our seminars, we provide examples and sample exercises that the kinesthetic learners can take back to their work areas and practice. This is a reasonable compromise that seems to work well as a best practice to follow.

Not all training has to include live presentations. For computer training, the education coordinator may include combinations of videotapes, audiotapes, and hands-on training where appropriate for the information conveyed. Other types of training include books, satellite, CD-based interactive training, web-based interactive training, seminars, and one-on-one training. Generally, novice users learn better with hands-on training, and intermediate and advanced users learn better by demonstration. Executive learners tend to make more progress by keeping a list of tasks that are a problem and receiving periodic instruction by an individual. I like the *personal trainer* approach, for busy executives with serious time constraints. Like personal fitness training, each executive session should focus on specific objectives. Keep the sessions short and to the point, and end with a positive benefit that has been achieved. If executives fail to benefit from a personal training session, they stop using them and often stop funding for staff training because they fail to see the benefits.

Very few software packages today come with extensive printed manuals. The preferred method, at least for software manufacturers, is to place manuals on the software CD. This is cheaper for them, and allows users to view manuals online and only print sections they need. However, many times users will call technical support for answers because they do not have the manual available to them, or do not know how to access it. A best practice is to create an online manual folder, or make the manuals available via the company's Intranet; then make sure everyone knows how to access the information. For the specialized software or custom programs developed in-house, write specific material that can be used to teach the business's best practices to users. Similarly, productivity software (word processing, spreadsheets, presentations, e-mail, and databases) needs to be taught the same way. It is easy to find books on Microsoft Office and similar tool type products, but these fall short when it comes to working with the templates and files used by a specific company. Written documentation on using such files will make users more productive. IT often misunderstands users' support calls, thinking they need help with *Excel,* when what they really want is help using a specific workbook file. Having resources available and documented is necessary to answer these questions.

Conducting a User Assessment

Best practice organizations create standards, by function, in different areas of knowledge. The organization should assess every individual against these standards, and then create a plan(s) of study for each individual, or group of individuals, and track it in a spreadsheet or a database. This is usually done as a function of the personnel or human resource department. Again, organizations are encouraged to pre-assess and post-assess all material taught to understand user progress. The assessment process may seem uncomfortable at first, but stick with it; learning effectiveness will be greatly increased over time.

Conducting an Information Technology Staff Assessment

IT assessment tends to be a very touchy area, and many IT managers are reluctant, or do not feel qualified, to assess the current skills of their staff. However, an honest assessment is necessary to ensure that the IT staff has the skills necessary to move the organization forward. An important part of the assessment process is to identify all positions and expertise that are needed. This assessment should include new positions, such as web content developer, web administrator, SQL database administrator, as well as the more traditional positions such as network administrator, help desk technician, and so forth. A previous chapter identified several of these positions, and provided a brief description of their responsibilities.

While the education coordinator will be active in developing training for the users, IT professionals will need specialized training above that of the average application user. This training will come from a number of sources. It is also important to provide IT professional staff continuous training to keep them current with emerging technologies that might prove economically beneficial to the organization. We see many occasions where IT department management is hesitant to recommend implementation of new technologies because they, or their staff, are not familiar with the new technologies. Frankly, they are afraid that if they fail, their jobs may be on the line. In a couple of recent cases, we recommended the deployment of thin client technology using Citrix, *www.citrix.com,* software solutions. IT balked and further discussions revealed that the technical staff was concerned with their knowledge and ability to implement the solution. After careful discussions with management, we were able to hire qualified installers, as well as send the IT staff to school for the necessary certification. With qualified IT staff so difficult to find and keep today, no organization wants to *throw away* the technical support staff they have. The organization must recognize the investment necessary to keep qualified staff and keep them sharp on the technology, to better serve the mission and objectives of the organization.

The first step for the IT manager, or perhaps even a higher-level manager, is to prepare an IT staff assessment. As with the user assessment, the idea of the IT staff assessment is to determine what expertise is present today, and what is lacking. From this assessment, management can easily identify where the weaknesses are and where additional skills are required. Exhibit 6.1 gives you an example of one possible assessment matrix. This example is meant only as a starting place for you to design your own.

Benefits of a Certified IT Staff

The arguments for and against the benefits of being certified have raged for the past decade. There are a number of truths on both sides. However, our own experience indicates that there are obvious benefits to hiring certified technicians and to having your existing staff certified. Now you must understand that your authors are somewhat prejudiced on the subject. Both of us are certified through a number of certification authorities. We both have prejudices toward higher education and the importance of both training and education for technologists.

Exhibit 6.1   IT Staff Assessment Form

Skills/Competencies	IT POSITIONS										
	IT Manager	Network Administrator	Help Desk Technician	Web Content Developer	Web Administrator	Communications	Technician	Analyst	Programmer	Other	
											Legend:
Technical:											5 = Completely Meets Expectations
Programming											3 = Partially Meets Expectations
Systems Analysis											1 = Does Not Meet Expectations
Database											0 = Not Applicable
Networking											
PCs											
Data Communications											
Voice Communications											
Internet											
Main Computer											
Other											
Overall Skills											
Management											
Planning											
Administration											
Training											
Other											

Consider this example. Almost everyone has worked with a certified public accountant, or, as they are lovingly called, a CPA. A CPA does your taxes. A CPA audits your books. CPAs audit the results of polls and contests and are generally considered the most trusted profession. (All Enron jokes aside, we believe this is still true today.) Now I know a number of accounting professionals who are at the top of their game and know just as much as an accountant who happened to sit for and pass the certification exam. In comparing two accountants with no prior knowledge of their ability or skill level, and one has CPA after their name and the other does not—is there an assumption to be made? Yes, that the CPA completed a battery of exams that tested his or her knowledge of the field and has proven their knowledge by passing those tests. In the real world, I know a number of non-CPAs who are very qualified. However, I also know several who have an accounting degree, but are not as knowledgeable as a CPA and have not met the requirement to continue their education past collecting a college diploma. With this example, you can immediately see some of the benefits of certification. Comparing two technicians, I have no way of knowing which is more qualified without trial and error (and sometimes the error part can be too costly and painful.) Yet, if one is certified and the other is not, I know that the one who is certified went the extra distance to prove their level of knowledge and expertise.

Qualifying technical professionals on certification alone can sometimes be taken to an extreme. Bob recently had a potential client ask if he was a Microsoft Certified Systems Engineer (MCSE.) Bob does not regularly install Windows NT or Windows 2000 operating system, so he did not see the value in sitting for the exam and keeping the certification up-to-date. Bob has a number of certifications from Microsoft, Novell, and other organizations in addition to several advanced degrees, including a Doctorate in Computer Science, but not the certification the client wanted. It is important to understand what certifications have value and under what circumstances each certification fits. If Bob does not spend the majority of his time deploying and supporting Windows 2000 users, then an MCSE designation does not have value to him, or his employer. Hiring a technician who is an MCSE for a position as web developer or SQL database administrator does not necessarily have value. While any certification is certainly commendable, the employer should look for certifications that pertain to the position the IT professional is intending to fill. For instance, for a position of Microsoft SQL database administrator, a Microsoft SQL certification would be of value. However, if the organization uses Oracle or IBM DB2 databases, while the Microsoft SQL would certainly have value, certification and experience for either Oracle or DB2 would have greater value.

There are also economic benefits in having staff certified. Certification usually involves specific training on the vendor's product. (Computer manufacturers and vendors provide certification training, sometimes for free, but usually for a cost.) The technician must also practice and study prior to taking the certification exam, so they are more familiar with the product. And finally, but most importantly, the technician learns the manufacturer's preferred methods during the certification process. For instance, as a follow-up to the example above, Bob was determined to get a Microsoft certification and went to Microsoft certified professional certification training for Microsoft NT. During the training Bob, who by this time had installed several dozen implementations of Microsoft NT, discovered a couple of installation steps that easily cut off 30 minutes of installation time, compared to the steps he had used previously. He learned the manufacturer's recommended process. Certification training can reduce time invested in learning about a product, improve the way a product is implemented, and make implementations more cost effective by reducing the time involved.

There is a downside to certification training as well. We constantly hear comments on the quality of training and how training differs across different regions. Many vendors evolve from an education and process improvement orientation for their products, to a cross-marketing approach to generate more sales, and make more money on certification. Thus, training becomes a profit center for their business. Most certifications have required renewals that occasionally pay good dividends, but many of them are unnecessary or redundant training. Carefully review the available programs and determine the programs that fit best in your organization.

Best practice IT departments will have a training plan for each person on staff as part of each staff professional's career plan. Tying certification to compensation helps give IT staff the incentive to continue training and reaching for higher goals. According to recent studies, bonus pay increased for IT certified professionals, but steadily declined for individuals with technical skills that had not been certified (This survey was conducted by Foote Partners LLC, an IT workforce research company.) The reports assessed the skills and pay of more than 29,000 IT professionals in about 1,800 North American and European companies. Certification bonus pay rose 4 percent from the fourth quarter (October through December) of 2000 to the fourth quarter of 2001, reaching a median average of 8.3 percent of base pay. That is slightly above the 8.1 percent average for skilled technicians that had not been certified. For the 83 skilled technicians covered by the report, bonuses fell 13.3 percent from the fourth quarter of 2000 to the fourth quarter of 2001. Eighty percent of certified IT professionals said they plan to pursue additional certifications in 2002. The best practice trend is for employers to cover the cost of certification. Foote estimated that half of employers covered all certification costs, up from 45 percent in 2001.

Project management professional certification provided the best bonuses, averaging 14 percent of base pay. Many of the fastest-growing certifications were security related, including GIAC Certified Intrusion Analyst and GIAC Certified Firewall Analyst. Siebel Certified Consultant and Siebel Customer Certified Consultant grew 17 percent and 14 percent respectively, between the third and fourth quarters of 2001. This suggests that companies are taking a more pragmatic approach to CRM installations and investing in having their staff properly trained.

A final word of caution on certification fallout. While best practice organizations are paying bonuses for certified IT staff, managers cite compensation as a reason not to require staff to be certified! For example, they cite that Microsoft certified engineers demand as much as 11 to 15 percent more than a technician without Microsoft certification. We have also been told that technicians demand huge raises after they receive their certification or threaten to go elsewhere. At face value, these seem like reasonable concerns. But, after further analysis, we found that, in those cases where the individuals requested raises after certification, they had been grossly underpaid all along. After being certified, they realized that they were more marketable and were able to cast off the shackles of oppression. These people would have eventually left anyway! In regard to hiring certified IT professionals versus non-certified, we have found that persons who have received their certifications are better trained and more committed to the organization. In a word, they are more professional. During the year 2000 crisis, we had clients who wanted to hire college freshmen to recode their systems because they were *cheaper*. In reality, a professional programmer could do the coding of three inexperienced temporary hires with fewer errors, so there was really no savings. Hiring cheap technology staff will, in the long run, cost the entire organization.

Key Industry Certifications

Cisco Career Certification allows candidates to become certified at various levels of technical proficiency across the disciplines of network design or network support. Cisco is well respected for the quality and depth of their training. Cisco certification has great value for IT professionals who are pursuing technical careers that are networking and communications specific.

There are several certifications along the Network Support path, including Cisco Certified Network Associate (CCNA), Cisco Certified Network Professional (CCNP), and two different Cisco Certified Internetwork Expert (CCIE) certifications:

CCIE-Routing and Switching, and CCIE–ISP Dial. CCNAs focus on relatively simple networks, and CCNPs have the expertise required to install, configure, operate, and troubleshoot more complex Cisco-based networks that encompass LAN/WAN routing and LAN switching.

CCIEs represent the highest-attainable certification level under Cisco Career Certifications and ideally represent at least two years of on-the-job experience, in addition to the knowledge associated with the CCNP level. There are two types of CCIE certifications: CCIE–Routing and Switching and CCIE–ISP Dial, which focus primarily on remote access technology and expertise.

MCP (Microsoft Certified Professional) is for individuals who want to demonstrate their expertise with a particular Microsoft product. Microsoft also has some specialty certifications such as *MCP + Internet* where individuals can obtain a certification with a specialty in Internet technologies. Individuals are qualified to plan security, install and configure server products, manage server resources, extend servers to run CGI scripts, or ISAPI scripts; monitor and analyze performance; and troubleshoot problems. Candidates must pass three exams: Internetworking MSTCP/IP, NT server, and Internet Information Server 4.0. The *MCP + Site Building* specialty is designed for website developers. Individuals with this certification are qualified to plan, build, maintain, and manage websites using Microsoft technologies and products. Candidates are required to pass two of the specialty exams: Designing and Implementing Web Sites with MS FrontPage 98, Designing and Implementing Commerce Solutions with MS Site Server 3.0 Commerce Edition, or Designing and Implementing MS Visual Interdev 6.0.

MCSE (Microsoft Certified Systems Engineer) designation is probably the most widely known and provides a valid and reliable measure of technical proficiency and expertise with desktop, server, and networking components. Candidates are required to pass four operating systems exams (Networking Essentials, Windows 2000 Workstation or Windows 95 or Windows 98, Windows 2000 server, Windows 2000 Server 4 in the Enterprise 4, etc.) and two elective exams.

MCSD (Microsoft Certified System Developer) is designed for developers who use Microsoft's development and programming tools to test the user's ability to build web-based, distributed, and commerce applications. Candidates are required to pass three core technology exams that include Solutions Architectures, Designing and Implementing Desktop Applications with MS Visual Basic 6.0 or Visual C++ 6.0, and Designing and Implementing Distributed Applications with MS Visual Basic 6.0 or Visual C++ 6.0 and one elective (FrontPage 98, Site Server 3.0, etc).

MCT (Microsoft Certified Trainer) is qualified instructionally and certified technically by Microsoft to deliver Microsoft Official Curriculum instructor-led courses to computer professionals. Only trainers who intend to deliver Microsoft Official Curriculum instructor-led courses at Microsoft Authorized Technical Education Centers are eligible to become Microsoft Certified Trainers. Once you have been approved as an MCT, your MCT credentials will be accepted in all Microsoft education channels.

MOUS (Microsoft Office User Specialist) is not as widely known as the certifications above, but might have a place in your organization. Candidates must pass all four of the expert exams for Word, Excel, PowerPoint, and Access.

We recommend visiting specific vendor websites and look for more information on certification programs that might have value to your organization, price these and then determine the quality of the actual training that is offered before making your decisions.

Ongoing Technical Education for IT Staff

Like many young people, I did not really enjoy school. If you had told me as a teenager that I would pursue a career that required ongoing continuous education, I would have questioned your sanity. But, that is exactly what happened. The technology profession, like tax accounting, medicine, or some fields of law, requires continuous education to keep up with changes. Best practice companies understand this and provide the appropriate training and education for IT staff to keep them current. These companies realize the power of technology has to leverage much more costly human resources. Technology increases productivity if used properly. New technology can sometimes be used to update processes and continue leveraging resources. Keeping staff up-to-date is important for another reason. Operating software and application software changes yearly. Business must protect its investment by keeping IT staff current on changes and ensuring that systems are running optimally. Finally, investing in IT staff adds to their value to the company and makes technology professionals better able to perform their mission.

While seminar presentations work very well for users, they seldom make sense for IT staff. Most IT departments do not have the numbers of staff to justify the cost of bringing in specialized presenters. The best practice method is to send IT staff to annual national or regional conferences where they can be exposed to a number of relevant seminars and talk with vendors over period of a few days. When it is not financially realistic to send all of your staff, send one or two to different conferences. Charge them to bring back the knowledge and present updates to IT in-house staff. Giving staff an assignment to train staff, or implement new technology upon their return, eliminates the urge to make such conferences a vacation!

Perhaps one of the greatest benefits I derive from conferences is the opportunity to network (socially) with other attendees. Time spent talking with peers and swapping business cards has incredible returns on the investment cost of attending the conference. Sometimes businesses are pretty conservative on travel expenses and what they allow staff to expense back to the company. We certainly do not encourage a blank check. But for some IT management level staff, it is appropriate to socialize with other attendees, perhaps invite a potential vendor to dinner, and participate in other networking activities.

Other than conferences and applications training, IT will get most of their information from trade journals and online resources. Only three years ago, I subscribed to as many as 30 weekly and monthly trade journals. I read at least half of these page to page, just to keep up with emerging technology and new trends. Today, I receive less than five hardcopy publications, yet I am more current on technology than before. Why? Today, I subscribe to online services that deliver content to my desktop daily. I review the ones I subscribe to and delete anything else that comes along. I find that a lot of duplicate content exists across publications and can be easily skipped. Another plus is that I get the information days, and often weeks, before it is in print. Here are a few recommended sites that support best practices:

www.infoworld.com/   *www.networkcomputing.com/*
www.iwsubscribe.com/newsletters/   *www.techweb.com/*
www.zdnet.com/   *www.nwfusion.com/*
register.microsoft.com/regsys/   *www.tsif.com*

MANAGING ELECTRONIC INFORMATION

Any best practice organization should have an appropriate acceptable use policy in place that dictates how technology is used. As mentioned earlier, such policies are not optional. The policies often do not go far enough in educating users on the proper use of technology, particularly electronic correspondence. Nearly all companies today have exposure to losses due to mismanagement or negligence in properly managing electronic mail or instant messages. We have seen a significant rise in the number of court cases where electronic mail is a deciding factor.

Today, we are afloat in a sea of information; the Internet seems to have made this almost nonstop. Add to that, cable TV news, e-mail, voicemail, faxes, pagers, cellular phones, other intelligent appliances and the recent explosion of newspapers, magazines and books. Most information workers are simply overwhelmed. Data glut has become a serious workplace issue during the past twenty years. One estimate says the average worker spends more than half of his or her day processing documents. Office workers can spend hours reading and answering e-mail, not to mention voicemail, faxes, and so forth. Whereas e-mail was deemed to be a boon to communication and a tool to make business more competitive, it has become a bane to people responding to inboxes filed with daily *FYI* messages and other information that would not have been responded to previously.

According to Paul Saffo from the Institute for the Future in Menlo Park, California, it is not the information glut itself that causes problems, but rather our inability to process information. "Information overload is not a function of the volume of information out there," Saffo says. "It is a gap between the volume of information and the tools we have to assimilate the information into useful knowledge." No one doubts that information overload fuels stress and promotes faulty thinking. Over time, information overload reduces our attention span, confuses us about what is really important, and causes us to ignore information that does not attract our attention immediately.

To effectively deal with information overload, users must be taught to prioritize what is important, which journals or information sources are of consistent quality and deliver the information needed. Users must make a conscious effort to focus on what is important and then begin discarding the rest. It is tempting to scan all the mail received and to spend time reading promotional subscriptions. Just because you have access to all the information in the world does not mean you have to process it all. A best practice approach is to move your organization to JITI—just in time information. This process involves weeding out anything not of value at the moment, realizing that users can easily search the Internet and find the information later, if needed.

In informal canvassing of seminar attendees, we found that less than a fraction of one percent had received any formal training on how to manage their electronic mail. None had received any advice on the use of instant messaging, yet the number of instant messaging users rose significantly beginning in late 2001. In 2001, Gartner Group projected that instant messaging would be used in as many as 35 percent of businesses by 2005.

There are a few best practice methods to manage the flow of information electronically, in hardcopy, voice, and data that IT should pass on to users. IT must also ensure that communication policies are properly documented, so that all users are aware of them and comply. These best practice methods are:

- When information comes in, whether via e-mail, the Internet, or fax, users should generally read and act on the item in a reasonable period, or discard it quickly. Users should not fall into the habit of creating a backlog of articles, faxes, and computer messages for future action. Doing this may allow action items that are time-sensitive to be missed or not be responded to.

- It is a best practice that users establish specific times to check e-mail and other electronic correspondence and not fall victim to the habit of allowing mail to constantly interrupt their activities. Best practice is to turn off mail notifications (those dings, pop-up messages, or voice notices), unless the user is truly expecting an important message. This should be the exception, not the rule! A reasonable schedule is to check mail at the beginning of the workday, again around midmorning, after lunch, midafternoon, and before leaving for the day. Pick one or two times during the day to actually collect and respond to messages; the other times should be a quick scan to see if there is something that demands immediate attention. Just as e-mail is distracting, so are phone calls. Many users answer every call as it comes in during the day. Most workers are much more productive collecting phone messages and responding to them as a group two or three times during the day. This takes an incredible amount of discipline and is not necessarily the right approach for everyone. There are, of course, many people whose job is to answer the phone and respond as calls are received. The real point here is to have a plan for managing time that is appropriate to each user. Educate the users to execute and stay with that plan.

- Mobile workers will be discussed more later in this chapter. If you are a road warrior, or simply have large reading files to keep up with, a best practice we have followed for years is to keep a *traveling* file of materials you want to read. Carry them with you to read and digest when you are on the subway, or waiting for appointments, planes, or clients. We also have no problem ripping technical journals apart and keeping the *good stuff* for more detailed review or filing later. This way, we can quickly wade through a stack of hardcopy journals and end up with a small folder of pertinent information. (Just ignore the strange looks of people sitting around you as you rip your magazine apart!)

- Whenever possible, have staff screen and summarize materials. It is a best practice that any document filed must have an expiration date and authority (who assigned the date) before it is filed. When it comes time to clean out the files, there is no question as to what to toss.

- IT has estimated that more than 80 percent of the information received today is in an electronic form. While this means less hardcopy documents to file, it also means that computer systems become cluttered with saved files that slow system processes and create problems. Policies and procedures for document retention should also apply to electronic documents.

- Educating users to not read electronic documents in the same way they read hardcopy documents is a difficult, but critical, task. Electronic documents should be scanned with the reader focusing on specific information relevant to them. I have observed many users attempting to read online journal articles, software application manuals and lengthy online articles as they would read the printed copy, line-by-line. Users who attempt to do this generally experience less retention rate and increased stress. Online information should be scanned or searched for specific keywords and knowledge.

Managing Electronic Mail

Here are some simple, but important best practice mail management tips. Microsoft Outlook is our example mail application, but the suggestions are valid for GroupWise and other electronic mail clients as well.

- *Turn off mail notification.* It is a distraction, as users are interrupted several times during the day. For every distraction, it is estimated that 5 to 10 minutes of productive time is lost. These interruptions add up over the day. What would be the annual benefit of recovering up to 30 minutes a day per employee?

- *Do not respond to every message when checking mail.* Sometimes simply reading the message and moving on without a response is appropriate. If the message happens to be contentious, it is always best to wait until a calmer head prevails and put the message in an action file for response when the user has had time to consider an appropriate response. This avoids the *Oh no* second! The Oh no second happens when you press the send key and realize that the response may negatively impact your career!

- *Stay on point.* Do not mix several topics in the same response; it can be too confusing. E-mail should be kept short and to the point. For instance, when responding to a question on the status of an order from a supervisor, do not add a request for a leave at the bottom of the response! Where there is a need to make multiple requests or inquiries, it is always a best practice to send multiple messages.

- *Include the original message in the response.* Most e-mail clients have a setup option to include the original message at the bottom of the reply, so the person(s) receiving the response can see it. Where e-mail is the predominant method of communication, this helps refresh the recipient's memory. If you have ever received a message back that says, "Yes, I agree with your idea," and you cannot remember what he is talking about, you can appreciate the importance of this policy.

- *Organize mail.* We often see e-mail users that are overwhelmed by the mail they receive. We also see users who keep mail in their inbox, even after they have read and responded to the messages. In one case, I noticed a client inbox with 1487 messages! The potential for missing an important message in a list this long is huge! Users have not been trained how to create mail folders and move messages to folders for later archiving. Archiving mail is important because, with mail clients such as Outlook, the software must load information about every message, and that slows the application down. This also creates large unmanageable files that impact the application's performance. Can anyone manage a couple of thousand e-mail messages? Messages that are to be discarded should be deleted immediately. The user can set mail options to remove deleted mail from the Deleted Items folder upon exiting the mail client. Turn on the auto archive features to archive mail on a periodic basis. The archive cycle may differ, depending on how much mail a user receives and sends. Ninety-day archiving cycles typically work very well. Archiving retires mail and other information from active mail folders and keeps the active folders clean.

- *Create a policy for mail retention.* Retention of mail is a major issue in organizations today. Most have no policy. Without instruction, users either keep everything, or delete everything; both actions are incorrect. Anyone who has followed major court cases over the past few years, such as legal actions against Microsoft, Enron, and Anderson, knows that e-mail is an important part of the evidence collected. Courts may subpoena e-mail and management may be liable if the e-mail cannot be produced. Any relevant business mail should be kept for an extended period of time. The appropriate period must be defined in written policy and procedures. Users must be advised of their obligation to maintain this e-mail. We advise that IT must also have methods in place for retrieving historical mail, if requested by subject or by key words. If you have doubts, consult legal counsel knowledgeable in the area of electronic evidence and maintain their response for future reference.

- *Backup e-mail for future restoration.* It is a best practice to backup user mail folders on a regular basis. There is an option in setup to backup mail folders. Where users store mail on personal workstations or laptops that are not under the immediate control of IT, this is extremely important.

MANAGING THE MOBILE USER

According to Cahners In-Stat Group, about 21 million U.S. workers are working from remote locations in 2002. By 2005, that figure is expected to top 35 million. Employers should know what to do when employees work remotely. IT must have policies and procedures in place to properly manage the mobile worker.

First, allowing workers to work remotely should not be done just because an exception comes up. If it is a good idea to allow employees to work at home from time to time, IT must have mechanisms to support mobile workers, as part of the way business is conducted. Temporary approvals to work at home are risky and may expose your organization to unnecessary liability.

Telecommuting, small office home office, and the latest term, mobile office, are ways of addressing mobile workers. Mobile workers also talk about their virtual office. Whatever term is used, the bottom line is that people do not only work in conventional offices, they work in alternative work environments. Some of these alternate workplaces are consistent, such as a homebased office. Some individuals may work for extended periods at a client's office. From an IT support perspective, wherever the worker is working is a remote office because the location is remote to the primary place of business. The remote office may be applied to the SOHO, which implies the worker is working from their home, or in a very small office space. Telecommuting tends to focus on the workers who work at home, perhaps part-time, and needs access to corporate data when working away from their normal place of employment. The remote office is really about the ability to work productively from anywhere in the known universe, at anytime!

In the late eighties and early nineties, telecommuting emerged as a concept for workers employed in large metropolitan areas. At that time, the driving economic factors were the cost of real estate and gasoline, and air pollution problems from commuting travelers. Large corporations began deploying employees to work at customer sites and many allowed workers to work, at least part-time, at home. While telecommuting proved to have value, it also resulted in a sudden distribution of the company's knowledge workers. Knowledge workers are workers who deal primarily with information in their job and do not have to be in a specific location where to perform their tasks. Accountants, salesmen, or typists are knowledge workers as opposed to shop foremen, mechanics, or technicians that must physically touch the product they are working on and must be where that product is in order to work. Telecommuting started a slow revolution in how and where people work that has evolved to how it is applied today, and will continue to evolve.

By the late nineties, another issue was driving the work force—the lack of qualified staff. It became very difficult to beg, borrow, or hire experienced accountants in the mid-nineties. Business owners and managers had to become more creative in their hiring and work strategies. Young parents asked for, and received, flexible office time and the resources to work from home. The search for qualified staff led to the discovery that businesses could extend the pool of available talent, and not only benefit from local employees, but also from talent and expertise from across the country, or around the world, that they did not have before. If a business needed an accounting professional, a financial planner, or a computer engineer with unique expertise for a specific task, they could hire that individual for a specified period of time. When the task was complete, that person was no longer on the payroll. For many companies, the concept worked well and yielded tremendous benefits.

More recently, following the September 11, 2001 terrorist attacks, many companies were forced to set up remote offices for their employees in order to stay in business. As companies rethink their business contingency plans, they are including remote access as a strategic option. Having IT methodologies in place that support remote access and remote offices, whether the remote office is a single user or many users, enhances a company's ability to respond, compete, and survive.

Obviously, not everyone has embraced the idea of employees working at home. For instance, many senior managers have an overriding fear of the mobile worker. They have concerns about their ability to *manage remote staff* adequately. Many employees, on the other hand, called this the *control factor* or the *control myth*, because managers do not really have control to start with! Without a written plan to embrace the mobile worker that includes well-developed procedures and policies to govern their actions, many users are simply allowed to proceed.

We do not intend to be cynical of all managers, or to imply that mobile workers are necessary in all organizations. We do believe that best practice organizations look closely at how mobile workers could enhance their ability to compete and provide services while reducing costs, and then create methods to manage these workers effectively. Mobile workers create a new paradigm for business. Not only do problems appear, but not having a clear understanding and well-developed processes in place may cause the traditional office processes to collapse as well. However, the need for alternative work environments is strong so that the idea of working at home and remotely continues to simmer, as more progressive companies continue to support the process and evolve the employees.

Most IT professionals believe that the mobile worker could not have happened without the personal computer and the Internet. The Internet made it possible for anyone to work anywhere at anytime and to be in constant communication with anyone. Technology has thus given birth to the concept of the distributed office; the traditional office where we once worked had been distributed out into multiple locations.

There are obviously drawbacks to having a distributed office. For instance, a distributed office also means there are distributed staff. Having distributed staff quickly affects the decision making process. According to French Caldwell, in his article "The E-Workplace and Distributed Decision Making," Gartner Group Resource ID 351168:

> *Decision processes that worked when executives gathered in one place, formally in board meetings or informally after work hours, can't operate once the workplace is distributed. Many executives find moving from a centralized environment to a distributed environment a handicap, and have difficulties making the transition. But a distributed operation brings powerful benefits.*

With experience, and the retirement of older managers, e-business companies are beginning to create *smart offices* that are truly virtual. According to the Gartner Group, there is a high probability that the proliferation of *smart* technologies for mobile and wireless offices, to including virtual team collaboration, media content management, voice portals, and personal knowledge management, will increase dramatically over the next three years ("New Focus on Knowledge and Collaboration Begins in 2002," *The Knowledge Management Advantage* [*www.kmadvantage.com*], January 2002).

What the Employer Should Know and Do

To create a mobile work environment, employers must address the work environment as well as legal issues. The most common remote work environments will be at a customer site, a traveling site, or at the user's home. In all of these cases, employers must address the ergonomics of the employees' *workplace*. Believe it or not, there is risk to the employer anytime an employee works away from the office. A number of these risks will be addressed in the employee section below. There have been a number of court cases over the past decade finding against employers who required, or allowed, employees to work at home, but failed to enforce a proper work environment, as they would have in company office space. In fairness, there have also been cases where the court found in favor of the employer when an employee brought a claim and the court felt that the employer, in fairness, could not enforce standards in the home. Because the employee is working away from your office space, either by direction or by choice, you cannot assume that you do not have a responsibility for the workspace that the employee is using.

The next major issue of the remote worker is that of employees taking confidential information off the premises, or employees having remote access to confidential information. You must ensure that there are written privacy statements in place that describe the employees' responsibility for protecting confidential, private information from falling into unauthorized hands. This information could be data files containing company confidential information, or the transmission of electronic mail containing information with restricted access. Electronic mail may be one of the most overlooked avenues for conveying confidential information. Employees must understand that whenever they are sending or receiving business e-mail, from personal computers or computers provided by the employer, they have a responsibility to protect the confidentiality and the privacy of the information contained therein.

IT must also consider the technology that may be provided by employers to employees who work remotely. This technology applies as much to the software as the hardware. Routinely, employers are expected to provide computers, printers, software, and to pay for remote communications. This includes licensed software for general tasks such as word processing and spreadsheets. Aside from providing the tools necessary to work remotely, the employer must also define what the employee is authorized to do with these tools. For instance, it is not acceptable, in most cases, for an employee to allow other members of their family or friends to use company-owned equipment. Why? The potential for inadvertent distribution of confidential information is one reason. Also consider the repercussions if a family member or friend uses a company computer and e-mail software to send inappropriate mail, or to visit websites that would be deemed inappropriate to the workplace. Employees using company-owned hardware and software are bound by the same acceptable use policies as employees working in the primary office. Employers are usually also bound by the same policies and legal requirements for the conduct of their remote employees as for the traditional office employees. When you update written policy and procedure manuals next, consider the ramifications of remote offices versus company-owned office space. Adjust any wording necessary to specifically reflect that company policy applies to both traditional office workers and mobile workers.

Employers must also make sure they have the right perception, and trust, of their mobile workers. If your managers are from the *old school* that staff must be supervised at all times and that good employees come in early and leave late (regardless of what they do in between), then you should stay away from a mobile work force. If, however, there are methods, procedures and policies in place to measure a person's performance and you trust your people to get the job done without being watched all day—you are a mobile worker candidate.

In considering allowing staff to work outside of the office, the first question has to be "Will the impact on productivity be positive or negative?" If positive, move forward with proper planning and documentation. If negative, investigate the negatives before saying no. The concern might be more from a lack of understanding, experience, or knowledge about how to measure the productivity of remote users. If you recognize the advantages of a mobile work force, you must be prepared to answer a number of hard questions. One common concern that should be addressed is "How will I manage mobile workers?" One good response is "How are you managing their productivity today?" If you have staff that requires constant supervision, then a remote office is not an option. For professional environments, supervision should not be an issue, and professional staff is often likely to benefit from a remote office. Schedules can be drawn up; conference calls held; and a number of other solutions can take care of times when it is necessary to communicate with a group of people.

Employers should also know that supporting a mobile user is usually more expensive than supporting a traditional office environment. A cost to benefit analysis should be done to determine if the benefits derived justify the additional costs. Additional costs include:

- *Hardware.* A mobile worker usually needs a more expensive laptop computer versus a stand-alone desktop system. There are also workers who will need a system in the office, as well as one for home or remote use, creating a double expense for hardware. A personal printer may also be needed. Today, a color ink jet printer may run between $200 and $300 for a portable model, while a personal laser printer runs between $400 and $500. Depending on the tasks assigned, the worker may also need a scanner, a microphone, a digital camera (for data conferencing), and a cellular phone or pager for communications.

- *Software.* Additional licenses in addition to those owned by the organization may be required for each mobile worker. Most site-licensed software is not applicable to workers who work away from the primary office. Review software licenses carefully. Users who work at home and have a computer may still require software upgrades and additional software to be compatible with the office. Software cost must be considered ongoing, as there are annual updates and modifications.

- *Communications.* Mobile workers require a way to communicate back to the office. While the Internet provides for secure virtual private networking, there is a cost to setting this up. Employers are usually expected to pay the cost of dial-up connectivity, about $20 a month, or high-speed broadband or DSL connectivity, about $50 a month. Additional expenses may include the cost of a separate phone line in the remote office, a calling card, or monthly cell phone usage fees. All of these depend on what the remote worker is expected to accomplish. Where remote users are provided access to company data via remote access, there is also a higher level of security required, incurring additional network communication and equipment costs.

- *Support.* Every organization must consider the additional cost of support. Where mobile workers routinely work from home, IT is often expected to support that user. A level of expectation must be established early on. For instance, many best practice companies now provide technical support to workers who routinely use home computers to connect to the office. As any IT professional knows, not all problems can be corrected remotely. So, IT must either dispatch a technician to an employee's home, or pay for third-party support where distance is a factor. Support costs are an important part of the analysis, often overlooked in the initial decision, and rarely funded in the budget.

Before examining each of these criteria and assuming that remote workers are too costly, employers must consider all the benefits, such as:

- Employees in certain positions are more productive in the field, at a customer's site, for instance, than they are in the office. An accounting auditor or field engineer are good examples.
- Where professional staff are in short supply, the cost of staffing an employee to work at home may be more beneficial that either replacing a very qualified person, or not being able to recruit qualified staff.
- Remote workers can often complete certain tasks more quickly and efficiently if they can *get away* from the office for a period of time and focus on the project to be done. Remember, there is no such thing as temporary remote workers. Methodologies must be in place before the need arises. Even when employees work away from the office sporadically for short periods of time, all the resources must be in place or errors and problems occur.
- The cost of supporting remote workers is often less than the real estate and overhead costs associated with the traditional brick and mortar office building. Particularly in larger cities, where the cost of real estate and commuting is almost prohibitive, more employees are being encouraged to work remotely and share a limited number of desks in the office when their presence is actually needed for face-to-face meetings or other group tasks.
- Sometimes there is a need for specific skills that are not available locally. Best practice businesses that are prepared to support temporary or contracted staff for *special* projects are usually ahead of the curve and therefore much more competitive.

Creating an environment for mobile workers should begin with management and not workers. Potential benefits should be listed along with a list of candidates. IT must work with management to identify the hardware and software the mobile worker will need, as well as the level of support that the organization is willing to provide (i.e. funds). IT must also develop procedures to support mobile workers in the field. The security aspects will be covered later in this chapter.

What the Employee Should Know and Do

Both of us actually work more from the road than in a traditional office. Bob spends so much time traveling and at clients' offices, that he operates his own office out of his Florida home. Bob only needs to visit his sister company's office in Kansas two or three times a year for business planning meetings when teleconferencing is not appropriate. While Randy lives in the same town in Kansas where the corporate office is located, when he is not traveling, he also usually prefers to work in the peace and quiet of his home office.

Bob has commented that potential clients may assume that because he has a home office, he might be somehow handicapped, or perhaps *less* professional, than someone whose office is located in a nice high-rise office building in the downtown of a big city. That thought passes quickly when clients realize that we have more technology at home than most high-end professional consulting firms have, as well as having all the other resources to run a professional office. What should a high-tech, state of the art, SOHO for the remote worker look like?

A mobile worker's office should be as well equipped as any traditional office with the latest and fastest computers for the work being done. The system should include CD/RW (compact disks that are writeable or rewriteable depending if they are to be used to backup files, or to create images for shipping or storage.) Iomega Zip drives are also appropriate for creating backups and storing large files. Most files, particularly graphic images, do not fit on floppy disks anymore. A full-size monitor is needed. Many users prefer flat screen monitors today; because of the smaller footprint, they take up less space. Power users who work with a number of applications simultaneously may use dual monitors to increase productivity. A quality printer is a must. Small remote or home offices often do not have the space for a number of individual devices, such as a fax machine, scanner, copier and printer; some of the new all-in-one-printers from companies such as Hewlett Packard might be useful. The G95 is an example of what HP calls their *All in one* printer. For about $500, the G95 offers quality color ink jet printing with copier, scanner and fax all built in. The G95 has a sheet feeder, a very nice feature, that works for both scanning and copying. The G95 is a medium duty unit, not meant for heavy printing, but works well for small jobs. We also recommend units such as the G95 because they are flat bed models. They are more like a copy machine, allowing books or larger tomes to be laid flat on the glass and scanned or copied. Other types of printers that have scanning and printing capability require individual pages to be sheet-fed and are not as flexible. For larger jobs, an Office Depot, Office Max, or Quick Copy is usually found close by and is more cost-effective than investing in high volume equipment. Companies should have methods in place for remote users to expense such costs easily and provide them with the authority to use outside resources. Outside resources should not be used for tasks that involve confidential information; employees must be able to protect the integrity of this information at all times.

Where higher volumes are routine or superior quality is important, laser printers should be used. The Hewlett Packard 4100 LaserJet printer is an excellent choice at 25ppm and 12 seconds to the first page out. These machines are fast and cost around

$1000. There are also lower cost options that might serve the user better, such as personal lasers like the Hewlett Packard 1250 personal Laser Jet. The 1250 is a 15ppm with optional scanner for under $400. Other options are listed in the hardware chapter.

It would be difficult for most mobile workers to work remotely without high speed Internet connectivity. There are a number of options depending on what is available and reliable in the area. The best practice choices, in order of preference, are DSL, Cable (broadband), and Satellite. ISDN is an option where the other options are not available. A 56K dial-up connection to the Internet should be a measure of last resort.

Most SOHOs will require some networking between systems. A traditional approach is to wire the office space for Ethernet cabling if the user plans to work at home regularly. Another choice is wireless connectivity. A small land wire network Hub (usually called a switch) costs under $50 for as many as five users. In the wireless network, these switches are called Access Points. The Access Point should include an Internet gateway for Cable/DSL and three or more RJ45 land wire Ethernet ports. The computers will need a Network Interface Card (NIC.) These cost less than $30. Wireless NICs cost a bit more, but should not be more than $100. For desktop units where wireless connectivity is desired, there are a number of USB compatible adaptors where the user never has to open the computer to insert a network card. Wireless is great for mobile devices, particularly if the user intends to work by the pool or in front of the ball game once in a while.

Companies considering going wireless might be interested in these points from a Gartner Group (*www.gartner.com*) white paper published in late 2001:

- By 2004, at least 50 percent of Fortune 1000 enterprises will commit 15 percent of all networking service spending to wireless voice and data solutions.
- By 2004, 40 percent of mobile workers will be compelled to carry technologies that offer instant voice response and hourly e-mail response.
- By 2004, 70 percent of new cell phones and 40 percent of new PDAs will use wireless technology for direct access to Web content and enterprise networks.
- By 2004, the average use of wireless bandwidth will increase from 8 kilobits per second (Kbps) to 56 Kbps, while the average price per Kbps will drop at least 30 percent per year.
- Through 2004, enterprises that do not correctly identify mobile users will decrease knowledge workers' productivity by at least 20 percent.
- Through at least 2003, 35 percent of knowledge workers will rely on a mix of three or more devices during the business day (e.g., laptop, mobile phone and PDA).
- Through at least 2004, 80 percent of all enterprises that do not engage a wireless management services provider will fail to meet their cost and performance objectives and will engender frustration among users and incur high costs (0.7 probability).
- Through 2004, wireless application protocol (WAP) will be the de facto standard for web delivery on smart phones.

Over the next three years, the rates for wireless services will continue to decline, which will fuel increased use of wireless networks. Competition between carriers will continue to grow through 2004, and prices will continue to drop about 30 percent per year. Competition will also drive carriers to differentiate offerings by adding data capability. The combination of lower prices and requirements for wireless data capabilities will drive individual users to consume seven times more bandwidth in 2004 than they do today (according to the Gartner Group.)

If the employee works out of the home on a regular basis, multiple phone lines are necessary to separate personal calls from business calls. There are a few tricks that may save money and make sense. If the worker needs a dedicated line for faxes, and the home phone is not used during daytime hours, the worker can use a phone feature called distinctive ring, an option that costs about $5.00 a month. Distinctive ring provides a second phone number that rings in on the same line as the home number. Most new fax/answering machines come enabled to recognize distinctive ring and will pick up automatically when the distinctive ring comes across your home line. In effect, this is a dedicated fax line for about $5 a month. With the distinctive ring, the ring tone is distinctive, so everyone knows not to pick up the phone when it rings. This seems to work well where there is not a high volume of faxes received and the home line is not often used during the person's normal business hours.

Another alternative is to use an Internet based fax service such as eFax, *www.efax. com*. There are a number of these services; a search of the Internet will provide more information. Faxing services such as eFax offer basic services for free, if you don't mind the pop-up marketing banners, and fee-based services that are more robust. For instance, eFax Plus is about $9.95 per month and offers a dedicated number for receiving faxes, a choice of a local or toll-free number in approximately 560 cities in the United States and the United Kingdom, plus other services. Internet faxing services offer an interesting alternative to traditional faxing. Some businesses use these services for remote workers to receive faxes from the office or customers.

The remote worker will also need call forwarding and call waiting. Most workers do not want to give out their cell phone numbers because it costs them money when someone calls them. However, in a small office, it is important to stay connected. Having the ability to forward office calls to your cell phone when you are out of the office is convenient and cost effective. The customer does not have to remember multiple numbers and the worker can better manage phone traffic. As a rule, it is not a best practice for workers to give out their cell phone number as calls may come in at embarrassing moments. Cell phone numbers are still very transient. If a company changes services, a new cell phone number is issued. Office numbers tend to be more static. Many companies provide dedicated company phone numbers that automatically forward when the employee is working out of the office.

Having a second line brought into a home for business use is fairly easy to do. The employee and employer must also have an agreement on how the line is to be expensed —how much of the installation cost the company will cover. When bringing in a second phone line that is not to be publicized, make it an unpublished number and remove it from local phone books. Another phone service to consider is in-house wiring maintenance. It costs about $1 a month. We have found that when maintenance is needed, the phone company usually says the problem is inside the home and not their responsibility. For $12 a year, the phone company will handle maintenance of wires.

Finally, what about the actual work environment? Home office workers must have a professional workspace that is maintained accordingly. Kitchen tables or folding tables in the corner of the living room or bedroom are not acceptable. Employers must ensure that the workplace is appropriate for staff working at home. There have been a number of lawsuits under disability acts where employees made claims for work related injuries that happened at home. Courts have decided both ways on these claims. Take this into consideration when allowing a worker to work at home for extended periods of time.

It is the responsibility of the employee to understand company policy for remote workers and to comply with those policies. If working at home, the remote worker should make sure that others who live in the same house understand that privacy and professionalism are important. A major downside to remote workers who work from home is the invasion of the workplace into the home environment. As people who battle this every day, we know it can be a serious problem. We love what we do and sometimes would rather be working at the computer than mowing the lawn (I know, hard to believe!) Working from home means setting regular office hours, taking regular breaks, and having a comfortable well-lighted and conditioned environment. It also means walking out and closing the door when the day is done!

Privacy and security are critical. Remote workers, home office workers, or mobile workers must understand that office systems are for work-related use. Inappropriate use is not acceptable. Only workers should have access to and use company-owned hardware and software. Friends, family, and neighbors are not allowed to use these systems. Employers must clearly state this in their policy and procedures manuals so there are no misunderstandings.

The Mobile Worker As Road Warrior

So far, the typical mobile worker discussed has been the home worker or someone working in a small remote office. Now let us turn to the road warrior, an affectionate term for those mobile workers with mobile offices. What are the tools of the mobile office? First of all, the mobile office is more often in a briefcase than a room in a building. The mobile office includes fewer resources, but is no less important to manage.

Unique Problems of the Road Warrior

Power is always an issue; if the mobile worker travels between countries, power is even a greater issue. Depending on the work environment, the user may need a special power supply tool such as a portable solar power generator; these are only slightly larger than a laptop and weigh about the same. The mobile worker should be issued spare batteries and make sure they are all fully charged before traveling. Based on the type of traveling the worker does, they will usually carry one or more spare batteries with them for in-flight use. Some employers balk at paying for extra batteries, but they are a great investment. The potential for lost time while traveling is great. But the potential for quality work time on long trips is also great. Do not depend on planes having power sources at the seats. Even in first class, this is rare for flights of less than three hours, the most common flights in the United States. It is better to be prepared. Mobile workers can sometimes find power sources in the airport, but will be much more productive if they are in a clubroom where business facilities, including work surfaces and Internet facilities, are provided.

Other accessories that the mobile worker needs include an extra power supply. Often, laptops stay in the office because a worker did not want to take the time to disconnect the plug, roll up the power cable and stuff everything in the briefcase. A spare power adaptor and mouse will cost less than $100 and make it much easier for mobile workers to disconnect their computers, drop them in briefcases and head out the door. Since security on the road is important, a steel cable with a lock to secure equipment is a good idea. Targus (*www.targus.com*) has steel cables and a number of other accessories for mobile workers.

Now that many companies have moved to wireless networking, it is getting easier to connect to customer and remote office networks, but still not as easy as most users would like. If the mobile worker routinely travels to locations with wireless access, supplying a wireless NIC makes sense. A number of airports had begun to offer wireless Internet access, but have backed off because of security issues. When traveling to visit a customer or remote site, the user should check ahead to see if network access is available. Network access not only provides Internet access for communications and e-mail but is also useful for having access to a printer. With the popularity of Hewlett Packard Laser Jet printers, it is fairly easy to print at a foreign location. While no one can load every printer driver needed, nearly all Hewlett Packard Laser Jet printers still support Laser Jet II print drivers. There may be reduced functionality, such as not being able to print some graphics and special fonts, but the worker can usually get by if there are no IT technicians available to provide the needed drivers. Printing is always an issue for road warriors. Always plan ahead for paper. Sometimes the mobile worker can sweet-talk a hotel night clerk out of a few sheets of paper. If a user does not have access to a printer and really needs to print something, they might try faxing the document to the hotel fax machine, to their attention. It is not pretty, but usually works. Most quality hotels now have business centers where travelers can check e-mail and print reports. A cup of coffee or bag of donuts has gained entrance into more than one hotel office to use the printer.

Many road warriors also carry a crossover cable with them. A crossover cable allows the user to network two computers without other equipment such as a hub or network switch. In any case, always carry a standard 10-foot Ethernet cable for connecting to a traditional network.

Portable Data Drives

CD/RW and DVD/RW are now available for most laptop systems and are highly recommended as a way to back up large data files and carry archived files on the road.

The Zip® drive from Iomega is a great choice to back up files and protect against computer failure. With millions of Zip drives out there, you can share and distribute files easily when on the road. The new *blue* 250MB Zip drive is powered via the USB port on a laptop, so there is one less power adaptor to carry. The blue Zip drive is under $200.

Iomega® has several solutions that provide high-capacity, inexpensive storage. The new sleekly designed Iomega storage systems are superfast, with transfer rates up to

15 MB/sec. This is the first true high-capacity removable storage medium with cartridges available in 10 and 20-gigabyte configurations. Pricing is under $400 and additional cartridges are around $200.

Managing Cell Phone and Communication Devices

Saving space is the mantra of the mobile worker. Combination PDAs that provide the functionality of a PDA, pager, and cell phone in one unit may be the best alternative for the mobile worker. The Samsung I300, the first generation of color PDAs and phones in one, is one of the latest in a long line of new entries. Microsoft and Intel will be entering the market heavily with GSM compatible phones based on the Pocket PC, WinCE operating system. Nokia and Samsung are already releasing competitive products.

Most cell phones do not ship with extended life batteries, but heavy travelers will need to carry one or two additional batteries. In most best practice organizations today, the IT department is responsible for phone systems and cell phones as well as all the phone and data lines. This puts all the company's technology under a single authority. IT has to carefully compare cell phone service programs to buy the right one for the company's employees. Cell service vendors are advertising lots of minutes. But, the minutes are useless unless they are daytime minutes. Carefully consider the users' travel areas. Most of the major cell phone service providers are offering national service, but IT needs to be careful of roaming charges. IT should consider e-mail services, paging, conference, and three-way calling. Caller ID is included on most services, allowing users to save minutes by not answering unwanted calls. Something as simple as the size of the phone can impact ease of use.

Headsets improve the quality of calls, make the conversation more private, and minimize the user disturbing others around them. Plantronics is one of the best solutions we have found, *www.plantronics.com*. They cost a little more, but are usually worth it. Headsets and ear buds are very personal items, so we suggest that you allow users to make the decision as to which suits them best. Establish a budget and then reimburse the expense.

Managing Personal Data Assistants (PDA)

PDAs are sometimes a personal choice, but companies are usually better off standardizing a specific PDA operating system. Doing so will create controversy because some users may have already purchased units on their own. IT will need to canvas users and carefully discuss options with management before making decisions. There are often some pretty heated arguments over the *best* PDA. Palm operating system based units have a large installed base. IT will find a wider choice of applications written for the Palm OS. There are also a number of developer kits and programming solutions for Palm units that make the development of custom applications relatively simple.

However, the market for the next closest competitor, Microsoft, is growing rapidly. The Microsoft PDA operating system is WinCE, also referred to as the Pocket PC OS. Early releases of this OS are reported to be slightly less dependable, and, as with many

Windows based products, require more support. This translates into a greater cost to support. Because Microsoft has licensed WinCE to several vendors including Compaq and Hewlett Packard, IT may find that applications and accessories from one vendor do not work with a PDA from another vendor using the same version of WinCE. This is usually not so with the Palm OS; applications written for the Palm OS tend to work on all Palm devices, with a few exceptions on combo devices that include cell phone capability.

One of the most important considerations that IT faces with the deployment of PDA devices is the information that is stored on them. These small devices are easily misplaced and lost, along with the sensitive information they contain. Users must be cautioned to use password log ins to protect company data and not to share their PDA with others. The organization must also have appropriate procedures for users to return PDAs, or to wipe company data from personal units should employment be terminated.

An alternative to the Palm or WinCE PDA is a device such as the Blackberry from Research in Motion (*www.rim.com*). The Blackberry has become very popular among mobile workers over the past few years and the more recent versions includes a small keyboard for thumb typing. The Blackberry is an advanced two-way pager that allows the user to receive and send e-mail, surf the Internet using a technique called Web-clips, and share information remotely. While these devices are less functional than Palm and WinCE PDAs, they do provide instant communication and are relatively inexpensive. With devices such as the Blackberry, and PDAs that use small thumb size keyboards, carpal thumb syndrome is a big concern. Typing with only your thumbs on the tiny keyboard is not good for your hands! The Blackberry has an embedded wireless modem and integrated e-mail/organizer software.

Deploying the right technology to each user is important to any organization. Just as one size does not fit all, there is no single PDA choice that fits all mobile users. IT should review the technology along with department representatives to determine which solutions to deploy. IT must also include estimates for long-term upkeep and support. Finally, IT must also consider that most mobile workers need to communicate with office networks and databases. The deployment of mobile workers means that additional security is needed.

Accessing Remote Information Securely!

Remote access to the company network is a part of what every remote worker expects. A mobile worker must to be able to access data from anywhere at anytime. IT departments, on the other hand, are less than enthusiastic about employees who work outside the office. A remote workforce sometimes makes it tough to secure centralized systems. Remote users accessing internal networks can be akin to locking the front door and then leaving all the windows open. As the number of remote workers has risen, so have concerns about security. Scott Scrogin, a technology consultant with Network Management Group, Inc., feels that clients are much more sensitive about security today. "It used to come up once in a while. But with recent media coverage of computer hacking and intrusions, questions about how to protect systems are being asked more," he says.

Having a safe means for workers to remotely access internal networks, without the fear of hacking, is keeping a number of businesses from allowing people to work at home and on the road.

There are tools on the market today, with more emerging, to help better secure the privacy of company networks and network access. Secure Computing Corporation's (*www.securecomputing.com*) SafeWord authentication and authorization software works with Citrix Systems Inc.'s MetaFrame application server. SafeWord allows users to securely access confidential information from anywhere by logging on to a secure, remote-access server. SafeWord secures the connection and web access to Citrix, and users authenticate themselves with the use of *tokens* that provide a one-time use key. User's access can be controlled, and detailed logs track all account activity.

RealSecure from the security vendor Internet Security Systems Inc. (*www.realsecure.com*) is another tool for companies considering remote users. Internet Security Systems has a suite of Internet security products, one of which is particularly targeted to the Small Office/Home Office (SOHO) worker.

Security vendor TruSecure Corp. (*www.trusecure.com*) estimates that the code red virus spread to more than a half million company networks last year when infected remote users logged on to the company networks. The majority of internal code red infections came, not from Internet-facing Microsoft Internet Information Services servers, but through notebook computers or systems connecting via virtual private networks. According to Russ Cooper, editor of TruSecure's security mailing list, NTBugTraq, once code red entered an internal network, it infected systems running Internet Information Services that had not been patched. True, the patch should have been done, and IIS had a hole. But, remote users who logged back in and infected the network intensified the problem.

Companies must take the security of their remote client access seriously. When the remote user becomes a corporate network access point, they provide as much of a threat as an internal user. One option might be for IT departments to continuously check remote systems, running a vulnerability assessment each time a remote desktop authenticates to the network, in order to ensure the remote system has not already been compromised.

As a best practice, IT must insist that remote users protect themselves with a personal firewall along with antivirus software, at all times, when working outside the office. Products like CyberArmor (*www.infoexpress.com*) help IT monitor and enforce secure connections. CyberArmor works with most virtual private network (VPN) products to detect and block attacks against the PC using the appropriate level of security at all times. CyberArmor detects where the system is located and what the user is doing, and then it enforces a security policy appropriate to the current situation. While the solution of the moment changes with the sunrise, CyberArmor has been getting a lot of attention lately as a solid, cost-effective solution to securing remote user access to corporate networks.

A Java-based client from AppGate (*www.appgate.com*) provides a standard based remote-access solution that is easier to deploy to PCs and notebooks than other solutions because it is browser-based. AppGate VPN and AppGate PowerBox enable you to choose how, when, where, and by whom critical applications are used. AppGate's technology integrates with any system or operating environment and is accessible via nearly any media.

SecurID tokens have also made their way into a number of businesses, such as health care where keeping patient records is not just good business, it is the law. The RSA SecurID Card and the RSA SecurID Key Fob operate identically. A device containing the RSA SecurID seed generates and displays a new token code every 60 seconds. This hardware device is shaped like a credit card and is easily portable and extremely durable. A system will have the decoding side accept the secure log in. At about $500 for the SecurID Card, this is not a cheap solution but a reliable one.

Netilla Networks Inc.'s (*www.netilla.com*) mobile worker service is another solution to consider. Netilla offers Internet/Intranet solutions for safe secure remote access to corporate information. Netilla Service Platforms (Internet Server/Super Firewall) can be purchased for internal use. Or, Netilla also provides the services in a hosted mode by subscription.

For companies that need to support a remote sales force, IT might consider FrontRange Solutions Inc.'s (www.frontrange.com) GoldMine sales and marketing software. Employees can access the contact database at the company headquarters, and download new data into GoldMine on a regular basis from home, in the office, or at a client site. Users do their own contact synchronization and keep up-to-date with tracking leads.

Intranets Support Users

Intranets are a strategic tool to help IT support users. Intranets facilitate the rapid flow of information within the organization, reduce delays in conveying information, and reduce costs associated with forms and data gathering activities. Dealing with forms, policies, and hard copy paper documents always leaves a wide margin for errors to occur. Intranets can solve many of these issues. Today, all best practice organizations have deployed Intranets.

The term Intranet is very broad. But basically, an Intranet uses the same tools as used to create an Internet site. Web-publishing tools, such as Microsoft FrontPage, Macromedia's Dreamweaver or Flash may be used. Small organizations, without technical resources to use these advanced tools, can create a simple Intranet using Microsoft Word 97, 2000, or 2002. Keeping the site simple and easy to maintain is more important than having lots of graphics and dancing bunnies, so FrontPage or similar tools will usually work much better than one of the more graphics-oriented products. Freeware and Shareware web development tools can be downloaded from TUCOWS, *www.tucows.com.*

Knowing that an Intranet looks and feels like any Internet site, and having selected the tools to create the site, the first step is for management and IT to define the objectives for company Intranet. Site design should not be done in isolation; it is important to get several users from a number of departments involved in the creation of the site. Getting users involved also means obtaining their commitment to use the site when it is done. IT will provide technical input as needed; IT should not forget that portions of the site might also contain forms and other pieces of information, such as online technical journals used by IT professionals. In defining the objectives, list the type of information and uses the Intranet might have.

While there are many things an Intranet may accomplish, here are a few of the best practice benefits:

- Company Information, such as contact information for senior management, department heads, and supervisors is important. Include office information, phone numbers, e-mail addresses and the like. Do not assume that information is not relevant. For instance, a long time employee may find rudimentary information not to be worthy of space on the Intranet; yet new employees would find background and other general information informative.

- The Intranet is a perfect place to post schedules for staff or work assignments. Several packages, including Microsoft Project, allow schedules to be posted as HTML pages on the Intranet. Users can view changes instantly from any system they can access their firm's Intranet.

- Use as a central repository for work papers, forms, and templates is a major benefit of the Intranet. When any form is changed, the change is immediate for the next person who accesses the site. Consider a leave request form. If personnel decides that a form needs a space for the immediate supervisor to sign off, a quick change to the form is made and the updated form is posted back to the Intranet site. The next employee who requests a copy of the form from the Intranet site will have the updated form immediately. This is much more effective than having many copies of the form lying around in various departments and going through the typical transition period every time a form is updated. An additional benefit is never having to print forms again, which means a huge cost savings.

- After all hardcopy forms are stored on the Intranet, the next step is to convert these forms so that employees can complete them electronically online. The completed data may be stored as data in a database, retrievable by the appropriate person, or sent as a completed form as an e-mail message for further action. Now users do not need to print anything and costs continue to decline!

- Intranets can also be used to store scanned images of documents. For instance, many organizations receive information from outside that must be disseminated internally. A common approach is to either make a number of copies and distribute them, or to place a routing slip on the document and hope the information makes it to everyone. An alternative best practice approach is to scan the document when it enters the organization and store the document in the Intranet. Send an e-mail to those who need to see the information that it is now available. Then, everyone is able to pull the document from the Intranet simultaneously and instantaneously. Imagine the benefits.

- Keeping procedures and policies current and deployed in a timely manner is a constant struggle. The following are just a few of the policies that can be posted on the Intranet. Think, for a moment about all those documents that exist in word processing that are sent to a printer each year. Then, calculate the economic value of posting these to an Intranet.

○ Acceptable use policy
○ Privacy statement
○ Security
○ Leave policy (sick, vacation, other)
○ Disaster recovery

• There are also a number of interactive pages that can be managed from the Intranet, such as:

○ Requests for leave
○ Firm chat rooms (for both official and unofficial virtual meetings)
○ Assignment request forms

The Intranet can quickly become an organization-wide internal newsletter as well. When an employee opens their browser, the Intranet home page should be the opening page. Important latebreaking news, alerts, or assignments should be posted here, or on links provided from this page. It is also common to have a hot links page of sites relevant to the business. These might include links to vendors, customers, and professional organizations

This may sound like a lot of information in one place; it is. Who should be responsible for maintaining the company Intranet? Intranets may be designed to be simple enough that technical staff, or third-party sources, like those that support the Internet site are not needed. An Intranet should not need that level of sophistication. A best practice is to keep the Intranet site simple and teach a few key people how to update pages that change often. IT technical staff or a web administrator will most likely set up the menu pages, create links, and fix small problems when they occur. But technical staff should not be responsible for preparing content or updating simple pages. If interactive pages are used for leave requests, interactive forms, and other information, technical people will set those up so that the appropriate staff can access the data and post information without constant intervention.

Keeping the Intranet simple and to the point is the secret of flexibility and of getting users to the site for information. Consider a couple of examples. If you are a Microsoft Outlook user, the latest 2002 version allows schedules to be published directly as a web page. Departmental calendars show what projects or meetings are scheduled when and who is to be where. The Intranet is a great place to post vacation and holiday information as well. Documents that are in Word today, such as policy statements and forms, may also be stored as Adobe Acrobat Portable Data Files (PDF). The Adobe Acrobat application creates PDF Files and costs under $300. Acrobat also integrates with Microsoft Office so that you can print to a printer using PDFWriter. Or, the user can create the file directly in the Intranet directory.

To post documents in hardcopy format to the Intranet site, give a scanner ($200–$300) to an administrative assistant or file room clerk and train them to scan these documents and post the image to the appropriate folder in the Intranet. The same person would then pull up a Word web page and enter the document title and a brief description on the table of contents page. The title would be hyper-linked to the scanned page. Today, images can be scanned to jpg, gif, or even PDF format easily. Again, keep this process simple. When a document is received, it is scanned and then forwarded to the person responsible for maintaining the Intranet site. Once completed, the form is posted. The person responsible will verify that the document is posted correctly and send out an organization-wide e-mail letting everyone know the document is there for them to review. They may even hyperlink the document in their e-mail to make access quick and easy. Thinking through the process, careful testing, getting input from users, and maintaining the Intranet will all lead to cost savings and increased productivity. With the inundation of information that accompanies the technology age, it is critical that firms learn to manage and benefit from the Intranet. No excuses. Now, go do it!

CONCLUSION

This chapter discussed methods and tools to assist IT in managing IT staff and users. This includes providing them with the right tools and training to make users more productive. We also gave evidence supporting the importance of educating both IT professionals and users to better leverage and manage technology for higher productivity and greater return on investment.

CHAPTER SEVEN

Software Selection and Maintenance Best Practices

SELECTING APPROPRIATE SOFTWARE

Through their ability to be completely changed by changing the software, computers have wonderful capability and flexibility. We will look at several levels of software selection that affect how end users are able to use their systems, as well as the capabilities of the systems. Most computers have firmware, an operating system, and application software.

Application software is the type of software that drives most business decisions. Categories of application software include: productivity software, accounting software, and other software tools or utilities. Evolving technologies are creating a transition in software. This transition includes the integration of personal digital assistants (PDAs), cell phones, web integration and browser enablement, and integration of other applications.

Tens of thousands of worldwide competitors make software in all categories. A few major companies try to have an offering in most of the categories of software. Because of the rise of web browsers, a simplification has occurred in the last 5–7 years. Many software products have been modified to work inside a web browser. This also allows a very simple operating system plus a browser to be used at the network edge. This strategy minimizes the different types of software needed on the desktop. There are many types of software in any complete computing software solution:

- Firmware and software drivers.
- Desktop and network operating systems.
- Database software.
- Productivity software.
- Internet software.
- Software tools and utilities.
- Accounting and financial systems.
- Other core business applications.

Occasionally, choosing one type of software automatically dictates some of the other choices. In other cases, the choices are largely independent of each other, but vendors will try to convince buyers that all of the solutions must come from a single source. Single source software can mean lower maintenance costs. But, it will often mean higher acquisition costs and may mean the software is not as good of a fit.

FIRMWARE

The very lowest level of programming in many systems occurs in firmware. Firmware is the software that resides in the basic input output system (BIOS) and communicates to the operating system and to the hardware. As a user of computing systems, it will be rare that your company or its technical people will ever program firmware. This occasionally happens with shopfloor data controllers, or specialized data collection devices. For most of us, part of what we get from our hardware supplier is their expertise in programming and updating their firmware. A key competitive difference between the larger suppliers, such as IBM, Compaq, HP, and to a lesser degree Dell and Gateway, is the level of firmware support that exists after the sale. White box clones almost never have any updates or repairs available at the firmware level. When an upgrade does occur, the software instructions are downloaded from the vendor, usually saved to a diskette or other removable media, and then applied in a cold boot of the hardware. Sometimes these fixes can be distributed by automatic means, or can be applied from a network server.

The most common software firmware fix is for BIOS updates that repair items like system timers, device support, and errors in the original programming. Other firmware fixes will be made for other system level components such as modems, network adapters, video drivers, input/output drivers and so on. Every possible hardware system can be updated with either firmware or driver fixes that are applied at the very low level of firmware. These updates are sometimes referred to as patches, upgrades, maintenance releases, FRU (field request for upgrade), or PTFs (program temporary fixes). Make sure all PC's have updated OS patches, for example Windows 2000 SP2 on a Windows 2000 system. Regardless of your operating system, we generally recommend that you apply the latest service pack if it has been out for more than 45 days. These operating systems service packs are usually repairs for errors in the original operating system.

Drivers are another type of low-level software used by operating systems. Drivers are usually operating system dependent. They are written for a particular version of the operating system. When software developers label their operating systems with numbers, they usually start with the major version number, followed by a revision number. Hence, a software product that is numbered V3.1 would be the third major version, and that version had one revision containing improvements and/or bug fixes. Low-level system drivers are revised much faster than operating systems or applications since minor changes can make them stop working, and these errors are easily missed in the testing process. The developers can make an additional change and release a new version of the driver quickly, sometimes in a matter of hours. We generally recommend that the drivers you install are certified drivers for that operating system. Drivers are available at both the firmware and operating system level. Firmware drivers are largely operating system independent, but sometimes will have to be modified to accommodate changes in the operating systems or version revisions. Both types of drivers can cause intermittent problems. Good technicians will troubleshoot problems by both updating to current versions and going back to old versions that work.

DESKTOP OPERATING SYSTEMS

The desktop operating system provides the primary interface from the user to the application software to the hardware being used. Microsoft has become the dominant supplier in this category. Historically, Microsoft was contracted by IBM to develop DOS that they purchased from Tim Patterson and Seattle Computing for a very low fee. DOS (disk operating system) was a character-based system that was created to compete against other popular character-based operating systems of the time like CPM and UNIX. Much of the structure of DOS was based on UNIX. Tim Patterson and his team did the bulk of the development in a very short period of time.

IBM wanted to have a standard operating system because they believed this would allow more rapid development of standardized applications. When the IBM PC was released in August 1981, it had several operating systems to choose from, and was serious competition at the time. DOS evolved from version 1.0 up through 2.0, which included disk support, to version 3.1 that was a very stable and capable operating system. DOS continued to add features with versions 4, 5 and 6, but during this time, Windows operating systems that started to work (V3.1) were introduced. IBM and Microsoft began to have disputes over direction and ownership of the operating system, and DOS began to fade in importance. DOS commands are still used in all Windows operating systems today.

Microsoft Windows

Microsoft began offering Windows in 1985, but it was an application-switching product at best. When Windows 3.1 arrived, and, more importantly, Windows for Workgroups V3.11 in April of 1992, the system became stable enough to use for business applications. Further, the addition of peer-to-peer networking in WFW was a significant technical gain since this reduced the cost of networking, and made resource sharing of printers, CDs and disk drives easier. The graphical user interface, the standardized menu, and the ability to run multiple applications at the same time were a great boon to productivity. Standardized device interfaces like printer drivers were also important. Instead of installing a print driver for every printer for every application, one driver could be installed for each printer, and used by all applications. System lockups and running out of system resources were common, but the gain was very significant. The largest competitor was IBM with their OS/2, which was also developed by Microsoft.

In August 1995, Windows 95 was introduced. It was immediately obvious that this product was far superior to the prior offerings. The most noticeable attribute was that the product was far more stable and introduced the hardware recognition feature of plug and play. Windows 95 evolved through several versions to add features like additional hard drive capacity (in Windows 95b). Windows 95 became a widespread corporate standard. Windows 95 was upgraded to the noticeably less stable Windows 98, Windows 98 SE (Second Edition), and Windows ME (Millennium Edition); each of these versions added features like support for Universal Serial Bus (USB). Windows 98 slightly modified the look and feel of the user interface. Strategically, Microsoft has positioned this operating system as a home operating system because of the lack of security features, and will discontinue the line completely.

A stumbling block to Windows 95 was incompatibility with existing applications. Windows 95 did a better job than most prior OS upgrades. But, it would still be at least six months before most applications were made compatible. This lag of application compatibility with the operating system is a very common characteristic that must be managed whenever a new operating system is introduced. We expect application compatibility to be an ongoing problem with introduction of operating systems regardless of the vendor.

A more stable, network operating system capable product known as Windows NT was on a separate development path. Network operating systems are discussed later, in Chapter 9. Windows NT was developed as a competitor to IBM's OS/2 and other UNIX offerings of the day. Much of the design came from the Digital VAX system, and from IBM's OS/2, although Microsoft routinely denied use of this intellectual property. Technicians of the day routinely looked at each other's development work to use new ideas and evolve ideas of their own. One of the chief architects of NT had helped develop the VAX operating system in a prior job.

NT was to become the mainstream of Microsoft's development work from the late 1980s to the early 2000s. NT 3.1, and the revisions of 3.11, 3.5, and 4.0 (September 1996) all helped make this product more reliable, and more compatible with applications. The 3.X versions of NT used the older Windows interface, and V4 of NT adopted the Windows 95 look and feel. Corporate users who felt that Windows 95 was too unstable to deploy were pleased with the stability and security features built into the NT version.

Windows 2000 became the best operating system release of the company to date. It was exceptionally stable and secure, and actually ran faster than older versions of the operating systems on the same hardware, a rare trend in the computer business. This product used the Windows 98 interface; the compatibility with both NT and 9X applications were notably good. Still, applications had to be modified to be truly Windows 2000 compatible, particularly with some of the driver controls enforced by Microsoft.

Windows XP is a follow-up product to Windows 2000 that changes the user interface, and adds more backward compatibility with applications. Windows XP (XP for experience) improves the user options, multimedia handling, and other operational characteristics. Some reviewers have called this Windows 2000 SE (Second Edition) to emphasize it is just a further modification to Windows 2000. This product does seem to be run faster on certain hardware, and can be much more problematic than Windows 2000. Reviewers compare this product to Windows 98 SE. Currently there is one more

Exhibit 7.1

Desktop Operating System	Networking Built in	Plug and Play	Graphical Support	Security (disk/user)	Year Introduced
DOS					1981
Windows 3.X	Only Word for Windows		X		1990
Windows 9.X	X	X	X		1995
Windows NT	X	X	X	X	1992
Windows 2000/XP	X	X	X	X	2000
OS X	X	X	X		1988
OS/2	X		X	X	1987
Linux	X	X	Some	X	1997

version of the Windows NT kernel operating system, known as Longhorn that will be beta tested during 2002, and possibly released in 2003. Exhibit 7.1 summarizes features in the desktop operating systems.

These desktop operating systems are evolving in the context of Microsoft's software architecture strategy known as .NET. Windows 2000, XP and Longhorn will all be modified to take advantage of .NET server strategies. .NET is Microsoft's attempt to put an overall architecture on software, just like IBM did in the 1970s and 1980s with their communications strategies of SNA (Systems Network Architecture) and SAA (Systems Application Architecture). The goal of .NET is to enable people to interact with computers with more than a keyboard and mouse for input, and a monitor for output. Additionally, it is important to make corporate data, application and user information and preferences accessible no matter where users log in, from their own machines or different machines. The users get to act directly on the information regardless of where it is. In our opinion, the largest goal is to make data available to all devices—PCs, pagers, cell phones, or PDAs—minimizing synchronization.

The handheld operating systems also fit into the Microsoft desktop strategies. These OS versions include the Pocket PC operating system known as Windows CE. This product is currently in version 3. The first version was a crude attempt to put the Windows interface in a handheld format so Microsoft could compete against the very successful Palm OS. Version 2 acted much more like Windows 2000 or Windows 98, but was still clumsy. Version 3 has evolved to act very much like the Windows XP interface.

For embedded controllers, another operating system, Embedded Windows NT, is competing for market share. The goal is to have a more stable, faster OS that can be used for industrial applications. There was early competition between CE and Embedded NT to rule the handheld market space, but Windows CE in the Pocket PC release seems to be gaining market acceptance.

The next evolution of the Microsoft desktop strategy is a new operating system already in development known as Blackcomb. This product will overhaul the core operating system, the kernel, and will introduce Storage+, a new relational file system that is combined with the registry, exchange and active directory. Microsoft considers Linux and other browser-based offerings as key competitive threats, and is trying to position the new line of products to defend the desktop operating system.

Linux

The most viable competitor for Microsoft on both the server and the desktop is the grass roots developed Linux operating system. What is Linux? This operating system is developed using open source, which means that the operating system is in the public domain or available as freeware (software without charge). Linux freeware operating systems are subject to the GNU license agreement. Doctoral student Linus Torvalds of Finland initially developed Linux. It is available for free as a download. Commercial distributions are sold on CD with setup and installation software. Many vendors have entered this marketplace by adding their own customizations or shells that add value to the operating system.

Linux has many attractive features, but some serious drawbacks as well. The Linux OS has some key competitive strengths. In a nutshell, the OS has very good stability, and similar throughput as Windows on the same platform. There are a limited number of applications but the number is growing. Currently, the Linux OS is not ready for prime-time on the desktop, but it is very close. But, Linux currently feels like the Windows of the early 1990s. But, Linux has much better server capabilities at this time.

There are some key Linux advantages. Among these are: low cost at $50 per CD, no per user licenses, a rapid development cycle, high reliability, solid performance, open source to give access to make OS modifications if needed, and low administrative overhead. Linux also has some key disadvantages. Among these are: a lack of hardware drivers, the need to know the command line OS instructions, confusing installation routines, inconsistent graphical desktops that include both X Windows and Windows managers, low-level tuning administration work that requires editing of configuration files, a lack of service and support, a lack of skilled and certified support technicians, a small number of applications compared to Windows, incompatibility of current applications, lack of control by single vendor (which some see as an advantage), and a lack of standards across commercial releases.

As of this writing, there are 15 English language distributions of Linux and all are slightly different. This makes application developers wary of incompatibilities across vendor's versions of this product. Commercial packages are available from Red Hat, Caldera, Corel, TurboLinux, and SuSE. Of the competitors in the market, Red Hat Linux is having the most success.

There are some very promising Linux developments in the marketplace. For example, Oracle reported 100,000 downloads of its Oracle 8i database for Linux. IBM has announced a Linux-based e-business strategy and server support. Several companies and industries have standardized on Linux, and there are many projects porting enterprise software to Linux. Of the major hardware vendors, Compaq, Dell, HP, and IBM, each support Linux on their servers although Dell discontinued desktop Linux support in August 2001. IT managers claim that Linux OS use will grow from 5% to nearly 20% by 2002. Ninety-two percent of managers in companies with revenues of $500 million or more say deployment is likely.

To improve support of the operating system will require more formal education and more widespread acceptance. Sometimes this feels like a chicken or the egg situation. Linux Professional Institute, with its members, Red Hat, Caldera, IBM, Linuxcare, and SuSE, has introduced certification exams. This should improve Linux Service and Support. Further, colleges and universities are choosing this as a teaching platform because of the sophistication, modification, and reduced costs.

The lack of Linux Applications is a key issue that is exceptionally important. Some of the products for productivity include Corel Office for Linux, Xinlan Evolution, and Sun StarOffice as well as Netscape Navigator/Communicator. In the accounting software arena, ACCPAC, Open Systems and others have made their applications available on Linux.

Linux currently functions better as a network operating system or NOS. It is really an offering of UNIX on an Intel platform that supports IPX and TCP/IP. It easily integrates with Microsoft NT/2000 and Novell NetWare networks. The product has good file and print services, and Samba provides SMB support for sharing other resources. Linux functions well as an application server, and shows promise of replacing Citrix MetaFrame or Windows Terminal Server for these application-sharing approaches. Web services are often implemented using Apache Web services. The Apache market share is approximately one fourth of the marketplace. FTP services, sendmail POP3 and SMTP services, NNTP support, DNS support, and scalability with SMP support are additional server features. Linux is often used as an eCommerce Server because of these capabilities.

Disadvantages of the Linux as a NOS include that it: can only support four processors; is limited to two GB of RAM; and that it doesn't support Fibre channel Storage Area Network (SANs). These characteristics of Linux change rapidly; refer to our web site for current technical information on the Linux family of products. Even with all of these negative sounding issues, Linux is still a very good NOS. An advantage of Linux as a NOS is the ability to have multiple servers with a large number of users per server. It fits well if you need Internet/Intranet functionality as well as file and print services. If you already have internal UNIX expertise and can support yourself, then this OS can be a great choice. There are many public resources available from books to web sites.

UNIX, Macintosh OS X, OS/2, and Others

There are still many other viable competitors in the marketplace, but their market share continues to decline. Each of these other competitors have an offering that has something unique as part of their solution. The UNIX offerings from Sun, IBM, Compaq, and HP, as well as the standard Berkeley editions, are all quite good operating systems that perform well and reliably. On the desktop, they can deliver higher performance than comparable Windows products, although there is a lot of marketing material to try convincing users otherwise. However, Windows offerings sometimes do perform faster than these other environments; their familiarity makes them a favored choice by users and support technicians alike.

Apple had the best potential to develop personal computing to the fullest, but focused on keeping their hardware and operating system proprietary. Since third parties had limited development support from both an operating system and hardware vantage point, Apple allowed their competitors, IBM, Microsoft, and eventually the entire PC compatible industry, to evolve. Apple continues to do creative engineering for both hardware and software, but has a limited, but loyal following. Their main markets are education, graphics, and video production. All of these markets are being threatened by applications running on the Windows platform.

The Apple Macintosh OS has better protection for the system drivers and dynamic link libraries (DLLs or software routines that are loaded on demand). The graphical interface has many features that can make it easier to use than Windows. The latest versions of the Mac OS are based on UNIX, and provide even greater performance than predecessors. Networking support has been included since very early on, and has worked acceptably since V6.5. Multiple monitor support is better than with the Windows OS. However, hardware, security and application support are far weaker with the Mac platform than with the PC and Windows environment.

IBM is another company that might have blown their huge market share lead with the introduction of their PS/2 hardware line utilizing Microchannel Architecture and OS/2 (operating system 2) on April 2, 1987. IBM wanted to introduce machines that were faster to repair, with fewer components to fail that had higher internal performance. The PS/2 was a great hardware design that the market was not ready to accept. The multi-tasking, multi-threaded operating system of OS/2 was a large step forward, but character-based DOS users were not ready to make the jump to a graphical environment at that time. A further complication was that many of the applications were not compatible (sound familiar?). Also, the cost of the hardware to run OS/2 was very high, with a fully configured PC with enough RAM and other resources costing $7–10,000 each. OS/2 gained good acceptance in corporate applications, particularly in IBM shops, but the more sophisticated applications for OS/2 failed to materialize. There is ample proof, and even more speculation, that vendors worked to make their products fail when running under OS/2 to keep IBM from becoming too powerful in the PC marketplace.

There have been other attempts to create desktop operating systems that include a revised version of CPM, a multi-user system call PCMOS, and many others, but the market saturation is so high for DOS, Windows and their related applications, that developers take a huge risk to create an application that runs on any platform but Windows. At least that was the case until the Internet web browser gained broad acceptance. We will look at this issue in the Internet software section of this chapter.

DATABASE SOFTWARE

A database is a software application that allows organized access to a large volume of data. There are many types of databases, but the most common database is currently the relational database. Relational databases are based on table structures, and have defined relationships between the tables. Relational databases have indexes that help with performance. Queries against a relational database are made through a common language called sequel or structured query language (SQL). SQL has become particularly common in the last ten years, but has been around since the late 1970s. SQL was used on databases that ran on IBM mainframes, and many other minicomputers. As smaller, personal computers became more powerful, SQL databases could run on this smaller hardware.

Several vendors have created database software including IBM, Oracle and Sybase. Databases are really a type of software utility that the operating system and the application share to access the data files. It is logical that the database should be a part of the operating system. This is exactly the strategy that has been used with Dick Pick's Pick Operating System. Other file management systems have effectively looked the same, such as Poise that was used on the Digital PDP-11 and VAX environments. IBM introduced the concept of a database implemented in hardware with the AS/400 environment. As this platform continues to mature, the database and application integration is very strong. We expect other vendors to combine database and OS operating systems in the near future. It is actually a superior design strategy, and Dick Pick was simply ahead of his time.

Microsoft SQL

In the PC environment, many vendors have current offerings on Windows, Linux, and other operating systems. Microsoft licensed, and then did further development work to create their current SQL database offering. As SQL evolved from 6.5 to 7.0 to SQL.NET, less and less manual administration was required, and greater performance benchmarks were achieved. In addition, Microsoft also worked with their own productivity applications to integrate SQL commands in their spreadsheets, personal database products, and development tools. They also marketed their database technology to software developers and encouraged them to convert to Microsoft SQL technology. Because of this, Microsoft SQL is the current PC database standard.

Competitive Databases

Microsoft has had competitors in database technology for years, including the Sybase product, IBM's DB2, and the file management system from Pervasive formerly known as Btrieve, and now available as either Pervasive 2000 or Pervasive.SQL. Most of these competitors have to overcome operating systems issues to help their product perform correctly, but all are good offerings worthy of consideration. PC databases are getting higher and higher processing volume capacity. The number of transactions a database can handle are typically measured in transactions per second or TPS. With higher-speed hardware, including faster disks, channels, controllers, storage area networks, multiple processors, and clustering, PC databases are performing like minicomputers. These hardware components can be purchased as needed allowing a company to start with a very simple, inexpensive hardware solution, and purchase more as needed. This scalability is a key reason behind the widespread acceptance of SQL databases on PCs. The other key reason for widespread acceptance is the price performance ratios of PC databases.

Larger databases running on minicomputers and mainframes are starting to feel some competitive pressure from the scalable PC databases. Informix, Progress (used in Frontstep Manufacturing), DB2, and Oracle are all far more capable of handling large volumes of transactions than the PC databases. Part of the performance comes from superior hardware capability, and part of the performance comes from superior disk mechanisms. As all three levels of hardware have started to use the same disk mechanisms, this hardware performance differential is being eliminated. PC databases will not replace all minicomputer and mainframe databases anytime soon. But, there are a lot of applications that are candidates for the simplicity, speed and cost advantages a PC database offers. Both IBM and Oracle are actively promoting their database products on smaller PC platforms, typically powered by Linux operating systems.

Older minicomputer and mainframe database technologies like IMS, Total, and Cullinane, have been replaced by relational technology. All of these technologies were databases of one type or another. One other technology deserves mention because of the low cost of ownership, and acceptable performance. The file management system Pervasive 2000 or Pervasive.SQL from Pervasive Software should not be eliminated from a PC based file strategy decision.

Pervasive

Pervasive's *customer-focused* business model leverages a global channel of independent software vendors (ISVs), OEMs, application developers, system integrators and value-added resellers. Based in Austin, Texas, Pervasive has offices in Europe and Japan, as well as 70 distributors. Pervasive has several characteristics that developers and managers of this product can use including:

- *Pervasive system analyzer.*   This eliminates deployment issues related to component management.
- *Network tolerance and recovery.*   This avoids minor networking issues by seamlessly reconnecting workstations to a server engine in case of a network error.
- *Cross-platform consistency.*   The file manager has common behavior across all platforms; this simplifies cross-platform deployment and administration.
- *Server/requester version independence.*   This dramatically simplifies deployments.
- *Highly scaleable.*   Pervasive is highly scaleable from 11MB up and is very stable in a multi-user database environment with little tweaking required.
- *Portability.*   Pervasive applications can be deployed with no code changes required. Existing client/server-based Pervasive.SQL 2000i applications can move to Linux without any code changes.
- *Cross-platform dynamic parameters.*   There is no need to change the database environment from platform to platform.

- *Server/requester version independence.* Linux can be integrated into an existing deployment without messy configurations.
- *Integration with Perl and PHP.* Documentation and samples leverage leading development environments.
- *Support for leading Linux deployments.* These include Red Hat, Caldera and SuSE.

Each of these different database technologies has its operational advantages and disadvantages. Most applications that require file systems will use one of these database applications to speed and ease their development work.

PRODUCTIVITY SOFTWARE

Applications that help with day-to-day tasks are collectively called productivity software. These applications often include word processing, spreadsheets, e-mail, presentation software, database, calendering, and more. For marketing purposes, many companies have grouped these applications together, and enabled them to work together as a suite of products. Microsoft Office is an example of one such suite. This product currently enjoys a greater than 90 percent marketshare.

When selecting productivity suites, it is important to cover the core functions used by end users. The products should work together with minimal effort (some would say seamlessly) and the application should be compatible with the customer or client base. This reasoning has driven the selection of Microsoft Office in many companies. But, other suites can be reasonable alternatives, such as IBM's SmartSuite Millennium Edition, Corel's WordPerfect® Office 2002—Professional Edition, or Sun's StarOffice.

Features included in Microsoft's Office XP are included in the following table:

Exhibit 7.2 Features in Microsoft Office XP

	Office XP Standard	Office XP Professional	Office XP Pro with FrontPage	Office XP Developer
Word	X	X	X	X
Excel	X	X	X	X
Outlook	X	X	X	X
PowerPoint	X	X	X	X
Access		X	X	X
FrontPage			X	X
Developer Tools				X

INTERNET SOFTWARE

The Internet has been used for over 30 years. But it was not until the development of the graphical web browser content that business applications of the web made sense. The Internet has many technologies available even though most of us only use the web or e-mail. Additional tools include: file transfer protocol (FTP), newsgroups, media players, instant messaging, collaborative tools, and many others.

Web Browsers

Web browser software was the key to the explosion of the Internet. The Internet has existed since 1969, but until Tim Berners-Lee invented the graphical web browser, the primary users were academics, government and the military. The early web browsers like Mosaic helped spawn Internet use by commercial enterprises. When Netscape was released, it was a much faster, and more fully featured browser. It quickly became the web browser standard, and users flocked to this piece of software. This rapid move to the graphical web interface also served as a wake-up call to Microsoft who had largely ignored Internet development. When Microsoft realized how much computing was going to be done by the web, they created and released their own web browser, Internet Explorer. This browser software was more tightly integrated into the operating systems over time, and became the standard browser of the PC desktop. Internet Explorer and Netscape Navigator or Communicator became the key web browsers across all operating system platforms.

E-mail

Another important growth area for the Internet was e-mail systems. E-mail was used since the earliest days of the Internet, but most of the e-mail products were character-based. The key e-mail products that popularized Internet e-mail were Eudora and Pegasus. These products combined both LAN e-mail and Internet mail into a single interface. Other popular commercial LAN products added Internet capabilities. These e-mail products, including Novell GroupWise (the old WordPerfect Office product), Lotus Notes, and Microsoft Outlook then began to dominate Internet mail. To make Internet mail even less complex to access, Microsoft also released an Internet mail product, Outlook Express. These software products were competing against easy, consumer solutions like America Online (AOL), CompuServe, Prodigy, Microsoft Network and their proprietary offerings. AOL went on to purchase Netscape and key Internet Service providers like CompuServe. AOL allowed their users to use standard software instead of the proprietary software products, although they continue to develop their software interface. Most users of the Internet expect and take for granted that they will have web browsing and e-mail access on all computers.

Plug-ins

Most additional features, such as audio support, were added to web browsers and other Internet software as plug-ins. Plug-ins are simply additional software features added using standard software interfaces. The software is downloaded and installed. The end-user typically has to do very little configuration.

Audio and Video Streaming

Since the early development of computing, there has been a need for a richer media interface. The ability to play back sound was primarily addressed by the company Real Networks. They released the Real Audio player that has been modified to play both audio and video. This software allowed real time, near real time, or stored for playback audio streams from radio stations, and other audio sources. The key to the success of this product was the ability to compress the audio enough to make it practical to play back high enough quality audio over dial-up connections that were commonly 19,200–24,000 bps. When further development allowed the same type of video compression, this product's success was assured. Most successful browsers incorporated Real Audio support directly, or were easily upgraded through the plug-in approach. Other competitors appeared, such as Microsoft with their Media player; all of these additional tools are integrated into the web browser. A key disadvantage to these types of media players for video is that they begin to take large amounts of network bandwidth.

PDF Files and Adobe Acrobat

In addition to the media player plug-ins, the ability to view rich, secure documents was needed. Adobe, with the Acrobat Reader, provided the best and most successful solution to this issue. Using the authoring and creation tool of Adobe Acrobat, companies and individuals could create a document in the PDF (postscript definition format) file type, and distribute the file, along with the reader, at no charge to the end user. The creation process amounts to no more than choosing a different printer type (the Adobe writing software). The output is a file that looks like a printed page. The file can be secured with a password to prevent manipulation or changes. Further, all of the original formatting is retained. This revolution changed the way documents could be distributed and posted on web sites. Adobe Acrobat was typically installed as a plug-in, but like Real Audio, became so popular that this support is often included by default with popular web browsers.

Other Plug-ins

Other plug-ins, like the Flash player, have been developed to support richer graphics and motion. Today, there are plug-ins for fax, search engines, and other special features. As web browsers and e-mail products become more sophisticated, more of these add-ins are incorporated in the software; or the plug-ins are automatically installed. When considering acceptable plug-ins for an organization, remember to consider security and network bandwidth issues. For example, a very popular Internet utility that evolved from a stand-alone utility to a plug-in was Pointcast. This product delivered information like news, weather, specific company information, and requested information to users' desktops. This product used so much network bandwidth that many organizations banned its use.

File Transfer Protocol Software (FTP)

Another early and primary application of the Internet was the ability to transfer files quickly and easily. The files were often information for research or from special projects. They were typically files or programs that needed to be moved from one computer to another to help further a project. The files did not come from standard applications, but that radically changed as the Internet became commercialized. Transferring files took separate software called FTP (file transfer protocol) software. The early versions of this software were clumsy, character-oriented, and required line commands to initiate the transfers. However, this was a vast improvement over writing files to tape or diskettes since communication was virtually immediate. The encoding, called UUEncoding (Unit to Unit Encoding), of these files to conserve space and speed often used 7 bit computer codes instead of 8 bit. This made standard application file formats in the 1990s corrupt. As the assumption became that all 8 bits were used, file formats, like those used in word processors or spreadsheets, could be transferred without special effort. The breakthrough in this area occurred when standard e-mail products allowed attachment of files. FTP software is still used with major competitors being CuteFTP and WSFTP. FTP products have become graphical, and transfer larger files much more effectively in both time and size than e-mail systems. This allows a user to see folders on both their own system and the remote system. They can then highlight, drag, and drop the files they want to copy.

Instant Messaging

Another handy tool for use on the Internet is instant messaging or IM. IM evolved from the chat room software to a graphically and voice enabled solution. Most people know about IM today because their children use IM to talk to their friends via the Internet. Instead of the old days of tying up a telephone line with a conversation to one friend, or the later days of 3-way calling and talking to two friends at the same time, many teenagers hold multiple conversations with friends from in town and all over the world. The key product that made IM popular was ICQ, but other software products like Yahoo Messenger, AOL IM, and Microsoft Network Messenger have gained popularity. A disadvantage to IM systems is that they can only talk to other users on the same IM system. During the development of this book, we used a consolidated IM product called Trillian to trade ideas while we were online, regardless of when and where we were working. Trillian can recognize multiple IM systems as well as multiple IM users at the same time. IM takes very little network bandwidth while providing users direct, inter-com-like access to other users. Although IM can be abused by workers, this can be a huge productivity tool with the right discipline and control.

Collaborative Tools

As bandwidth increased on the Internet, new collaborative tools began to appear. The goal was to create an interactive environment where files, video, and voice would flow in real time between users. Some of the early tools only allowed remote manipulation of the computer, and are still useful for support purposes. Popular products in this class include pcAnyWhere, Carbon Copy, Remotely Possible, and GoToMyPC. This type of support is also in remote control products like Citrix or Microsoft Terminal Server. A better example of products in this class is Microsoft NetMeeting or the support provided in video conferencing products, when the power of interactive voice and video allows small workgroups interactive collaboration on projects. The number of simultaneous users should be limited to 3 to 4 people although by design this technology will support up to 24 users.

Conferencing Software

Another software category that is popular for remote training and demonstration is conferencing software. This software allows a host site to run an application and/or a presentation. Everyone who has security access and is signed on to the session can see the results. Placeware and WebEx are examples of products in this class. The software products can support a wide variety of applications. The key to both conferencing and collaboration software is that users can see the application running in near real time, and need nothing more than a web browser loaded. This can help minimize travel and other business expenses. More importantly, this type of instruction helps visual learners see what a product can and does do with a minimum of preparation. Further, by using screen captures (press the ALT PRTSC keys on the keyboard), and pasting these screens into a word processing document, you can quickly document procedures, and use this information to train others.

Newsgroups

Another function that was frequently used before the Internet was commercialized is the newsgroup function. Typically, a newsreader was installed. But, today most of the popular browsers do a good job of providing a newsgroup interface. Newsgroups exist for tens of thousands of topics. Some of the best technical support that is available can be obtained through newsgroups. There is rarely a charge, and good technical users with a wide variety of expertise frequent these groups to provide answers. This function of the Internet is one last bastion of free, shared knowledge without a lot of commercialization. Many commercial companies are adding newsgroup support for their commercial products. Of course, the challenge is how to charge for the support. But, customer satisfaction is increased, and developmental staff can assess the success, issues and opportunities with the products.

OTHER SOFTWARE TOOLS

There are also many other software tools that can have a significant impact on productivity. For example, a key software product to use for documentation of networks and processes is Microsoft Visio. This product helps with diagramming, using shapes, arrows and words. Since this list of software changes so frequently, we recommend checking this book's supporting website (*www.technologybestpractices.com*) for our current recommendations.

ENCRYPTION

Encryption is another class of software so important to business operations that it is a major section of a later chapter. Encryption takes files, and encodes them with mathematical calculations that can be reversed on the receiver's end. While the information is passing over the Internet, it cannot be read with simple text tools. The goal is to make the data inaccessible by all but the intended recipient. Encryption software can be as simple as PGP (pretty good privacy); included as options in both e-mail and web browser software through digital certificates; or be integrated into hardware. Organizations should have a direct plan for creating a secure, encrypted environment.

CONCLUSION

Software drives the use of computers to solve business problems. The marketplace drives some software choices. In other cases, software selection has to match the business philosophy and approach. In all cases, poor software choices can damage the ability of a business to operate, and good software choices give the business the tools that are needed to operate smoothly. However, implementation and training are still key to helping staff use software to solve business problems.

CHAPTER EIGHT

Hardware Selection and Maintenance Best Practices

SELECTING APPROPRIATE HARDWARE

If there is a computer solution, there is hardware to run it. As stated in earlier chapters, the first mission should be to define the business problem; then to select appropriate software and procedures. Finally, select the hardware to run this solution. Occasionally, a great new piece of technology, like a handheld scanner, will prompt users to look for a business problem to solve using this piece of technology. Part of the job of the information steering committee should proactively watch evolving or new technology to see how technology *toys* can be effectively used in the business.

We believe that higher quality hardware will reduce the total cost of ownership. The cost of hardware purchases is typically less than 25 percent of the lifetime ownership cost of technology. But hardware and software are frequently the only hard costs that can be tied to technology purchases. In general, larger vendors like IBM, Compaq or Hewlett Packard will spend more on engineering for their products than most of their competitors combined. This extra engineering will generally mean more reliability and more innovation over the long term.

The intent of this chapter is to describe each of the common computer hardware categories today, and give guidance for selection. Remember that our online presence gives current opinions of products in these different categories.

There are many components in any computing hardware solution:

- Printing solutions.
  - Types of printers.
  - Personal printing saves money.
  - Multi-function devices.
  - Network.
  - Color.
  - Adobe as an alternative to printing.

- Client workstation solutions.
  - PC developments.
    - Pentium IV.
    - Major brands.
    - Recommended configuration—RAM, Disk, CD/CDRW/DVD/DVDRW.
  - Thin clients (the network computer).
  - Browser based clients.
  - RISC computers.
  - No home computers.
- Monitor solutions.
  - Flat screen.
  - Short neck.
  - Multiple monitors.
- Portable solutions.
  - Lightweight, middleweight, heavyweight.
  - Screen size.
  - Drive size.
  - Docking stations.
- Server solutions.
  - Stand alone versus rack.
  - Processors.
    - Itanium.
    - Multiple.
  - Windows terminal server and Citrix.
  - Internet servers, firewalls, proxy.
  - Remote access.
- Network hardware infrastructure.
  - Switches, routers and hubs.
  - Cabling and wireless solutions.
- Storage options.
  - Small (Iomega).
  - Mid.
  - Large (fiber options).
  - Dataspace (remote Internet based storage).
  - Calculating space requirements for embedded image applications (i.e., inventory systems).
- Developing a data management schema.
  - Flat files.
  - Databases.

- Backup solutions for servers and clients.
  - Server backup.
  - Desktop file backup.
  - Desktop imaging.
- Extending the life of hardware.
  - Continuous care.
  - Third-party warranties.
  - Use of replicated drive images.
  - Replacement of mice and keyboards.

Many of these components are combined into a system unit selection, or the decision is made to use products only from a single vendor. We will treat the components separately, noting where there are dependencies.

PRINTING SOLUTIONS

The first consideration is the device that creates the final output from the systems, the printers. Consistency is the watchword in printer purchases. Buy from the same manufacturer to minimize support and driver issues. We prefer leading brands like Hewlett Packard, Lexmark or Xerox. Most printers come in several different types and styles as shown in Exhibit 8.1.

Each of these types of printers serves a specific function in the business application. As a general rule, it is less expensive to use laser printers. The following discussion reviews each type of printer.

Exhibit 8.1

Type of Printer	Black and White	Color	Photo Quality	Multi-part (Impact)	Operational Cost	Initial Cost
Laser	X	X	X		Low	Medium
Ink Jet	X	X	Some		High	Low
Thermal	X				High	Low
Thermal Transfer		X	Typically high quality wax		Very High	High
Dot Matrix	X			X	Medium	Low
Line Printer	X			X	Low	High

First, we recommend *laser printers* wherever they make practical sense, including lasers at the desktop, or personal laser printers. Laser print costs between 0.6 cents and 1.2 cents per page, and is often less expensive than using a copier. Laser printers create higher quality images by fusing toner to paper with high heat. Personal laser printers print at speeds between 4 and 15 pages per minute (PPM), and shared network laser printers print at 8 to 50 PPM.

Personal laser printers will keep most workers from leaving their workspace, particularly if the laser printer has copy capability included. Some vendors refer to combination laser printers and copiers (and occasionally faxes) as *multi-function printers* or *multi-function devices*. Placing a multi-function printer at each worker's desktop is a sure way to drive productivity up. These units cost between $350 to $950 for a laser device, and between $150 to $750 for an inkjet device. Even if the worker does not stop to have a copier, water cooler, or coffee break discussion just once per day, the cost will be justified rapidly. One caution is needed—there are indications that many office workers need to get up every two hours to prevent physical problems like blood clots in the legs. Do not spend extra money on technology just to keep a person in their work area, and to keep them from moving. Personal printing saves money (primarily through saving time) compared to most shared network printing approaches. However, if the print job is much larger than 30 pages, using a shared network printer saves more time.

Shared network attached laser printers can be very productive in small work groups. Networked laser printing is faster than using serial or parallel cables to make the attachment. Some vendors, like Hewlett Packard, have created an entire product line of network cards for their laser printers, the Jet Direct cards, to enable shared laser printing across the network. Network attached printers are faster because they eliminate the speed bottleneck of either parallel or serial cables, since they can accept the data at network speeds (10 or 100 Mbps today instead of 9600 bps for direct cables). Further, they remove the burden of print spooling from the local workstation or the network servers. Additionally, some of the more sophisticated shared network laser printers use hard drives to retain multiple copies of a document for printing, or to keep the most commonly used fonts. Using a hard drive in a laser printer reduces network traffic, and is almost always a great value.

Today, everyone seems to want laser printing. It is very affordable and is required by tax and image processing. Not all users on a network understand how shared printers work, so specific additional training will be necessary. A specific class teaching about network use, including shared printers, should be implemented in most organizations. A default printer should be selected at log in time by the network system. A network system log in script can make multiple printers continuously available. Software should be configured to support multiple printers. Network shared printers should include a printer to handle a letterhead paper tray (switchable to $8^1/_2 \times 11$ bond, legal size or second sheet letterhead), $8^1/_2 \times 11$ plain white paper, and an envelope feeder.

Each business should own at least one *color laser printer* to print important client or customer documents and proposals. Replacement of some business forms is possible by using color laser technology as well. Today the typical color laser cost per page is 3 cents. Color laser technology continues to improve in quality while reducing price per page. Small color lasers currently cost around $2,000, and print at 4 PPM. High-speed models run about $4,000 and can print 16 PPM. Most color lasers can print in color or black and white. Black and white print speeds will commonly be four times the speed of color printing, since most of the printers use four different colors of toners and four print passes to make a single image. Further, with the improvement in quality, color laser photo quality is now a reasonable substitute for traditional photographic images.

Control of color printing will be a cost consideration in the future. Color images that show negative numbers in red can be very helpful in a presentation piece to drive home a point. Likewise, printing a web page in color can make the page more readable. However, users may be tempted to print everything in color without regard to the cost per page or the speed. These issues will need to be part of your training program.

Ink jet printers are more expensive to operate, and much less expensive to purchase. Ink jet printers usually have a separate black ink cartridge; they may have either a combination cartridge or multiple separate cartridges to produce a color image. Ink jet printers spray an image onto the paper in the pattern of the letters or lines that correspond to an image. The high cost per page is the big objection to ink jet printers—approximately 7 cents per page for black, and between 12 and 30 cents per page for color. We discourage ink jet printer selection except for very limited and occasional use. If there is a low volume of color work done in an office, a high-end ink jet printer may produce a good enough quality of print that the organization will be satisfied with the results.

One breakthrough in color print technology is resolution high enough to make the printing of photographic images acceptable. The resolution continues to climb about 1000 dots per inch (dpi) and is headed above 2400 dpi. High quality magazine pictures, like those in *National Geographic,* are produced at 2400 dpi. Additionally, some models of these printers have the ability to take a memory card from a digital camera, and to read directly from that card to create photographic prints. There is minimal editing capability today, but this is improving. Further, with photographic paper, the ink jet image appears to be quite acceptable. Smearing due to moisture is another traditional ink jet problem that is becoming less common. The formulation of inks used today, along with the type of paper that is being used to accept ink jet print, is helping with this issue.

Another category of printers, the *thermal printer*, is used for specialty application. This class of printer requires special supplies, and is usually more expensive to operate. The paper used in this type of printer is usually heat sensitive; heating a pattern of dots on the paper creates characters or images. Fax machines, card printers, time clocks, airline printers, and other specialty devices use this technology. The disadvantage of thermal printers is that the image will fade over time.

On the other end of the quality spectrum is *color wax transfer printers.* This class of printer uses sheets of colored transfer material that will lay an exceptional color image on paper. This technology is used for some of the best color images today in advertising, architecture, and design work.

Finally, the traditional workhorses of data processing have been the *impact printers.* These come in two categories, the dot matrix printer, and the line printer. Impact printers can strike through multi-part forms, sometimes as many as six copies. Additionally, impact printers still dominate continuous forms production. The dot matrix printer is used for small print jobs where quality is not as important, but speed, reliability and cost is important. The speed of dot matrix printers is usually measured in characters per second (CPS), and these products typically do 80 to 700 CPS. Aircraft manifests and shopfloor work tickets are two examples where the dot matrix printer still dominates.

The line printer can be built using several different technologies from band to hammers, but the key to this technology is high-speed output for low cost. These printers are usually measured in lines per minute (LPM), and the typical printer in this category will do anywhere from 20 to 880 LPM. Multipart reports, and green bar paper reporting is the chief realm of the line printer.

An alternative to printing is the use of software to create images. *Adobe Acrobat* PDF (postscript definition file) *Writer* is a reasonable alternative to printing images. This software acts like a printer, and is available as a printer choice once it is installed on the desktop user's machine. The software creates small files that can be secured with passwords, and easily sent as e-mail attachments. Further, the images can be stored on Intranet and Internet sites, and looked at with a typical web browser that has the Adobe Acrobat Reader plug-in. Other software products, such as document imaging, can also minimize the number of printed pages.

To properly manage the print environment, keep a log of the expenses to create a printed page such as the one shown in Exhibit 8.2. This will warn you of waste, a printer that has an operational problem, theft, and the cost per printed page. Consider a simple spreadsheet or log sheet that contains the following factors: date (to show when a component was changed), initials of the person who made the change, page count when the change was made, type of item used (toner, drum, fuser, cartridge), and the cost of the item, if known. This log sheet should be located near each printer, and updated when a change is made. The log sheets should be gathered (or the spreadsheets summarized) on a quarterly or annual basis to establish usage patterns and costs of operation.

There is one final note on printed images. It is generally less expensive to print an image, and recycle the paper when done than it is to file a printed document. There are several factors affecting this statement; one factor is currency of information. How many incorrect decisions have been made from looking at old paper that does not have all of the latest facts? Additional factors include the time and the cost of filing and retrieval versus the cost of a printed page, the ease of editing on larger monitors, the personal preferences of looking at documents on paper for review, and the editing of a document.

CLIENT WORKSTATION SOLUTIONS

There are many different types, brands, styles and capabilities of computers in today's marketplace. We currently recommend replacing desktop computers every three to four years, laptop computers every two years, and servers every three to five years. When making a computing decision, the needs of the user must be balanced with the needs of the organization.

Computer capabilities change continuously and radically from year to year. There are cycles of price reductions based on reductions in components such as CPUs or memory.

Exhibit 8.2   Log of Expenses

Date	Initials	Page Count	Item Used	Cost if known

Further, upgraded CPU capabilities have been introduced every calendar quarter for the last twenty years. A major change in CPU capability occurred in 1979 (8088, product in 1981), 1982 (80286, product in 1984), 1987 (80386), 1991 (80486), 1993 (80586 or Pentium), 1996 (Pentium II), 1999 (Pentium III) and 2001 (Pentium IV). This is a major change every three years. As shown in Exhibit 8.3, Intel maintains a roadmap of their projected product line, and new system introductions can be anticipated within two to three months of the introduction of a new CPU. Check Intel's website, *www.intel.com/eBusiness/products/roadmap.htm,* for current information on new systems.

Exhibit 8.3   Intel processor road maps

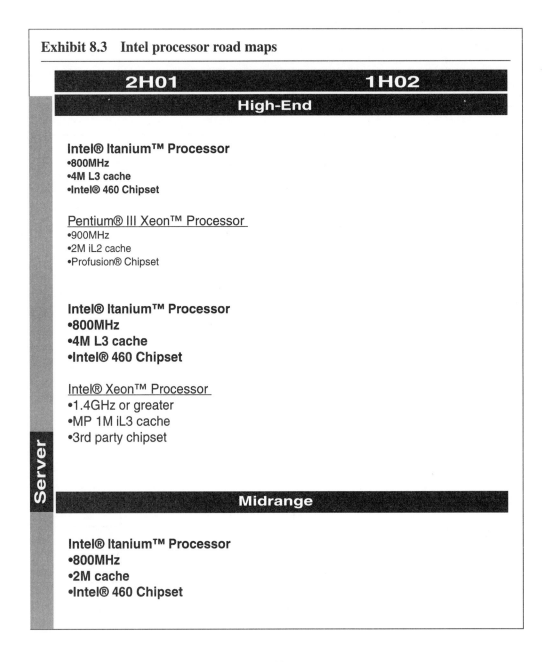

Pentium® III Xeon™ Processor
•700MHz
•1M & 2M cache
•Intel® 440GX Chipset

Intel® Itanium™ Processor
•800MHz
•2M cache
•Intel® 460 Chipset

Intel® Xeon™ Processor
•1.4GHz or greater
•MP 512K iL3 cache
•3rd party chipset

Entry-Level

Intel® Pentium® III Processor
•1.26GHz or greater
•3rd party chipset

Intel® Xeon™ Processor
•2GHz or greater
•Intel® E7500 Chipset

Intel® Pentium® III Processor
•1.26GHz or greater
•3rd party chipset

(continues)

Exhibit 8.3   *(continued)*

2H01	1H02

Desktop

Intel® Pentium® 4 Processor
•**2GHz or greater**
•**Intel® 850 Chipset**
•**Intel® 845 Chipset**

Intel® Pentium® III Processor
•greater than 1GHz
•256K on-die L2 cache
•133MHz system bus
•Internet Streaming SIMD Extensions
•Intel® 815/E Chipset
•Socket-based and Slot designs

Intel® Pentium® 4 Processor
•**greater than 2GHz**
•**Streaming SIMD Extensions 2**
•**400MHz system bus**
•**Intel® 850 Chipset**
•**Intel® 845 Chipset**

2H01	1H02

Mobile

Mobile Intel® Pentium® III Processor-M
•**1.2GHz**
•**Intel® 830M/MP Chipset**

Intel® Pentium® III Processor
•1GHz
•256K on-die L2 cache
•Internet Streaming SIMD Extensions
•Intel® SpeedStep™ technology
•Intel® 815EM Chipset

Mobile Northwood Processor
•**1.5GHz or greater**
•**Intel® 845MP/MZ**

Mobile Intel® Pentium® III Processor-M
•1.2GHz or greater
•Intel® 830M/MP Chipset

Workstation

2H01   1H02

High-End

Intel® Itanium™ Processor
•733 / 800MHz
•4M L3 cache
•Intel® 460 Chipset

Intel® Xeon™ Processor
•2GHz
•Intel® 860 Chipset

Intel® Itanium™ Processor
•733 / 800MHz
•4M L3 cache
•Intel® 460 Chipset

Intel® Xeon™ Processor
•2GHz or greater
•Intel® 860 Chipset

Midrange

Intel® Itanium™ Processor
•800MHz
•2M cache
•Intel® 460 Chipset

Intel® Xeon™ Processor
•1.7GHz or greater
•Intel® 860 Chipset

Intel® Pentium® III Processor
•1GHz or greater
•256K iL2 cache
•Intel® 840 Chipset

Intel® Itanium™ Processor
•800MHz
•2M cache
•Intel® 460 Chipset

Intel® Xeon™ Processor
•2GHz or greater
•Intel® 860 Chipset

(continues)

Exhibit 8.3   *(continued)*

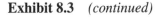

Midrange
Intel® Pentium® 4 Processor
•**2GHz****
•**256K iL2 cache**
•**Intel® 850 Chipset**
•
<u>Intel® Pentium® III Processor</u>
•1GHz or greater
•256K iL2 cache
•Intel® 840 Chipset
•
•
Intel® Pentium® 4 Processor
•**2GHz or greater****
•**256K iL2 cache**

The current mainstream desktop processing chip is the Pentium IV by Intel. As it continues to increase in speed and decrease in price, Pentium IV will become the dominant desktop CPU technology. Pentium IV is key to the next generation of the Internet with enhanced sound and graphic processing capabilities. It is also likely that when enough processing power is available, voice recognition will begin to work correctly. Intel has competitors in the CPU chip marketplace such as AMD. There are generally compatibility issues with CPU chips when they are first introduced; but operating systems, BIOS (Basic Input/Output Systems) and other system level ROM changes usually resolve the problems after three to six months.

We support the notion of buying major brand computers, particularly from vendors like Compaq, IBM, Hewlett Packard, Dell, and Gateway. The key issue is the amount of engineering that the major vendors do before releasing a product. Companies that primarily assemble machines from parts (like Dell, Gateway, and white box clone manufacturers) are counting on other vendors to perform their engineering. They may buy high quality parts, like system boards from Intel, or they may buy the cheapest parts they can find in the world. However, since no engineering of system BIOS is done, compatibility issues may be the price of being first to market.

Today's desktop computers should include a high speed processor like the Pentium IV; a generous, high-speed hard drive 40 Gigabyte (GB) or larger; ample memory or RAM (512 MB plus); a diskette drive; and at least a CD ROM drive. As the market matures, expect DVD drives with write capability to become standard items. A combination drive that is a CD/CDRW/DVD in one unit is available now. The ability to create CDs on a personal computer is good for temporary backup purposes, and can help with the transportability of data. A CDRW (read-write) drive can create both read-only (CDR) and rewriteable CDs (CDRW). CDR is more reliable than CDRW, but the media can only be written one time.

Other types of computers such as the PC Client (sometimes called a *fat client,* discussed in earlier chapters) have just as much use in business as those described above. The *thin client,* also called a network computer, does not have all the hardware resources of a standard PC. The thin client still has a CPU, memory, and usually a hard drive. However, devices that allow access to the data or computer are usually not included. Therefore, most of these units do not have a diskette drive, removable media drives, such as an Iomega Zip® drive, or a CD of any kind. The processing may still be done on the thin client, or the processing may be more dependent on the network server, depending on the software. This type of technology has a very low cost of ownership, because so little can go wrong at the desktop. Technicians do not need to spend as much time dealing with desktop issues, setup, or configuration.

Browser based clients are similar to thin clients, but nothing more than a browser is loaded. These units will not include a hard drive, and will only load a web browser. All applications are accessed through a web browser, and only minimal processing is done locally.

More powerful computers, called *workstations*, are usually based on RISC (reduced instruction set computer) CPUs. These specialized CPUs do not have the more complex instruction set of a typical PC CPU (formally called a CISC or complex instruction set computer). With fewer instructions that can be chosen by a program, these CPUs can accomplish more computation in a smaller amount of time, making them much faster for applications like computer aided design (CAD), engineering or design work. These computers are actually faster in day-to-day productivity use as well. In addition, workstations usually have the fastest RAM available at the time as well as having very high-speed disks installed. These units also have far more sophisticated video cards to handle complex graphics. A workstation will cost 1.5 to 3 times the cost of a typical PC based client.

There is one final caution in the area of client workstations. Most manufacturers create a special home edition of their personal computer brands. *Home computers* are designed to work in homes, and business computers are designed to work better in business. For example, the current home computer lines are: IBM—Aptiva; Compaq—Presario; and HP—Pavilion. These computer lines have software bundling and other features that make them work far better in a home environment. The big disadvantages are complexity of networking; equipment that doesn't make sense in the business marketplace; and hardware that will take less day-to-day abuse. Other vendors do not configure their lines as home versus business, although they are sold that way. In general, home or small business configurations are made from lower quality components.

MONITOR SOLUTIONS

Monitors, sometimes called CRTs (for cathode ray tube), are needed for all of these client workstations, although a few models will have the monitor integrated in the system unit. Monitors come in three major varieties today: standard CRT, short neck CRT, and flat screen CRT. CRT size is a major consideration for most organizations. Today, we recommend 19 inches as the minimum monitor size, but understand that acquiring new, larger monitors can result in the political issue of monitor envy. Large monitor sizes in CRT formats take a large amount of desk space, commonly a 20-inch cube. To lessen the amount of desk space taken by a large monitor, manufacturers have come up with a short-term alternative called short neck monitors. This CRT design minimizes the depth of a CRT, so that the monitor is no more than 6 to 8 inches deep, and still has the advantage of image brightness. CRT solutions are between $150 and $750.

Flat screen monitors have the key advantages of taking very little space and being very glare tolerant. Further, flat screen monitors give their full value in viewable area. For example, a 21-inch CRT design may only give 18 to 20 diagonal inches of viewable area. A 21-inch flat screen will be very close to giving 21 inches of viewable area. Flat screens also tend to be not quite as bright as their CRT cousins. This lack of brightness is improving as the large chip that makes up the flat screen improves. Software tuning tools exist to improve the output of flat screens in conjunction with video cards. Many flat screen designs are digital designs instead of the analog design of the CRTs. Digital flat screen monitors may be difficult, if not impossible, to configure without temporarily having a regular CRT installed during the setup process.

Flat screens have also been more expensive than the CRT alternatives, often costing 2 to 3 times as much as the same size CRT. Even with these considerations, flat screen monitors are often worth the money, just for the recovery of desk space alone. Some users report less eyestrain using a flat screen compared to a CRT. Further, flat screen monitors emit less radiation than CRTs. Most people who use flat screens do not want to return to CRTs.

Both the authors use *multiple monitors* for our development work. Multiple monitors allow looking at several documents with a simple head or eye movement. It is common to have a web resource on one monitor while using the word processor on the other monitor. If a single document or spreadsheet becomes too large, it can be spread over multiple monitors. If document imaging is being used, the document can be pulled up on one monitor while work in an accounting system continues on the other monitor. It is a simple task to have multiple monitors for Windows 98, later Windows operating systems, and Linux. Simply install an adapter that supports two or more monitors, install the drivers, and attach the monitors.

Having multiple monitors reduces eyestrain but increases radiation. One unconfirmed caution is in order: There are indications that multiple monitors may be produce enough radiation to cause complications during pregnancy. For safety reasons, until the research is clear, we recommend having loaner flat screen monitors for pregnant workers.

PORTABLE SOLUTIONS

Portable solutions are reducing in weight and size while increasing in power and capacity. As in the case of desktops, we prefer the major vendors for laptops, but there are some additional competitors who have nice products. Most laptop vendors have a good product every other year. There is certainly plenty of engineering required to have a great laptop design. The key design issues for laptop engineering are weight, heat, and battery life.

Most portable computers are in the laptop format today, and come in three sizes: lightweight, middleweight, and heavyweight. The different sizes carry different price tags and feature sets. The best value is the middleweight class since these computers have a little more weight, and use slightly less expensive components to get the job done. Most middleweight portable computers are $1300 to $2200 and weigh 5 to 6 pounds. They often have a three spindle design. This means there is a diskette, hard drive and CD/DVD drive included in the unit.

Lightweight portable computers are usually in the 3 to 4 pound range, and are thin in appearance. They have not given up performance or hard drive space, but usually only have a one or two spindle design. This means that the diskette drive must be hooked up separately when needed, or an additional docking module may be needed to add the functionality of diskette or CD/DVD. These machines are usually more expensive than the middleweight computers, and may not be as durable.

Heavyweight computers are the most powerful of the laptop portables. These machines will have the most comparable desktop features, and will typically feature the largest screens, a docking station, and other equipment to give them desktop functionality. These machines are usually slightly heavier than middleweight machines, commonly weighing in at 5 to 8 pounds. These machines also tend to be the most expensive of the laptops with prices ranging from $2200 to $3500.

Most manufacturers have several different screen sizes available for every model they sell. Today's laptop screen size varies from 11 to 16 inches, but 13 and 14-inch screens are the most common. If the laptop is to be a full-time desktop replacement, a larger screen is certainly preferable. The screen in a laptop is actually quite durable and can be cleaned with a soft cloth or a paper towel moistened with a glass cleaning solution like Windex.

Hard drive sizes continue to increase in laptops with 6 to 40GB being common right now. Laptop drives tend to be slower than desktop drives; this can affect performance for certain applications. We recommend larger, faster hard drives, but this one factor alone can affect the price of the laptop by $300 to $500 and more. Being able to remove the hard drive is another factor in the price of the units. Most middleweight portable computers do not have removable drives, although most light and heavyweight machines do have removable hard drives. Removable media is important if the machine is going to be used for many different applications that require different operating systems or configurations. Removable media is also important if the laptop is going to be shared by multiple users. We recommend acquiring a drive for each user or class of user so the laptop is always configured for that user. Most laptop users are fine with a non-removable drive.

Today's portable computers include parallel, serial, and USB ports, network connections, wireless capability, and modems. They also have at least a CD, a CDRW, a DVD, or a combination device that serves all three functions. The laptop will also have one or two PC card slots to allow connection of card-based devices to the computer. Older laptops used this slot for network adapters, SCSI adapters, or removable storage. Most new laptop technology is first introduced via a PC card adapter.

Most portable computer manufacturers have *docking stations, docking slices, port replicators,* or some other device that allows the portable computer to be easily and quickly reconnected to the corporate network when the user returns to the office. The docking device often has network connection, keyboard, mouse, and monitor connections as well as the ability to hook up other equipment like additional hard drives or multiple monitors. Since there is no standard interface defined for portable computers, docking devices are usually only good with the computer with which they were purchased. Some manufacturers have families of computers that use the same docking device.

SERVER SOLUTIONS

The core processing capability and capacity of today's computing is the server solution. The technology industry's current philosophy is to refer primarily to LAN based or personal computer servers as servers. But, we believe that any computer that shares its resources is a server. Servers can share disk, printers, fax, communications, and processing power with other computers. Using this definition, all minicomputers and mainframes, as well as workstations, are servers. Logically and for planning purposes, it is fair to consider all of these machines as comparable. But, there are key operational differences between different classes of servers, as shown in Exhibit 8.4. We will begin with the physical layout of servers.

Servers have traditionally been purchased as separate stand-alone units that were initially tied together with slow communication lines. Today, they are tied with local area networks, high-speed communication lines such as a wide area network, or VPN, or fiber optics. Each of these servers has its own operating system, disk and so forth. Many organizations still deploy servers the same way today.

To drive down the cost of ownership where there are two or more servers, we suggest buying the rack mount versions of the servers such as the one in Exhibit 8.5. The electronics industry maintains a standard 19-inch rack definition for mounting high-density

Exhibit 8.4

Type of Server	Processor Fault Tolerance	Disk Fault Tolerance	Power and Processing Redundancy	Self-Correcting Memory
Mainframe	X	X	X	X
Minicomputer	X	X	X	X
Workstation	X	X	Some	Some
PC Based	Some	X	Some	Some

Exhibit 8.5

electronics. By using the rack mount approach, more equipment can be placed in a smaller space, and maintenance can be done easier and faster.

Further, the rack can hold keyboard, monitor, disk or storage area network, tape backup, battery backups, and occasionally even switches or routers. The idea is to create a clean environment with properly labeled equipment to make the computer operation cleaner and more reliable.

Properly designed server computers are different than stand-alone desktop computers. Many server features appear later in desktop computers. For example, a well-designed server today will have one or more of the following features: multiple processors; server clustering; disk array (RAID) controllers, at least disk mirroring; redundant power supplies; hot swappable (can be physically exchanged while the equipment is running) drives; power supplies and mother boards; higher speed network cards; disk channels; disks; memory; fault notification cards and/or software; specific integration to the operating system in use; and self-correcting memory. The table in Exhibit 8.6 summarizes some of the common fault tolerant features in servers. Each of these features is typically purchased as a separate upgrade to the server capability and thus each carries an initial acquisition price. Organizations should assess the cost of downtime versus the initial price and maintenance spread across the life of the product. Since we tend to favor reliability, speed, and price (in that order) for computing in general, we

Exhibit 8.6

Feature	Processor Fault Tolerance	Disk Fault Tolerance	Power Fault Tolerance	Speed	Availability
Multiple processors	X	X	X	X	X
Server clustering	X	X	X	X	X
Error correcting memory	X				X
Disk array controllers		X			X
Hot swap drives		X	X		X
Hot swap power supplies	X		X		X
Hot swap system boards	X				X
Redundant power supplies	X	X	X		X
Disk mirroring		X		X	X
RAID		X		X	X
SAN	X	X	X	X	X
Hot standby drive		X			X
Tape array		X		X	X
LAN communications				X	
Channel speed		X		X	
Self-correcting memory	X				X
Remote management hardware	X	X	X		X
Remote management software	X	X	X		X
Specific engineering to match operating systems	X	X	X	X	X

have a strong preference for purchasing these fault tolerant features in mission critical servers, and often in the entire server farm.

The processing chips used in servers may be proprietary, specialized workstation processing units, or standard processors from companies like Intel. The speed of the chip is only one factor in rating the processing capability of a CPU chip. Other design factors, like processor cache, will also affect the capability of the CPUs used in servers. Even smaller, slower processing chips like Intel Pentium III chips may be sufficient for some server applications, although we recommend server specific chips like XEON or Itanium designs.

One of the leading ways to gain processing horsepower is to use multiple CPU chips in a single server machine, if the operating system supports this type of hardware. All of the common Microsoft Windows server operating systems support multiple CPUs (NT, 2000, .NET) as do Novell NetWare and Linux. Other evolving technologies include machines that use arrays of CPU chips in a single server. It is not uncommon right now to find 8, 16, and 32 CPUs in this configuration. Some companies have announced designs involving 128 processors and more.

PC servers continue to gain more and more power. In some cases, they are replacing minicomputer and mainframe technology with similar processing horsepower and a lower initial acquisition cost. PC server operating systems are supporting hundreds and, in some cases, thousands of users simultaneously. Realistically, there is a practical operational limit of a few hundred desktop PCs for every server deployed, even though the operating systems and directory services can support much larger numbers. Since many organizations are obviously larger than a few hundred people, the strategy most frequently used with PC servers is to have departmental level servers. These servers should be centralized in groups even if departmental control is allowed. As operations increase in size, more professional data processing management is needed to protect the organization.

PC servers run not only file and print services, but can run additional services as well. Beyond file and print services, specialized services such as SQL databases, DNS (domain name services), communication servers including proxy and host services, mail, web, e-commerce, productivity enhancement services, software management consoles, and system monitoring servers may be added to larger networks. It is not unusual to limit PC servers to a single function, improving reliability, but driving up the cost of ownership. This can make midrange and mainframe solutions more cost-effective than banks of PC based servers. A fairly recent evolution in this competition is the creation of blade (single card) servers where one or more servers are inserted in a housing.

The PC industry has tried to reduce the cost of ownership, including upgrades to desktop software and limiting purchase of new desktop hardware by providing thin client software solutions. Two popular solutions include Citrix MetaFrame, and Microsoft Terminal server. There are products that run on UNIX, and in hardware as well. This topic is so broad as to merit separate coverage in Chapter 11.

Servers can also perform specific functions such as firewalls, proxy servers, and communication gateways. We generally recommend that these functions are implemented in routers or specialized concentrators rather than at the server level. But, for an inexpensive, workable solution, implementing the software to do these tasks on a server can minimize the cost of implementation in branch offices. When these services are run on server products, they tend to be less reliable and slower than comparable solutions on specialized pieces of hardware.

A few other cautions and admonitions about server acquisition are important. First, drive speed and capacities are important considerations. Today's better server drives run at 15,000 RPM. This faster rotation speeds up the transfer of data. As soon as faster technology is available and reliable, we recommend the fastest server drive available.

Next, because of changes in technology announced by IBM and others in 2001, server drive capacity will increase radically. This *pixie dust* technology allows data to be stored more densely than ever before on drives. Today's standard size of 18 and 36GB spindles will commonly become 72 and 144GB and more.

The interface of the server drive is also changing. The most common electrical interface for a server drive has been SCSI (Small Computer System Interface). This technology has evolved from 8 to 16 to 32 to 64 to 128 bit technology, with several variants in the naming such as SCSI-2, SCSI-3, Wide SCSI and Ultra Wide SCSI. This interface may be nearing the end of its useful life; but every time that seems to be the case, some smart engineer figures out how to improve the performance and capacity. There is a new version of SCSI that is trying to compete with Infiniband, Fibre Channel, and other high-speed Input/Output transfer technologies in servers. The key thing to watch is the new high-speed I/O technologies for servers that will affect server performance, reliability, and server interconnection.

Memory in servers is another consideration. Memory technology changes fairly frequently in servers, and it is best to acquire a high-speed memory solution that complies with the evolving standards. Some marketing efforts will try to convince customers that a particular vendor is using proprietary memory. That is a bad strategy and we are not convinced of this argument. If cost seems reasonable compared to other alternatives; if long-term ability to get replacement memory seems probable; and if the memory has attractive performance or self-correcting capabilities, we support using this technology at the server level.

Finally, all server gear should be supported by Uninterruptible Power Supplies (UPS) technology. Based on the cost of a UPS compared to the cost of being down, not having a UPS on a server is almost always a bad business decision. It can be a wise business investment to place UPS in front of almost all computer gear, including servers, workstations, routers and switches. Laser printers are the only exception to this rule, since they require too much power for their protection to be cost effective. But they should at least have surge protection. Learn more about power protection later in this chapter.

STORAGE SOLUTIONS

Although disk storage received some coverage in the context of servers, there are many more smaller and larger solutions available. This section will start with smaller and go on to discuss larger solutions available today. As always, organizations should monitor changes in these technologies.

One of the leading vendors in small removable storage is Iomega. Products from this company represent a wide variety of solutions. Very small amounts of removable storage can be stored on the 2-inch square Pocket Zip media, which currently holds 40MB of storage on removable media for less than $10. This technology can be used in PC Cards, in specialized drives, in cameras and in MP3 players.

The next larger removable drive is the Zip drive. This product has increased in size from 100 to 250MB, and could be increased even more. This media is a good value, is approximately the size of a 3.5-inch floppy, and is often used as a floppy replacement. Many BIOS and hardware manufacturers, as well as operating systems, have been modified to support booting from the Zip drive. The company recently discontinued the larger Jaz product that at 1 and 2GB was a reasonable hard drive substitute during its life cycle.

Inexpensive writeable CDs (CDR and CDRW) have made some of this removable storage less valuable and obsolete. But, these different types of storage solve different problems. The CD format stores around 600MB for thirty cents. The devices that create the CDs are routinely less than $200, and often less than $100 today. CDR (CD Read means can only be written once) is more reliable and less expensive than CDRW (CD Read/Write). A new trend is technology companies is to leave the CD writing business and to head for the next generation of DVD (Digital Video Disk) writing. Furthermore, devices that do CDRW and read DVD media are now small enough to be included in laptops.

DVD media today can hold 7 to 8GB. The amount of data this media can hold will increase as new standards are adopted. Expect DVD capacities of 18GB and 36GB. The increases in capacities are similar to what occurred historically in the diskette market place. The technology evolves from single sided, single density, to double sided and double density, up to quad density. Another issue in the DVD market place is the encryption standards needed by the motion picture industry. DVD recording and playback is currently a mixture of hardware and software capabilities. This technology is evolving at the time of this writing.

An older, but similar technology to CD and DVD is WORM (Write Once, Read Many) technology. This technology holds 400MB to 2.2GB, and is usually used in document imaging and COLD (Computer On Line Document) solutions. Because of the evolution of CDR and CDRW, as well as the reduction in cost, WORM is primarily used where it has been deployed historically.

Medium size storage solutions are primarily hard disk today. There are two primary interfaces being used, IDE (intelligent device emulation) and SCSI (small computer systems interface). There are many other interfaces available. Although some consultants incorrectly recommend it, IDE is primarily used on the desktop; and SCSI is used in high performance workstations or servers. Although some consultants recommend it, IDE tends to be too slow to be used in servers. Make sure to review the discussion of server drives above.

Because of reduced cost, increased speed and increased capacity, the way hard drives are used is getting more creative. Drives are commonly hooked to controller cards with cables in the simplest approach, but new styles of deploying hard drives are changing this mechanical approach. The controller card may (IDE, SCSI or array adapters) or may not (IDE) have intelligence on the controller card. Further, the controller card may or may not be programmable, have memory, or for that matter have a full-scale computer system on the adapter card. Most desktop purchases will include a simple controller card integrated into the system board, or a separate card that is used for the disk interface.

More sophisticated disk attachments will include drive array controllers that will probably have two or more communication channels, memory buffers, and processing power on the card. When a controller card has processing power on the card, this relieves the main CPU from processing disk I/O. Disk array controllers can control one or more hard drives at the hardware level. These controllers should not be used unless you intend to deploy at least a pair of mirrored drives. Drive mirroring allows data to be simultaneously duplicated on two drives. A better use of an array controller is to create a RAID (redundant array of inexpensive disks). RAID configurations must have at least three drives, but usually have more. RAID writes data redundantly across all physical disk spindles. A complete hard drive failure can happen without shutting a system down. Performance will be slower as data is recreated from the remaining drives using CRC (cyclic redundancy check) technology, but it is rare that a drive failure stops operations. The highest speed disk controllers today have throughput between 160 and 320 Mbps, but slower speeds of 40 and 80 Mbps are more common.

Additional safety is available for RAID units by having a hot standby drive configured. This drive can be plugged into the drive enclosure, but not be included in the RAID. If a drive failure occurs, the RAID can be reconfigured in software to use the hot standby, taking the failed drive offline. Data is written to the new drive added to the array, and normal operations can resume. The failed drive can then be replaced when the replacement drive arrives (typically the next day), and become either a hot spare, or be included in the RAID again. Some vendors, Compaq for example, have hardware and software that will notify their service parts distribution automatically that a failure is beginning to occur, based on failure criterion like bad tracks on a drive. They will ship the replacement drive automatically to the server location for a replacement operation. Most RAID units use hot swap drives that be unplugged and plugged in while the computer is running. RAID units containing terabytes of data can be built today.

If disk performance is an issue in servers, there are two options available. Solid-state drives can radically improve server performance. Solid-state drives are a combination of very high-speed memory backed up by batteries to hold the value placed in the memory, if power fails. Solid-state drives are not system RAM, but a different style of disk. The concept is that 5 to 10 percent of files are used all the time, and significant performance gains can be had beyond RAM caching. These files represent over 50 percent of the I/O activity. Solid-state drives are around 1,000 times faster than regular drives. SANs are the other high performance option for drive storage.

Even more sophisticated than RAID units are SANs (storage area networks). This technology uses a different approach than hard-wired controllers, disks and RAID. The strategy is simple. Instead of building complete disk subsystems in every computer, consolidate the disk storage. Include simple disk support (single disk or mirrored pairs) at the server level, but use a network card over a separate disk I/O network for the majority of the storage. This separate network is much higher speed than disk controllers today. The most common implementations are done over 1 or 2Gbps Fibre Channel. A new competing technology using 10Gbps Ethernet is being built.

To build a SAN, each server that is going to be attached needs to have a SAN adapter (typically, 2 Gbps fibre channel). Fiber optics connect the adapter to a SAN switch or hub. This device implements fibre channel arbitrated loop technology to allocate appropriate processing time to each server and device on the SAN. The software used in this device is very sophisticated and represents the majority of the cost involved. The software also allows the SAN to be used by different operating systems.

There are several key advantages to SANs. They are faster, more reliable, and cheaper than building multiple RAIDs when there are three or more servers involved. Entry level prices for SANs have fallen to around $7,000 today. Multiple operating systems can be supported on the same SAN, including Linux, NetWare, Window NT, Windows 2000, UNIX, OS/400 and MVS. Because the connection to the SAN is over a fiber optics, the physical disk storage can be up to 18 KM from the servers. Furthermore, backup management is much easier because the backup is centralized on the SAN instead of distributed across multiple RAIDs and servers.

SANs have the devices to connect the new generation of technology to legacy technology. As in Exhibit 8.7 below, a SAN gateway can be used to connect Ethernet to Fibre Channel. This allows workstations and older servers without Fibre Channel

Exhibit 8.7

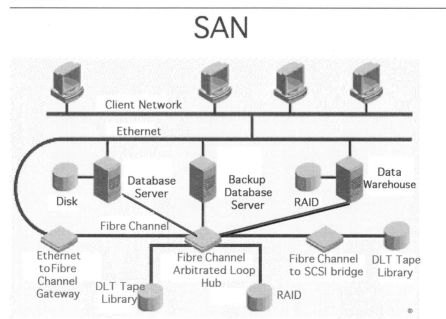

SAN

adapters to connect to the SAN. A Fibre Channel to SCSI Bridge allows older SCSI technology to be preserved. This is sometimes needed to preserve investment in older tape or RAID technology.

NAS (network attached storage) is a competitive technology to a SAN. NAS is less expensive and slower than SAN technology. There are some vendors who are combining their SAN and NAS technology. NAS units typically have an Ethernet LAN adapter that gives access to a single drive or RAID unit in a self-contained housing. This device is limited by your LAN speed. The good news is that these units are very inexpensive. If you need to rapidly expand your server-accessible disk, these units can give you 18GB of storage for less than $500 today.

Data is currently being stored in large volumes over large geographic distances by using private networks or the Internet for storage purposes. We believe that less confidential data, and possibly even very confidential data, will be able to be stored this way in the future. When the Internet is used as the transport mechanism, this is referred to as Dataspace. The connection to these file systems is using the Internet technology of IP to access the drives.

Several technologies will force storage space requirements to skyrocket. Embedding an image in accounting systems for inventory, personnel, and even simple documents will require more storage space. In a product like Microsoft/Great Plains eEnterprise, picture images of inventory items are only taking about 10K of storage for each picture. Document imaging should also drive storage demand up. With today's compression techniques, 1 million documents can be stored in roughly 36GB of disk. As a final example, data marts and data warehouses are keeping a large amount of data for analysis purposes. This application was impractical before cheap disk, server, database and manipulation tools.

DATA MANAGEMENT SOLUTIONS

Even small organizations are increasing the amount of data that is being stored. From accounting systems to e-mail to e-commerce to proprietary systems, more and more data is being stored and analyzed. Traditional systems used file systems that had to be accessed through proprietary or third party mechanisms like Pervasive 2000 (the old Btrieve). Some of these flat file systems were very slow, while others were exceptionally fast and can still outperform relational (SQL) databases today. Pervasive 2000 and Pervasive.SQL represent some of the best flat file technology available today. The design of the data in most of these systems is not as obvious as relational database definitions, unless there is very thorough documentation. Organizations will want to maintain the definitions of the data format as they build their data storage systems. This is particularly important if the data stored becomes large in volume.

Relational databases have been around for more than 25 years, but have only recently become inexpensive enough to deploy that SMB (small medium business) could afford the technology. The primary competitors are: Oracle, IBM with DB2 and other technologies, Microsoft with SQL, and Sybase. These products use relations between tables to store and process data. The statements that access these tables are based on an ANSI (American National Standards Institute) standard that defines the format (rules) of the database instructions. These instructions are called structured query language, commonly referred to as SQL. These standard statements are included in application programs that access the relational databases, as well as in productivity software like Excel. Furthermore, there are development and reporting tools written to use with the major database products, often using SQL as well.

This part of the technology has become so important, that it is wise to employ people with specialized talents to manage the data of the business. This position is usually called a database administrator (or DBA). Refer to Chapter 3 for a complete description of the DBA's responsibilities.

BACKUP SOLUTIONS

Appropriate backup procedures and hardware are mission-critical to every business. If you only learn one item from this entire book, and that is to create and monitor the proper backup of your system, your investment in money and time is more than repaid. Even technology professionals who should understand the importance of backup procedures routinely make errors in this portion of their technology management. Improper backup is the number one error we see in the field. This chapter includes a section on backup methodology to serve as a minimum guide. Additional coverage is included in Chapter 3. You can see how important this topic is to us!

Tape backup units come in three major styles: DAT, DLT and XIO. DAT (digital audio tape) has capacities of up to 24GB, and is very inexpensive hardware costing less than $500. DLT (digital linear tape) has greater speeds and capacities, but is more expensive with units ranging from $1000 to $5000. Capacities are frequently 40 to 200GB or more. A new generation of DLT, called Super DLT promises expanded capacity and speed. XIO (Extended Input Output) units can handle 2 terabytes of data and more, and currently cost around $10,000. All of these technologies are cartridge based. Reel-to-reel tape drives are still available and being used, but they are becoming more rare all the time.

Tape drives can be used independently or in RAID units just like disk drives. Because tape capacities often lag behind disk capacities, it is not unusual to upgrade tape units from one technology to another just to handle routine backup. We usually see physical capacities (too much disk capacity to back up) or time windows (back up takes too long) motivating these changes.

Tape arrays can also be used to minimize user intervention. When a tape array or loader has 7, 14, or 31 tape capacities, the array may be used to backup daily without changing tapes. This strategy calls for a multiple tape array or loader call for a backup to be made on a different tape every night, and all tapes to be exchanged one day of the week.

If tape drives are used in a harsh environment, they may become dirty. Further, if poor quality tapes are used, the tape media may leave residue on the tape drive. We recommend cleaning tape drive units. Different vendors make different recommendations about cleaning; look for and follow the vendor's recommendations.

A few warnings about tape media are also in order. Tapes wear out after use. We recommend rotating tapes into permanent archival storage before they become questionable. This means that tape replacement will need to be budgeted for on an ongoing basis. Further, tapes may need retensioning after some use. This is usually an option in and controlled by the tape backup software.

If there is not tape backup technology built into the operating system, a separate tape backup product will need to be purchased. Even if a backup facility is included in the operating system, you may want to acquire special software because it is more comprehensive, easier to use, and can cross multiple platforms. The major products in the PC marketplace are ARCServe and Backup Exec. These products are available on a wide variety of platforms. Some of the software products are sophisticated enough to manage a tape library, and will handle archiving and cataloging the backups.

Another issue with backup software is that open files are usually not backed up. This is part of the reason that users should log out from systems at least nightly. This helps remind users to close applications and files. When you are acquiring backup software that will back up a relational database, make sure there are the appropriate drivers to backup the database software while it is open. It is unlikely to be able to close down the database for backup purposes.

Another strategy that works for a temporary backup is to copy from disk to disk or RAID to RAID. For example, if you have a SQL database that is being used constantly, you may want to build another SQL database server, which is wise for redundancy purposes, and replicate the primary SQL database data to this server. The redundant server(s) can be taken off-line for backup purposes, and backed up normally. This same type of strategy can be used for servers that are connected in a cluster.

An additional variant of this thinking is duplicating key data on a server in an alternate location. With high-speed Internet access, even small businesses can afford to do this. The business owner will typically have high-speed Internet access in their home, and an additional server can be installed there with a duplication completed on a regular basis.

Desktop File Backup

Another major consideration that is often overlooked is backing up desktop data. Most data should be centralized on servers for backup purposes, but much data is improperly stored without backup on local hard drives. It is a rare day when an end-user has the discipline to backup this data to the centralized network storage. Furthermore, some desktop configuration files are not maintained in a logical place. If a complete desktop hard drive is lost, a comprehensive backup of each desktop drive's contents would have to be maintained. In large organizations, this is not very practical. The installation of new desktop hardware is difficult without an organization-wide strategy.

The IT professional has several strategies that can be used to solve this problem. They are:

- *Desktop backup on:*
  - ○ Internal backup devices.
  - ○ Portable backup devices.
  - ○ Removable media—Zip, CDRW.
  - ○ To file server storage.
- *Desktop management software.*
- *Master images of desktops* (next section).
- *Hardware level drive duplication technology* (also next section).

Internal backup devices give individuals control of when and what gets backed up. This is great for a literate user, but risky for all other users. The user selects the files that need copied, and uses standard commands to write data from the primary drive to something that is removable: Zip, CD, or a removable hard drive.

IT professionals can carry portable backup devices, and rotate through the user base to create a backup either on a schedule or on demand. The issue with this approach is that backups may not be made consistently or on a timely basis.

Backups from the desktops can be made to file server storage. But, for space considerations, usually only desktop data is copied. If the desktop configuration is done properly, the user settings can also be made during this copy. However, with today's desktop drive sizes, the data requirements may become quite large, requiring unanticipated increases in server disk and tape requirements. It is fine for these items to need expansion for backup purposes, but it may require complete server I/O system replacements.

For organizations with more than 75 users, it is clear that some of the desktop management software products are very cost-effective. Software management products like Altiris, CA, BMC or Tivoli will distribute updated software to the desktop automatically, unattended, or on demand. System BIOS, operating systems, applications and virus signatures can all be distributed automatically through the system console.

Presently there are effectively four levels of management capability for PC systems. The first is simple network management protocol (SNMP) that is enabled in the operating system. This tracks the basic network layer functions and basic system level functions. SNMP relies primarily on the network card for support and messaging. SNMP does not provide CPU, Memory or PC configuration information. The next layer, where there is real management power for a desktop, begins with Desktop Management Interface 2.0 (DMI) capability. DMI is O/S independent as it is part of the PC hardware. DMI provides the ability to start a PC up remotely, get component information including memory and drives, as well as complete PC configuration information. DMI communicates via SNMP for events and alarms. Windows Management Interface (WMI) is an additional layer; it is a software agent that provides additional O/S level diagnostic information. The fourth level is a specific agent like the Altiris, CA, BMC or Tivoli agents, which provide an advanced level of detail including process and file details.

The bottom line for desktop management software is that PCs should be SNMP and DMI 2.0 compliant. With these capabilities, additional agents are not needed on PCs. This saves management dollars. We utilize Compaq hardware that is SNMP and DMI 2.0 compliant. It does not appear all IBM PC hardware is DMI 2.0 compliant.

Desktop Images

Software utilities can help the network administrator recreate desktop images from master images of desktops. The idea here is simple, and execution is also straightforward. Once a desktop has been completely set up and tested, a copy of the drive is made with image software like Ghost from Symantec. This software will make a complete image in a smaller space on the server that can be reused on multiple hard drives. The software can also be used to copy one hard drive to another directly. For a 20GB laptop drive, the duplication time is around 15 to 30 minutes. This can be a huge labor savings, and a huge productivity gain for organizations because of the consistency that is automatically enforced at the desktop. No confidential files (like password files) should be copied, and if it is possible to set up system parameters to be updated during the installation or after the duplication, this is a wise strategy. Under *no* condition should this technology or technique be used to violate software license agreements. This issue was discussed in Chapter 7.

A hardware level duplication is similar in logic to the software duplication technique of drives. This approach is more practical on removable drive laptops, but can also be used on desktop drives that can easily be removed and reinstalled. Again, once a master image has been created, the drive is placed in a machine (or occasionally copied to the duplication machine). Depending on the duplication unit, 2, 4, 8, or 16 and more drives can be duplicated at the same time. Duplication time is 10 to 20 minutes for all drives combined. These units vary widely in price and begin at $3,000.

BACKUP METHODOLOGY

We recommend that the tape backup function be performed during nonbusiness hours (as covered in the backup topic in Chapter 3 on procedures). Businesses should develop a system recovery plan for catastrophic failure for their servers, data and network system since they will become very dependent on these systems. Taking the precaution of testing the procedures is an excellent idea. A reciprocal agreement with an outside company or firm in case of failure would allow critical data to be recovered and used. This could provide additional safety to supplement the support provided by the vendor.

The current methods of backup most organizations use can be improved. Monitoring the tape drive(s) and procedures carefully can do this. Scheduling the time of day the backup is done, reading the tape backup logs daily, using backup tapes in rotation, and periodically checking the off-site rotation all help to make for a more reliable backup.

The network tape software should allow backups at specific times of day. With proper use of tape, data could be restored to an appropriate drive depending on the type of failure. The proper use of this software and device(s) will be the best long-term solution for your organization. In many organizations, backups are done on a regular basis, but more control needs to be exercised. This lack of control and testing is an inadequate approach. In general, the system should not be used during backup. This lack of system availability affects productivity if the backup is performed during normal business hours. Unattended backup should be scheduled for 1 a.m. This allows the system to be available during the key hours of 7 a.m. to 7 p.m. If the system backup takes more than 1 tape to complete, this tape can be inserted first thing in the morning to complete the backup, although it is much better to replace the tape drive with one that has a larger capacity. Using this method, the system can be left on 24 hours a day.

Methods of backup to consider include:

- *Grandparent, parent, and child.* This is a rotating scheme that allows some degree of safety for files. A backup of files is made and kept for later use. The next time a backup is made, another set of media (tape) is used. This makes the first set one generation older or a *parent*. The third time a backup is made, a third set of media is used. The first copy has aged another generation and become a *grandparent*. Each time a backup is made, a complete copy of all relevant files are copied to the media. By the time a backup has become a grandparent, the value of the information has decreased because it is not current enough. For the next backup, the grandparent set of media is reused or *born again* as current data is written in place of the first backup made.

- *Another scheme similar to grandparent, parent, and child.* This scheme uses one set of media for each day of the week. On one particular day, perhaps Friday, one set of media is used for each Friday of the month. At the end of the month, a special set of media is used and kept as the end-of-month copy. This method requires 10 sets of media to function correctly. Media used daily should be rotated out over time as the end-of-month copy and archived for whatever period is desired. We recommend this methodology.

Backup media should be stored in a safe place not only in the place of business, but also in an alternate site, such as a bank safe. This allows the support team to recover the data in case of a major catastrophe such as a fire. Try to make the alternate site safe from other natural events like floods and tornadoes.

Backups can be taken of all programs and data files or of only certain files. Complete backups take more time, but contain all programs and data in case any item fails. When making a complete backup, the selective option should be used to allow individual restore of any file. An alternate backup style backs everything up on a particular day (let us say Saturday) and only those files are changed on subsequent days until the next complete backup. We discourage incremental backups because of the increased risk of media failure and the possibility of end-user confusion.

Organizations should use a strict rotation style. If an organization cannot decide, we recommend the second method above that uses 10 sets of tapes, and takes less effort from the operator should it be selected for implementation. This 10-set tape method also allows for more flexibility in recovering data lost further back in time. Additionally, it is important to remember that tapes wear out over time. The tapes in this scheme can be retired by using them as the permanent end-of-month archive. All tapes are then replaced every year, which we also recommend. Implementation of this method is recommended with the current system of backup.

NETWORK HARDWARE INFRASTRUCTURE SOLUTIONS

In the early days of computing, infrastructure standards varied widely, and there were several competitive solutions that worked. Today, the decisions seem far easier and clearer from our perspective. This section is to help orgaizations understand how to make infrastructure decisions. We will look at cabling, wireless, switch, hub and router technology.

Cabling Solutions

Cabling comes in three primary types: twisted pair, coax and fiber optic. Twisted pair comes in both shielded and unshielded twisted pair. Cabling also has different types of jackets that enclose the wires. These outside coverings can be a standard material (like PVC), but if they are not enclosed in conduit, some building codes will require that the jacket be plenum-rated. A plenum rating simply means that the cable will not melt as quickly, nor give off as many poisonous fumes during a fire as a standard cable. Occasionally cables will be gel-filled, particularly in the case of fiber, to give them some resistance to freezing or other physical damage. The average cost of installing a network drop is $250, which includes labor, cable, and termination parts. Some cabling contractors can do the installation for as low as $75 per drop, but remember that you get what you pay for. It is important to have a certified cable drop, including the printed page of proof of performance.

Far more common today is the unshielded twisted pair (UTP) technologies. The most common types of unshielded cables are referred to as CAT 3, CAT 5 and CAT 6. These names refer to the number of twists, and the specification that the UTP cable will meet. CAT 3 cable supports 10Mbps speeds, CAT 5 supports 100Mbps speeds and CAT 6 supports 1 Gbps speeds. There are attempts made to run higher speed technology over lower speed wire, and this meets with marginal success. This strategy is like placing more cars on the freeway without adding lanes. It works for a while, but eventually the traffic backs up, and will no longer flow. Match technology speed with the appropriate wiring specification. For a direct cabling recommendation today, we recommend CAT 6 to give your cabling plant the longest life cycle. Occasionally, UTP cable is referred to by the name *Level* instead of CAT (category). Level simply means that the cable is a proposed standard where CAT is an accepted standard.

To minimize the cost of maintenance, a structured wiring scheme should be implemented using rated CAT 6 unshielded twisted pair wire for new runs, utilizing punch down blocks and connectors. CAT 6 wire will support speed up to 1 Gbps, and we suggest converting some of the operations to this higher speed.

The wiring in all locations should be clearly labeled, the wiring racks grounded, and each cable run should be tested and certified to be at least CAT 6 capable. The minimum target is 568B (100MB) CAT 5. The certification tests will provide a baseline of each connection for future testing as well as documentation of the installation. Most testing equipment will provide a summary printout showing the performance characteristics of each cable drop.

When the cabling infrastructure is completed correctly, it will look orderly and neat like the illustration in Exhibit 8.8. Cabling systems in all locations should be rack mounted, clearly labeled, and tested with both the test documentation and the wiring diagrams on file as part of the system documentation. Small wall-mount racks are also available in addition to the floor rack pictured. The organization will be at risk if anything less than this strategy is used.

The most common of the shielded twisted pair (STP) wiring was the IBM cabling system, which had Type 1, Type 2, and Type 6 cables most commonly deployed. The IBM cabling system is quite capable of handling 100Mbps traffic and can easily be used with today's network technology by using baluns to convert the universal data connectors (UDC) to the more common RJ45 connectors. It is not necessary at this time to remove the older IBM cabling system and replace it with unshielded twisted pair technologies as so many ill-informed consultants have recommended. Cabling infrastructures when properly done should last for 10 to 20 years. Most IBM cabling systems

Exhibit 8.8

were installed between 1980 and 1990. They may never have to be replaced if wireless technology evolves as promised.

Coax cables were traditionally used for Ethernet, ARCnet, security camera, and TV operations. The most common of these cables came in different types (RG58A/U, RG58C/U, RG59, and RG6). Today, RG6 is most commonly used to distribute security camera and closed circuit TV signals, as well as to distribute cable TV signals throughout a building. Coax cable is also used to bring signals from antennas down to the receiver or transmitter devices. For the AS/400 family of computers, IBM used a special variant of coax cable, called twinax. We have not found any way to cost-effectively use or convert coax or twinax cables for LAN operations. However, there are baluns to convert UTP or STP for use in coax or twinax environments.

Fiber optic cables are the third common type of cables in use today. Fiber optic should be chosen when:

- A large amount of electrical interference present—large motors, and so forth.
- The connections are between floors in buildings.
- There are connections between buildings. Each building needs to be isolated electrically to minimize ground voltage potential differential. *Always* use fiber optics between buildings, if possible. Never connect buildings using any type of copper wire.
- When distances exceed 100 meters. Fiber optic can support up to 2 Km without amplification, and can have up to 7 repeaters in standard deployment which gives up to 16 Km of distance without special repeaters.

Fiber optics have two major types that can be installed: single mode and multi-mode. Multi-mode fiber is easier to work with in LAN applications and is easier to terminate (install the ends on the cable). Single mode has greater distance capability, and generally will have greater throughput.

Wireless connections show the most promise for the near future. Encryption is currently at 40 bits and is being upgraded to 128 bits. Stronger encryption is expected. Authentication is improved by being tied to operating system directories and MAC address of the card and wireless access point. Wireless standards are:

- Bluetooth—a short range personal area network with a range of 10 Meters initially at 1Mbps, and increasing to 11Mbps.
- 802.11b or WIFI—LAN replacement running 11Mbps.
- 802.11a—LAN replacement running 22 Mbps.
- 802.11g—LAN replacement running 54 Mbps.
- CDPD—WAN infrastructure in about 3000 US Cities running 19.2K.
- 3G—WAN infrastructure running 2Mbps.

WIFI or 802.11b wireless networking is commonly built into laptop computers today, and is working reliably enough for deployment. Some airports, like the Minneapolis–St. Paul International Airport, have the technology deployed throughout the terminal. This technology can also be used in homes to give home users access to their broadband cable, DSL or satellite without having to wire the whole house.

Hub, Switch and Router Solutions

Many organizations have built infrastructures over a period of years. They commonly purchased the best technology available at the time. Because of current network speed and capability constraints, many organizations' current network architecture is not capable of supporting what they are trying to accomplish and will require major upgrades. Radical overhauls in internal infrastructure can pay dividends in speed and reliability. The current hubs and switches will probably need to be upgraded. There are likely to be some cabling issues that need attention. Wireless technology should probably be implemented as well. Infrastructure needs are reviewed annually, and major upgrades tend to occur every 5 to 7 years.

As networks converted from coax to unshielded twisted pair cables, organizations installed the wiring of the day, often CAT 3 or CAT 5 wire. Each of these wiring types has speed limitations (of 10Mbps or 100Mbps respectively), and may cause bottlenecks in network performance. It was common to buy network hubs, which share communication bandwidth among all devices attached to the hub. A key recommendation today is to replace all hubs with switches. A switch gives a dedicated, two-way communication path on each port. Better designs will be able to aggregate all ports to an even higher speed backplane or communication channel, as the traffic is carried from switch to switch.

Simplistically, you could think of a hub as sharing 10 or 100Mbps between all ports. This would mean that a 12 port hub has, on average, only .83 Mbps for a 10Mbps hub and 8.3Mbps on a 100Mbps hub. A switch has twice the LAN wire speed dedicated to each port because of two-way wire duplexing. Therefore, most switches effectively run at 200Mbps per port.

It is also important that switches are connected together using some form of backplane communications, not a port in the switch. Performance is the reason for this. Using a port in the switch or hub is all right for a temporary connection, but this type of connection is known as cascading. Cascading hubs or switches can cut performance in half every time they are used. A backplane connection might be a special cable assembly, or it might be a special port in the switch dedicated for this purpose.

All locations should use the same brand of switches for each maintenance. The current market leaders are Cisco and 3Com. Based on size and sophistication, a company will select one vendor over another based on internal capability or the availability of a network infrastructure contractor. 3Com switch and router products are easier to configure and install in smaller network environments. Cisco products tend to be more sophisticated with more ability to be configured. If making a switch (and card) conversion, match the cards to the switch vendor and be consistent in subsequent purchases, if possible.

Routers will be used for communications to the Internet and to other locations as you build out your own WAN. Routers should have enough sophistication that firewall and virtual private network (VPN) software can be added. Cisco is currently dominating the router marketplace for these products, and is a good vendor to consider in this category of product.

Power Protection Solutions

Finally, all server gear should be supported by uninterruptible power supplies (UPS) technology. Since servers need to be available whenever the business is operational, not having a UPS on a server is almost always a bad business decision. Improper power protection is the second most common problem we encounter consulting in the field.

The UPS should have an automatic shut-down capability that is configured and attached to the computer being protected. The connection is often made through a serial or USB cable. When power is lost, monitoring software matches the operating system then watches the UPS, so that an orderly shut down of the computer can be done. This orderly shutdown closes all applications and all open files, protecting the data. When power is restored, the UPS will automatically restart the computer system it is protecting. All of the parameters for shutting down and starting the system again are under user control. We particularly like the UPS logs that show losses of power and are a long-term log of power problems.

One style of UPS is the desktop UPS. This unit has a stand-alone form factor or enclosure, and often sits beside the device being protected. Closely related to the stand-alone UPS is the rack-mounted UPS. This device complies with the 19-inch rack form factor, and is usually only 2 to 6U high. A rack mount UPS may support one or more computers, and have separate shut down facilities for each computer. A third style of UPS is the room or building UPS. This type of power protection will keep an entire room or building supplied with power in case of a major outage. This class of UPS will often have a diesel engine backup that starts automatically after a loss of power to keep generating electricity for indefinite periods of time. Most fuel reserves on the diesel generators are designed to run at least one week.

Beyond protecting all servers with UPS units, we recommend that all units but laser printers are protected. If you do not want to invest in UPS units for every computer, router and switch, the minimum protection at all workstations, printers, and all other computer devices is to have surge protection. The surge protectors should have all computer-related devices attached. The goal is to have all power in the entire operation passing through either a UPS or a surge protector. Occasionally, to protect UPS units, you will need a surge protector in front of the UPS. This is to minimize the outages caused by bad power losses or lightning strikes.

Finally, surge protection can be used on network cables, phone lines, and other network connected devices, like wireless antennas. The goal in designing a network should be to isolate the network 100 percent through surge protectors or UPS devices. End users will often want to plug printers or other devices directly into the wall, bypassing the power protection scheme. Network technicians will be trained to continuously watch for these types of issues.

EXTENDING THE LIFE OF THE HARDWARE

The life of a hardware infrastructure can be extended by continuous care strategies. It is important to have every technician and every end-user proactive in caring for a technology investment. Simply cleaning monitors every Monday morning can make the use of the computer more productive every day. It is important to teach end-users the proper way to care for their equipment, including the proper cleaning techniques; and what can cause damage. If the end-user knows how to clean a keyboard, monitor, and mouse and keep the dust off of a CPU, you will wind up with fewer service calls.

When a technician repairs a machine, doing preventive maintenance on the machine can help the system run better. Since we are recommending longer life-cycles for systems, it is wise to schedule routine, preventive maintenance to clean and service the unit.

We have long been proponents of having spare units for mission critical functions. These spares can be immediately deployed in the event of a failure. However, this strategy is very capital intensive. A positive economic change in system maintenance is the pricing of third-party warranties. It may be cost-effective to purchase third party warranties on key technologies like laser printers, servers, and laptops since they tend to be the devices that require more service or are mission critical to the business. The table in Exhibit 8.9 illustrates some current maintenance pricing. You may want to investigate your vendor's offerings in these areas.

One of the goals in desktop maintenance is to save the user's data while making them productive again as quickly as possible. A prior section discussed the advantage of restoring replicated drive images to the desktop. An additional element of frustration for most end-users is input equipment that does not work. We reiterate again that bad mice and bad keyboards should be routinely and quickly replaced to keep end-users produc-

Exhibit 8.9

Server	Notebook	Laser Printer
Compaq ProLiant	N400C	HP 4100
Next Day, 3 years	Depot, 3 years	Return to Hewlett Packard, 3 years
Compaq	**Compaq**	**Hewlett Packard**
$199	$99	$199
Third Party	**Third Party**	**Third Party**
$150	$99	$99

tive. You have probably seen end-users picking up mice and trying to make them move when a mouse ball is dirty or the mouse is becoming defective. It would be common to replace keyboards and mice two or three times during the time you keep a system unit in service. This is a very inexpensive way to improve end-user productivity.

CONCLUSION

Purchasing hardware in today's market involves many sources of supply: local resellers, direct sources, mail order, and the web. Selection of the right products will reduce the cost of ownership. The initial price of higher quality products is usually greater, but the cost of owning the products will be lower, and end-user satisfaction will generally be higher.

Selecting products in any category is tricky, but this chapter has tried to show the major considerations in each category. Make sure to look at the online resources to see current recommendations and cautions on buying technology hardware products.

CHAPTER NINE

Network Communications Best Practices

NETWORKS GIVE COMPUTERS MORE CAPABILITIES

Networking computers makes them more powerful tools. Being able to share information from one computing resource to another amplifies the power that any one computer brings to its end user. Simple computer networks have existed since the 1960s in mainframe and minicomputer systems. These systems initially used proprietary communications, and the connection equipment was very expensive. Eventually these systems evolved to use some communications standards that are still found today. The protocols are asynchronous, Bi-Sync, HDLC, SDLC, and many more. Remember that a single character stored in a computer is stored using either ASCII or EBCDIC format, and that it takes seven or eight bits to make a single character. These communications protocols would operate at 2400 to 9600 bits per second if working at their optimal speed. This style of communications is largely replaced today with either Wide Area Networking (WAN) or Virtual Private Networking (VPN) discussed later in this chapter.

The real power of networking started to appear with the addition of generalized standards-based networking in the late 1960s, particularly with the definition of TCP/IP (Transport Control Protocol/Internet Protocol). This allowed vendors to write communications programs for their equipment, connect to modems, and talk to each other over these communication channels. TCP/IP was the first major building block of the Internet.

The next major step in networking occurred in the late 1970s and early 1980s with the linking computers, on a limited geographic basis, to communicate with one another at high speed. These local area networks (LANs) would change the way computers could talk to each other in a building or a group of buildings. The idea was to get away from the slower communications standards, and create new, faster standards. The introduction of new, smaller computers for less than $10,000 each emphasized this need!

There were distance limitations and disadvantages with all of these technologies, but it was clear to us in 1978 that LANs would change the computing landscape from mainframes and minicomputers to networks of computers ranging in size from the smallest computers available to the largest. It is still evolving this way today.

There were many local area network competitors, such as ARCNet, Ethernet, and Token Ring. ARCNet was one of the cheaper and more reliable products to install its infrastructure of active and passive hubs, and its use of active, token passing protocols. Ethernet regularly failed because of faults in the coax cabling systems. Token Ring was much more expensive than the competition, but radically more reliable. Even with some problems, local area networking was radically changing the communication landscape. LAN technology was connecting computers of all sizes together. Having one or more computers connected was becoming a mandatory business practice, not an expensive option. Until 1985, it was unclear which technology would win in the long haul, although by 1990, it was clear that ARCNet would not. As networking evolved, many of the developments seemed to have three-way competition, as summarized in Exhibit 9.1.

These technologies originally ran at speeds of 2Mbps, 10Mbps, and 4Mbps respectively. Token Ring increased in speed to 16Mbps, which has the equivalent speed of Ethernet running at 100Mbps. Ethernet increased in speed from 10 to 100Mbps, and today is available in 1,000 and 10,000 Mbps (1 and 10 Gigabit) speeds. But the key differential became price. Texas Instruments and IBM controlled Token Ring technology, and both were reluctant to reduce their pricing to generate additional demand. The more competitive Ethernet marketplace continued to drive prices down. Most new LAN technologies are introduced at about the $700 price point, and the technology is adopted in large volume as the price per adapter falls below $200. Any new technology in networking tends to follow this same pattern of introduction and decline in pricing as the development costs are recovered from the early adopters.

Cabling, Cabling, Cabling

Each of the three major LAN technologies used their own cabling system that was not compatible with any of the others. Selecting technology meant a commitment to a

Exhibit 9.1

LAN Technology	Cabling	Topology	Communication Access Method
ARCNet	RG59A/U Coax	Distributed Star	Token Passing
Ethernet	RG58C/U Coax	Linear Bus	CSMA/CD or Contention
Token Ring	Shielded Twisted Pair	Structured Ring	Token Passing

cabling infrastructure that was expensive, and dictated the technology the organization could use in the future. Further, these cabling systems were fragile and susceptible to failure from small components such as terminators. Standards for cabling were needed, and many companies and people developed ideas. Two companies drove the market in the United States to standardize cabling. This paved the way for rapid evolution of local area networks.

During the late 1980s, both AT&T and IBM promoted the concept of structured cabling systems. AT&T's Premises Distribution System (PDS) used unshielded twisted pair wires as its primary distribution approach on a single floor of an office, claiming that 97 percent of all offices in the world were within 300 feet of a wiring closet. Wiring closets were hooked together with fiber optics. To build a computer network using their system, it was possible to simply use existing telephone wire; add computer connection technology in the wiring closet (called a hub); and have a star distribution system. Star distribution systems are the least expensive to maintain. Further, IBM claimed that each change, add, or move would cost $200 (in 1988 dollars), so it was easy to justify a structured cabling system. AT&T wanted their system to be easy to change, not requiring special equipment once it was in place. They adopted the RJ45 connector for data, just as they had begun using the RJ11 connector in phone applications. The RJ45 connector is currently the standard connector at the desktop and throughout the cabling system.

IBM created their structured cabling system to consolidate all known cabling technologies. They wanted one cabling system that used multiple cable types (Types 1 to 9) that each handled a different situation, from voice and data (maintained separately in Type 2 cable) to fiber optics to a flat cable lying under carpet. Their technology used universal data connectors that were very easy to install with no special equipment. Converters called baluns (balanced/unbalanced) could be plugged into the UDC connectors to support technology ranging from phones to coax to twinax to LAN twisted pair. Both of these strategies have been used by a large number of companies and are still in use today. At this time, there is no real need to replace these cabling systems, although upgrades to faster cable types or wireless may be needed.

Cabling standards evolved from these technologies for unshielded twisted pair (UTP) run from standard phone cable (CAT 3) through a series of standards that gave greater and greater speeds. These standards included CAT4, CAT5, CAT5e, and CAT6. In October of 1990, CAT 5, using the 568B international standard, became a widely accepted standard. Most properly built cabling infrastructures installed since that time have followed these standards. The best cabling installers attend schools and obtain certifications for understanding these standards. It is important to use a certified cabling installer. Two of the certifications to look for are: registered communications distribution designer (RCDD) and a certified fiber optic technician (CFOT). Companies with these certifications can address and solve the client's needs in category 5, category 5e, level 6, and single mode/multimode fiber optic cable.

In very small LANs in businesses or in homes, pre-assembled patch cables will be pulled throughout the facility to establish a LAN. However, the first problems with any network are cabling problems. The second problems with most networks are cabling problems, and the third most common problems are cabling problems. Yes, if there is a technical problem with a network, be careful not to overlook a cabling issue before trying to solve the problem with a software change. A problem with a LAN will tend to be cable. If a cabling problem cannot be found after an initial search, it is wise to reassess and try to determine what cable problem has been overlooked. If a second attempt to find a cabling problem has not been able to locate it, a third attempt with outside help should probably be made before beginning to pursue software problems, unless there is something obvious like a hard drive failure.

A good cabling installer knows and understands standards from the small details like the number of twists per inch in a CAT3 or CAT5 cable to the minimum distance from a power circuit. A common error in architectural design or cable installation is that the jack for the network connection is placed adjacent to the power plug for convenience. Cabling paths are important too; major electrical interference should be avoided. For example, wiring directly over fluorescent fixtures, near escalator or elevator motors, or near the back of big copy machines can cause unnecessary problems. Although this is not a comprehensive list, here are some considerations that all quality cabling installers know and practice about network cables:

- Maintain a minimum of three feet from ac power and lighting fixtures.
- Kinks in cables will cause future failures, and less than optimum performance.
- Each cable circuit must be tested not only for continuity, but also for other electrical characteristics like cross talk interference and signal fade. This testing equipment can cost $3,000 to $5,000 or more.
- Patch cables (the cable from the wall jack to the device) should be as short as possible, but never less than three feet. Most patch cables come in standard lengths that were originally based on a metric length (seven feet patch cable was really two meters).
- Cables should be exceptionally neat and well labeled. Cable systems should then document the labeling and associate the cable runs with physical locations in the building.
- While trying to make cables neat, be careful not to pull wire wraps too tight, because pinched cables will not perform properly or will fail later at this point.
- The twists in a wire cannot be undone to make it easier to crimp on an RJ45 connector. This affects the throughput of the patch cable.
- Always design more capacity than needed, and install all of the cable at one time if possible. The majority of the cost is in the labor of the installation, not in the cost of the parts.
- Always use punch down blocks, RJ connectors, patch or distribution panels, and tools that match the specification (CAT5, CAT5e or CAT6). Even though the components look similar, they have different electrical characteristics. Unscrupulous or unknowing installers will often install a CAT 5 or 6 job with cheaper CAT 3 parts since they know the consumer cannot tell the difference.
- Make sure that there is one and only one system ground. When a ground is needed, different soil conditions under different buildings or parts of buildings will cause

electrical potential differential. If more than one ground exists, transient voltages can cause erratic network performance and unpredictable problems.

Cabling infrastructure investments vary from $75 to $250; $200 is a good planning average for all of the components needed (connectors, cable, faceplates, distribution racks, and installation labor). Fiber optics and wireless technologies are just beginning to replace or minimize the need for structured cabling systems.

Even in medium sized LANs, certain minor types of test equipment may be desired. A budget should be provided for cable testers that commonly cost from $700 to $5500. These cable testers can save significant amounts of time in the event of a major system failure on the cabling side.

Network Operating Systems

Operating systems developed on top of this hardware base of networking adapters and cabling. Besides the major host environments developed by IBM, DEC, Burroughs, NCR, and others, PC-based operating systems also evolved from vendors like Corvus, Novell, 3Com, Artisoft, Banyan, Apple, and Microsoft. These operating systems fell into three major categories:

1. Multi-user
   - Linux
   - Unix
   - MOS
   - Pick
   - Proprietary
     - VM, MVS
     - OS/400
     - Many others
2. File Server
   - Corvus Omninet
   - Novell NetWare
   - Banyan Vines
   - IBM OS/2 LAN Manager
   - Microsoft LAN Manager, which evolved to Windows NT 3.1, 3.5, 4.0, Windows 2000 Server, and .NET servers
3. Peer to Peer
   - Artisoft Lantastic
   - NetWare Lite
   - Windows for Workgroups, which evolved to inclusion in Windows 95, 98, ME, Windows 2000 and Windows XP

○ AppleShare

○ And many other good competitors

There is wonderful computing history involved in many of these products, such as the:

- Evolution from disk sharing to file sharing driven by competition between 3Com and Novell.
- Price performance and reliability issues including:
  ○ Dedicated versus non-dedicated servers.
  ○ High performance and large disks—starting with 5MB.
  ○ Specially designed servers.
  ○ Running multiple services on a single server.
- Integration of the networking application into the operating system by IBM and then by Microsoft.
- Evolution of directory services from Banyan and Novell and then, Microsoft.

A good management view of this network operating system technology is that desktop operating systems generally have peer-to-peer sharing built into them. For greater performance and reliability some of the computers on the network need to be servers. Servers share their resources with other computers on the network. Servers will be more reliable if they are only used for a single network service, and are not used as a workstation by the end user.

The major competitors in the PC market today are: Microsoft with Windows 2000 and .NET servers, Novell with NetWare, and several vendors with Linux offerings. All major minicomputer and mainframe vendors have made resource sharing a part of their operating systems. These host environments can be treated logically as large file and application servers. They share their printers, disks, run applications, run web servers, and other functions faster and, in many cases, more cost-effectively than a PC-based server. But, the initial investment and ongoing maintenance costs can be greater.

Protocols, Standards, and Other Communications Strategies

Protocols are the low-level communications standards used by servers and desktop operating systems alike. Common protocols in use are TCP/IP, IPX, and NetBIOS/Net-BEUI. Most network administrators have evolved their LAN protocols from IPX and NetBIOS to TCP/IP. Each of these different protocols has its own unique advantage or function. For example, IPX is an active protocol that will look for the existence of servers on a LAN, and will make sure that a connection between workstation and server continues to exist. NetBIOS has the ability to share resources such as files or printers with more user-friendly names, but it is a passive, non-routable protocol. TCP/IP is a low overhead, passive protocol. Most corporate networks are being changed to be TCP/IP only with an eye on future changes in TCP/IP definitions to support new features such as more addresses.

Standards groups like the Institute of Electrical and Electronics Engineers (IEEE) control the communications that are done at a low level. In Europe, the Commission Internationale de l'Eclairage (*www.cie.co.at*) controls some of the standards definitions. As protocols have evolved and have been used more around the world, worldwide definitions are developed. These definitions usually go by their standards number, such as low-level standards of 802.11 or X.25. These definitions are important when selecting new communications gear, because vendors can choose to comply with standards or create their own proprietary technology. Most vendors try to accommodate the standard, as they understand it. Some vendors will comply with the base standard, and extend the standard with proprietary features. This can be more risky to consumers of their product. But, many times these extensions often become part of a future revision of the definitions. Unfortunately, extending the standard may make a vendor's product features not compatible with other vendor's products that are following the standard.

Access Methods

Standard protocols use access methods to do their communication work. There are three primary types of access methods: polling, contention, and token passing.

- *Polling.*   This method allows a centralized computer to ask other computers or terminals on the network if they need to communicate. Polling mechanisms can be tuned. More frequently used machines or devices on the network can be polled more often. This access method gives the greatest control for performance.
- *Contention.*   This method is often implemented as Carrier Sense Multiple Access/Collision Detect or CSMA/CD. This mechanism is like a human conversation. Each station listens to the cabling system to see if there is any activity. If there is no activity, the individual workstation can speak. But, as in a human conversation, multiple workstations can speak at the same time. When this happens in a human conversation, people normally stop talking, and wait a random amount of time to resume speaking. Occasionally, we must deal with the human (or computer) who will not stop speaking.

    Continuing with the analogy, if there are just a few people in a conversation, it is fairly easy to speak individually and be heard. As the number of people (stations) increases, the difficulty of establishing an individual conversation also increases. If you are in a party of 15 people, think about how hard it is to speak and be individually heard. Think of a party of 100 people and imagine how hard it is to speak and be individually heard. Without overstating the problem, this example holds true for technologies that are implemented using CSMA/CD. An example of this technology is Ethernet. Caution must be used when building larger networks with Ethernet, particularly if connection technologies like hubs are used. Hubs propagate the conversations throughout the network. Routers and switches can stop the excessive or repeated traffic.
- *Token passing.*   This access method uses a signal (token) that is passed around the network. Tokens are either busy or free. The free token is passed from station to station and any station can remove the free token and put a message on the network (the

busy token). This message has a destination address, message, and an area in the message to confirm that the message was received. When the message arrives at the station, a bit acknowledging receipt is sent. The sending station then has a definite confirmation that the message was received.

In IBM Token Ring, each network adapter has a circuitry called the monitor that insures the tokens are passing properly. The monitor function is very effective and keeps token ring networks running under very poor conditions. On the other hand, ARCNet networks do not have any mechanism to watch the token and it can be easily lost. A lost token equals a network that is down.

Transmission Medium

There are three common transmission mediums (cables) today. These are: twisted pair, coax, and fiber optics. Additional options of wireless technologies include: infrared, spread spectrum, microwave, and satellite transmissions.

- *Twisted pair.* Twisted pair wires are the most popular method of connecting computers to LANs today. Both unshielded twisted pair (UTP) and shielded twisted pair (STP) are used as described in the cabling section above. These wires have the ability to carry signals at 4 mbps, 10, 16,100 and 1000Mbps. New technologies might allow faster speeds, but fiber is usually recommended for speeds above 600Mbps. Most twisted pair technologies are limited to 330 feet or 100 meters in length.

- *Coax.* Coaxial cable has been used for computer communications for 40 years or more. These cables all have a central conductor, an insulator around the central conductor, a shield around the insulating material, and a jacket. Different coax technologies allow different cable lengths. 608 feet to 20,000 feet are common.

- *Fiber optics.* Fiber optic cable continues to fall in price and should be considered in new building construction and remodeling projects. Two major types of fiber optics are available: glass and plastic. Glass fiber has an almost unlimited life; we still recommend it. Plastic fibers tend to yellow over time, affecting transmission. Long distances are usually supported. Two kilometers is a common fiber optic maximum length without a repeater (amplifier). Further, fiber is either single mode (carrying a single frequency) or multi-mode. Single mode usually gives greater distances and higher speeds. But, multi-mode may give greater throughput since it can transmit multiple frequencies (transmissions) at the same time.

- *Wireless.* Most wireless LAN technologies are expensive and slow compared to wired standards today. Products complying with the 802.11b standard achieve 2 to 11Mbps performance. These wireless technologies generally have the same distance limitations as twisted pair wires (330 feet). However with special antennas, distances of up to five miles can be connected using wireless technologies.

  New microwave towers that have increased the common distances of 10 to 12 miles to 40 miles or more are available from some manufacturers. This development significantly reduces the cost of high-speed communications.

- *Satellite.* Several providers are now making satellite uplinks bridged to landlines available, and are providing two-way earth stations for $5,000 to $7,000. Small two-way satellites have been covering most of the United States since January 2001. These cost $50 to $70 per month. The dish size continues to shrink from 6 to10 feet, to 2 to 3 feet, to 12 to 18 inches. As the space shuttle delivers new satellites into orbit with more capacity, the costs of using a satellite will continue to fall. Some locations can be connected for $300 to $500 per site.

The technologies are summarized in Exhibit 9.2.

Topologies

Topologies are the logical design of the networking standards, or how the stations are interconnected. Topology is usually chosen according to the transmission medium and the physical layout of office. It is most commonly dictated by the manufacturer based on product choice. The physical designs of networks today are almost all star-wired, and run over UTP cable as described above. The logical designs are Star, Bus, and Ring.

- *Star.* Using one or more centralized wiring closets, the star topology gives greater reliability and control than the linear bus approach. Each workstation communicates

Exhibit 9.2

PRIVATE Types of Cables	Cost	Distance Limit	Connection Devices	Advantages	Disadvantages
Twisted Pair	.05-.17/ft .35-.45/ft	330'	Concentrators/ MAU	Cheap, Common	Interference, Low Speed
Coax	.17-.75/ft	608' - 1000' (Ether-net) 2000' (ARCnet)	Hub	Less Susceptible to Interference	Single Cable fault can take network down
Fiber Optics	.80-1.25/ft	2 Km	Hub	No interference, secure	Cost
Wireless	$500-800	330' - 5 miles	Antenna	Installable where wire can't go	Lower speed, signal interference

with the wiring concentrator (a hub or a multi-station access unit) and the communication proceeds to the next appropriate computer. This wiring scheme is used with ARCNet, 10,100, or 1000BaseT Ethernet and with IBM Token Ring.

- *Linear Bus.* Using a linear bus topology, the workstations are connected to a single transmission line with a beginning and an end. They communicate directly with each other through this line. Since the workstations have passive connections, a workstation may fail without affecting the other network stations. Coax Ethernet is an example of a linear bus. The risk with this technology is that a single break in the cable can (and usually does) take the entire network down. Even when Ethernet is running over twisted pair with hubs, the logical design of Ethernet is still linear bus.

- *Ring.* Ring technologies connect computers electronically in a circular fashion. Messages are passed from one computer to the next computer in line. This happens with Token Ring implementations. Usually rings are the most reliable. Other examples of ring technology are: Fiber Data Distributed Interface (FDDI), Fibre Channel Storage Area Network Technology, and Asynchronous Transfer Mode (ATM). Rings are deterministic, and will guarantee slices of performance making it easier to guarantee quality of service (QOS).

THE INFRASTRUCTURE: LOCAL AREA NETWORK

Once the technology is selected and the cabling is in place, devices to hook up servers, workstations, printers, and other devices need to be selected and implemented. Connection devices include hubs, switches, repeaters, bridges, routers, and gateways.

Hubs

Hubs can be used in most of the LAN technologies. In the case of Ethernet, the hubs can be purchased with or without network management. In the Ethernet world, hubs come in several port configurations; the most common configurations are four, eight, twelve, twenty-four, and forty-eight ports. When adding hubs to a network configuration, remember that hubs are devices that share their bandwidth (the total communication capacity) with all devices that are attached. For planning purposes, it is fair to take the speed of the Ethernet network, and divide by the number of ports in the hub to get the average speed per port. For example, a 12-port 100Mbps hub would have an average port speed of 8.33Mbps.

When designing networks, never have a single point of failure. We recommend that you have multiple devices for network connection to minimize the risk of failure. For example, if the total devices attached to the network will be 20, it is a natural temptation to purchase a 24-port hub or switch. However, it is a much safer business decision to buy two 12-port switches for this situation. If one device fails, at least half of the network will still be functioning. Many organizations make another common mistake when they properly choose to have multiple connection devices. They incorrectly connect the multiple devices together by daisy chaining them. *Daisy chaining* is the technique of hooking hubs or switches together by using a cable out of one of the standard ports. This results in delays waiting for each device to cycle, effectively doubling the network transmission time. A simple connection cable can radically slow performance. Many crossover ports make it easy to daisy chain devices. This technique should be avoided if there are other alternatives. What are some of the other alternatives? Devices can have back plane connections or specialized communications cables that make multiple devices appear as a single managed unit. Either of these approaches is superior to a daisy chain attachment.

Dual speed hubs are another popular competitor in today's environment. Dual speed hubs allow for devices to communicate at different speeds to the same hub. The most common speeds are 10/100, but some options are appearing for 1000 as well. Dual speed attachment is a convenience, and allows 100Mbps workstations or printers to communicate at their full speed; this does not overcome the shared capacity of the device.

Because of price and performance, one of the best business decisions you can make today is to avoid hubs. We do not recommend hubs for performance reasons, as well as the improved management that is included with most switches. A simple recommendation for an organization is to replace all hubs with switches, creating a 4- to 20-fold improvement in speed. This will be most noticeable if there were a lot of daisy chain attachments and on high-speed computers. Hubs and switches can be stand-alone, rack mount, or chassis format devices. For organizations from 30 to 1000, we recommend the rack mount format. All connection devices should always be protected with a UPS.

In the case of Token Ring, there are actually two types of connection devices. First is a MAU or multi-station access unit. The standard MAU has eight ports plus a ring in (RI) and a ring out (RO) port. Competitors to IBM have developed MAUs that have four, sixteen or thirty-two ports as well, but most models have eight ports. MAUs are not managed units. If a workstation is producing errant behavior, there is no way to shut that particular MAU down. Second is a CAU, the controlled access unit, that addresses this particular problem. In the Token Ring world, management is available in the CAU. The CAU is really broken down into multiple parts with the CAU being the main controlling unit. To make CAUs complete, you have to buy LAMs (lobe attachment modules). CAUs are commonly configured with thirty or sixty ports.

In the case of ARCnet, hubs are usually configured with the number of ports needed. The original standard was eight ports per hub, although ARCnet active hubs eventually became available with 8, 16, 24, 32, and 64 ports. These hubs can be simple hubs, or they can have more intelligence in them. With ARCnet, they are actually called intelligent hubs, which reflects the status of the link of an ARCnet adapter. Hubs selection should be made based on reliability, speed, warranty, flexibility, and expandability.

Switches

Switches should be used in all network environments where performance and system reliability is an issue. Only rarely is there enough price differential to recommend hubs.

This is usually for a few specialized small LANs or temporary installations. Today, we do not recommend hubs.

Switches usually support multiple speeds with 10/100 very common and 10/100/1000 starting to appear regularly. Occasionally switches will be a single speed, such as all 10 or all 100, but this is rare. A switch allows dedicated two-way (duplex) performance on every port. This means that a 100Mbps link will have 200Mbps of net throughput. Further, the speed of a switch is usually an aggregate (multiplication) of the ports, not a division of the speed as seen with hubs. Therefore, a 12-port switch will have 12*200 or 2.4Gbps throughput. The internal design will usually include a statement about the speed of the back plane. A very common back plane speed would be 2.2 Gbps.

Switches are becoming more sophisticated as more control, processing power, and memory is being placed in the devices. The ability to segment the network for security and performance purposes can be accomplished with many products. This segmentation is done with VLAN technology, and use of Layer 3 and Layer 4 switches. Layer 3 and 4 switches gain capability through software configuration.

Management in Hubs, Switches, and Routers

Another feature to consider purchasing is management in hubs, switches, or routers. These devices can be purchased with or without network management. Management of the network hardware and software can be controlled on either a hardware and software level. The management techniques revolve around SMNP (Simple Management Network Protocol). To implement management requires not only the hardware support in the connection devices, such as the hubs, but also software to drive it. Smaller devices are usually available without management. If the size of the network is going to be greater than 50 stations, management is generally recommended. For less than 50 stations, unmanaged hubs are probably acceptable. The bottom line for management is pretty simple. The software and hardware have very little incremental costs, but give the network administrator or outsourced technician the ability:

- To shut down a single port where a failing component (workstation, printer, etc.) is causing problems. This keeps the rest of the network running or performing normally during the repair.
- See the statistics on usage by port.
- To control for usage monitoring if desired (required in the banking environment under the current regulations).
- To optimize the device performance by allowing software configuration of the device.
- To repair network communications issues remotely.

Repeaters

If distance limitations, as outlined in the cabling section above, are not great enough, then devices called repeaters can be used. Repeaters are really simple amplifiers. They receive the signal, retime it, and retransmit. There are different limitations in different technologies. For example, in the Ethernet world, depending on which standard is being followed, either two repeaters (the original standard), or four repeaters (the newer standard), allow hooking multiple hub or switch stacks or segments of coax cable together. The overall maximum distance for thick Ethernet becomes 3,280 feet times three (or 1,000 meters times three). For thin Ethernet, the distance limitation is five times 608 feet. Similar restrictions apply for CAT 5 cables.

Repeaters can also be used for token ring, but in the token ring environment copper repeaters or fiber optic repeaters are the choices. Copper repeaters will give an additional 1,000 feet of distance. Fiber optic repeaters will give an extra two kilometers. There is a maximum of seven repeaters or sixteen kilometers of distance that can be achieved by using repeaters.

In the case of ARCnet, which has maximum 2,000 foot active hub cable segments and a 20,000 foot overall length, no more than nine hubs can be used. In that scenario, these hubs function as repeaters.

Bridges

Bridges are devices that allow us to hook multiple segments of LANs together. Bridges may convert from one technology to another, such as from Ethernet to Token Ring. But they are commonly used to allow Ethernet to Ethernet or Token Ring to Token Ring style of connections. Bridges perform the repeater function with an additional feature. That is, they filter out network traffic that does not really need to cross the bridge. If a message is being sent from station A to station B on a network and those two stations are on one cable segment, station C (which might be on the other side of the bridge or on a different cable segment) does not see the traffic that is generated by messages being passed back and forth from station A to station B.

Bridges can be implemented in software, but are implemented more efficiently in hardware. During the last ten years, the prices for bridges have radically fallen, from $15,000 per bridge down to $200 to $2,000 per bridge. Bridges should be selected based on reliability, speed, flexibility, and expandability.

Using bridges is a way to design a larger network, particularly one that is spread over multiple floors of a building and/or between multiple buildings. Bridges can be purchased to operate in either a local environment where there are no telecommunications involved or they can be purchased as remote bridges. However, because of price, routers are almost always used instead of bridges. This is the same situation for hubs and switches.

Remote bridges allow us to begin the process of wide area networking, which is where we get telecommunications involved. Most of the bridge products interface to digital modules or digital modems known as CSU/DSUs (Control Service Unit/Digital Service Unit). CSU/DSUs in the United States commonly give speeds of 56K or T1 speeds. WANs running on 56K are adequate to do mainframe terminal emulations or pass data in e-mail messages, but are not really adequate for running applications. However, communications done at T1 speeds allow programs to be downloaded down the T1 lines for small remote network nodes, eliminating the need for a file server in a remote location.

Routers

Routers are devices that are very similar to bridges, but they have the additional capability of taking the shortest, least expensive, or fastest path to get a message transferred from one segment to another segment. If one communications path is not available, routers are smart enough to pick alternate paths for the communications traffic. An operative rule of thumb is that routers should probably be chosen rather than bridges, if there are more than five segments involved. Routers may also have more than just the two ports common in bridge configurations. Bridges can also have multiple ports. But, routers may have three, four, and more ports, allowing a single device to connect to multiple different LAN segments or wide area network segments simultaneously.

Further, routers are becoming more sophisticated. Router vendors are adding switch capabilities, as well as other segmentation, firewall and remote monitoring capabilities. Since the price of routers has fallen from around $30,000 to $5,000 and less for sophisticated units, and less than $200 for small edge routers, routers are used almost everywhere in communications networks. Since so many LANs are connected to the Internet, a router is needed to make this connection.

Gateways

Gateways are hardware and software combinations that allow a LAN to provide terminal emulation services to a minicomputer or mainframe. There are many styles of gateways available. A common configuration today requires a hardware communications device or controller, or a dedicated PC or service running on a server. Gateways provide the controller emulation that the mainframe or minicomputer recognizes as a common controller in the family of supporter controllers.

There is also workstation software that runs on DOS, Windows, or Macintosh OS that connects to the Gateway, and subsequently to the host, to provide a terminal emulation session. Emulations available include 3270 in the ES9000 family environment, 5250 in the AS400 environment, and the VT100 in the Compaq/DEC environment.

Gateways often provide the ability for LAN stations to share mainframe resources such as printers and files. Gateways may also allow downloading of mainframe files to PCs for PC based processing. As gateways become more sophisticated, cooperative processing between mainframe, minicomputer environments, and PCs is becoming more common.

The second common gateway configuration puts a network adapter, such as Ethernet or Token Ring, in a minicomputer or mainframe, and then does a direct attach to the minicomputer or mainframe. In this case, the terminal emulation software runs on the PC and talks directly to software that is running inside the minicomputer or mainframe. This type of attachment results in even faster communications to the host than were available through terminal emulation. The only significant disadvantages to direct attach are increased costs and overhead on the mainframe or minicomputer that is driving the emulation. Host overhead is greater because, in most implementations today, the individual PC acts as a separate controller unit that significantly adds to overhead on the host environment.

A reasonable price allowance for acquiring a gateway today is approximately $3500 per gateway protocol required. If both IBM 3270 and IBM 5250 emulations are required, the total cost allowance ought to be at least $7,400.

THE INFRASTRUCTURE: WAN AND VPN

Wide Area Networking (WAN) is private communication built between multiple sites of a business. The WAN structure is often private, but could be built using the public communications structure of the Internet using Virtual Private Network (VPN) techniques. First, let us understand some of the options for WAN communications.

WANs need to be cost-effective for organizations and can represent a significant ongoing cost for businesses. These costs should be justified by reduced long distance charges with voice-over data, increased communications, or other benefits. WANs generally require the use of external third-party communications services, such as public phone companies or satellite communications. Typically, WANs serve to interconnect LANs in different cities, states, and countries. Specialized hardware or hardware and software combinations called bridges are required. More sophisticated connections are made with devices called routers. The line speeds will be discussed later in this chapter. WAN requirements are shown in Exhibit 9.3.

To make a typical WAN connection, a port should be taken from the switch and plugged into the WAN port on a router. From the router, a cable connection will be made to the communication system connection device, which will be a broadband modem, CSU/DSU, or a FRAD. Occasionally, these devices will be built into the router, as Cisco and 3Com are trying to do. But, separate connection devices function just as well.

One of the ways to justify permanent high-speed communications is to include all of the organization's voice traffic between locations on the data lines. Carrying multiple signals on the same communication line is called multiplexing. Multiplexing voice and data can be done on communication lines as slow as 56K. If faster lines like T1 lines are used, specific channels on the T1 can be used for voice. The device that makes this

Exhibit 9.3

WAN Technology	LAN to WAN Connection Device	Connection Device to Communication Line	Common Speeds
2 and 4 wire	Router/Bridge	CSU/DSU	56K, T1 (1.5Mbps)
Frame Relay	Router/Bridge	FRAD	56K,128K,256K,T1
Wireless	WAP/Router	Antenna	1,2,11 Mbps
VPN	Router	Internet	56K,128K,256K,T1

possible is called a Mux (multiplex), and is only slightly more expensive than CSU/DSU or FRADs. Phone line access out of many of these devices is presented as a standard analog or digital voice line.

There are many vendors competing for the business of communication gear, but the dominant player is Cisco. Other players like 3Com, Lucent Technologies, and IBM have offerings as well. For the connection devices of CSU/DSU or FRADs, the key players are AdTrans, Digital Link, BlackBox, and Paradyne. For Mux gear, Micom and NewBridge (owned by Cisco) have nice offerings.

Videoconferencing

Another advantage of owning a private communication system is that additional features can be added with very little incremental cost. Videoconferencing reduces travel costs and adds the additional element of seeing and speaking to someone in another location. Videoconferencing has established standards, just like local area networks have standards. The key standard is H.323 that defines standard video and data interchanges between different vendor's products.

To do business quality videoconferencing, 128K of bandwidth is needed. Many organizations chose to implement videoconferencing over ISDN lines since these provide dial on demand digital capability at 128K. More speed is needed to get higher quality videoconferencing. For example, to get medical quality imaging where a patient's eye dilation could be observed, 384K communication speed is needed. For most of the data communications world, the communication pipes are broken up in 64K pipes. Standard business videoconferencing would take two 64K channels, and medical quality videoconferencing would take six channels.

Videoconferencing is normally considered a point-to-point connection. However, in the last few years, using a company's private WAN or using the public transport of the Internet has been successful. Further, having more than two locations in a videoconference is often desirable and needed. To connect three or more locations together, video bridging is needed. Some vendors offer units that will bridge 4, 8, 16, or more locations together. Polycom is a good example of a vendor with simple products that have these capabilities. These units cost from $5,000 to $20,000. The larger the video bridging unit, the more expensive the device. As an alternative, video bridging facilities can be rented on an hourly basis.

During a videoconference, the attendees of the call can share voice, video, data, and documents simultaneously. Specialized pieces of equipment may be required to add capabilities like document sharing, but when contrasted to the expense of travel and the time savings possible, videoconferencing is a technology bargain, not a technology luxury.

Bandwidth Options

For WAN connections, there are several types of data lines to consider. For home office or small branch office communications, refer to Chapter 11 on remote communications.

Exhibit 9.4

Line Type	Speed	Initial Installation	Monthly Cost
ISDN - BRI	128K	$300	$90+$30
56K – 4 Wire – DS0	56K	$75–$1100	$50–$1900
Frame	56K-T1	$250–$700	$200–$1500
T1- ISDN - PRI	1.5Mbps	$700	$800–$1500
T1 – 4 Wire – DS1	1.5Mbps	$700	$700–$1500
T1 – OC (Fiber)	1.5Mbps	$900	$500–$1800
T3 – 4 Wire	45MBps	$2,500	$12,000–$20,000
OC3 (Fiber)	45MBps	$3,000	$9,000–$25,000
OC12	192MBps	$2,500–$4,500	$6,000–$35,000

For permanent high-speed connections, the fiber lines shown in Exhibit 9.4 are the most common options.

As you can see, there is a premium paid for faster lines, but the prices increase less rapidly as the line speeds increase. There are several factors to consider when selecting and negotiating contracts on these dedicated lines. First, the initial installation fee is often waived in the negotiation. There is actual work done to test the lines; this can take several hours to several days. However, if the carrier wants your business badly, they will often concede installation costs. Additionally, if you need to make adjustments to the speeds of your lines, it is not unusual to have to pay the installation fees multiple times. Sometimes you can negotiate to have all future changes in the lines to be exempt from installation fees. This is a particularly good option if you are unsure of the capacity needed for your application.

Notice also that the lines are supplied on either copper wire or fiber optics. The fiber lines are generally more reliable; their cost will vary more widely, both higher and lower than copper pricing. Many communication systems have been built by private concerns on oil pipeline or railroad right of ways, and try to compete on price against the regional bell operating companies (RBOCs).

A good rule for judging the amount of capacity needed is that ten heavy users will require about 56K of bandwidth. Applications like Internet web browsing or remote access through products like Citrix MetaFrame require less bandwidth than file transfers or applications that have not been optimized for thin client technologies. Additionally, once the needs exceed 512K, pricing makes it an easy business decision to jump to a full T1. With a T1, consider dedicating a few channels to voice and a few channels to video-conferencing. Twenty channels of a T1 will feel like a full 24 channels to most users.

Note that there are also a couple of options involving ISDN technology. Popular belief is that ISDN is a failing technology, but this is an incorrect assumption. ISDN services are a special packaging of a T1 line that can be particularly helpful if the line is used primarily for voice or dial-in services. A standard T1 line has 24 channels. If it were used for voice only, this would net 24 channels on standard equipment, and perhaps as high as 96 voice channels if heavily multiplexed. Voice quality will deteriorate when more multiplexing is done.

Computer Telephony

Since PRI ISDN has a different technical construct (23 channels, plus 1 signaling channel), the line can be used in different ways. Each of the 23 channels natively supports two voice lines, so immediately there are 46 voice or dial-in circuits available. Further, features like caller ID are included with a PRI packaging of a T1. A PRI T1 can give more flexibility to integrate call center operations, CRM (customer resource management), or other phone integration into computer applications. You can also easily supply individuals with their own unique inbound number.

As PBX (private branch exchange) and KSU (key service unit) phone systems are replaced with new generation CTI (computer telephony integration) systems, the use of PRI T1 or DS1 with phone feature overlays for Caller ID and other features will be required to take full advantage of the phone system's features. CTI systems will either run on the old phone system wires or over the LAN cabling system. The central switch for the CTI system may be computer based, or specialized processor based. The phone sets may be traditional in format, or tied through the desktop computer using USB phone sets. Currently the best approach to CTI based systems is to use phone system technology for the central switch, and traditional phone hand sets over the old phone wire. This technology changes rapidly; it should be reviewed within a few weeks before a purchase.

Virtual Private Networking

Virtual Private Networking (VPN) is another way to connect multiple offices. This is discussed in the context of remote networking in Chapter 11. For organizations that need access to multiple locations; cannot justify the on-going cost of permanent communications; and are willing to accept some risk on data being compromised, a VPN is a viable solution.

For WAN applications of VPNs, firewalls must be installed in every location. Additional software for the VPN is installed in the firewall. The firewalls communicate over a secure channel from one location to another using the Internet as the communication path.

The biggest disadvantage to using VPNs for a WAN application is speed. The encryption and decryption that must occur at each firewall add overhead and delay the speed of the transmission. The second disadvantage is that the data may be at risk. This is a relatively low risk since the data is encrypted, but from a security planning vantage point, we believe that all encryption can be broken. If someone has access to the data that you are transmitting over the Internet, is this a problem for the organization? Once you can answer this question, you can decide whether or not a VPN is acceptable as a WAN solution for your business.

CONCLUSION

All businesses that have two or more computers should connect their machines using LAN technology. Today the best approach is to use Level 6 cable with 10/100 Ethernet adapters tied to 100Mbps switches. However, higher speed Ethernet or wireless technology should be considered in new installations.

Once the LAN is established, a connection to the Internet and other locations should be created. After passing through a router and a firewall, using communication lines does this. If multiple locations exist, there may be better control if you create your own WAN, and limit Internet connection through a single, controlled connection.

With communications established between all locations, you are a candidate for videoconferencing and computer telephony (CTI). In some cases, the reduction of long distance toll charges justifies the installation of the WAN lines. In other cases, the additional functionality and savings of videoconferencing and CTI is justification enough. Certainly, when all of these factors plus the factor of remote workers are considered, creating universal access via LANs, WANs, and the Internet makes sense.

CHAPTER TEN

Network Management and Security Best Practices

MANAGING AND SECURING INFORMATION TECHNOLOGY RESOURCES

Business networks continue to become installed and accessible almost everywhere. This includes the main office and branch office locations, and for home-based and mobile workers. These networks might be private using Local Area and Wide Area Network technology; semi-private using Virtual Private Networking and Internet technology; or public using Internet and wireless technology. Regardless of the way networks are built, they must be manageable and secure. Even with the best planning, careful execution and maintenance, most networks have security holes. Viruses have become very expensive to individuals and businesses alike because of the large cost in time from loss of productivity. It is imperative that businesses and individuals protect their computers from viruses at all times. This chapter provides an overview of each of the risk areas that must be continuously monitored. LAN and WAN administrators frequently handle network management and software updates. Many larger organizations have a person in charge of security, a chief security officer.

DATA AND NETWORK SECURITY SOLUTIONS

Data and network security includes all of the hardware and software to protect data including, but not limited to:

- Backup
- Firewalls
- Virus checking

- Content control
- Encryption
- Directory management

INTERNET SECURITY RISKS

Internet security almost always ranks near or at the top of the list when people are questioned about Internet issues and concerns. Network administrators are usually concerned about hackers, privacy, and reliability, while consumers are concerned about the confidentiality of financial transactions. These concerns are increased by news stories that often exaggerate the risk with misleading headlines designed to gain readership. On January 7, 1999, *USA Today* ran a story with the headline "*U.S. Networks Most Vulnerable of Any Nation*" followed by the tagline "Cyberterrorism InfoWar Electronic Pearl Harbor." In a recent study conducted by the Computer Security Institute (CSI) (*gocsi.com/*) and the FBI, released in 2001, the CSI estimated that "Sophisticated cyber crooks caused well over $377 million in losses last year." This is hardly the equivalent of World War II. The U.S. military has airplanes alone that cost over ten times as much.

Internet security issues are best managed if they are viewed as just another category of business risk. In other business areas, such as cash disbursements and inventory, the risks are evaluated and internal control procedures designed to provide reasonable assurance. The same thing should (and can) be done with Internet security risks.

As with other business risks, the risks associated with using the Internet vary depending on the size of the organization and the nature of its operations. High profile organizations like the *The New York Times* and organizations that represent a *badge of honor* if broken into, like the CIA, are obviously at much higher risk than small local businesses that are using the Internet for e-mail and WAN applications. Financial institutions and other organizations with valuable confidential information obviously have a higher level of risk than other organizations of similar size.

Accordingly, we should deal with Internet security risks in the same way we deal with other business risks. Step one is to clearly define, for the particular business, all the different risks resulting from using the Internet. Step two is to design internal control procedures to reduce this risk to an acceptable level (i.e. provide reasonable assurance). Step three is to set up procedures to monitor these controls on a continuing basis to make sure an acceptable level of risk is maintained.

AREAS OF INTERNET SECURITY RISK

Internet users are subject to four possible areas of risk.

1. Viruses
2. E-mail privacy

3. Commercial transactions

4. Network attacks

Viruses

Can you or your employees get a computer virus by using the Internet? The answer is yes. However, there are only a few clearly definable ways you can get a virus by using the Internet, and the procedures for defending against viruses are simple and well established.

First, you can get a virus as an attachment to an e-mail. Most viruses are some type of executable file. Internet e-mail, by definition and protocol, is clear text. Therefore, you will not get a virus from opening your e-mail if you do not open the attachments. Attachments from questionable sources should never be opened. Attachments from other sources should be saved to disk without opening them, and then scanned with anti-virus software.

It is technically possible, although extremely unlikely, to get a virus by surfing Web pages. Some Web pages contain Java applets, Java script, and/or Active X controls. These run as little programs on your computer when you browse pages that contain them. This is often done without your express permission and depending on your level of technical expertise, perhaps without even your knowledge. While these types of attacks are technically possible, they are just not happening. If you are afraid of this type of attack, you can disable Java and Active X in your browser. Both the Netscape Web browser and Microsoft's Internet Explorer Web browser allow the user to turn off Java and Active X.

A third way to get a virus from the Internet is by downloading a file. Once again this is not a large risk, if you are downloading files from known sources. For example, downloading a service pack from Compaq or Microsoft is safe. However, when downloading a file from a questionable source (a game someone recommended), first save the file to disk without opening it. Then, scan the file with anti-virus software before trying to use it.

A macro virus is a macro embedded in an otherwise harmless document. The Microsoft Office applications are particularly susceptible to these types of viruses. These macros generally auto execute when the file is opened and do not let the reader know they are executing. Since the Microsoft Office applications have such a powerful macro language (i.e. VBA—Visual Basic for Applications), it is possible to do some pretty powerful things with their macros. Microsoft did put some protection in Office 97 by warning users when a macro is contained in a file. Anti-virus programs are designed to detect macro viruses.

Control Procedures for Viruses

Today viruses are simple to control. Organizations should run anti-virus software all the time on every computer. The virus software signature file should be updated frequently (normally once a week) to make sure it is scanning for all the latest viruses. The anti-virus software should load whenever the computer boots so that it is always checking every file that comes on to the computer from any source.

For organizations that are at a very high risk of a virus attack (e.g. universities and other organizations where people are frequently bringing in disks from other locations), more aggressive measures may be needed. Anti-virus software services will proactively contact users when they discover a new virus strain.

Managing Mail, Messaging, and FTP Services

E-mail, instant messaging, and file transfer protocol (FTP) are all possible security holes in the MIS system. Each of these functional areas need protection, but the most common business asset that needs to be managed is e-mail. This involves managing both viruses and the security of the information. The basic principles discussed about e-mail apply to FTP services, and to a lesser degree to instant messaging.

Outlook and E-mail Viruses (e.g., the ILOVEYOU Virus)

All of the Microsoft Office products provide built-in support for Visual Basic applications. A modified version of Visual Basic called VBA (Visual Basic for Applications) serves as the programming language for the Office applications. Unfortunately, Visual Basic is such a powerful programming language that it can be used to do some evil things, such as deleting all the files on a hard drive, or e-mailing a password list to someone else. Worst of all, these evil tasks can be done without user approval, if someone can find and execute the Visual Basic program on another user's machine.

With applications like Excel and Word, the most common approach of these despots is to create an *autoexec macro* that runs without permission when the user opens the file. The macro runs in the background and the user is not even aware it is running. All the virus creator has to do is to get the user to open the Excel or Word document. These viruses are called macro viruses. Both Office 97 and Office 2000 have built-in protection to prevent macro viruses from being unleashed. When a user opens a Word or Excel (or Access or PowerPoint for that matter) document that has a macro, they receive a warning (unless they have disabled this feature) and can choose to disable the macro or not to open the file. WARNING! Do not enable macros in files unless you are aware that a macro should be in the file and you know and trust the creator of the file. Office 2000 even allows macro creators to digitally sign their macros, so the user can be sure the macro came from a trusted source.

Macro viruses were not the source of the significant e-mail virus outbreaks that occurred in the first half of 2000 (i.e. the Melissa and ILOVEYOU viruses). These were Visual Basic programs that were attached to harmless looking e-mail. If the reader of the e-mail opened the virus, the Visual Basic program was executed, yielding disastrous results. For example, the ILOVEYOU virus purportedly caused over 10 billion dollars in damage in the first day alone.

Microsoft has received a tremendous amount of criticism for not designing their products to prevent these types of viruses. Unfortunately, this is a case of not being able to have your cake and eat it too. Scanning and deleting e-mail attachments that potentially contain Visual Basic programs (or other types of programs) would prevent users from exchanging perfectly legitimate files, such as Word documents with macros or any other executable files. Microsoft has come out with a fix for these types of viruses. But, the fix is so restrictive that many users are not willing to load it.

SECURITY OF HOME PC AND SMALL OFFICES ATTACHED TO THE INTERNET

With the widespread availability of DSL and cable Internet connections, more and more people are getting persistent (i.e. always on) connections to the Internet. These always on connections are a much more serious security risk that dial-up connections because the user has a fixed IP address rather than a dynamic IP address. With a fixed IP address, the user is always at the same address, so hackers can try for days, weeks, or even months to break in.

Cable modems offer a particularly serious problem because the user is often not separated from others in his or her neighborhood by a router. Routers provide some level of security because they can only route TCP/IP packets and cannot route IPX or NET Bios packets. This means that Novell NetWare packets and Windows Network packets cannot go past the router and onto the Internet. Without routers, Internet users can see machines using these protocols.

The Internet provider will supply a connection device called a DSL modem or a cable modem. These devices are essential to the service provider's ability to manage the network because they contain ROM chips that provide for remote network administration. Users will generally not be allowed to replace these devices even though ROM chips provide no protection against hackers.

Appliance Hardware Firewalls

The solution is to either place a third party hardware firewall device behind the Internet provider's device or to run firewall software on the computer. The first solution (i.e. using a third party hardware device) is clearly preferable, because it provides a higher-level solution that is less susceptible to software attacks, and does not use up any of the RAM or processing capabilities of the user's PC.

Several companies now produce inexpensive (under $500) firewall solutions known as security appliances that are completely self-contained and easy to implement. These solutions not only block hackers; they can do content filtering and block viruses at the point where the system connects to the Internet rather than within the system. The SonicWall SOHO Firewall pictured in Exhibit 10.1 is an example of such a device.

Exhibit 10.1

Software-based Firewalls

If you have a stand-alone PC and do not feel you can justify the cost of a hardware firewall, you may want to consider purchasing a software product to block hackers. The following are three popular products:

- BlackICE Defender *www.networkice.com/.*
- Norton Internet Security 2000 Family *www.symantec.com/sabu/nis/nis_fe/.* This software offers: a personal firewall, privacy control, anti-virus protection, and parental control.
- ZoneAlarm (free for nonprofits and for personal use) *www.zonelabs.com/.* The Norton Internet Security Home Edition product is a good choice for homes because it provides not only security from hackers, it also provides parental control, anti-virus software, and blocking software. Several of the recent reviews of security software have rated it either the best or near the top of the pack because it is easy to user interface.

Exhibit 10.2

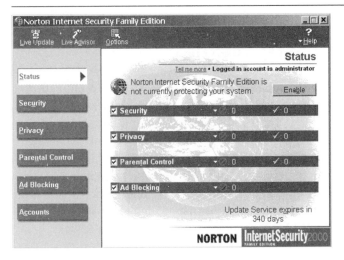

SECURITY OF NETWORKS ATTACHED TO THE INTERNET

Businesses often start out accessing the Internet though dial-up modem connections that are initiated whenever someone needs to browse Web pages or check e-mail. Most businesses have Web pages hosted by someone else on a remote computer (such as their ISP) rather than doing this work in-house. As Internet usage increases, this arrangement quickly becomes inadequate.

Even relatively small businesses quickly develop a need for a permanent, dedicated, high-speed connection to the Internet. Such a connection allows them to access e-mail, browse the Web, and download files in a small fraction of the time it takes to do the same tasks with a dial-up modem connection. Furthermore, the single, high-speed connection often results in significant cost savings because the business does not need multiple telephone lines and modems.

Some of the compelling reasons many businesses attach their internal networks to the Internet are:

- Immediate access to both incoming and outgoing e-mail.
- Control of the mail server which provides copies of all mail sent and received. E-mail data can be archived and backed up.
- Use of the Internet as a wide area backbone for connections to small and branch offices.
- The need for a permanent high-speed Internet connection for live voice and video conferencing.
- The need to accept and process orders live and online.
- Information access to databases on the Web becomes such an important part of operations that dial-up access is no longer adequate.
- The need for dynamic pages (i.e. Web pages that come from live data off the internal network).

USING THE FIREWALL TO CONTROL CONTENT

The term firewall refers to hardware and/or software that is used as a front end to an office's Wide Area Network (WAN) connection (i.e. usually the Internet). A firewall is designed to block unauthorized or devious communications. It is a company's primary defense against hackers and unauthorized entry. Recently, the process of content filtering has been incorporated into some of the hardware based firewall solutions. The Sonicwall or 3COM firewall hardware devices are an example of such firewalls.

3COM's content filtering features work by scanning requests from Web browsers to determine whether or not they are trying to access restricted content. First, a new connection is scanned for the *GET/* or *POST/* command at its beginning. If this is found, then the connection is assumed to be a Web connection. Note that it is not enough simply to scan packets on TCP port 80, since Web servers are often run on nonstandard ports. Some filtering is also provided for NNTP, FTP, and Gopher.

When a new Web connection is initiated, several pieces of data are used to determine whether it should be rejected.

- Server IP address
- Server port number
- Filename field
- Host field

Various combinations of these elements are used to provide a number of different content filtering functions.

One of 3COM's main content filtering features is based on a dynamically changing list of sites. This list is maintained by Microsystems Software (a subsidiary of The Learning Company). Information on Microsystems blocking criteria is available online. Information about the group of people that maintains the list is also online. The group is known as the *CyberNOT Oversight Committee*.

The Content Filter List provides human-generated categorization information about Web sites based on IP address and filename. The 3COM administrator can choose to block or allow access to sites based on these categories. The list also includes network news transfer protocol (NNTP) newsgroups, file transfer protocol (FTP) sites, and gopher sites that are categorized in the same way.

Since sites on the Internet are constantly being added and removed, the Content Filter List changes frequently. Currently, list updates are available once a week. It is not uncommon for a few hundred new entries to be added in one week. Outdated sites are removed as well.

Of course, this process cannot be 100 percent effective (due to the vastness of the Internet, and because of the arbitrary nature of the categorization). Some clearly objectionable sites may not be blocked (for instance, if they were created a few hours ago). In addition, some sites may be blocked which contain no objectionable content.

This may happen for several reasons:

- A new site is using an IP address that was abandoned by an adult site, but has not yet been removed from the Content Filter List.
- A site is being run on the same host as an adult site.
- A page may be blocked at a site that contains other blocked pages. For instance, all home pages at an ISP may be blocked, since some contain adult material.

There are two ways of dealing with these problems. The first is to control the site manually by using SonicWALL's *Forbidden Domains* list or the *Trusted Domains* list. Alternately, you can ask Microsystems to review the site and either add it or remove it. There is an online form at their Web site for submitting *site reviews*.

Note that blocking a fragment such as *alt.sex* may actually block hundreds of newsgroups. For example, if the group name is matched against *alt.sex*, then all NNTP newsgroups in the *alt.sex* category would be blocked by the single filter.

Unfortunately, NNTP services are often abused. People occasionally broadcast advertisements for such things as phone sex to all the newsgroups they can, including ones that have nothing to do with sex. For this reason, SonicWALL allows the option of blocking all NNTP traffic, simply by not allowing traffic to TCP port 119.

ACTIVE CONTENT FILTERING WITH SOFTWARE— FDIC COMPLIANCE VIA ETRUST

As computer networks expand to include more machines and applications, and the number of users continues to grow, managing security across the enterprise is increasingly complex. Computer Associates offers a product line called eTrust to help manage the enterprise security. eTrust security solutions suite protects the business with complete authentication, VPN, firewall, intrusion detection, antivirus, content inspection and policy management tools. eTrust security management tools are flexible, scalable, and robust. They automate routine management tasks, automatically enforce security policies, and make it easier than ever for administrators to monitor security events. The result? Better, more cost-efficient safeguarding of systems enterprise-wide. There are several software products in the product line; but the key is that this software provides active monitoring of intrusions down to the workstation level. The FDIC requires this type of monitoring in all banks, and we expect more organizations to be regulated in the same way.

For example, because of increased HIPAA regulations, this type of monitoring will be required in the healthcare industry. Today, the healthcare industry faces a time-critical challenge: protecting the privacy of patient information. The Health Insurance Portability and Accountability Act (HIPAA) requires protecting patient information and imposes strict deadlines for getting it done. CA's eTrust portfolio of security solutions, combined with strategic third-party offerings, help health care organizations meet HIPAA standards. At its core, HIPAA is about taking steps to protect the confidentiality of patient information. Achieving HIPAA compliance means implementing security standards that govern how healthcare plans, providers, and clearinghouses transmit, access and store health information in electronic form. The stringent standards and deadlines apply to any health information about an individual that is electronically maintained or transmitted. Civil and criminal penalties may be imposed for non-compliance. In effect, healthcare organizations must take precautionary steps to:

- Avoid giving unauthorized user access to confidential information (*authentication, authorization*).
- Make sure that healthcare professionals are held accountable for compliance (*auditability*).
- Restrict access by professionals to only such information as they need to do their jobs (*need-to-know basis*).

This monitoring is just good business. The tools in the eTrust family include:

- Access control—regulating access to critical business assets.
- Admin—total enterprise user administration.
- Audit—audit log repository.
- Policy compliance—risk assessment and policy audit.
- Single sign-on—a user needs only one ID and password.
- CA-Examine Auditing—identify and control OS/390 security exposures.
- Access Solution Set—extending the boundaries of the enterprise.
- Defense Solution Set—defending against Internet threats.

eTrust Access Control provides an essential eBusiness element—regulating access to critical business assets. In a world where business systems are all too accessible, eTrust Access Control provides policy-based control of who can access specific systems, what they can do within them, and when they are allowed access. Policies can be created, managed, and distributed on an enterprise-wide basis, or customized to meet the security requirements of specific applications.

This best-of-breed solution can be deployed in small individual departments, such as payroll, or the largest enterprises—and everything in between. Its hardened operating system security, complete audibility, and cross-platform access control secures everything from LANs and web servers to mainframes. eTrust Access Control's built-in baseline policies give organizations immediate results right out of the box. Open and extensible, this powerful solution supports all industry-standard platforms, databases and applications and includes published interfaces allowing it to secure any resource. Ease of use, combined with centralized user and access administration, enables organizations to confidently exploit eBusiness.

eTrust Administration helps enable eBusiness by simplifying user and resource administration, making it less complex, expensive, and error-prone. Typically, each system, groupware, database, and application in the environment maintains its own user/resource information. Most of this is inconsistent across systems. eTrust Administration remedies this situation by providing a single point of control from which you can create, modify, and remove users and related objects across multiple environments. A single console allows you to manage all security systems and directories, with support for industry standards such as LDAP(v3) and X.500. eTrust Administration enhances flexibility by supporting all network operating systems, electronic mail systems, and groupware. It provides consistency across the enterprise with policy-based administration.

eTrust Audit collects enterprise-wide security and system audit information without the reduced performance and overwhelming network traffic caused by other auditing products. It consolidates data from UNIX and Windows NT servers—as well as other eTrust products—and stores it in a central database for easy access and reporting. Administrators use eTrust Audit for monitoring, alerting, and reporting information about user activity across platforms. Companies need to implement vulnerability assessment tools, develop and enforce enterprise-wide security policies, and provide appropriate audit-ready documentation. eTrust Policy Compliance enables organizations to prepare for unauthorized usage or attacks by:

- *Identifying potential weak points in an organization's security policies.*   For example, eTrust Policy Compliance will identify policies that do not specify exact read/write rights for a file.
- *Automatically generating appropriate corrections.*   By creating a script to fix identified vulnerabilities and policy breaches, eTrust Policy Compliance helps companies respond without delay.
- *Monitoring the network of systems and databases on an ongoing basis.*   eTrust Policy Compliance immediately identifies systems that have security-related changes and generates audit reports.

CONCLUSION

Data management and security have never been optional in MIS systems. But, small computer systems have frequently been installed without the appropriate management and security tools installed. We suspect that this is sometimes from a lack of knowledge, occasionally a lack of funding, and always an incorrect judgment call when the risks are weighed against the costs. Data management and security for small computer systems is still difficult to install and use, but continues to improve in functionality and features.

Internet security issues pose real risks to almost all businesses that use the Internet. While these risks are not nearly as great as described by the press, they are real business risks and they are increasing daily. These risks should be addressed the way we address any other risks. Information managers and systems administrators need to understand exactly what types and levels of risk their particular business faces. Then they need to design and implement internal control procedures to reduce these risks to a reasonable level. As with other internal control procedures, we are looking for reasonable, not absolute, assurance. See *www.technologybestpractices.com* for supplemental materials.

CHAPTER ELEVEN

Remote Technology Best Practices

SUPPORTING REMOTE USERS

Remote workers are a fact of business today. These people may be full-time employees working from a small office/home office (SOHO) or they may be temporary part-time employees. They may be professionals who spend most of their time on the road, and need support from hotels or client offices. The speed of the remote access should not dramatically affect the productivity of the remote worker, although there are cost/benefit tradeoffs. There are ways to support remote workers that won't break your budget or bank account. The techniques discussed here will work in most parts of the world, with slight regional variations. You can manage a project to get this work done in a few short weeks, and recognize the gains shortly thereafter.

There are four primary components of any remote computing solution:

- Communications—types of access.
  - On demand—Analog, ISDN, occasionally DSL.
  - Permanent—DSL, cable, satellite.
  - Roaming—wireless.
- Security—needed to link multiple locations.
  - Firewalls—hardware and software.
  - Virtual Private Networking.
- Software required.
  - Thin bandwidth client—Citrix, Microsoft Terminal Server.
  - Remote control client—pcAnywhere, Carbon Copy, Remotely Possible, Timbuktu.
- Hardware required.
  - Communications hardware.
  - PC Hardware options.

Although decisions about any one of the components is frequently related to decisions about one or more of the other components, the goal is to make the remote worker's connection technically easy and fast enough that they can do their work.

WHAT IS THE BUSINESS GOAL?

The first step in designing any remote computing solution is to consider the business goals to be accomplished. Here are some possible choices:

- Enable work from home.
  - How frequently?
    - Telecommuting.
    - Occasional Access.
    - Permanent Access.
  - Applications needed.
    - E-mail.
    - File access and transfer.
    - Accounting or other business applications.
- Enable work from on the road.
  - Hotels, airport clubs.
  - Client or customer sites.

Let us assume, for example, that you want to enable everyone in the office to work from anywhere around the country, as if they are sitting in the office. You want them to be able to run all applications securely, and cannot predict where they will be working. Sometimes they will be working at home, sometimes traveling, sometimes at a client site. Since long distance could be a factor if access to systems is allowed from many different places by many different people, you also want to minimize communications costs.

First, assume that you want to use the Internet to minimize your communications cost. If the Internet (as opposed to dedicated private leased lines) is to be the communications medium, you must be concerned about security, speed, and access. Assume the software side of the problem will be solved with some software called Citrix MetaFrame. The whole solution will contain the following parts: communication lines; access to the Internet through a national class dial-up provider or permanent Internet connection; remote computer with the Citrix MetaFrame client loaded, as well as a modem and network interface; a Citrix MetaFrame server in the office on the outside of the firewall; and a hardware firewall.

COMMUNICATIONS OPTIONS FOR MOBILE WORKERS

Today, there are dial-up, permanent connection, or roaming Internet connection options available. A pool of modems that can be used for dial-in purposes by remote workers can also be built. Dial-up access is slow; but keep this as a viable alternative for mobile workers since much of the United States only has dial-up access available. Since national dial-up Internet access is available in most parts of the country, is there an easier way for remote users to connect than dialing the office directly?

To solve the dial-up, remote user need, a national ISP such as CompuServe, AT&T, Microsoft Network, and so forth is the best solution. The charge for this service is between $20 and $30 per month. The idea here is to have local numbers that can be accessed in many different marketplaces. Further, these vendors all have 1-800 capability, if all local access options fail. The cost for the 1-800 dial-up support is approximately $6 per hour. With this type of access, most users will have a safety net they can use anywhere in the United States, and occasionally in other countries.

On the other hand, if your people are telecommuting from a limited number of known locations, contact your local ISP to see if they have reciprocal arrangements with local ISPs in locations that would allow your people to use local numbers when they are traveling.

Why use a national ISP instead of your own dial-up facility? The easy answer is cost. Paying for a national class Internet account can eliminate most of long distance communications cost for dial-up purposes. You can build a dial-in facility for your office. But, a key question is how many lines are needed at one time? We could use the ISP rule of thumb, which is one phone line for every 16 users. But, we believe that any formula used will cause you to not have enough lines at one time or another. If you are generous enough with the number of lines available, then you will have extra ongoing costs hidden in the business communication costs after a period of time. Unless special circumstances exist, this approach is generally not a cost-effective solution.

Wireless Internet access is another solution that is coming of age and should be considered in some areas of the country. Today there are competing wireless service providers, in addition to digital cell phone connections, that can give mobile workers good quality Internet access. The primary competitors are Mobitex (major US cities at 9.6K) and CDPD (3000 cities at 19.2). Check the coverage maps at *http://www.compaq.com/products/wireless/wwan/index.shtml* to see if coverage exists in your market. Both AT&T and Sprint offer nationwide digital service that can be used for low speed wireless connection. Other third party products like OmniSky are also providing this technology. Some communities have high-speed metropolitan area access at reasonable speeds and rates.

Hotels have discovered a new revenue opportunity by providing both wireless and high speed, broadband access in their properties. Upscale hotels frequently have the service today. The daily charge of $9.95 is quite justifiable if the mobile worker is going to be attached for some period of time. These services can also be contracted on an annual basis. When a mobile worker is attached at the hotel, the service will usually be connected in one of several ways: Ethernet network, USB, or Firewire. The most common connection method today is using the computer's Ethernet adapter.

COMMUNICATIONS OPTIONS FOR THOSE WORKING AT HOME

Those working from home can choose not only from the above options available to mobile workers, but also have additional options such as ISDN, DSL, Cable Modem, and two-way satellite. The table in Exhibit 11.1 gives rough costs and speeds for these different options.

Each of these different solutions could be used for the home office. But clearly, the last two are too expensive, and not very practical for a home office application. Accordingly, the five primary choices for home office remote communications around the country are: Analog, ISDN, DSL, Cable, and Satellite.

ISDN (Integrated Services Digital Network) technology is fading in popularity. But, if you cannot get DSL or Cable service, it is significantly better than analog and is probably the best option. Basic Rate Interface (BRI) ISDN lines will provide a 2-channel link (one voice and one data, or two data or two voice lines) to connect to the Internet. With ISDN, you can be sending data over the same line used for talking. Therefore, the cost of the ISDN line can be partially offset by the reduced cost of not needing a separate voice line.

ISDN service is offered in two primary forms, measured and unmeasured. Measured service usually provides a base number of service hours (typically five) and is paid for

Exhibit 11.1

Type of Communication	Speed	Cost (Line plus ISP)
Async Analog	56K, V.90, V.92	$40+20
ISDN - BRI	128K	$90+30
DSL	1.5Mbps/384K	$30-70
Cable	1,2,4,10Mbps	$30-60
Satellite	400-500K/100K	$50-70
Wireless	19.2K	$60-90
Dedicated	56K	$300+150
T1 – 4 Wire, Frame, PRI	1.5Mbps	$800+200

by the hour (typically $6/hour). If the user forgets to disconnect a measured service ISDN, the large bill can be an unpleasant surprise. We recommend unmeasured service wherever possible. Unmeasured ISDN typically has no limitation on the number of hours that can be used for a flat rate. When ISDN is installed, there will be an initial installation fee. An ISDN terminal adapter (modem) or router will need to be purchased.

DSL (Digital Subscriber Line) service provides as much as ten times the speed for as little as one-third of the cost of ISDN. We generally recommend using the local Bell operating company as a DSL provider, although there are several good competitive companies, such as New Edge, offering DSL nationally.

DSL home service will vary from $25 to $75 and DSL business service will cost from $40 to $120. DSL speeds will vary from 256K to 1.5Mbps with most of the offerings today. A common asymmetric DSL (aDSL) line speed would be 1.5Mbps download and 384K upload speed. Most of the time when DSL lines are discussed, asymmetric DSL is assumed. Symmetric DSL (sDSL) has the same upload and download speed and usually costs a premium. For home applications, we do not recommend sDSL.

DSL will often provide one or more static (fixed) IP addresses to allow configuration of certain types of Internet services, like firewalls, VPNs, Lotus Notes servers or Citrix servers. The availability of the IP addresses and the consistency of speed are key features of DSL.

When considering DSL, be aware of the distance to the Central Office (CO) or Wiring Closet (WC). The most reliable and highest speed connections are those that are less than 5,000 feet from the wiring closet or CO. Acceptable connections are found for distances from 5,000 to 12,000 feet from the wiring closet or CO. Questionable, but often usable, are connections from 12,000 feet to the current DSL distance limitation of 18,000 feet. AT&T has reported that 98 percent of all U.S. homes and businesses are within 18,000 feet of a CO or WC. Note also that heavy population bases in the major cities skew these percentages. Expect slower speeds, and more reliability issues with these longer lengths of connection. There are some DSL technologies being tested that will support connections of up to 100,000 feet.

Cable modems can be very cost-effective for home-based workers. The costs vary from $25 to $40 for home applications and $30 to $120 for business offerings around the United States The speeds of cable modems vary by marketplace and provider, but commonly are 1, 2, 4 or 10 Mbps. The disadvantage of most cable offerings is that no static IP addressing is available. However, for home-based usage connecting back to the office, this is usually not a factor. Common vendors are AT&T, @Home, and Time Warner with their RoadRunner service.

Either DSL or Cable Modem is recommended for a permanent connection to the Internet. If both are available, DSL is generally a better business choice because of the availability of static IP addresses as well as superior support service coverage hours. DSL providers are generally business-to-business organizations that have support 24 hours a day, 7 days a week. Cable operators are business-to-consumer operations and are more difficult for businesses to reach, particularly on weekends and at night.

If neither of these two high-speed products is available, a third permanent connection to consider is two-way satellite. Satellite is much better for web browsing, but can be used for two-way remote communication as well. This has been commercially available since January 2001, and has been remarkably reliable. Satellite response will be better than dial-up in most cases, and the benefits will be noticeable when Internet access such as web browsing is used. Common providers of satellite services are Intercom Online and Starband. Intercom Online typically has faster connections such as 2Mbps available for $299. Starband usually offers slow connections such as 400 to 500K for $49 to $79.

With prices falling and availability increasing, the rule of thumb is get the fastest service available as soon as possible. The installation costs are generally small and it is easy to switch from one communications provider to another if a better option comes along. Because of the significant improvements in productivity that are often associated with high-speed remote access, even more expensive leased lines dedicated to the home are sometimes justified. However, usually the best high-speed values are found in DSL and Cable. Web resources can be found at *DSLReports.com, GetSpeed.com* and *Get-Connected.com.*

LINKING MULTIPLE LOCATIONS

It is often desirable to link the main office location and other remote office locations. Another common link is from the main office to the SOHO offices of people working at home. The communications lines described in the prior sections provide the basic infrastructure. But, it is important to make these links to the office secure. The main technology considerations to make these links secure are firewalls and virtual private networks (VPNs). Using remote access software will speed these links up for the end user.

SECURITY

If a connection to the Internet exists, there is risk of attack. Even on dial-up links, caution should be exercised. Firewalls protect a single computer or an entire network. Firewalls can be hardware- or software-based. For most business applications, including telecommuters, we recommend hardware-based firewalls. Many of these products are so simple to install and use that a computer literate user can install the device in less than 30 minutes. However, under a few conditions, most notably with DSL, outsourced technical help may be required. Firewalls are covered in more detail in a later section.

On the home or mobile user side of this issue, there are several small units about the size of a VHS videocassette available. SonicWall has a Telecommuter, SOHO 10 and SOHO 50 version of their firewall. The Telecommuter or SOHO 10 units are quite affordable for a single home user or a small remote office LAN. Occasionally we recommend that the mobile worker carry this type of product if they frequently have access to high speed Internet, and want to protect their system with their own firewall.

We recommend products from vendors like: SonicWall, 3Com, Intel, LinkSys and others who have appliance firewalls in their product mix. An example product for a home user might be a SonicWall SOHO3-10. These products typically cost $200 to $700, but very sophisticated versions might be $2000 to $9000. The firewalls used in the main office should be faster and more capable. An example of this type of firewall today would be the SonicWall Pro. This product can support up to 1,000 users, and has other features available such as content filtering, virus scanning, and the ability to implement a virtual private network (VPN), which allow the Intenet to be used in a secure, encrypted fashion to connect an office network to workers outside the office.

REMOTE ACCESS SOFTWARE

If PC applications need more speed for remote users, the best products in the market today are Citrix MetaFrame and other related competitors. Citrix servers run applications on larger servers in the main office and users run a Citrix Neighborhood client on their workstation. Different operating systems (Apple OS, UNIX, etc.) can be supported in addition to most of the Windows platforms. Note the table of compatibilities in Exhibit 11.2.

In many cases, the use of Citrix can eliminate or reduce the need to upgrade local workstations, allow the purchase of thin client terminals, and allow remote users to run at high speeds even over dial-up lines. In our own application (RoadRunner cable modem via SonicWall firewall remotely hooked into SBC DSL filtered by a SonicWall

Exhibit 11.2

	MetaFrame XPs	MetaFrame XPa	MetaFrame XPe	Windows 2000
Native Clients				
Win32	ü	ü	ü	ü
WinCE	ü	ü	ü	ü
Pocket PC	ü	ü	ü	
EPOC	ü	ü	ü	
Active-X	ü	ü	ü	ü
Win16 (WFW 3.11)	ü	ü	ü	ü
Win16 (Win 3.1)	ü	ü	ü	
DOS (16-bit)	ü	ü	ü	
DOS (32-bit)	ü	ü	ü	
Java (JDK 1.0 & 1.1)	ü	ü	ü	
Plug-In	ü	ü	ü	
Mac	ü	ü	ü	
Linux	ü	ü	ü	
Solaris (SPARC)	ü	ü	ü	
Solaris (x86)	ü	ü	ü	
HP/UX	ü	ü	ü	
AIX	ü	ü	ü	
SunOS	ü	ü	ü	
Tru64	ü	ü	ü	
SGI	ü	ü	ü	
SCO	ü	ü	ü	

Pro using Citrix MetaFrame), we can run applications faster remotely than from the office. Our frequent temptation is to also use the Citrix server while we are in the office. Many businesses and firms have eliminated servers in remote locations and avoided Novell and Windows server upgrades by installing more Citrix servers.

Citrix MetaFrame has the following requirements and costs:

- Server class hardware.
  - Budget for 12 users per server, although more can be practically run.
  - Dual processors better for more than 5 users.
  - Memory.
    - Base for OS 32 MB.
    - Allowance per user 16 to 64 MB.
    - Typical total memory 1GB RAM.
  - Connections can be made via local LAN, Internet, or dial-in modems.
  - Disks.
    - Mirrored disks minimum.
    - Separate paging disk for memory swaps increases performance.
    - Multiple disk controllers better.
    - RAID for data, but we recommend loading applications and having data storage on a separate server.
- Costs.
  - $4,995 for 0 to 15 users, additional 5 user packs available.
  - $1,995 for maximum of 5 users—non upgradeable.
  - $1495 for load balancing—a feature that supports multiple Citrix servers and provides users with a higher level of fault tolerance.
  - Typical total costs.
    - For a 5-user system: $6,000.
    - For a 12-user system: $18,000.

Citrix MetaFrame clients can be widely distributed and used by many different users without many restrictions. Competitors like Microsoft have far more restrictive licensing. On the surface, using Microsoft Terminal Server may look less expensive, but check the license agreement carefully. More importantly, Citrix MetaFrame has some very distinct advantages over Microsoft Terminal Server. Note the following:

- Better security.
- Higher performance.
- Better control of printers.
- Shadowing—support of end users by watching and assisting their actions.
- And more, as shown in Exhibits 11.3 to 11.5.

Exhibit 11.3

	MetaFrame XPs	MetaFrame XPa	MetaFrame XPe	Windows 2000
Application Management				
Anonymous user support	?	?	?	?
Application publishing	?	?	?	
Push icons to desktop (Program Neighborhood™)	?	?	?	
Push icons to Web page (NFuse™)	?	?	?	
Web Application Access				
Access desktops via Web page	?	?	?	?
Access published applications via Web page	?	?	?	
Centrally "publish" applications to Web page	?	?	?	
Web-based client installation	?	?	?	
Printer Management				
Printing bandwidth control	?	?	?	
Printer driver access control	?	?	?	
Printer driver replication	?	?	?	
Printer auto creation log	?	?	?	
Shadowing				
One-to-one shadowing	?	?	?	?
One-to-many/many-to-one shadowing	?	?	?	
Cross-server shadowing	?	?	?	
Shadowing administration task bar	?	?	?	
Shadowing indicator	?	?	?	
Shadowing activity log	?	?	?	
Permanent shadowing configuration option	?	?	?	
Centralized Administration				
Active Directory support	?	?	?	?
Auto client update	?	?	?	
Support for > 32 servers in server farm (up to 1,000)	?	?	?	
Cross-subnet administration	?	?	?	

Exhibits 11.3 to 11.5 illustrate the depth of features present in Citrix MetaFrame that are not yet in Microsoft Terminal Server, in addition to the features that are in different versions of MetaFrame. By using a Thin Bandwidth client like Citrix, the bottom line for operations is improved performance and reduced administration of software.

A less expensive way to connect to the office from a remote location is to use a remote control client like pcAnywhere. This generally requires one or more machines in the main office that can be controlled by one user at a time. The applications will generally run so slow as to be unusable, but an application can be run in a desperate pinch. These types of products do allow for secure transferring of files, and running enough applications to make repairs or modifications. This product is also usable as a remote support tool.

FIREWALLS

Firewalls are nearly mandatory for making remote connections today. A firewall is a combination of hardware and software that protects a computer or network from other computers or networks. Today, we usually think of firewalls in the context of protecting

Exhibit 11.4

	MetaFrame XPs	MetaFrame XPa	MetaFrame XPe	Windows 2000
Universal Connectivity				
Windows clients	?	?	?	?
Non-Windows clients (Mac, UNIX Lirux, Java, EPOC)	?	?	?	
Support for TCP/IP	?	?	?	?
Support for IP X SP X and NetBios	?	?	?	
TCP-based browsing	?	?	?	
Support for direct asynch dial-up	?	?	?	
Seamless User Experience				
Seamless Windows	?	?	?	
High-/true-color depth & resolution	?	?	?	
16-bit audio support	?	?	?	
Multi-monitor support	?	?	?	
Client time zone support	?	?	?	
Pass-through authentication	?	?	?	
Panning and scaling (handhelds)	?	?	?	
Access to Local System Resources				
Auto printer creation	?	?	?	?
Clipboard redirection	?	?	?	?
Automatic drive redirection	?	?	?	
Native client drive letter access (c:)	?	?	?	
COM port redirection	?	?	?	
Priority packet tagging support (Q oS)	?	?	?	
Performance				
Persistent bitmap caching	?	?	?	?
Advanced bandwith compression (SpeedScreen™ 3)	?	?	?	
Text-entry prediction	?	?	?	
Instant mouse click feedback	?	?	?	
Security				
RSA 1 28-bit encryption	?	?	?	?
SSL encryption	?	?	?	?
Cross-subnet administration	?	?	?	

Exhibit 11.5

	MetaFrame XPs	MetaFrame XPa	MetaFrame XPe	Windows 2000
Advanced Load Management				
Server-based load balancing		?	?	?
Application-based load balancing		?	?	
Load balancing based on resource utilization		?	?	
Load balancing reconnect support		?	?	
Schedule application availability		?	?	
Instant load balancing feedback		?	?	
Specify client IP range for application access		?	?	
Load balance across unlimited subnets		?	?	
System Monitoring and Analysis				
Perform system capacity planning			?	
Real-time performance graphing			?	
Set custom resource thresholds			?	
Receive pager, S M S, and e-mail alerts			?	
Application monitoring			?	
Server farm monitoring			?	
Customized reporting			?	
Schedule automatic server reboots			?	
Application Packaging and Delivery				
M S I support			?	?
Centrally install and uninstall applications			?	
Distribute service packs, updates and files			?	
Schedule application delivery			?	
Support for unattended installs			?	
Inventory installed applications			?	
Network Management (multi-user)				
Integrate with third-party network management platforms			?	
S N M P monitoring agent			?	

our LAN from the Internet, but a firewall could easily protect the payroll department LAN from the corporate LAN. Firewalls come in multiple types:

- Software-based—both server and desktop.
- Router-based.
- Appliance.

It is important that remote workers have a firewall protecting them at all times. An inexpensive approach to protection is to use a software-based firewall on a single computer. Sample products using this type of protection are the Symantec Norton Internet Security Suite, the Network ICE BlackICE Defender and ZoneLabs ZoneAlarm. These products are installed on the desktop computer, and can be updated to protect from the latest hacker threats.

These software products protect an individual machine, but can cause some operational difficulty for the end-user. Further, since the attack is stopped at the machine level, the attacker already has reached the machine at the hardware, OS or application software level. These products provide a safe enough barrier, but must be monitored for upgrades or changes. New hacker tools can put these software products at risk. The appliance firewalls also need their software upgraded routinely to close newly found vulnerabilities. Choose either a hardware- or software-based solution to protect internal and external resources.

Software-based firewalls will cause most users some interruption in work, and will often conflict with other applications that are running. Be prepared to train people on how to use the products, how to update the products, and how to work around issues caused by the firewall software. Software firewalls work with both dial-up and permanent connections to the Internet.

Router-based firewalls, such as the Cisco PIX firewall, add firewall protection through software on top of the functionality of the router. Routers provide minimal protection from intrusion attempts. A traditional type of protection from a router was Network Address Translation (NAT), but this is not sufficient protection today. The firewall software will perform all of the sophisticated functions of a firewall:

- *Address filtering*
- *Packet filtering*
- *Boundary routing*
- *Proxy server or application server*
- *Address translation*
- *Stateful inspection*

What do these different functions do? *Address and packet filtering* examines packet headers for IP addresses and ports. They then process according to rules created by the creator of the product and the network administrator. The feature of *boundary routing* is designed to prevent IP spoofing. During this process the firewall examines IP headers, and blocks those that are on the wrong side of the boundary, given their header information. A *proxy or application server* acts as a server to the application client and a client to the application server. This allows inside computers to never deal directly with outside computers. *Address translation* shields internal IP addresses from the outside world. Finally, *stateful inspection* examines IP packets, compares packet contents to known bit patterns and allows *friendly* packets in while blocking *unfriendly* or unknown packets. Router-based firewalls have more control and configuration capability than most desktop server solutions.

However, highly configurable firewalls are also available to run on PC and RISC based hardware to do the same job as the software added to routers. The software-based firewalls that are run separately on computer platforms can be even more powerful than the firewalls based in routers. Examples of products in this category include: Check-Point, Symantec Enterprise Firewall (formerly Raptor Eagle firewall) and the MacAfee Gauntlet Firewall. Both the router-based firewalls and the software-based firewalls have added Virtual Private Networking functionality that will be covered in a later section.

Finally, we recommend appliance firewalls for the SOHO user. These firewalls are simple to install and maintain, and provide good protection with minimal intrusion. The appliance firewall generally has a WAN port, a LAN port, and a power plug. Occasionally there may be additional functionality like network switch or hub ports, or wireless access point support. All configuration of the appliance firewall is done with a web browser.

Installation time is very short, typically less than 15 minutes. IT personnel can configure the firewall in advance. Installation is usually nothing more than connecting the Ethernet cable from the DSL, Cable Modem or Satellite into the WAN port on the firewall. The LAN port of the appliance firewall is then connected to a small switch, hub, or directly to the computer in the home-based office or hotel room. The appliance firewall is usually configured to dynamically allocate internal IP addresses for users inside the firewall. Appliance firewalls can be purchased to support 1, 5, 10, 25, 50, 100, 200, 300, 500 or 1000 users. Good vendors of products in this category include SonicWall with their Tele3 or SOHO3 units, 3Com with their OfficeConnect Internet Firewalls, Intel AnyPoint, and on the low end, LinkSys. Appliance firewalls can add Virtual Private Networking through software.

VIRTUAL PRIVATE NETWORKING

Virtual Private Networks (VPNs), another approach to remote access, is beginning to work well, and has some unique advantages. Virtual Private Networking is a way to use Internet communication lines securely for private use. This outside connection could be another network or an individual on the road. VPNs are faster when implemented in hardware like a firewall or router. VPNs can also be implemented in software on individual computers. Our recommended approach to implementing a VPN is to have a major firewall in the main office location with VPN software installed, and to have smaller appliance firewalls in remote locations and home offices. If mobile workers are willing to carry some support hardware, appliance firewalls can also be used on the road. However, most users don't want the extra bulk. It is acceptable to allow these users to implement a VPN in software. The key technology to watch for is IPSEC (Internet Protocol Secure). This technology began to stabilize a few years ago and is quite good, quick and secure. Make sure to implement at least IPSEC V6.

VPNs allow you to communicate at long distances at minimal charge. Traditionally, long-distance data communication has cost businesses and firms money for private lines. VPNs use a combination of hardware and software to encrypt one or more communication paths, called pipes, which can then carry private data over the public Internet lines, protecting the communications from outside intrusion. These pipes are secured using Internet standards, like IPSEC. The latest version, version 6, is the most standard and fastest implementation of IPSEC yet. Because of this new standard, many vendors of hardware and software are able to work together to allow building a private network. In effect, LANs and mobile workers can be connected together as if they are all on one big (virtual) network. The users of the VPN can share resources in accordance with their normal networking rights. If they have rights to printers, servers, data or applications as a user of the regular network, they may be granted similar rights as a VPN user.

VPN functionality is commonly added to any of the firewall types being used today. It is often included in the sophisticated software-based firewalls. It can be added as an additional piece of software to the router or appliance based firewalls as well. Further, VPN capability has been built into the Microsoft operating systems since the late 1990s.

If you are considering implementing a VPN, we recommend that you look at the hardware-based solutions first because of better speed. Even in a SOHO environment, we think it is worth the extra money to use a hardware firewall plus VPN software to get the best ease of use and greatest speed. Even with these cautions, we know that some implementations cannot justify the hardware costs when software VPN clients are either free or range in price from $30 to $70.

When a VPN is implemented, remote workers or remote offices can use the network in the main office transparently, as if they were all on the same network. The VPN extends the reach of the LAN securely. With client-server applications, this technology is very effective. The problem? With traditional PC applications, it is slower than we prefer, so sometimes we are forced to accelerate the connections with thin client technology.

PROVIDING TECHNICAL SUPPORT TO REMOTE AND HOME USERS

Remote and home users will need to be supported just like office-based workers need support. As in the office, some users will take more support and others will require less support. Home-based users will become frustrated without proper support from the office.

Remote users should have a single point of contact via e-mail and at a phone-in help desk staffed by knowledgeable support people. This support team should have a similar, if not the exact, configuration as the remote worker. The first line of defense should be e-mail. But it is clear that if the remote worker is having technical problems, e-mail may not be available. However, when e-mail is available, it gives the remote worker round-the-clock support in addition to documenting the problem. If web-based help desk software is available, the remote user may be able to log their own issues on the help desk, and be taught to do some simple queries against the help database. Many problems will be solved through electronic exchanges via e-mail or the web.

However, unusual technical problems are much harder to solve without a conversation; a phone call can often produce faster results. The help desk should be staffed to give remote users a reasonable turn-around time on their calls. Common response times are 15 minutes to 4 hours. You may set your own standard. But, to a remote user who is down, a 30-minute wait can seem like an eternity. If the problem is not resolvable in a few hours on the phone, it is clear that one of three strategies should be used. Some companies allow a maximum of 30 minutes before implementing one of these three strategies. The support strategies are:

- Dispatch your own technicians to the remote worker's location. This can be expensive and time-consuming. But, it is often faster than continuing a phone conversation and getting nowhere.
- Do an exchange shipment. Ship working product to the remote worker, and have the remote worker ship the defective product back to the main office in the same boxes.
- Dispatch national support technicians to the remote worker's location. The disadvantage of this strategy is that these technicians won't know the specific hardware or applications used, but will be technical enough that the technical support team can explain what has to get done, and they can serve as remote eyes, ears and hands.

BUY QUALITY HARDWARE AND SOFTWARE

The hardware used for the remote worker is the easiest decision to be made. For a home-based worker, desktop PCs make financial sense. For mobile workers, portable computers have become quite affordable. Portables today come in three basic sizes: lightweight, middleweight, and heavyweight. The middleweight products are probably the best value, but the lightweight machines are certainly attractive for only slightly more money. The heavyweight portables are the most powerful and flexible. The use of the computer should determine the type of computer purchased.

Since cable modems, DSL and Satellite (collectively referred to as broadband solutions) are all usually connected using Ethernet technology, this should be included in both portable and desktop computers, and is often built-in. We also recommend a modem for dial-up to use as a backup communications method if the permanent, broadband connection is not available. Appliance firewalls are important, and this technology should be considered for the remote worker. The key items to consider for the remote worker are a high-speed, hardware-based modem that supports V.90 and V.92 and an Ethernet LAN connection to connect to all of the available high-speed options.

There are several good ideas to follow for supporting remote and home-based users. But, the first line of support should be prevention. Do not buy cheap technology for the remote or home user. Cheaper technology products will tend to break more and will wind up costing the organization more money because the product costs more to support. Time wasted waiting on or repairing cheap technology can be financially devastating and make your life miserable. Always purchase high quality, brand name, popular products. This gives a much better chance of avoiding any compatibility or support issues. When Microsoft comes out with a new version of Windows, which printers do they create drivers for and test first? We recommend products from vendors like Compaq, IBM, HP and Dell for CPUs. We recommend products from HP and Lexmark for printers.

A remote or home office worker must have access to the same type and quality of business equipment that is found in a traditional office setting. Run this home office as you would run a main office location. Provide for all of the following:

- Computers—portable or desktop.
- Printers—consider laser and/or color.
- Copy capability—possibly as part of your multifunction printer.
- Power support—including UPS and Surge protection.
- Virus protection—updated routinely.
- Backup—performed frequently or unattended and an off-site archive.
- Fax capability—possibly as part of your multifunction printer.
- Ergonomic workspace—proper monitor and keyboard position, seating.
- Calculators—not on the computer.
- Proper lighting—light over workspace.
- Extra phone lines—with forwarding features and for fax.
- High-speed Internet access—DSL or cable modem is best.
- Firewall—probably an appliance firewall.
- Disaster recovery plan—could be for both the remote worker and the office.
- Access to critical software installation disks—for reinstallation or upgrades.
- Complete copy of installation codes and licenses—for reinstallation or upgrades.
- Organized filing system—perhaps integrated to an office imaging system.

This equipment can be purchased, leased, borrowed, or found at locations such as copy centers, and so forth. But, it must be available at all hours. One real benefit of ownership is not worrying about the copy center being closed late at night when there is great pressure to get something done.

Now that the remote worker is properly equipped, technical support can be provided. We can use remote access support tools, which will be discussed in the next section.

REMOTE SUPPORT TOOLS

Hardware problems used to be the majority of remote support issues. But today, hardware is far more reliable. Hardware can still break and will need to be replaced. But it is more likely that the support team will encounter software and configuration errors than hardware problems—assuming the company has followed the recommendation to buy quality equipment.

Hardware replacement can be handled by cross-shipping replacement gear, or by using company or nationally contracted support technicians to take a part to the remote worker and replace it. If the part being replaced is not the hard drive, then the remote worker should regain all key functionality once the replacement is made. If the hard drive is the failing part, the replacement drive will need to have a copy of all of the user's critical applications, and if possible, critical data. These master images can be made using products like Symantec Ghost. More sophisticated remote support and software distribution tools from vendors like Altiris, Computer Associates, BMC or Tivoli (IBM) can provide ROM updates, OS updates, application updates and distribution of data.

Simple solutions include remote tools like pcAnywhere, Carbon Copy, Remotely Possible, and Timbuktu. These products allow the remote user to start access. Then the support team can temporarily take over the desktop, make repairs or changes, and return control to the user.

An intermediate solution is using one of the thin client products for remote support. Citrix MetaFrame allows a remote technical support user to modify settings on the remote user's computer including copying files, and making keystrokes as if they were sitting at remote user's site. Microsoft Terminal Server has similar capabilities, although it is not as flexible as the Citrix MetaFrame approach.

CONCLUSION

If they are provided the right communication tools, remote workers today can work as effectively at home or on the road as they can in the office. Fortunately, the right tools now cost less than $100 per month in most cases, and initial capital investments in the communications technology is also less than $1000 per user. Speeds and reliability are likely to increase, but for most people in the United States, this technology is affordable now.

Remote computing is a requirement of today's computing environment. It is necessary to build these links securely using firewalls. It is preferable to use high-speed communications to help keep the remote worker as productive as possible. Finally, it is important to have support procedures in place to keep the remote worker productive at all times.

CHAPTER TWELVE

Emerging Technology Best Practices

Throughout this book, we have attempted to stay with best practice approaches for the here and now. But what about the future? What trends are developing? What new technologies should we expect over the next few years that could dramatically affect how we use technology and how we work?

TECHNOLOGY TRENDS

We have noticed recently, for the first time in 20 years, that management is asking for a more long-term view of technology. Rather than viewing technology as tactical, like a stapler or a desk is tactical, technology is becoming strategic to success. Perhaps one of the greatest benefits that emerged from Y2K (remember that issue over dates rolling over correctly?) is that management understands technology better than anytime in our past. That is, they understand that technology costs a lot and that the investment should have significant returns. Now, rather than IT coming to the chief financial officer (CFO) or controller and saying, "We need new Pentium IV with the latest this and that," management expects IT to develop strategic technology plans that define the future, and the cost of that future, with the benefits the new technology will bring.

Management is less enthused by the "next big thing" and more interested in the economic life cycles of what they are purchasing. Best practice companies are investing in education and requiring users to be accountable for achieving greater productivity. It is clear that technology must be viewed, not in terms of the most recent announcement, latest computer, or cheapest price, but in terms of developing trends. What will be the long-term return on investment (ROI) of today's technology purchases and developing trends that should be explored in the future? We have already discussed planning, documenting, and educating in previous chapters. Now here are the top technology trends, as we see them evolving. We feel mainstream business should be aware of these evolving trends:

Extend the Useful Economic Life of Technology

The consensus of best practice organizations is to focus on extending the economic life of existing hardware and software, making better use of installed technology, instead of continually paying the expense of newer technology without deriving additional benefits. Up until early 2001, technology advisors and consultants were recommending that IT cycle technology every three years, and some were even championing every 24 months. The idea of extending the economic life of workstations and servers is well-received. We discussed some of the hidden costs of software ownership in Chapter 5 when we advised that the cost of deployment should be included in the total purchase cost estimates. We also advised that the cost of education as discussed in Chapter 6 must be considered as a part of the total investment costs.

Extending Hardware Life

Experience with Pentium IV, 1.x GHz processor based systems, indicates that we can expect an economic life of four to five years for general applications, such as accounting and manufacturing. The use of thin client or web-enabled applications could extend the useful life even further. Even running software not optimized for the Pentium IV processor will still yield performance improvements. This is because Pentium IV based systems also tend to have higher quality, faster disk drives, controllers, and memory— all adding to an overall improved performance. Comparing the quality of hardware now to quality just three years ago, we see better quality monitors, such as the new flat panel displays, and faster hard drives and printers.

Extending Software Life

Whereas extending the economic life of hardware was a plus, software vendors are attempting to go for the opposite. Driven by the need for continuing revenue streams, software companies attempt to create obsolescence by adding new features that we cannot live without! Another approach is to retire older versions of their software and no longer provide support. Many of the accounting software vendors have started either not providing support for older versions of their software, or charging a surcharge that makes it more practical to upgrade than pay the higher support fees. In their defense, our experience shows that a company is more often better off upgrading each year, rather than staying with an older version for several years. Still, most managers would like to have the option of deciding for themselves!

Microsoft, in late 2001, took the position that they would retire older versions of their operating systems and published a planned life cycle for their desktop products (which corresponds to their server versions as well.) Visit *www.microsoft.com*

Use of Personal Digital Assistants Will Rise Dramatically

The use of Personal Digital Assistants (PDAs), such as Palm, HandSpring, and the Pocket PC, will continue to rise. A March 2002 survey (The NPD Group, *www.npd.com*) of the sale of PDAs and the portable software that runs on them shows portable software sales were up over 200 percent in 2001. Over an estimated 900,000 PDA units were sold through retail channels during 2001, up from approximately 225,000 in 2000.

M-commerce Will Supplant E-commerce

Moving processes outside the traditional computer environment is a serious trend in technology. Those close to the cellular industry understand that the potential of the cellular market is only now being tapped. Some of the features and functionality being integrated into PDAs are related to wireless communication. M-commerce (the M is for mobile) makes use of the cellular, wireless, and PDA technology to execute transactions ranging from checking inventory remotely to ordering tickets for a concert. The United States is actually lagging a little behind the rest of the world, but catching up quickly. Visit *www.technologybestpractices.com* for supplemental information on PDA productivity software.

Instant Messaging Popularity to Increase

Over the next three years, the use of instant messaging (IM) will move into mainstream business. Younger workers entering the workforce, as well as the need to respond to customers before the competition does, will drive this trend. IM will also evolve to incorporate voice instant messaging (VIM), as well as text, which will take place on your cell phone, PDA, and computer. The larger trend here will be for IM to merge into the traditional telephone service. Traditional phone use will evolve into a much different environment where your calls will be made via IM.

As the use of instant messaging grows, so does the concern over security and improper use of the technology. In the last several months, viruses have appeared that attach through instant messaging communications. Of course, antivirus vendors are moving to develop countermeasures, but the playing field has been established.

Best practice organizations are not ignoring the potential benefits of IM. But, they are moving quickly to manage the new technology before it takes hold. Policies must be changed immediately to document what is acceptable and what is not. Users should not be allowed to install and use IM until a policy for usage has been defined. This may seem harsh, but IM has much potential to cause harm, as well as to bring benefit. IT cannot allow the lax acceptance and deployment of electronic mail to be repeated.

Looking for the Next Dominant Operating System

For nearly a year now, we have noticed best practice organizations that are beginning to select alternative solutions to mainstream server and desktop operating systems. Organizations that were once extremely loyal have begun to deploy Unix and Linux based solutions. Businesses are no longer convinced that economic benefits are being derived from constantly upgrading to the vendor's latest version of an operating system. Many professionals disagree with, and are frustrated over, recent changes in licensing and upgrade policy from such firms as Microsoft Corporation. As a result, many IT professionals and business owners will continue to look for alternatives to Microsoft OS based applications and platforms.

Transferring Data between Vendors Will Become Seamless

The evolution of Extensible Markup Language (XML) is a significant trend in nearly all professions. There are many implementations of XML. For instance, in the accounting field, XML has evolved into Extensible Business Reporting Language (XBRL.) XBRL is an agreed-upon method to *tag* data elements so that data can flow between applications transparently. (See *www.xml.org* for more detailed information.) XML and XBRL will further support the platform independence mentioned above. It will take several years for XML to be everywhere. But, the trend, at the moment, is clear and building momentum. There are entire countries legislating that data will be stored and transmitted according to XML standards. It is important that IT professionals follow this trend closely and that any new application acquisitions be XML compliant.

Paperless Offices Are Driven to Less Paper

The office will not be completely paperless for decades to come. However, with the trend to store and maintain more information in digital or electronic form, newer applications to manage electronic data are emerging. The future will drive us to an office with *less paper,* versus a paperless office. In the accounting environment, there is renewed interest, for instance, in electronic workpapers. In the retail market, the use of electronic workflow applications are replacing the old bill of lading, shipping request, invoice, and other paper-based forms. Electronic invoices, even in low-end applications, are becoming an accepted method for billing customers. From utility bills, such as phone and power bills, to retail sales via e-commerce, the trend is not to print and mail invoices and statements. Many service providers, such as Sprint and AT&T, for example, give discounts to customers who receive their statements electronically. Most accounting systems now give users the ability to either e-mail or fax invoices directly from their computer to the customer's computer or fax machine. Best practice businesses realize the benefits of cost savings (no printing, packaging and postage fees), and increased speed of delivery over conventional methods.

Mobile Workers Will Become More Prevalent

As discussed in Chapter 6, the deployment of mobile workers and mobile offices has tremendous benefits. Best practice companies are poised to reap the benefits of a mobile workforce. Within a few years, remote computing or mobile computing will be as accepted as flextime and job sharing are today. Savvy employers will use technology to accommodate employees who need to be home during certain hours, or who live in another city or state. Expect the trend for remote computing to continue evolving, as the physical location where people work becomes less important than the talents they bring to the company.

Centralized Computing Will Reemerge as the Dominant Technology Trend

What is the one fundamental foundation that is needed to support the trends discussed above? The answer is access to information from anywhere at anytime. After nearly three decades of decentralizing automated systems, beginning with products from Digital Equipment Corporation (DEC) and Wang, today's technology is rapidly developing to support, not only widely distributed databases, but is also returning to centralized information warehouses.

This does not mean that there will be only be one gigantic database containing all information, as there was thirty years ago. It means that centralized databases will be well defined and managed centrally for rapid and easy access. For instance, inventory, sales, marketing, and accounting data will be stored centrally. Multiple companies will share a common platform, down to and including, a central computer room so that information can be updated from anywhere at anytime. Flexibility and access is the name of the game in the future. Just as JIT (just in time) became the buzzword for the post-World War II industrial era, "anytime anywhere" will be the mantra of the decade to come.

Return of the Clone Computer

Beginning in late 2001, we have seen a surprising trend toward returning to no-name cloned systems developing. While the price differences are not as dramatic as they once were, many technicians have told us they are more comfortable standardizing at the component level and either building, or having a third-party build, systems to their specification. The jury is still out on whether this truly represents the return of the clone system, or is just a bump in the technology road.

Wireless Everywhere!

One emerging technology that is easy to predict (we think!) is the area of wireless communications. As more communication bands are opened to high-speed wireless communications, more vendors are entering the wireless market. Since we discussed the security issues of wireless technology earlier in this book, we will assume that new products will solve the security issues. We believe that the advent of 802.11b, 802.11g and even 802.11e (think of the 802.11 communications protocol as the foundation; each of the letters designates an improvement in the functionality of how 802.11 works) will all serve to extend our use of wireless technology and provide higher speed network access. It is conceivable that all networks will be wireless in five to ten years. The next couple of years will see tremendous growth in similar technology.

64-bit Desktop Systems

Intel and IBM are poised to bring us faster processors. Late last year, Intel released Foster to manufacturers. This means the benefits of newer, faster, and more reliable servers should be seen by the time you read this book. For the past several years, the flagship of Intel's processors for server class machines has been the Xeon processor. *Xeon* became as recognizable for server or professional workstation users as the *Pentium* did to small business and home users. After the design of the original Pentium processor, Intel designed an early successor to it, codenamed P6. The P6 was heavily optimized for 32-bit applications, which were not really available for the desktop market at the time. The Xeon was built on P6 technology that began with the Pentium Pro in 1995. (Much of the design and development work on Intel's server class processors was done in cooperation with engineers from Hewlett Packard.)

CONCLUSION

We struggled constantly with what information to include in this book and what to eliminate. More than half of the original content had to be taken out, just to meet printing requirements. As technology continues to evolve and new best practice methods become known, we invite you to visit our web site at *www.technologybestpractices.com* for the latest and greatest information. Share with us, as well, your own technology best practices.

Index